A Living Theology of Krishna Bhakti

A Living Theology of Krishna Bhakti

Essential Teachings of
A. C. Bhaktivedanta Swami Prabhupāda

TAMAL KRISHNA GOSWAMI

Edited with Introduction
and Conclusion by

GRAHAM M. SCHWEIG

OXFORD
UNIVERSITY PRESS

OXFORD
UNIVERSITY PRESS

Oxford University Press, Inc., publishes works that further
Oxford University's objective of excellence
in research, scholarship, and education.

Oxford New York
Auckland Cape Town Dar es Salaam Hong Kong Karachi
Kuala Lumpur Madrid Melbourne Mexico City Nairobi
New Delhi Shanghai Taipei Toronto

With offices in
Argentina Austria Brazil Chile Czech Republic France Greece
Guatemala Hungary Italy Japan Poland Portugal Singapore
South Korea Switzerland Thailand Turkey Ukraine Vietnam

Published by Oxford University Press, Inc.
198 Madison Avenue, New York, New York 10016
www.oup.com

Library of Congress Cataloging-in-Publication Data
A living theology of Krishna Bhakti : essential teachings of
A.C. Bhaktivedanta Swami Prabhupada Tamal Krishna Goswami /
edited with introduction and conclusion by Graham M. Schweig.
p. cm.
Includes bibliographical references and index.
ISBN 978-0-19-979663-2 (hardcover : alk. paper)
1. A. C. Bhaktivedanta Swami Prabhupada, 1896–1977.
2. International Society for Krishna Consciousness—Doctrines.
I. Schweig, Graham M., 1953–
BL1285.892.A28L58 2012
294.5′512092—dc23
2011050785

1 3 5 7 9 8 6 4 2
Printed in the United States of America
on acid-free paper

Contents

List of Abbreviations

BG	*Bhagavad-gītā As It Is*, 1989 ed. unless otherwise noted, translation and commentary
BRS	*Bhakti-rasāmṛta-sindhu* by Rūpa Gosvāmin
BTG	*Back to Godhead* Magazine
CB	*Caitanya Bhāgavata* by Vṛndāvana dāsa Ṭhākura
CC	*Caitanya-caritāmṛta* by Kṛṣṇadās Kavirāja, 9 vols., translation and commentary
KB	*Kṛṣṇa, the Supreme Personality of Godhead*, 3 vols.
MMW	M. Monier-Williams, *Sanskrit-English Dictionary*
NOD	*The Nectar of Devotion*
OED	*Oxford English Dictionary*, 2nd ed.
SSR	*Science of Self Realization*
SPL	*Śrīla Prabhupāda-līlāmṛta*, 6 vols., by Satsvarūpa dāsa Goswami
SB	*Śrīmad Bhāgavatam* 12 cantos (*Bhāgavata Purāṇa*), translation and commentary
TLC	*Teachings of Lord Caitanya*

The above abbreviations are followed either by a page reference, a volume and page reference, a chapter and verse reference, or a canto, chapter, and verse reference. The letter "P" following a verse number indicates a citation from Prabhupāda's Purport: his commentary upon that verse.

Prabhupāda's *personal letters* and *conversations* have been coded to their electronic version, available through the Folio database Bhaktivedanta VedaBase # 1.[1] Personal letters are coded according to their date (year, month, day), preceded by the name of the recipient. Thus, Mandali Bhadra 720120 indicates a letter to

1. They have also been printed. The five-volume Letters edition is now out of print. According to the director of the Bhaktivedanta Archives responsible for the thirty-seven-volume printed edition of *Conversations with Śrīla Prabhupāda*, only a dozen sets remain in stock and there is no plan to reprint owing to the exclusive demand for the electronic version.

Mandali Bhadra dated January 20, 1972. Room conversations (rc), lectures (le), interviews (iv), morning walks (mw), meetings (me), evening *darśan* (ed), *Śrīmad Bhāgavatam* classes (sb), press conversations (pc), and so on are indicated by the date, followed by one of these or other abbreviations, as well as a three-letter extension indicating the place. Thus, 690511rc.col. indicates a room conversation in Columbus on May 11, 1969.

Note on the Spelling of Personal Names

While the standard English transliteration for Sanskrit has been used (with some modification for Bengali quotations), personal names have been spelled according to an individual's or a publisher's preference; thus, Bhaktivedanta Swami Prabhupāda rather than Bhaktivedānta Svāmī Prabhupāda, and Satsvarūpa dāsa Goswami rather than Satsvarūpa dāsa Gosvāmī.

A Living Theology of Krishna Bhakti

Introduction: Moving between Worlds

Graham M. Schweig

General Remarks

This book presents a carefully conducted theological study. It focuses on the rebirth and transmission of an ancient faith tradition coming from sacred India to the West and ultimately the rest of the world. It is about the emergence of a sophisticated traditional theology centered on the divinity of Krishna, or Vishnu. It is about this faith's dramatic global blossoming that was launched by the actions and practices of one teacher in the second half of the twentieth century, and how his presentation contributed to this ancient tradition a "living theology"—a theology that assumed new dimensions that would reach and engage the faith of persons born to other traditions in the world's major cultural centers.

Faith is what stirs most deeply within human hearts. It is fully trusting in the highest thing we know and in what we most love. It moves out from the heart into the subtle realms of inner thought and then into engagement with the world. Its very depths are aligned with one's most profound sense of purpose and meaning in life. Even death becomes its handmaiden. The intricacies of faith, its innermost workings, and that form of discourse in which we examine it and illuminate it are the unique tasks of theology. While human faith takes numerous forms, while it may manifest as a very personal vision or as a collective vision within particular traditions or faith communities, each expression of faith in its own way reveals and articulates something of its mysterious nature.

The author of this work cultivated a deep faith as he became an intimate disciple of the guru on whose teachings he focuses in this book. Tamal Krishna Goswami (hereinafter referred to simply as "Goswami") was a monk and a renunciate, and one of the major religious leaders and teachers of the worldwide

Hindu-Vaishnava order. He fully dedicated his life to the practice of offering the heart to the supremely beautiful, loving, and playful divinity of Krishna—the practice known as "Krishna *bhakti.*" Goswami, in the last several, very fulfilling and vibrant years of his later middle-aged life, was close to completing the doctoral degree in theology at the University of Cambridge. Goswami had written a nearly completed doctoral thesis before his life ended abruptly and unexpectedly in an automobile accident in India in 2002 at the age of fifty-six.

In this work, consisting of five substantive chapters, Goswami discovers essential aspects of the core theological teaching of his own revered teacher. He does this by closely examining the significant ways in which certain life events of the religious mission and example of his guru unfolded, particularly in the first two chapters, and by exploring key themes embedded in his writings and translations that fueled his mission, for the purpose of revealing his theological contribution—that which constitutes his "living theology"—in the remaining three chapters. I append, in addition to these introductory words, a concluding chapter that is intended to frame Goswami's work and carry some of the momentum of his ideas through to completion.

The way of life, the practices, and the traditional teachings of Krishna *bhakti* were established in the West and then in major cultural centers of the world for the first time in history by Goswami's teacher, A. C. Bhaktivedanta Swami Prabhupāda (hereinafter referred to simply as "Prabhupāda"), and his disciples. This importation of Krishna *bhakti* began as Prabhupāda, at the age of seventy, came to New York City in the mid-1960s, when he formalized its practices and teachings in the institution he founded, commonly known as the Hare Krishna movement, legally registered as the International Society for Krishna Consciousness (ISKCON). His movement arises from and represents an extraordinarily rich theological school and life practice of Krishna *bhakti*, which had developed in India over many centuries. The origins of this *bhakti* practice can be seen as going back as far as the sacred hymns of the Vedas, at least three thousand years ago, and the vision of *bhakti* has been elaborately developed in Indian religion, philosophy, literature, poetry, and drama. It is a tradition out of which emerges the famed sacred text, Bhagavad Gītā, possibly the most read scripture of world literature next to the Bible and the Qur'ān. It has truly been one of the most powerful forces in the world of religion, and certainly one of the most compelling among the traditions of sacred India.

Although Tamal Krishna Goswami was born and raised in the United States, as a young man he became a fully committed practitioner of Krishna *bhakti*. Goswami entered serious academic study only in his later years. The religious practice undertaken by him has its origins in the ancient Hindu sect known as Vaishnavism, that tradition centered on the worship of the divinity as Vishnu or Krishna. It is the largest of several primary religious traditions that make up the Hindu complex of religion. ISKCON is a branch or sect of Vaishnavism, and Goswami was part of the history on which this book in part focuses. Vaishnavism, since the second half of the last century, moved into various cultures different from that in which it originally arose. In the last twelve years of his life, Prabhupāda along with his disciples transplanted an authentic devotional tradition of India in foreign lands, but not without challenges and difficulties. Goswami himself was an intimate associate of Prabhupāda and certainly one of the most important close disciples working under him as the movement experienced dramatic growth and expansion into unchartered territories.

Goswami himself assisted and witnessed the movement's founder as he envisioned the immediate and future expansion of the society he founded, traveled and lectured on fourteen world tours, and published dozens of volumes of translation and commentary. In the latter half of the 1960s, when Goswami was in his early twenties, he committed himself to the life of Krishna *bhakti* as taught by Prabhupāda and served his guru's movement with all his energy. And he was with Prabhupāda during Prabhupāda's final months and his last days in Vrindāvan, India, personally serving him until mid-November 1977, when Goswami's guru left this world. Goswami was therefore a key disciple, an intimate associate of Prabhupāda's, who at the highest level of ISKCON would carry forward his teachings, establish centers, and initiate disciples, to keep alive Prabhupāda's living theology of Krishna *bhakti* over the two and a half decades following Prabhupāda's departure.

The Focus of Goswami's Work

Presented here is a careful study of core aspects of the "living theology" of Bhaktivedanta Swami Prabhupāda. Goswami argues that Prabhupāda's theological contribution has gone unappreciated and even unnoticed by the academic community and deserves consideration. Professor Edwin Bryant summarizes well Goswami's project:

> *A Living Theology of Krishna Bhakti* is a sophisticated historicized analysis of the Movement's teachings, adopting, on the one hand, a hermeneutical schema inherent in the tradition itself, and excavating, on the other, progressively more focused layers of embedded context external to it. Goswami's survey touches upon the initial colonial/missionary context of Hindu studies in the nineteenth and early twentieth centuries, and the revisionistic Hindu apologetic strategies of response that this provoked, both of which were formative influences in Prabhupāda's orientations. It also analyzes the counter-culture context Prabhupāda encountered in the West, with its Abrahamically-derived conceptual structure in matters of

> religion. Goswami brings great penetrative insight to his task of tracing the effects that these contexts had on the language Prabhupāda uses in translating certain key terms and concepts from the centuries-old tradition into English, and the aspects of it he chose to emphasize.[1]

Goswami examines essential elements in the life and teachings of his teacher that are significant for understanding his "living theology" and sees these elements as dramatically embedded or culminating in two *mahāvākyas*, or "great principles," that recur over and over throughout his written work. The first *mahāvākya* is "Krishna, the Supreme Personality of Godhead," a highly embellished translation of at least two specific, original Sanskrit words or phrases, namely *bhagavān* and *kṛṣṇas tu bhagavān svayam*. The other *mahāvākya* is "devotional service," a unique and telling translation of the Sanskrit word *bhakti*.

Goswami crafts an elaborate analysis of these embellished translations and brings out the theological richness and significance of their constituent elements. He brings to the reader's attention the tremendous frequency of these two *mahāvākyas* throughout Prabhupāda's work, and the significance of their repetitiveness. It is Goswami's contention that if one understands all that is behind these two *mahāvākyas* and the theological and meditative power behind them, one can better appreciate the living theology of Prabhupāda. I believe that Goswami's analysis of Prabhupāda's *mahāvākyas*, the very principles in which Prabhupāda was obviously invested, is successful in revealing the inner theological intentions at work in the writings of a teacher who would most powerfully move traditional Vaishnava practices beyond India and create centers of worship for the first time globally, especially those of the Chaitanya sect.

The reader will be fascinated to witness Goswami's rigorous level of scholarship, and his tremendous knowledge of the primary sources into which he probes deeply. When this work was in the form of a doctoral thesis, Julius Lipner, his mentor at the University of Cambridge, had this to say about the focus and quality of Goswami's work:

> In his thesis Goswami shows a fine ability to blend "insider" and "outsider" views in a balanced approach of criticality, enriched by deep personal experience of Prabhupāda and a wide knowledge of the secondary literature. The reader will have numerous occasions to note Goswami's deep familiarity with his material, coupled with the insights of subtle and penetrating analyses. But what also impresses is the integrity of his appraisal,

1. Quoted from Bryant's peer review of Goswami's manuscript for the publisher's consideration.

> in keeping with the highest standards of intellectual honesty. The gist of Goswami's thesis is a study in depth of central features of the "living theology" of Swami Prabhupāda. To this end Goswami analyses the background of Prabhupāda, the cultural context in which he began his mission in the West, the intellectual and social opposition he encountered, the way he sought to marry personal and conceptual integrity with the need to adapt his message, and the content of this message in terms of its sources, means and ends. The result is a work of impressive insight and scholarship.[2]

Goswami constantly pondered the challenge of performing at the highest scholarly levels while living the tradition he was to submit to academic scrutiny. Lipner's words attest to Goswami's ability to maintain his integrity in both the academic and religious communities, and to demonstrate that not only is it possible to be genuine to both the religious and the intellectual but there are clearly advantages for advancing theological scholarship for the benefit of both. Barbara Holdrege appreciated how Goswami challenged the academy to appreciate the synergy of the two:

> Tamal Krishna Goswami's presence in the academy—albeit for too brief a time—invites us to break open the Hindu studies guild and to provide hermeneutical and institutional space for the multitude of voices.... This memorial volume honors the legacy of Tamal Krishna Goswami as one of the courageous pioneers who helped to open the guild to important new voices and alternative discourses. (2003:136)

My hope is that this work can exemplify the kind of rigorous scholarship that can be expected by scholar-practitioners in Hindu studies within the academy, so that one day, such scholars will be accepted along with their counterpart Jewish, Muslim, Buddhist, and Christian colleagues.

To give a better sense of the focus of this work, I will extract some of Goswami's words from the book and also revisit statements about his work from academic colleagues. But first, I wish to call attention to a key phrase in this volume's title: "living theology." I have employed the phrase because it appears several times throughout Goswami's work, and with it, he characterizes the nature and locus of Prabhupāda's theological contribution. It should be noted, however, that the phrase is loosely and informally applied by many current Christian denominations in Europe and the United States, and that their application of it must be distinguished from ours. In the phrase's popular setting, the word "living" is

---

2. These and subsequent comments from Lipner are from a rough draft of introductory notes he prepared for Goswami's thesis at Cambridge in 2005.

roughly equivalent to the meaning "contemporary," and the word "theology" generally refers to "doctrine" or "beliefs." Indeed, since its original use by the Greeks, the word *theology* has been claimed by Christian sects for hundreds of years. In modern times, the word is being applied, appropriately, more and more by scholars to non-Christian traditions.[3]

Goswami's application of the phrase "living theology" is for a serious purpose. With its first appearance in the book (25) we gain a glimpse of Goswami's definition. He uses the phrase "theological wholeness" when speaking of the slanted or incomplete examinations of his teacher's work by scholars. Furthermore, Goswami points out that studies of the psychological, political, sociological, and other aspects of his work have not considered the way Prabhupāda's intense dedication to his tradition's innermost theological thought and vision have inextricably and most powerfully motivated his work in these more external arenas. The author wishes to negotiate the delicate theological balance achieved by Prabhupāda as this very fine, very subtle space within which he moved between two worlds:

> We must discover an approach that makes Prabhupāda's theology the locus of our attention, that can negotiate the two worlds out of which Prabhupāda's thought arises—the contemporary and the cumulative tradition—and that juxtaposes their claims and their standards of scholarship without being naive toward their respective presuppositions. (84)

The way Goswami examines Prabhupāda's theological contribution reflects an awareness of how the aliveness and growth of faith is presented to the currents of diverse cultures in the contemporary world: "Tensions arise when a self-consciously traditional movement, fixed by the mammoth literary canon of its founder, is confronted by the ever-changing conditions of time, place, and circumstance" (86). Thus the discovering of a living theology for Goswami is a delicate task. It requires careful examination of the many factors surrounding the life of the person from whom the traditional theology comes and in whom the theology is seen to be lived and exemplified. And thus much attention in this work is given to certain important biographical factors that illuminate the powerful life force of this theology. As he makes clear:

> I have traced Prabhupāda's birth and upbringing, his college education, and his discipleship through sketches of his father and mother, professor, and guru.... My purpose, however, is not to produce a comprehensive

3. In the concluding chapter of this book, I discuss further the appropriateness of applying the word *theology* to Hindu thought and reflection, specifically to that of the Vaishnava school of Chaitanya.

> biography. Rather, I have identified the main currents that feed into the theological stream of his thought. So prepared, we are now ready to follow his theology as it eddies about, flowing to and fro, shaping itself around an audience isolated geographically, culturally, and linguistically from the tradition's origins. (119)

Goswami defines "living theology" as the contemporary manifestation of a long and "vital" theological tradition (71). Furthermore, the phrase refers to a theology capable of bringing the whole practice of Krishna *bhakti* fully into the lives of persons not only in modern times but around the globe in various cultures (86, 122, 170). Here Goswami expresses one intended meaning as Prabhupāda's unique capacity to breathe new life into the tradition (170). Goswami's interest is in understanding what it is about Prabhupāda's theology that makes the Vaishnava tradition come alive in the latter half of the twentieth century, to the extent that it is able to spread to and take root in foreign lands.

This book is really a study of the transmission and continuation of a strong theological tradition on foreign soil. Throughout, the reader witnesses a scholar carefully navigating the myriad of primary sources with the aid of scholarly approaches:

> I make for Prabhupāda no maverick claim of doctrinal inventiveness; Vedānta traditions eschew the notion of theological originality. Nevertheless, that the basic Gauḍīya Vaishnava system of thought enshrined five centuries ago can still be spoken of as normative is to be credited not only to the resilient craft of its original chief architects but to their descendants as resourceful preservationists. And preservation is rarely a passive receptivity.... In Prabhupāda's case, to engage the text as part of a larger project of cultural transmission is to mine its rich repository of customs, values, and so on, so that it may produce a living theology in the West and around the world. (122)

Here the reader will find that the author reveals what is needed: both a gentle and creative innovation relevant to what is happening now and the maintenance of an informed literalism nourished by a long-standing commentarial tradition. He finds that Prabhupāda sustains this healthy tension. If there is too much innovation, the power of the original and its depth of vision are lost. If there is too little innovation, the tradition becomes lifeless, replete with empty ritual, formulaic doctrine, and routinized practices. Thus the balance between too much and too little innovation is critical and delicate.

Two colleagues and friends with whom Goswami would express his passion for his work illuminate so well what he wished to achieve in this study that I quote their words here. Their reflections illuminate how Goswami's presentation of Prabhupāda's living theology involved precisely this navigation between two worlds. Rachel McDermott recalls:

> Goswami's intellectual passions sprang from his artful ability to live in two landscapes at once. He was a respected *guru* and teacher in the ISKCON movement and was also about to receive his Ph.D. in the academic study of religion. He was fervent about both commitments and wanted them to come together, not only in his own person but also in both arenas separately. More specifically, (1) he wanted ISKCON devotees to shed some of their theological and practical rigidities—things he felt limited the movement in light of his deeper study of the Hindu tradition and other world religions—and (2) he desired that scholars take ISKCON more seriously as a mainstream expression of Hindu faith and practice. (2003:29)

The two worlds between which Goswami navigated are described above as the religious and academic communities. McDermott articulates well the author's desire to have these two communities, in some sense, meet in his own experience, in his own person. Indeed, it was into and between these communities that he moved with respect and affection. Francis X. Clooney, S.J., echoes McDermott's words:

> My hypothesis then is that Tamal Krishna's contribution—as matters stood at the moment of his untimely death—was to foster respect for the academic world in ISKCON, and to show that ISKCON devotees could also negotiate successfully the challenges of academe. ISKCON members could step into the academic world and succeed as scholars; scholars could also enter the community of devotees wholeheartedly. (2003:57)

Again, Holdrege, also a colleague, understood Goswami's challenges and his accomplishments:

> Tamal Krishna Goswami's life's work, as a leader of the International Society for Krishna Consciousness (ISKCON) and as a scholar of the religion, was that of a 'master mediator' who sought to mediate between the world of ISKCON and a variety of intersecting religious and cultural worlds: the world of South Asian Hindus in India and the diaspora, the world of American culture with its dominant Protestant Christian ethos, the world of his own Jewish heritage, the world of Buddhists in China, and, in the final phase of his life, the world of academia. (2003:113)

Clearly, Goswami's work, in what would later become his dissertation, was something about which the author's colleagues would be informed. Goswami held serious discussions with scholars in the field, and particularly pursued the topic of his moving between the two worlds in which he found himself, as an academically trained scholar and as a leading religious practitioner.

A Sketch of Goswami's Life

Even as adults, we never entirely leave the world of our early childhood. We take much of it with us and in various ways emotionally revisit it throughout adulthood. So was the case with Goswami as he, again, was moving between worlds. He moved from the personal, familial world into the world of the sacred retaining certain character traits exercised during his childhood experiences—indeed, he would draw from them. After looking into Goswami's background, I realized that two significant relationships in his childhood especially influenced his relationships with those in the religious order to which he committed during his early adulthood—his relationship with his father and his relationship with his younger brother.[4]

The separation of Goswami's mother and father early in his life, when he was eight years of age—particularly his father's departure from the family—ultimately moved Goswami to search for the true and wise father figure as spiritual preceptor in the religious realm. And the emergence of a baby brother, whom he adored, in his father's new family, when Goswami was nine, formed the world in which he naturally developed the intensely caring, loving, and guiding personality that would lead others in the spiritual quest. These two relationship dynamics would be archetypally revisited by Goswami throughout his spiritual journey.

Goswami's birth name was Thomas George Herzig. He was born on June 18, 1946, in New York City, the son of immigrant parents who raised him in the Upper West Side of the City, near Harlem. Although each of his parents was Jewish, neither was seriously committed to the faith into which they were born. His father, James Joseph Herzig, was Austrian and had been active in the Austrian Socialist Youth Movement, and when he moved to New York, he remained involved in socialist activism. He worked first in machine shops and then as a printer for New York newspapers. Goswami's mother, Lore Garrick, came from a well-to-do Jewish family in Germany. After attending boarding school in England, she immigrated to America, where she met Goswami's father and, after marrying, became a jeweler.

When Goswami was eight, his parents split, amicably, most likely due to incompatibility. His mother's more intellectual, artistic lifestyle did not match the worker and the political organizer that was his father. Shortly after the breakup, James married Bertha Simon, who gave birth to Goswami's much-loved younger

4. I am indebted to Professor Carl Herzig, Goswami's brother, for providing most of the biographical information on Goswami's early life for my writing of this section of the introduction.

brother, Carl. Goswami immediately claimed his brother as "his own," and the two grew very close. It is significant that Goswami was always guiding, teaching, and caring for his younger brother. Indeed, he was especially paternal toward him, from the time his brother was a mere infant throughout their lives. Goswami adored his younger brother, and his love for him is evident in Carl's own words:

> Right from my birth he was the most loving brother in the world. I wasn't just a little brother; I was his baby. He was not quite ten years old, but he embraced me fully and entirely, took possession of me to the point of wanting to take physical care of me, even change my diapers. Soon after I was born, he collected together his childhood toys and announced, "I'm not a child anymore; these are his," and gave all the toys to me. A child's toys—especially those personal ones, like his stuffed animals—can mean a lot to the child, but he wanted to hand them over. It was a coming of age for him, and a sacrifice, but one that he offered with love.[5]

As a younger brother, Carl greatly admired and looked up to Goswami, whom he witnessed moving into the world in various admirably adventurous ways. There were several periods during which they would be out of touch for years, but when they reconnected, the heartfelt affections for one another remained and increased with each meeting. This early experience of familial leadership, in relation to a sibling, set the stage for so many of his other relationships in Goswami's later life and especially within the religious order to which he committed for a lifetime.

In his late teens, Goswami began his college studies, an education that he would eventually take up again and complete over thirty years later. For two years he attended Queens College of New York, where he studied philosophy and music. He sought in his professors the guiding light and wise fatherlike figure who would practice in life what was taught in the classroom. But he was disillusioned with his instructors, who appeared to him to not live the lofty philosophy they taught. He discontinued his college study, and became involved right at the heart of the countercultural movement of the 1960s, which was very active in New York City.

Goswami would spend days playing his flute in the open, with audiences that would naturally gather in Washington Square Park in Greenwich Village and Tompkins Square Park in the East Village. Coincidentally, during this same period, the person Goswami would later recognize as his spiritual teacher performed *kīrtana,* songs chanted from the heart to the Lord, in Tompkins Square Park. One time, the crowd listening to Goswami's playing dispersed, drawn by the nearby strains of *kīrtana,* which he, too, could hear. But their paths did not

---

5. Taken from a transcription of a talk given by Carl Herzig in Carpinteria, California, on June 18, 2006, entitled "The Older Brother."

cross then, and neither of them knew the other at the time. It would be a couple of years later, in 1968, clear across the country, that they would finally meet.

Before that decisive meeting, Goswami, in his early life, was very creative and pursued fine art drawing and ceramics. And in his college years he loved music and became proficient at playing the flute. He supported himself as a production manager for newspapers and magazines. But whatever he did, his inborn leadership and managerial qualities would naturally emerge to enhance the situation, and people, wherever he was, would naturally follow his lead. Goswami can easily be characterized with a certain intensity of intention, commitment, and perfectionism and as a very serious and sober person, yet at the same time amicable, caring, and attractive.

After two years of college, and after at least the one year following, at the age of twenty-two, Goswami entered a yet more radical countercultural religious world for the rest of his life. Though he was not raised with any form of Jewish practice, he discovered a practice and a religious way of life that was deeply fulfilling. It promised a fresh vision of the world, and he found it to be something to which he could be fully devoted, and something in which he would become fulfilled philosophically and artistically. It was an exclusive world within the greater world, an arena in which he felt he could satisfy his perfectionistic tendencies beyond his previous philosophical or artistic pursuits. This form of spirituality was a form of devotional mysticism from India, known as Krishna *bhakti*.

But Goswami did not merely discover a way of life and a profoundly inspiring way of life. He became part of a burgeoning missionary movement that was to spread, for the first time in history, the way of life of Krishna *bhakti* to major cities around the globe. He did not retreat to an Indian ashram or mountain cave to take up his newly found ascetical and devotional practices. Rather, he discovered them in San Francisco when he first met with his teacher and spiritual master, Prabhupāda. There, in the spring of 1968, Thomas Herzig was initiated and received the Sanskrit name Tamal Krishna Das.

From the start, Goswami was made one of the leading disciples who would be responsible in a major way for the movement's penetration and spread into Western culture and also to countries in the East. First, he became a key figure in the expansion of the movement on the West Coast; then he was sent to London (fig. I.1), then to Hamburg and Paris, to do the same. In 1970, Prabhupāda formed the highest managerial ecclesiastical board that would oversee the movement. Goswami was an original member, and remained a leading member for the rest of his life (thirty-two years). In the early years, he oversaw the development of major centers in India, especially the Vṛndāvana, Mumbai, and Mayapur temples. He single-handedly acquired the land for the movement's world headquarters in Mayapur, the place he last visited, from where he would leave this world, where his body was entombed. Most notably, Goswami led and organized the movement's early outreach activities in North America, Europe, India, and China.

FIGURE I.1 Prabhupāda, Goswami's teacher, conversing with Goswami in London in the late 1960s. (Photograph courtesy of the Bhaktivedanta Book Trust)

In 1972, he traveled with Prabhupāda to Jaipur, where he was initiated into the renunciate order of *sannyāsa*. His name as a peripatetic monk was now Tamal Krishna Goswami. In 1974, he returned to the United States to develop the movement throughout the country. In 1977, for almost a year, he assisted and attended Prabhupāda in his last year of life, until Prabhupāda's departure in November that year (just two months after Goswami learned of his father's passing). In 1978, he began accepting, initiating, and training his own disciples.

Goswami found himself in the midst of a movement going through many growing pains. Indeed, he was a pivotal figure around whom significant movement-wide theological and ecclesiastical discussions took place. The specific regions for which he was responsible were themselves extensive and impactful. He made his base in Dallas, Texas, where he developed a temple into a very active thriving center, together with a renowned restaurant. He focused especially on developing the movement in the states of Texas (fig. I.2), Oklahoma, and Arkansas, and he was also responsible for the areas of Mayapur, Calcutta, Hong Kong, Taiwan, Fiji, Korea, and the Philippines.

As Goswami was tending to his extremely active and intensive responsibilities around the world, a scholarly side to him emerged. In the 1980s, he published two books: *The Drama of Lord Jagannātha: Jagannātha-priya Nāṭakam* and *Prabhupāda Antya Līlā*. And in 1996, at the age of fifty, he returned to college and became a student at Southern Methodist University (SMU), close to his Dallas-based center. In 1998, he graduated with a BA degree from Dedman College, SMU, with departmental distinction in religious studies. From SMU, he applied to the doctoral program in theology at the University of Cambridge, and he was

FIGURE I.2 Photo of Goswami taken in 2000 at the ISKCON Temple in Houston, Texas. (Photograph courtesy of Radhacharan Das)

accepted. In October 1998, Goswami began his doctoral studies in theology at Cambridge under the tutelage of the preeminent Indologist Julius Lipner, professor of Hinduism and the comparative study of religion in the Faculty of Divinity. Only two months later, he was diagnosed with cancer, which he had treated by doctors immediately and from which he completely recovered. Over three years, Goswami completed the five main chapters for his doctoral dissertation.

Goswami would take his last pilgrimage journey to the holy site of Mayapur, in the province of Bengal, India, in March 2002. At the end of February, he packed his bags, including several scholarly treatises on the theme of death and dying in Hindu traditions. He had been asked to contribute a chapter to a scholarly volume on Hindu devotionalism being edited by two scholars in England. How strange that the subject on which he would focus his chapter was the theme of death. The title he had already given to the essay was "Dying the Good Death: The Transfigurative Power of Bhakti." He would leave only random notes and scraps on the subject before he passed away, and thus he never contributed the chapter.[6]

6. This assignment was one that I accepted on behalf of Goswami, and my chapter retains the title that Goswami originally gave to it (Schweig 2005b). A slightly modified version of this chapter also appears originally as an article of the same title (Schweig 2003).

In the early morning hours of March 15, 2002, Goswami was being driven from Mayapur toward Calcutta airport. When the driver fell asleep at the wheel, the car went off the road in the District of Phuliya, West Bengal. The vehicle, while overturning, hit an extremely large tree, at which point Goswami died instantly, along with another passenger. The funeral rites were prepared for an immediate burial in the holy site of Mayapur, as stipulated in his will, on the land, as mentioned earlier, that he acquired. Since Goswami's visit was an annual pilgrimage made by many hundreds of *bhaktas* and the members of ISKCON's managing ecclesiastical board, his funeral was attended by many of his dear friends and devotional colleagues. His disciples and friends later built a memorial shrine on the site (fig. I.3).

One can observe in the mid-1980s the beginning of Goswami's serious pursuit of Vaishnava thought and writing. In addition to the many activities of his dedicated life of practice, managerial responsibilities, and leadership in ISKCON, Goswami produced several books, two of which, already mentioned,

FIGURE I.3 Goswami's tomb at the ISKCON Chandrodaya Mandir in Mayapur, India. The memorial tomb for his teacher, Prabhupāda, is seen in the background. (Photograph by and courtesy of Braja Sorensen)

are particularly worth noting here, as they anticipate his later academic pursuits and the work of this volume. *The Drama of Lord Jagannātha: Jagannātha-Priya Nāṭakam* (1985) is a creative and scholarly presentation. The work represents a serious study and remarkable application of the conventions of Sanskrit poetics to the writing of a drama, not in Sanskrit but in English. The first part of the book is his original drama written in English, based on purāṇic sources and the laws of Sanskrit poetics. The second part of the book is virtually a catalogue of poetic conventions and techniques that were meant to help the reader appreciate the ways in which the drama was constructed according to traditional practices. I had solicited the foreword to that book from Gary Tubb (of Harvard University at that time), who later reflects on the elaborate study of poetics in the second part of the book: "The impressive extent of this catalogue might lead one to suspect that each detail of Tamal Krishna Goswami's allegiance to the Sanskrit tradition in his English play has been accounted for, but in fact his achievement was a good deal more extensive" (2003:145). Goswami's work at this earlier stage of his scholarly pursuits was extraordinary, as Professor Tubb observes.

The second book, *The Final Pastimes of Śrīla Prabhupāda: Prabhupāda Antya-līlā* (1988), is also a drama that engages traditional poetics.[7] It represents Goswami's experience of the final days of his guru, again using a traditional form of drama. From these works it is clear that Goswami had a passion for the highly technical field of Sanskrit poetics as well as for dramatic expression of the theological tenets of his tradition. I believe that these works exercised Goswami's sensitivity to and propensity for exploring especially a "living theology" of Krishna *bhakti,* as both works deliver through dramatic expression a Vaishnava theology that has been lived and continues to be lived.

During the years that Goswami interacted with the academic world—finishing his bachelor's degree in the study of religion at Southern Methodist University and then completing the requirements for the doctoral degree in theology at the University of Cambridge—he unfailingly attended and became active at the international annual meetings of the American Academy of Religion. At these professional meetings he would present papers, participate on panels, and attend sessions of colleagues in his fields of interest. He would meet and establish connections with scholars in his field, develop friendships with colleagues, and in some cases make close friends. Goswami stood out at these meetings as a shaven-headed monk in the traditional garb of bright saffron robes, often gently smiling and always gracious, cordial—often hosting colleagues at meals

7. These two books were edited and produced by me. For a complete bibliography of Goswami's written work, see *The Tamal Krishna Goswami Memorial Volume,* a special issue of *Journal of Vaishnava Studies* 11, no. 2 (2003), 207–209.

cooked by attending disciples, while consistently maintaining a demeanor of deep intellectual interest and sobriety in dialogue.

It is no exaggeration to say that Goswami's academic and evident spiritual maturity, along with his untiring interest in the views and opinions of his colleagues and the personal generosity that he always extended to them, was unforgettable to those colleagues who knew and loved him. Compassion and affection are attributes by which he would be often remembered. Anna King recalls Goswami's caring personality, when she writes, "I remember feeling that despite his highly disciplined and busy lifestyle, Goswami found time to care deeply for others. His attention to my needs was compassionate and sensitive, his words of advice wise and considered" (2003:184).

Many colleagues appreciated Goswami for both his scholarship and his personal qualities. C. Mackenzie Brown writes, "I will always be grateful for having met Tamal Krishna Goswami, not only for the marvelous insights he gave me into ISKCON, but also, and primarily, for my having had the opportunity to encounter such a compassionate, intellectually open, and thoroughly selfless individual" (2003:40). McDermott ponders Goswami's devotion, reflected in his generous nature and kindness: "As I am sure anyone who met Goswami, even briefly, sensed immediately, his own rootedness in love for and by Lord Krishna allowed him to express himself freely. He was an incredibly affectionate person, offering his friends books, advice, honesty, and compassion" (2003:28). And Julius Lipner, as Goswami's doctoral mentor, appreciates Goswami's personal and scholarly integrity when he writes, "Here speaks a man of integrity: integrity with respect to his own personal commitment, and integrity with respect to his commitment to critical scholarship. Goswami's thesis succeeds in combining both" (2003:25). Goswami was appreciated and beloved as a person and a colleague, and therefore expressions of bereavement at the time of his departure were numerous.

I, too, easily corroborate these experiences and many other experiences of Goswami's character along with appreciations of his intellectual acumen, only some of which I have presented above. Although I knew Goswami before he entered the academic life, having produced both his dramatic works, it was during the final phase of his life, especially those years in which he was pursuing his doctoral work, that I came to know him in these ways. It was certainly during this period, when we would meet at academic conferences and over many long phone conversations, that my own relationship with Goswami solidified into one of the dearest friendships in my life.

On the Preparation of this Book

Immediately following the time that Goswami left this world, the executors of Goswami's will appointed me to oversee the completion of the dissertation and the editing and general preparation of the manuscript for publication. My first task was to provide support to Goswami's very generous doctoral mentor, Professor Lipner, who voluntarily contributed some careful editing to Goswami's chapters. Lipner wrote in his introductory notes of his task in preparing the final thesis:

> My task has been to edit the whole. I have checked the text for typographical consistency, corralled some of the material under different chapter divisions, and edited text marginally here and there so as to show, in a way I believe Goswami would have approved in the circumstances, the self-standing nature of the whole. But the work is his work entirely.

Lipner wanted to ensure that Goswami's valuable work would be in the best possible condition as a doctoral thesis so that it could be carried forward for publication. The submission of the thesis to a University of Cambridge doctoral examination committee by Lipner on behalf of Goswami was not ultimately an option because the five chapters lacked a concluding chapter. So rather than attempting to seek official acceptance by the university, Lipner determined that his editing would better serve Goswami's remaining work, which is what he did as described above. Even if Goswami had left a completed thesis, Cambridge, however, does not award posthumous doctoral degrees, and therefore Goswami could not have received his doctorate in such a way.

After Professor Lipner had passed the now refined and nearly completed doctoral thesis on to me in 2005, about one year later I had the opportunity to meet with Lipner in Cambridge. At that meeting, Lipner gave me a tour of all the places where Goswami would walk, and where he would meet with him in his office to discuss his work. When we shared our remembrances of Goswami, it became obvious why Goswami had disclosed to me how much he admired and respected his doctoral mentor. Goswami found in Lipner a scholar of great integrity and penetrating insight, someone in whom he could have complete confidence to guide him in his work. I was always delighted to hear Goswami speak of Lipner and their enlightening interactions. I therefore wish to acknowledge here the very significant place Lipner had in the final phase of Goswami's life and work, and to thank him for all the time, expertise, and friendship he gave to Goswami over the years, and the care and energy given to his work before I even began preparing it for publication.

My task, following Lipner's work, was to take Goswami's dissertation and turn it into a book that could be accessible to a wider readership than the academic arena in which it was produced. And this task of preparing the book for a wider readership was included in the detailed book proposal. After I submitted my proposal to several publishers, Oxford University Press in New York accepted the work for publication. Here I wish to acknowledge Cynthia Read, senior editor, with whom it has been a pleasure to work on this project. Cynthia and I put our thoughts together about meeting some of the unusual challenges of preparing a manuscript by a deceased author.

Cynthia Read and the reviewers of the manuscript thought that it needed something introductory and something conclusive to be complete. Lipner insisted that as far as the work as a thesis was concerned, it was missing not a substantive chapter, but only a concluding chapter that would present mostly summary statements and thoughts for further research. After careful consideration, and taking into account comments made by Bryant and Clooney, the peer reviewers of the work, I decided that this introduction and a concluding chapter would, in effect, "frame" the theological portrait of Prabhupāda that Goswami painted in his five chapters.

It appeared, however, that Goswami intended to take his work further after its thesis phase. This intention of Goswami is evident in some of the notes that remained and in some comments on this matter of his doctoral advisor. Moreover, the very titles and subject focuses of the penultimate and last chapters of his work tacitly indicate Goswami's intention to perhaps develop the subject beyond the dissertation's content to the ultimate book stage. I derive this conjecture from the titles and topics of the penultimate and final chapters that draw from three well-known theological categories: namely, *sambandha,* which Goswami translates as simply "relationship" in *bhakti*; *abhidheya,* or "execution" of *bhakti* practices; and *prayojana,* or "the goal of love of Krishna (*prema*)." It is on the first two of these terms that Goswami focuses in his two last chapters. The third phase on love, or *prema,* one can assume he was going to further work on. In my concluding chapter, I make no pretense about presenting what Goswami would have done on this subject, though I discuss aspects of and explore some directions for this very rich third and ultimate topic within *bhakti.* Goswami himself expresses several times how he hopes that his work will catalyze other scholars to further explore the very complex topic that he begins to tackle in the five chapters that follow:

> In ways that previous scholarship has to a large extent lacked, these chapters are meant to sensitize us to the many voices of Prabhupāda. The amalgam of past and present in a cumulative tradition is never entirely homogenous. Tensions arise when a self-consciously traditional movement, fixed by the mammoth literary canon of its founder, is confronted by the ever-changing conditions of time, place, and circumstance. I hope that this study will lay the foundation for a future constructive scholarship that, while selecting and exploring questions, acknowledges the theology from which they emerge. (86)

In this book's concluding chapter, I offer some ways to understand and appreciate some of the inner workings of *bhakti* theology intended to enhance the work that Goswami leaves us. I provide the reader with thoughts and reflections on the theological themes to which Goswami's five chapters naturally bring us, ideas that constitute in some sense what Goswami urges us to ponder, with the voice that comes through his words here, and in more subtle ways, as a voice that now speaks to us from beyond this world.

In the process of preparing Goswami's thesis for publication, I consulted many persons with whom Goswami spoke about his work and consulted a few persons about my tasks as the editor of this volume. These tasks, in addition to the contribution of the introductory and concluding chapters, consisted of making subtle adjustments to its contents to make it readable as a book rather than a thesis; adding section breaks to chapters 3–5 and giving them titles; making minor corrections and updating specific information in the work; adding editorial notes where Goswami's notes required further explanation; overseeing the construction of the book's index; working with Oxford's copy editor; adjusting the book's overall format; and so on. It should be noted that Goswami's words and ideas have been preserved with the utmost care, and that any editing was executed only to bring out more clearly what the author was putting forth.

It is also worth mentioning that Goswami did not leave us with a title for the dissertation, or a title for what would become the book. I carefully pondered what title would do the work justice. After reading deeply into the manuscript many times, and after consulting with Oxford's editor, I created a title that is intended to give the essential thrust of Goswami's accomplishment in his five chapters, as well as its place within the intersecting fields of study on which the work touches. The phrase "Essential Teachings" does not preclude the existence of other important dimensions of Prabhupāda's thought, nor am I claiming that Goswami has exhaustively covered Prabhupāda's essential teachings. I did want to communicate that Goswami analyzes, constructs, and interprets specific theological concepts and teachings of Prabhupāda's work that bring out the very core of Prabhupāda's living theology.

I am grateful to so many for supporting me through this long process of carrying Goswami's work through to completion. I am especially indebted to Tattvavit Das, with whom I closely worked, reviewing his tireless efforts in carefully going through the work to enhance its intellectual clarity and good American English usage. Additionally, he and Rembert Lutjeharms, the librarian at the Oxford Center for Hindu Studies, where Tamal Krishna Goswami's personal library is now held, tracked down many incomplete bibliographic details to meet the publisher's standards. I am also very grateful to Carl Herzig for contributing important editing suggestions and essential biographical information on Goswami, and to Giriraja Swami for his support and invaluable help at key points. Also, my gratitude goes to Edwin F. Bryant and Francis X. Clooney, S.J., for their in-depth peer reviews of the work for the publisher. Many thanks go to Michael Gressett and Steven Rosen, who were very helpful with their comments and suggestions. Others, along the way, played their parts: Ferdinando Sardella and Shaunaka Rishi of the Oxford Centre for Hindu Studies, Braja Sorensen, Radhacharan Das, Henry Schoellkopf, Jonathan Edelmann, Kenneth Valpey, Hridayananda Das Goswami, Abhishek Ghosh, Jayadvaita Swami, and Travis Chilcott. And still other friends, colleagues, and devotees, too numerous to list here, were very supportive and encouraging along the way. However, I wish to especially thank Rasikendra Das, the treasurer of and fund-raiser for the Tamal Krishna Goswami Memorial Foundation, for his unrelenting financial and emotional support and faith in my efforts to see Goswami's work through to completion, and to Maria Angelina Shaheen for her financial contributions to the foundation for covering many of the project's expenses. And my thanks go to Yudhisthira Das, one of three executors of Goswami's will and personal secretary of Goswami for nearly twenty years, who has always facilitated my connection with Goswami. And finally I would like to acknowledge Catherine, my life partner, for her loving support, unfailing encouragement, and invaluable insights at some of the critical stages in the writing and time-consuming preparation required of me to produce this book.

1

In Quest of the "Theological" Prabhupāda

SINCE ITS ESTABLISHMENT in the mid-1960s, the Hare Krishna movement, officially known as the International Society for Krishna Consciousness, or ISKCON, its acronym (used hereinafter), with its street chanters, pamphleteers, and fund-raisers has attracted considerable, though not always favorable, public attention.[1] Public vacillation is understandable considering the movement's exotic character. As one eminent historian notes, "for the first time since the days of the Roman empire, an Asian religion is being openly practiced by people of Western origin in the streets of Western cities" (Basham 1997:497). Scholars, though less ambivalent, are no less divided. Their ability to contextualize the movement's beliefs and practices within their defined areas of expertise has polarized responses both

---

1. Here I speak particularly of the reception from indigenous Western populations. For the British reception, see Knott 1986:75–84; for a historical survey of the American reception to Hinduism generally, see Melton 1989; for Christian and Jewish responses, see Saliba 1989. Indian expatriates, while generally appreciative of ISKCON's activities, may find certain aspects disconcerting: see Tamal Krishna 1999a.

[The phrase "Krishna consciousness" in the name of Prabhupada's organization is also a phrase used numerous times throughout his books. It is important to note that it is Prabhupāda's uniquely coined phrase that is often interchangeable in Prabhupada's works with the more traditional phrase "Krishna *bhakti*." Goswami, too, in the spirit of his teacher, uses the phrase to refer to this concept, as he understands Krishna consciousness to include the range of states in *bhakti*, from the beginning practical stages to the stage of perfect love, *prema*. Even so, from an outside perspective, it could be observed that the phrase "Krishna consciousness" carries a distinctive yogic, metaphysical, or Vedāntic flavor, while the phrase "Krishna *bhakti*" carries more of a theological sense, a meaning broad enough to contain within it the meaning of "Krishna consciousness." To be merely aware or "conscious" of Krishna is certainly prior to *bhakti*, or the offering of all one's heart to Krishna, or what is often more simply put as "devotion to Krishna." And since Goswami's work here explores Prabhupada's living theology, which clearly goes beyond merely metaphysical or Vedāntic discourse, I therefore have included in the title of Goswami's work the more traditionally known key phrase "Krishna *bhakti*."—ed.]

within and between disciplines.[2] While this may be a necessary outcome of specialization, the varying and inconsistent responses largely arise from an inadequate assessment of the movement's founder, A. C. Bhaktivedanta Swami Prabhupāda (1896–1977), particularly with regard to his intellectual legacy. In this book we are on a quest for the intellectual or specifically theological contributions of the founder of the worldwide Hare Krishna movement.[3]

The name "A. C. Bhaktivedanta Swami Prabhupāda" is itself an encoded history. The initials A. C. are an abbreviation for Abhay (fearless) Charan (feet), a name given by Rajani and Gour Mohan De, his parents, which indicates that the Lord's feet grant fearlessness. Bhaktisiddhānta Sarasvatī (1874–1937), his guru, at the time of Abhay Charan's initiation in 1933, added *aravinda* (lotus) to his name, since the Lord's feet are compared to the lotus. Thus his spiritual name was Abhay Charan Aravinda, though judging from his earliest authored publications, he seems to have preferred the simpler Abhay Charan.[4] "Bhaktivedanta" (*bhakti,* or devotion, and *vedānta,* or culmination of Vedic knowledge) is an honorary title awarded to him in 1939 by elders in the tradition, in tribute to his piety and scholarship. "Swami" (actually *svāmī,* or spiritual preceptor) was added in 1959 upon his entering the final Hindu life-cycle stage of *saṁnyāsa* (renunciation). From this time, "A. C." is substituted for Abhay Charan. Finally, we come to "Prabhupāda" (the feet of the master), the respectful address used by his followers from mid-1968 onward and reserved for only the most accomplished gurus in the line.[5] As the epithet "Prabhupāda" enjoys currency with devotees and an increasing number of scholars, for simplicity's sake it is used in this work, unless historical contexts demand otherwise.[6]

---

2. This is a primary concern of the next chapter.

3. The modernization of any historical subject has its risks. The methodological failure of improper historical contextualization can shape apparent findings into unrecognizable ideological distortions. Nowhere is this more clearly presented than in Albert Schweitzer's classic, *The Quest of the Historical Jesus.* Scheitzer finds that amid the babble of misconceived modernizing, Jesus remains a chimera to his eighteenth- and nineteenth-century biographers. Nearly a century separates his *Quest* and ours, while twenty centuries separate our subjects. We share a common problem, but each has a different challenge. Schweitzer's historical subject "comes to us as One unknown" (Schweitzer 1911:401) and remains a stranger to our time, smothered by a morass of historical assumptions. Ours, though still within the living memory of many, is also enigmatic, "as one unknown." Our challenge, unlike Schweitzer's, is not one of forced historicizing, but of theological inertia. If we but rouse ourselves theologically, our search may well be fruitful.

4. See any of the *Back to Godhead* magazine mastheads from 1944 to 1960.

5. The use of this title provoked strong objections from his godbrothers in India; see SPL 4:94–95.

6. Works that primarily trace Prabhupāda's history generally use a variety of names according to the setting; see SPL. For a scholar who alternates names to suit changing

Prabhupāda traced his lineage to the ecstatic mystic Śrī Chaitanya (traditionally 1486–1534), considered by the tradition to be the embodiment of the Godhead. The various branches of Vaishnavism are clearly monotheistic, in that they worship Vishnu or one of his prominent manifestations. For the Chaitanya school of Vaishnavism, or Gauttīya Vaishnavism,[7] Krishna is the supreme deity, not merely an incarnation of Vishnu. This school extends its lineage back to the teacher Madhva (traditionally 1238–1317)[8] and into the primeval past to Brahmā, the universe maker and progenitor, and ultimately Krishna, the Godhead. As a translator and interpreter of Sanskrit and Bengali texts, Prabhupāda served as a medium between these distant authorities and his modern Western readership. As founder, prophet, and priest of a new religious movement,[9] he saw his writings as more than exegesis, as blueprints for spiritual change, as cathartic agents meant to foment a revolution in consciousness. His purpose was to transplant an entire culture—root, trunk, branches, and all—into alien soil. He had to speak the language of a people vastly disparate from the scripture's original recipients, without compromising fidelity to the tradition.

The Need and Aim of This Study

The distinctiveness of this cultural transplantation, its unique conveyance, is credited by a majority of scholars to the specific social and psychological conditions that influenced its recipients, on the one hand, and to Prabhupāda's unparalleled blend of charisma and traditional authority on the other. Much has been made

---

contexts, see Knott 1998:88 n. 1. Scholars using the epithet "Prabhupāda" include Rochford, Knott, Shinn, and R. P. Das, to name a few.

7. The term *Gauḍīya* generally refers to the eastern region of India known as Gauḍadeśa, located in Bengal, where this sect of Vaishnavism originated. Some scholars, therefore, prefer to call the sect Bengali Vaishnavism, but since the tradition spread southward throughout Orissa, as well as northwest to the region of Mathura-Vrindaban and Jaipur, I will use Gauḍīya Vaishnavism, or on occasion, Chaitanya Vaishnavism. Graham Schweig offers a further nuance: " 'gauḍa. . . .,' apart from its geographic designation, means 'prepared from sugar or molasses'. This is appropriate, since Chaitanya's school is known chiefly for promoting *mādhurya-bhakti,* or literally, 'devotion in sweetness', referring to the loving intimacy that the devotee experiences with God" (Schweig 1998a:7).

8. The South Indian theologian Madhva was born in a small village near Uḍipī, now in Kannāḍa, and founded the Dvaita (dualistic) school of Vedānta. Opposed to Śaṅkara's Advaita (nondual) philosophy, Madhva believed in the distinction of the self and matter, both from each other and from the Lord upon whom both depend; see B. N. K. Sharma 1962:15–25. He worshipped Vishnu in the form of Krishna as the supreme deity.

9. "Founder," "prophet," and "priest" are three categories drawn from Joachim Wach's typology of charismatic leadership in his *Sociology of Religion* (1944). Wach extended Max Weber's dichotomous categories of magician and priest in primal religions, and prophet and teacher in developed religions, into a more elaborate typology. For their application in illuminating Prabhupāda's religious leadership, see Tamal Krishna 1999b:11–16.

of Prabhupāda's organizational command, his persuasiveness, and even his role as an exemplar saint. Yet he considered his books his primary legacy.[10] While the importance of philosophy in recruitment figures has been clearly documented,[11] his authorial talent and productivity have received surprisingly little analysis. Books were the final mandate from his guru, books the means by which he began his mission, books the object of his nightly labors. Although remarkably few scholars have probed his dictated writings in depth, it is his books, most of all, that he hoped they would approve. That he wished to be understood through his books is evident from a statement made shortly before his demise: "Whatever I have wanted to say, I have said in my books. If I live, I will say something more. If you want to know me, read my books" (Tamal Krishna 1998c:66). Unlike the two-millennia-old disagreement surrounding Jesus, another disruptive religious figure, *who* he is and *whether* he said what is attributed to him is not really the problem. The problem is simply that *he said too much*.

Fifty volumes of translation and commentary, sixty volumes of lecturing, thirty-seven volumes of conversation, five volumes of correspondence, each approximately four hundred pages in length, printed, reproduced electronically, and when possible audibly and visually, are a gigantic, daunting corpus. The "historical" Prabhupāda looms large on the horizon, buttressed by undisputed "canonical" texts.[12] It is the "theological" Prabhupāda, hiding in his shadow, who solicits our attention. We see the person, but his mind still eludes us.

No professional scholar can be expected to devote the time required to comprehensively critique all of Prabhupāda's thought. Some have argued that a sampling suggests the whole, inadvertently an admission that to survey all his work could require a lifetime. Others have drawn on their familiarity with the tradition to compensate for an abbreviated reading. Still others have preferred to focus on the "institutional" Prabhupāda, upon his charismatic leadership viewed through

10. "My first concern is that my books shall be published and distributed profusely all over the world. Practically, books are the basis of our Movement. Without our books, our preaching will have no effect": Mandali Bhadra 720120. See also Satsvarūpa 1982.

11. See, for example, Rochford 1985:ch. 3. While Rochford warns that members' accounts of the reasons influencing recruitment and conversions cannot be accepted uncritically (autobiographical stories are constantly being revised, redefined, and reconstructed), he reports that one-third of devotees interviewed ranked the philosophy as the primary reason for joining, while another one-third considered it among the most significant factors. Certainly ideology is an important factor in sustaining those recruited.

12. Historian Thomas Hopkins comments, "There are no significant questions in [Prabhupāda's] case about what he said and where he said it, as there clearly are in other religions. His teachings have been published in books, magazines, records, videotapes, and CD-ROMs, and are accessible to anyone who wants to read, see or hear them. By analogy with other religions, the canonical scriptures of ISKCON have been established" (1998:4).

the varied lenses of the social sciences. All of these are legitimate strategies. Still, the collective portrait of Prabhupāda till now is not an image of theological wholeness, but more a pastiche of fragmented, sometimes incongruent elements.

Giving less importance to the movement as a "living theology," the social-scientific studies, by far the most numerous, have presented Prabhupāda's mission as a psychological, political, and social phenomenon. Those whose primary concern was Prabhupāda's thought have evaluated the accuracy of his text translation or his fidelity to the tradition as a whole, some proffering high praise, others raising serious objections. The latter have generally failed to either systematically evaluate his arguments or properly contextualize them within the broader Chaitanya tradition. And in neither group has a comprehensive appraisal been attempted. Probably the only category of persons with enough time and devotion to give Prabhupāda a full reading is his followers, but their scholarship to date has been either pious accounting or else limited to specific issues. The field emerges level: Neither "insiders" nor "outsiders," despite their respective advantages, ultimately appear more privileged.[13]

It is my contention that all three categories of investigation (social scientific, philosophical, and "insider") have failed to identify, much less explain, the presence of a powerful interpretative device—a *mahāvākya,* or "great utterance"—*that pervades and governs Prabhupāda's thought,* and accounts in no small measure for the success of his mission. For Prabhupāda, the wide range of "Vedic"[14] subject matter is governed by one axiomatic truth: *Krishna is the Supreme Personality of Godhead.*[15] This is Prabhupāda's "canon within the canon," similar to Luther's focus on Christ as the unifying principle of biblical literature. As his "root metaphor," with strength to marshal a multitude of models, it informs the entire content of his religious thought, which would radically change without it. *Krishna, the (Supreme) Personality of Godhead* appears no less than 7,926 times in his teachings.[16]

---

13. The insider-outsider distinction often becomes blurred, as a number of scholars examining ISKCON have noted. See Young 1985:29, Rosen 1992c:2, Knott 1998:87–88.

14. See Das 1998:149. Das summarizes three uses of the term by Prabhupāda: "'Vedic 1' approximates most closely to what the Western classical Indologist would understand by this term; 'Vedic 2' refers to texts containing what is to Prabhupāda Vedic thought and which are hallowed inasmuch as they are derived from Vyāsa; and 'Vedic 3' is a narrower application of 'Vedic 1', referring only to the *Saṁhitās* (as contrasted to the *Upaniṣads*) and thus continuing an ancient usage of the term."

15. Graham Schweig briefly reflects upon Prabhupāda's translation of the Sanskrit word *bhagavān* as "the Supreme Personality of Godhead," noting the profuse application of this phrase throughout his writings. See Schweig 1998b:106–107.

16. This figure was obtained by searching the Folio databases, "The Bhaktivedanta VedaBase #1—Prabhupāda" and "The Bhaktivedanta VedaBase #3—Historical," version 4.11, 1998a and

The necessity of a unitary semantic thesis—whatever it may be—is common to all Indian schools of thought (Mumme 1992:70). With at least one good interpretative device, apparently contradictory passages can be brought into conformity with canon. Not only does this allow a work such as the Bhagavad Gītā to be seen as a single, unified text but then all the canonical texts may appear as a simultaneous revelation supportive of a single meaning and even anticipating all future change and development.

It was Jīva Gosvāmin (traditionally 1513–98), the great medieval theologian and disciple of Chaitanya, who first identified the governing *sūtra* of the Bhāgavata Purāṇa, the tradition's foremost canonical literature, as *kṛṣṇas tu bhagavān svayam* (1.3:28), translated by Prabhupāda as "but Lord Śrī Kṛṣṇa is the original Personality of Godhead."[17] Prabhupāda employed this richly theological phrase to guide his entire thought and mission from the very start, as the early evidence hints. There is, for example, the initial, apparently sectarian act of naming his institution the International Society for *Krishna* Consciousness rather than accepting the suggested, seemingly more generic and inclusive "International Society for *God* Consciousness."

Again, anticipating that he might not live to complete his life's work, the translation of the Bhāgavata Purāṇa, he first published a two-volume study of its most important tenth canto under the title *Kṛṣṇa, The Supreme Personality of Godhead.* Also, in composing an invocational prayer to himself for the society's liturgy, he demarcated the highly personalistic theological and geographic boundaries of his mission by the use of explicitly nontheistic references: "Our respectful obeisances are unto you, O spiritual master, servant of Sarasvatī Gosvāmī. You are kindly preaching the message of Lord Chaitanya and delivering the Western countries, which are filled with *impersonalism* and *voidism.*"[18] This strongly personal brand of Krishna monotheism, predicated upon a pivotal theistic *sūtra,* is the key to understanding the delicate theological balance Prabhupāda achieved

---

c. The search was conducted for "Krishna" or "Kṛṣṇa" in combination with either "Supreme Personality of Godhead" or "Personality of Godhead."

17. The Bhāgavata Purāṇa, the most popular of the traditional Purāṇas (ancient books), is the source of many of the most famous and loved stories of Krishna. Jīva refers to text 1.3:28 as a *paribhāṣā-sūtra* (according to Pāṇini's grammar, "a rule or maxim that teaches the proper interpretation or application of other rules" [M. Monier-Williams, *Sanskrit-English Dictionary*, s.v. *paribhāṣā*]). Jīva explains, "A *paribhāṣā* restricts what would otherwise be unrestricted, limiting it to a specific interpretation. In any treatise, it may be stated only once, not more. Thus, even tens of millions of statements can be governed by a single one" (Jīva Gosvāmin 1986b, *Kṛṣṇa-sandarbha, anuccheda* 29).

18. For a comment by Prabhupāda on the Sanskrit of this invocation, see Pradyumna 700409.

by seeking, in the process of transmission, to preserve the tradition by making subtle adjustments to it.[19]

As one who has been seriously engaged in the academic study of religion and has been practicing and giving instruction in Gauḍīya Vaishnavism for over three decades, I can here speak to those "outside" the tradition, as well as to those "inside." Central to the needs of this study, my extensive personal association with Prabhupāda as his private secretary and managerial representative allows me what is possibly a unique insight into how the particularities of history have enmeshed themselves in the development of his theological vision. Although the primary focus of this study will be theological, it attempts to plumb the gradual evolution of Prabhupāda's thought for its historical and sociological antecedents. My intention is to offer scholars of the academic community a clearer access to what has for many seemed a bewildering maze of sectarian discourse. By speaking from within the tradition, yet ever mindful of those outside it, I hope to address not only academe according to the accredited norms of scholarship but also other religious traditions of theistic temperament. Finally, I have a sense that this work may be of value to those within the Gauḍīya Vaishnava community, particularly the members of ISKCON.

The Approach of This Study

How should a search for the "theological" Prabhupāda proceed? While reading Prabhupāda in his entirety is a good beginning, isolated reading that ignores contexts can produce a flat and potentially misleading image. Prabhupāda is clearly working through a cumulative tradition, one that is dynamic and observable.[20] We need to know precisely what he inherits, and from whom, and what he creatively adds to that tradition. Equally important, which formative events lead to his recovery of the tradition, and which events influence his interpretation of it? The six-volume authorized biography, *Śrīla Prabhupāda-līlāmṛta*, gives sketchy answers to these essential questions.[21]

---

19. I elaborate on this later in this chapter.

20. W. C. Smith introduced the term "cumulative tradition" to indicate "the entire mass of overt objective data that constitute the historical deposit, as it were, of the past religious life of the community in question: temples, scriptures, theological systems, dance patterns, legal and other social institutions, conventions, moral codes, myths, and so on; anything that can be and is transmitted from one person, one generation, to another, and that an historian can observe" (1978:156–157).

21. In a conversation with me in 1977, Prabhupāda approved the idea of a biography, but hinted that it should not be done while he was alive. A year later, after Prabhupāda's demise, ISKCON's Governing Body Commission authorized Satsvarūpa Dāsa Goswami to write the biography.

A frequent problem with hagiography is that supporting characters and events are devalued while the principal subject towers with Bunyanesque proportions against a two-dimensional backdrop world too small to contain him. We want a human portrait of Prabhupāda—not divested of its otherworldly dimension, to be sure—but taking seriously his place in a human history that includes the formulations of his religious convictions. Our study should be equally alert to both traditional voices and those of contemporary scholarship, delighting in the polyphony, respecting each for its uniqueness, appreciating as much their discord as their harmony. This spirit of mutual respect will help carry us safely through the fiery volleys between Prabhupāda and his most heated critics.

Because our project is to read Prabhupāda critically and theologically, it is appropriate to say something about reading habits. Francis Clooney has had considerable experience doing comparative theology with the texts of Śrī Vaishnavism, a sister tradition to the Gauḍīyas.[22] He uses reader-oriented literary theory as a methodological approach for a task that in part resembles ours. According to Clooney, the Vedānta traditions have a built-in hermeneutic, a "right reading by right readers" ethic (Clooney 1994:140). Canonized texts are not only privileged and given a well-defined status, they are protected by a code that prescribes right ways of reading, interpreting, and arguing them. The implicit expectation, beyond mere reader sympathy, is an openness to being personally recomposed (Clooney suggests the slogan "no information without transformation" [160]). Undergirding all of this is the Vedānta notion that there is an arguable, defensible truth. This is a claim that directly challenges modern and postmodern critiques, and Clooney, of course, realizes that. His discussion of scholarly aloofness is worth citing because it begins to explain why some critics find Prabhupāda problematic:

> Contemporary scholars are for the most part content with modest contributions to the understanding of the original, contextual meaning of such texts and with a concomitant dismissal of various erroneous, overly exegetical to theological interpretations; they decline to affirm or deny the larger truth value such texts might hold for those who study them carefully with open minds. Frequently skeptical and even dismissive of the theological interpretations with which the Vedāntins invested the Upaniṣads, and reluctant to take sides in debates that begin from the premise that truth and moral implication can be identified, scholars are often in the

22. Śrī Vaishnavism's leading exponent is Rāmānuja (traditionally 1017–1137), born near Madras (now Chennai) in South India. Opposed to Śaṅkara's Advaita (nondualism), Rāmānuja's school, known as Viśiṣṭādvaita (nondualism of particulars), teaches that the one ultimate reality is composed of the world of matter, unlimited individual living beings, and Brahman, who is known personally as the Lord, Vishnu.

> position of knowing a great deal about the great texts, and of being able to catalogue quite skillfully various actual and possible interpretations, while nevertheless remaining comfortably distant from the categories such as "true meaning," "right interpretation," and "the right way to live one's life according to the text." Though a scholar may know a great deal about a text and about why others thought it important, she or he may have little to say about whether it is, or ought to be, important today in any way that stands in recognizable continuity with the tradition. (140)

Clooney does not suggest that scholars should disregard contemporary standards, but ideally that "these standards must remain open to modification and in explicit juxtaposition with those of the tradition" (161). That some of Prabhupāda's harsher critics fail to do this should not surprise us. Clooney's frank assessment alerts us to the potential misalignment of traditional and scholarly foci. Taking exception to Prabhupāda's strident truth claims may be less an aversion to his overt, sectarian missionizing than a failure to recognize how strictly the systematization of the text binds its exegetes to fixed boundaries. In fact, any propaedeutic to a fair assessment of Prabhupāda's thought must acknowledge the conscious location of his chosen texts within a cumulative tradition that strongly militates in favor of a particular hermeneutic. Clooney's summary of a text tradition's components serves well to elucidate Prabhupāda's interpretative frame:

> 1) a series of readings, accompanied by the teachings and rules that govern them; 2) a set of commentaries which serve as exegetical, doctrinal, and pedagogical loci; 3) a set of accumulated loyalties to the smaller and larger choices made by one's own teachers and their teachers—choices about topics such as patterns of language, the norms and precedents of argument, and the idea of tradition itself. (150)

Even if Vedānta (via Prabhupāda) is read without the liability of openness to being "recomposed," how can one ignore the tradition with its determined canon, which has invested the texts with such authority? Impoverished reading that masks other doctrines and commitments beneath a veneer of disinterest makes for poor scholarship. Clooney remarks: "the defining difference is between scholarship that makes its presuppositions explicit and scholarship that does not" (157). A tradition's presuppositions are clear (which is not to infer reflexivity in its advocates), but scholars are not always so clear about their presuppositions (neither necessarily reflexive). A productive reading of Prabhupāda demands that the criteria of contemporary scholarship be balanced against an appreciation for traditional and often equally rigorous standards. Viewed in this light, Prabhupāda's contribution may be that of a respected "colleague" rather than of a theologically biased traditionalist.

And now we must rescue "tradition," "traditional," and "traditionalist" from being fossilized, that is, something incapable of change, in contrast to "modernity," that provocative harbinger of change. Having constrained Prabhupāda to the "fixed boundaries" of tradition, we must set him free to "dance as a dextrous hermeneute," transforming tradition in the process of translating it.[23] Fortunately, the interplay of tradition and modernity is already well established. They are not antithetical, and either may be a source of change or stasis.[24]

I shall argue, following the lead of Marilyn R. Waldman, that Prabhupāda harnessed traditions as a process, a "modality of change":

> In this sense, tradition is not a fixed code or pool of techniques and values but rather a particular style exemplified in certain actors. As a sentiment, it expresses fidelity, continuity, and solidarity with the past and with others. An alternative to it is the sentiment of radical discontinuity or the ideology of antitraditionalism. As a modality of change, "tradition' is more related to adaptation and modification of the prescribed social order, whereas radical discontinuity, often represented by revolution, is oriented to fundamental changes in the prescribed social order. (Waldman 1986:326)

Prabhupāda is not a radical innovator or reformer (though, no doubt, he may appear so to those unfamiliar with the tradition). His accomplishment is the distinctiveness of his cultural transplantation, its unique conveyance. He discovered in various "Vedic" themes, embedded in key Sanskritic terms, a pliability and elasticity that allowed him to make changes while claiming just the opposite. Waldman's discussion is most germane to a consideration of Prabhupāda's project:

> Change can be future oriented and identified with novelty, but it does not have to be.... In pre-modern societies change was often past oriented, not based on newness but rather on a new rediscovery of oldness; the ideology of tradition produced and validated change by providing a vision of the ideal order to which people were motivated to "return" through reform and renewal. There are, of course, even traditions of reforming in that way. Out of its sense of reconstructed continuity, then, tradition can be a source of legitimation for change even if its contents have to be adjusted to be compatible with change. Even if its contents are in fact changed, they will have

23. For Prabhupāda, scriptural transmission is always as much a transformation as it is a translation, an exercise in preserving the canon's authority while extending its boundaries; see Tamal Krishna 1998a.

24. See Lawrence 1998:340. For a summary of forty years of literature on the subject, see Waldman 1986.

> the advantage of being thought of as unconsciously adopted, normative, unanalyzed, and ancestrally recognized. (326–327)

How this process worked within the Vedānta tradition, where "change" can be regarded not as a virtue but a deviation, is explained by Julius Lipner:

> It was no virtue to be seen to be 'doing theology in an original way', to be offering a new interpretation of the ancient wisdom. . . . Theological originality, expressly claimed as such, lacked authority and therefore any claim to illumination in the eyes of the faithful and of rival teachers. The professed aim of the sound exegete and theologian (unlike that of, for example, the poet, the dramatist, the military strategist) was not innovative but essentially preservative: his to perpetuate in an increasingly relevant and perhaps systematic way the teaching that had been handed down—not to change it. It was more important to be regarded by one's contemporaries as standing within the continuum of tradition than to be credited with an 'original' but deviant mind (1986:3).

Still, there is wriggle room, as Lipner clarifies:

> Nevertheless, in spite of the binding respect a theologian had to show his teaching-tradition, he had ample scope if he was so minded to contribute fresh insights, by the creative organisation of his material, the penetration of his arguments and even by doctrinal innovation. . . . But such originality had to be cloaked by the pretext of only bringing to fruition or reflecting faithfully what was already in the tradition from the beginning (3).

One whose function includes the act of translation has even more possibility of making "new" contributions. Prabhupāda's translation of *bhagavān* as "Kṛṣṇa, the Supreme Personality of Godhead" galvanizes a common Sanskritic term for "God" with sufficient potentiality to stimulate the "reform and renewal" about which Waldman speaks. By polarizing two of God's most striking attributes—divine greatness, communicated by the word "supreme," and divine intimacy, conveyed by the word "personality"—Prabhupāda surcharged the otherwise normative term *bhagavān* with the highly suggestive, metaphorical tension required to provide it with radically new meaning.[25] In explaining the meaning of this dynamic, I shall

25. The discussion of divine polar attributes is the theme of John Carman's *Majesty and Meekness*. Carman defines "polarity" as "the link between two apparently opposite qualities that belong to or describe the same reality" (1994:11).

turn to the work of Janet Soskice, Sallie McFague, and others who focused on the use of metaphor in religious language.

If Prabhupāda is to be spared from the charge of naive literalism, we will need to examine his constant use of metaphorical language (semantically, not just syntactically) and his equally frequent deployment of models when speaking of God. In doing so, we shall have to consider the nature, function, and cognitive status of those models to determine, as far as possible, the reality to which they refer. Do his models and metaphors commit "violence to genuine religious conviction by vulgar anthropomorphism," which Soskice so abhors (1985:149)? Is their predication "cognitively fruitful rather than cognitively misleading," as Julius Lipner reminds us such language must be? Does it deny "the literalness of the attribution by an act that is on the whole what Śaṅkara calls an imaginative ascription" (1989:181)? In seeking answers to these questions we will be led to the heart of theology, which is relational, as McFague emphasizes: "the critical models of the great theologians—their root metaphors—are not about God or about human beings, but are concerned with the relationship between them" (1982:125). We should expect, therefore, that in an examination of Prabhupāda's use of metaphors and models, many of the key elements in his systematics will come to light.

I have outlined some broad approaches that will shape this study, the lenses through which I intend to focus it. Obviously, there are others. Valuable studies have been done on the movement, and, of course, Prabhupāda has figured prominently in these. Despite their strengths, however, it is their deficiencies that motivated my investigation. Highlighting these areas of dissatisfaction will yield a collectively important interpretative key. My selective analysis of the relevant scholarship to date is meant to create a conceptual platform for launching a serious quest for our elusive subject, the "theological" Prabhupāda.[26] To contextualize both Prabhupāda's thought and the scholarly reflection on it, it is necessary initially to offer a brief account of Prabhupāda's history up to the opening of his first "temple" in America. Then our quest can begin in earnest.

Background of the Pre-ISKCON Prabhupāda

A. C. Bhaktivedanta Swami Prabhupāda was born on September 1, 1896, the day after the traditional lunar-calendar date of Lord Krishna's birth, no doubt a contributing factor to his parents' naming him Abhay Charan.[27] Gour Mohan, his

26. I will not include scholarship responding to translations of Prabhupāda's works, only those dealing with his original English publications and that claim to shed new light.

27. Many of the details of Prabhupāda's early life are crucial to the development of his thought and will be examined at length later. For now, only a brief overview is intended. For

father, was a cloth merchant in the respected *suvarṇa-vānik* trading community, with family connections to the wealthy Mulliks of Calcutta, who for about two hundred years had traded gold and salt with the British. Abhay Charan's parents raised him according to their own orthodox Hindu Vaishnava faith. They had an altar in their home, and they also took him to the Mulliks' temple to worship Krishna. Growing up under the British Rāj, he developed strong sentiments for Indian independence, which led him to refuse the university diploma offered upon the completion of his studies in philosophy, economics, and English literature (along with compulsory Bible classes) at Calcutta's Scottish Churches' College. While still in college he married Rādhārāṇī Datta, and afterward he developed a business career in pharmaceuticals to support their five children.

None of these "threads" of life is in itself enough to suggest the richly religious tapestry of his later career. True, he credited the shaping influences of his father's early guidance and his mother's extraordinary affection as the foundation of his life's work. The value of his English Christian education is also seen in his later writings, as are the effects of growing up amidst the Bengal "Renaissance" and the struggle for independence. Nor can his disappointement later on with family and business be undervalued for inducing in him a spirit of detachment and renunciation. But above all, it was his meeting with the Vaishnava *saṁnyāsī* (renouncer) Bhaktisiddhānta Sarasvatī in the twenty-sixth year of his life that was to have the greatest impact.

At their first meeting, Bhaktisiddhānta dismissed his young visitor's concern for India's political independence, and instead proposed a far grander vision: "You are an educated young man. Why don't you preach Lord Caitanya Mahāprabhu's message throughout the whole world?" (Satsvarūpa 1980–83:1.39). This command to start a global mission was not the unique idea of Bhaktisiddhānta. Rather, Bhaktisiddhānta saw himself globally expanding Chaitanya's own prophecy that "[i]n as many towns and villages as there are on the surface of the earth, My holy name will be preached" (CB).[28] The tradition connects Chaitanya's words, in turn, to an older citation from the Bhāgavata Purāṇa.[29] While other methods of redemption were previously possible, now only chanting of God's holy names will be

elaborate detail, see SPL 1, the well-researched hagiography entitled *A Lifetime in Preparation: India, 1896–1965*.

28. *Pṛthibīte āche jata nagarādi-grām/sarbatra pracār haibe mor nām.* (CB Antya 4:126)

29. "My dear king, although Kali-yuga is an ocean of faults, there is still one good quality about this age: Simply by chanting the Hare Krishna *mahāmantra*, one can become free from material bondage and be promoted to the transcendental kingdom.

"Whatever result was obtained in Satya-yuga by meditating on Vishnu, in Tretā-yuga by performing sacrifices, and in Dvāpara-yuga by serving the Lord's lotus feet can be obtained in Kali-yuga simply by chanting the Hare Kṛṣṇa *mahāmantra*" (SB 12.3:51–52).

effective, owing to the unparalleled degradation of the present age (*kali-yuga*, the last and worst age of the cycle of four ages). Chaitanya's followers spread his message through *kīrtana*, ecstatic public chanting; only with the facilities of modern communication and transportation could his most recent disciple-descendants attempt to realize his prediction beyond the subcontinent. Bhaktivinoda Ṭhākura (1838–1914), the father of Bhaktisiddhānta, sent some publications to universities and intellectuals abroad;[30] when his son succeeded him, missionaries were sent to Europe.[31] But these efforts met with minimal success.

Forty years would have to pass before Abhay Charan's ocean crossing. First, Abhay would have to taste bitter disappointment in his personal life and business career. Although he was primarily occupied initially with these engagements, Bhaktisiddhānta's order was never far from his mind. If anything, his circumstantial inability to immediately act on his guru's words only deepened their significance. They became his constant meditation, gestating for eleven years, until 1933, when he received formal initiation from Bhaktisiddhānta and vowed to dedicate his life to the service of his guru's mission. In 1939, his godbrothers conferred on him the title Bhaktivedānta, signifying that in him were found both devotion and learning. In 1959, having already set to rest all worldly concerns, he entered the *saṁnyāsa* order, the stage of renunciation. A. C. Bhaktivedanta Swami was now poised to launch his worldwide mission.

Living in Vṛndāvana, the North Indian pilgrimage town of Krishna's childhood, in extremely simple residential quarters within the medieval Rādhā Dāmodara Temple established by Jīva Gosvāmin, he told doubtful visitors about temples and devotee communities spread throughout the world, with only time separating them from him (Brooks 1989:76). He had received a final confirmation from Bhaktisiddhānta just days before the guru's demise: "I have every hope that you can turn yourself into a very good English preacher if you serve the mission to inculcate the novel impression of Lord Caitanya's teachings to the people in general as well as philosophers and religionists" (Satsvarūpa 1980:1.61). Bhaktivedanta Swami was aware that he stood in a tradition in which he could well be the one chosen to accomplish what others before him had only dreamed of. There was no pride in this recognition. Rather, he was humbled by it, as he

30. Copies of a short collection of Sanskrit verses summarizing Chaitanya's teachings, which included a forty-seven-page English introduction, reached the bookshelves of McGill University in Montreal, the University of Sydney in Australia, and the Royal Asiatic Society in London, sometime after 1896. The London-based Sanskritist Reinhold Rost and Ralph Waldo Emerson in America were among the individual recipients of an earlier Sanskrit work printed in Bengali characters, a theological reassessment of the life of Krishna in the light of modernity. Emerson, in a brief letter dated May 10, 1896, while grateful for the gift, apologizes for his inability to read the language. See Shukavak 1999:89–92.

31. Bhakti Pradip Tīrtha, Bhakti Hriday Bon, and Sambidānanda Dāsa were sent to the West.

noted in his diary while crossing the Atlantic aboard the ship *Jaladūta* bound for America in 1965:

> Śrī Śrīmad Bhaktisiddhānta Sarasvatī Ṭhākura... is that great saintly spiritual master who bestows intense devotion to Kṛṣṇa in different places throughout the world. By his strong desire, the holy name of Lord Caitanya will spread throughout all the countries of the Western world. In all the cities, towns, and villages on the earth, from all the oceans, seas, rivers, and streams, everyone will chant the holy name of Kṛṣṇa... Although my Guru Mahārāja ordered me to accomplish this mission, I am not worthy or fit to do it. I am very fallen and insignificant. Therefore, O Lord, now I am begging for Your mercy so that I may become worthy, for You are the wisest and most experienced of all (Prabhupāda 1995:70–71).

Recognizing that his mission was time bound—he would turn seventy while still aboard the ship—he saw his success as dependent upon his guru's and God's mercy. Rather than beg alms like other mendicants in India, he would begin to finance and simultaneously propagate his mission by selling the two hundred copies of his three-volume translation of the Bhāgavata Purāṇa's first canto, stowed in the ship's hold. Apart from these books, forty rupees was the extent of his start-up capital, a most unlikely beginning for any success story.

His plan was fourfold: (1) to translate the essential Vaishnava scriptures; (2) to train a core of dedicated disciples; (3) to create an organization; (4) and to conduct widespread propaganda. Although the results of his teaching in India had yielded little (e.g., a disciple and a failed League of Devotees in Jhansi), he had single-handedly translated and produced the first canto of the Bhāgavata Purāṇa, and in 1944 he had begun publication of *Back to Godhead,* an English magazine. Books, therefore, would be the basis of his mission. How else would a public largely unfamiliar with Chaitanya's teachings be attracted and thereafter educated? Rather than limiting himself to the specific texts written by Chaitanya's followers, he chose to reach behind them: He translated the Bhagavad Gītā and Īśopaniṣad as consistently devotional, countering the prevailing translations of the monistic Śaṅkara school.

Outside India, Bhaktivedanta Swami did most of his literary work in the hours after midnight, sitting down with the commentaries of prominent predecessors before giving his modern audience a fresh translation and a "purport" in the light of the succession of disciples.[32] Although clearly within the Gauḍīya tradition, his

32. Except in the case of three summary studies, texts are given a verse-by-verse treatment. They are presented in their original Sanskrit or Bengali script, followed by a roman diacritical transliteration. Each word is then glossed in an English lexical study, followed by an English

commentaries had an unmistakable missionary agenda. His unabashed advocacy of India's ancient culture challenged the notion of Western cultural hegemony. His "purports" were designed as the intellectual framework on which the society he founded would be built. Having established his first storefront temple in New York's Lower East Side (in what was formerly a curio shop, whose signboard, "Matchless Gifts," was befittingly retained), he set about shaping his fresh recruits into useful assistants.

While the external appearance of an elderly Bengali *sādhu* was commonplace in India, his flowing ocher robes and rubber shoes were news in New York. Bhaktivedanta Swami, however (as A. L. Basham was to note), was not one of the "streamlined swamis" who glutted the market with "a streamlined kind of Hindu mysticism designed to appeal to modern, jet-age disciples: levitation of a few months or even weeks, *mokṣa* (final liberation) in a few easy lessons—a Hinduism without class, without worship, without rigid taboos, and so forth" (Basham 1983:166). In the great American permissive society, where "do your own thing" was the norm, his four prohibitions—no meat, fish, or eggs; no gambling; no intoxication (which even includes alcohol, caffeine, and tobacco); and no illicit sex (even within marriage if not for procreation)—were puritanical. An early admirer, historian Thomas Hopkins, offered his retrospective view:

> It's an astonishing story. If someone told you a story like this, you wouldn't believe it. Here's this person, he's seventy years old, he's going to a country where he's never been before, he doesn't know anybody there, he has no money, has no contacts. He has none of the things, you would say, that make for success. He's going to recruit people not on any systematic basis, but just picking up whomever he comes across and he's going to give them responsibility for organizing a worldwide movement. You'd say, "What kind of program is that?" There are precedents perhaps. Jesus of Nazareth went around saying, "Come follow me. Drop your nets, or leave your tax collecting, and come with me and be my disciple." But in his case, he wasn't an old man in a strange society dealing with people whose backgrounds were totally different from his own. He was dealing with his own

translation of the entire verse and a "Purport," or commentary, that unpacks its meaning (in this book, references to purports are indicated by a "P" after a verse number, e.g., BG 1:1P). The summary studies are *Teachings of Lord Caitanya* (a summary of Kṛṣṇadāsa Kavirāja's medieval Bengali classic *Śrī Caitanya Caritāmṛta*), *The Nectar of Devotion* (a summary of Rūpa Gosvāmin's canonical treatise of devotional aesthetics, *Bhakti-rasāmṛta-sindhu*), and *Kṛṣṇa, The Supreme Personality of Godhead* (a summary of the Bhāgavata Purāṇa's tenth canto). His principal commentaries, with verse-by-verse treatment, are to the Bhagavad Gītā, Bhāgavata Purāṇa, and *Caitanya Caritāmṛta*.

> community. Bhaktivedanta Swami's achievement, then, must be seen as unique (1983:127–128).

Others have made a comparison with Jesus, often based on Max Weber's understanding of charismatic prophecy.[33] Joachim Wach's fuller typology helps illuminate the distinctive qualities of Bhaktivedanta Swami's religious leadership.[34] Offering "old wine in a new bottle" (a favorite self-description), he is a renewer rather than a founder of a religion—a Weberian distinction, meaningful to scholars and fellow Indians, no doubt, though easily lost on those hearing his message for the first time. Although his written message appears to be a prophetic recovery of a depository of ancient wisdom—what Wach describes as "lost contact with the hidden powers of life" (Wach 1944:348)—it is, in fact, a deeply pondered textual commentary, methodically drawn from the works of previous commentators. His is the enterprise not only of a prophet but of a teacher "who transmits acquired, not revealed knowledge, and this by virtue of a commission and not on his own authority" (M. Weber 1964:52–53). He is his movement's first and foremost priest. While not necessarily an accurate indication of his temperament, the category of "priest" accommodates the sweeping reach of his accomplishments. In readying himself for his mission and in the later, similar training of his disciples, he exhibits the preparation and education that has come to be associated with the priesthood. This includes ascetic practices, meditation and prayer, instruction, and study. Bhaktivedanta Swami is, in Wach's terms, simultaneously his fledgling movement's high priest, guardian of traditions, keeper of sacred knowledge, custodian of the holy law, chief justice, administrator, teacher, scholar, patron of the arts, *and theologian* (1944:365).

33. See M. Weber 1964:46–59 and, for example, Shinn 1987:40. Focusing on Prabhupāda's charisma and religious innovation, Selengut 1996 has also cast him in the role of a charismatic prophet.

34. See n. 9 earlier in the chapter for Wach's typology of charismatic leadership.

2

The Travails of Illegitimacy: Historical Setting

Counterculture Discourse: The Mid-1960s to Mid-1970s

"At first they will laugh at you,..."

A welter of youthful elation, parental dismay, public perplexity, cult deprogramming, and establishment opposition followed in the wake of ISKCON's emergence as a new religious movement. The storm of media coverage and the social-scientific studies that attempted to make sense of this riotous tableau stand in stark contrast to the paucity of serious scholarship that has attended Prabhupāda's actual thought. If a review of the scholarship was made, the lack of any sustained systematic in the treatment of his theology would at once become clear.

A careful survey, even though not exhaustive, recommends itself for a number of reasons. A broad, more or less chronological overview will add depth to our theological portrait by placing our subject directly within the sociocultural environment that so shaped his mission. As one observer notes, "the history of movements like Hare Krishna *is* the history of the society and its culture" (Bromley 1989:287). The major sociological and psychological studies of the movement set him among his most important audience: the disciples for whom he especially tailored his thought. The dateline of Prabhupāda's career transects the earliest studies; to observe his interaction with them will help to flesh out our portrait by exposing the issues he and his critics considered important. Emerging themes essential to his theology can then be catalogued for later treatment. These advantages suggest that a review of ISKCON-related studies, perhaps the inevitable focus of such a survey, will decisively invigorate our quest, both by what is revealed about our own subject, the "theological" Prabhupāda, and even more tellingly by what is omitted.[1]

1. This survey does not include studies betraying obvious bias, for example, religious apologia or anticult literature that is not up to academic standards.

The main obstacle to a full assessment of Prabhupāda's thought has been its voluminousness. This chapter will expose other obtrusive elements, some circumstantial, but most either scholarly constructions or the hapless creations of ISKCON. If the history of religious movements "*is* the history of the society and its culture," equally so is the history of scholarship. That Prabhupāda's triumphalism emerged in response to a past colonialist and Orientalist confinement is a matter we shall duly consider; that it encountered an equally disempowering discourse of Occidental scholarship, well meaning yet no less colonizing, is the subject of our immediate survey. ISKCON's own role as an active rather than passive agent, and in quite another way Prabhupāda's as well, completes a pattern of domination aptly described as the "postcolonial predicament" (Breckenridge and van der Veer 1993).

I am not suggesting that the subject-object relationship of scholarship be solely interpreted in terms of power. Ideally, the study of religion should be one of dialogue rather than mutual suspicion, as Gavin Flood has most recently argued, pursuing the thought of Mikhail Bakhtin (Flood 1999). That research on ISKCON has generally lacked sufficient reflexivity and hence failed to be power sensitive, intertextual, and intersubjective will soon be apparent. With some notable exceptions, most of the conversation has been monologic. Under a facade of neutrality and objectivity, researchers routinely failed to critique the grounds on which they stood, and instead imported value-laden theories and methods that to a large degree determined their observed data. "All academic inquiry is from a place," Flood asserts (1999:144); "the data of religious studies are not innocently self-revealing" (33). He adds, quoting June O'Connor, "It's not enough to tell me what you see. I want to know where you are standing as you see and speak, and also why you stand there" (37).

From this viewpoint, with an awareness of historical contingency, to survey the history of scholarship about ISKCON is to identify the binding narratives that have sought to illuminate particular questions raised by ISKCON's presence.[2] By emphasizing narratives as bases for the subject and object of religious study, outsider narratives are deprivileged and made to compete, or better yet, complement those of the insider. To reconfigure this balance, I am going to intentionally divide the material of this chapter into a constructed narrative order that as much places ISKCON's enquirers within the broad context of culture and history as it does those who stand inside the tradition.[3] In the language of Paul Ricoeur

2. [What the author means by "binding narratives" is "narratives," or accounts of events, as perceived by entities external to the movement that have powerfully influenced the conception of its identity to the point of fixing it, or "binding" it, significantly altering or adding to the conception of the movement. The author, in this chapter, discusses three categories of binding narratives: discourses about the counterculture, discourses about cult controversies, and a discourse of indifference.—ed.]

3. An alternative, entirely "object"-oriented structure would tell us little of what informs the "subject's" inquiries. For example, Kenney 1976 organizes his study around

(1984), this "organization of events" into "plots" has the distinct advantage of highlighting how scholarship about ISKCON has been as much a response to public perceptions as to ISKCON itself (and by extension, Prabhupāda and his thought).

The epigraphs at the start of this and the following two chapter sections are the voice of the "other"—possibly Prabhupāda's—acknowledging this force of history by anticipating the public's response to his movement.[4] Prabhupāda so closely identified himself with ISKCON (declaring "ISKCON is my body") that the question of legitimacy was deeply personal. The chapter title suggests the impossible: legitimating a misfit "other" conceived in the conflicted alliance of Prabhupāda/ISKCON, the public, and scholarship. I will do my best to remain unobtrusive, for as Wendy Doniger suggests, "If a scholar selects her texts carefully and places them in a sequence that tells the story she wants to tell, she will need relatively little theory to explain why they belong together and what sort of argument they imply together" (1998:60). Doniger also asserts that the best theory is "like the mortar that is all but unnecessary to hold together carefully constructed stone walls in Ireland" (quoted in Llwellyn 2000:43). I trust my own location is clear: I am inside, though trained to look from the outside in, equally bound to subject and object, and no less to the outcome of their dialogue.

In 1968, Collier Macmillan in New York published an abridged edition of Prabhupāda's *Bhagavad-gītā As It Is* (1968a). Bards, appropriately, were assembled to herald its release. Allen Ginsberg, Thomas Merton, and Denise Levertov, as dissimilar in temperament and style as alike in their appreciation for poesy and for things Indian, take turns acquainting Macmillan's readers with that ultimate Indian philosophical poem, the Gītā. Ginsberg begins by introducing its latest interpreter:

> Swami Bhaktivedanta came to USA and went swiftly to the Archetype Spiritual Neighborhood, the New York Lower East Side, and installed intact an ancient perfectly preserved piece of street India. He adorned a

Prabhupāda's manifestation as "swami," then "guru," and at last "avatar," while in Kenney and Polling 1986, the authors survey ISKCON's history by dividing the material into four periods: "beginning," "organizational," "expansion, legitimization," and "crisis of leadership."

4. Taken together, the phrases form a popular statement disciples attributed to Prabhupāda. Although a thorough search of the VedaBase (Prabhupāda 1998 a, b, c) did not conclusively establish its authorship, events certainly have confirmed its veracity. Early ISKCON devotees "became the subject of numerous cartoons and provided comic relief in many movies and television shows" (Melton 1989:91). One scholar observes, "The movement is looked on by most of the Western public with some amusement, and its members are thought of as harmless cranks" (Basham 1997:497).

> storefront as his Ashram and adored Krishna therein and by patience and good humor, singing, chanting and expounding Sanskrit terminology day by day established Krishna Consciousness in the psychedelic (mind-manifesting) center of America East. He and his children sang the first summer through in Tompkins Park. Upaya—skillful means—is the Sanskrit word for this divine Tact. To choose to attend to the Lower East Side, what kindness and humility and intelligence! (Ginsberg 1968:15)[5]

Denise Levertov is far more restrained. She appreciates the cathartic effect of the *Gītā As It Is* on a young adherent she has met, while simultaneously being "appalled by his fundamentalism," his belief in the Gītā's "exclusive wisdom" (Levertov 1968:16). Levertov also worries about the movement's attitudes toward social injustice and war (she has the Vietnam conflict in mind). Thomas Merton registers a similar concern, but for the readers: Will they see a justification for violence in the Gītā's example of war as religious duty? Both view the battlefield as symbolic, the battle as interior. Neither reads the Gītā literally: Krishna is *not* a charioteer, Levertov tells us, but the God within. "God-consciousness," Merton explains, is "(n)ot concentration on an idea or concept of God, still less on an image of God, but a sense of *presence*, of an ultimate ground of reality and meaning, from which life and love could spontaneously flower" (Merton 1968:19).

Prabhupāda could not have disagreed more. In his "purport," or commentary, on the Gītā's opening verse, as if anticipating and then defying the preceding introductions, he identifies Arjuna's friend and charioteer Krishna as the full-phrased, verbal icon, "the Supreme Personality of Godhead":

> It is understood that this philosophy evolved on the Battlefield of Kurukshetra, which is a sacred place of pilgrimage from the immemorial time of the Vedic age. It was spoken by the Lord when He was present personally on this planet for the guidance of mankind.... [O]n the Battlefield of Kurukshetra, the Supreme Personality of Godhead was present on the side of Arjuna. (BG 1:1P)

Although the poets intend to introduce Prabhupāda's Gītā, their approach to the text is preconditioned by metaphysical assumptions directly at loggerheads with

5. Ginsberg, in fact, helped popularize Hare Krishna, chanting publicly (with Prabhupāda on occasion), and offered help in various ways: financing an immigration lawyer to secure Prabhupāda's American residential visa, arranging a psychiatrist to rescue Prabhupāda's first disciple from Bellevue Hospital, donating musical instruments, and introducing celebrities to the movement. See SPL 2 and Hayagriva das 1985. For transcripts of four of Ginsberg's conversations with Prabhupāda, May 11–14, 1969, in Columbus, Ohio (on the occasion of their joint program at Ohio State University) see 690511(12, 13, 14).rc.col.

Prabhupāda's.[6] This will remain a thorny problem for Prabhupāda: The cries of exclusivism, social disengagement, and literalism loudly echo in future scholarly critiques.

Macmillan published the *unabridged* edition of the *Gītā As It Is* in 1972 ("requested by many scholars and devotees," Prabhupāda informs us in his preface). The bards are gone, and in their place the Chaitanya scholar Edward C. Dimock, Jr. contextualizes Prabhupāda's commentary within the Gauḍīya school of thought. Therein *bhakti,* devotion, acts as a powerful, transformative force, gradually enabling one to come face to face with the Lord. Considering Dimock's renown, it is worth noting what he values, and his legitimation of the "insider's" viewpoint, especially in light of what others will later argue:

> (I)n this translation the Western reader has the unique opportunity of seeing how a Kṛṣṇa devotee interprets his own texts. It is the Vedic exegetical tradition, justly famous, in action.... It allows us to listen to a skilled interpreter explicating a text which has profound religious meaning. It gives us insights into the original and highly convincing ideas of the Gauḍīya Vaishnava school. In providing the Sanskrit in both Devanāgarī and transliteration, it offers the Sanskrit specialist the opportunity to re-interpret, or debate particular Sanskrit meanings—although I think there will be little disagreement about the quality of the Swami's Sanskrit scholarship. And finally, for the nonspecialist, there is readable English and a devotional attitude which cannot help but move the sensitive reader. (1972:ix–x)

Always alert to whatever might further (or retard) his movement's progress, Prabhupāda used Dimock's unequivocal endorsement as an imprimatur in meetings with intellectuals, while he distanced himself from Ginsberg.[7] When Frits Staal, the distinguished University of California (Berkeley) professor of philosophy and of South Asian languages, was interviewed by the *Los Angeles Times* for

---

6. Sent Ginsberg's and Levertov's forewords in advance of publication by Brahmānanda (New York temple president and Collier Macmillan interface), Prabhupāda approved their inclusion for purposes of sales. But, "[s]o far as their study of Bhagavad-gita is concerned, that is completely nil"; see Brahmananda 680406. Merton is not mentioned, though on one occasion, when reminded of Merton's foreword, Prabhupāda doesn't comment; see 760617mw.tor.

7. Originally, Dimock's foreword was less positive, but he agreed to edit some of his more critical remarks. In a letter from Hamburg, Prabhupāda mentions that Indologist Franz Bernhard mistook the devotees for hippies because of seeing Ginsberg's name on their meeting's notice board: "In our papers nothing should be published which has even a small tinge of hippy [*sic*] ideas" (Hayagriva 690827). The OED defines hippie as "a person, usually exotically dressed, who is, or is taken to be, given to the use of hallucinogenic drugs."

refusing to accredit a Krishna consciousness experimental course on campus, Prabhupāda seized the opportunity to publicize his own views through a letter to the editor.[8] The *Times* reported that Staal thought the devotees spent too much time chanting to develop a philosophy. He also expressed surprise that converts from Western monotheistic religions that stress faith in a personal God should take to an Indian cult that does the same (rather than an Indian philosophy that stresses an impersonal absolute). Prabhupāda sent Staal a copy of his letter and then turned their personal correspondence which followed into a small pamphlet: "The Krishna Consciousness Movement Is the Genuine Vedic Way."[9]

Although the obvious opportunism spoils any chance of their published exchange being a piece of savvy publicity, it does highlight contentious issues for scholars and Prabhupāda. Differences arise when Prabhupāda insists, in pursuance of his tradition's views, on valorizing one above all other aspects of long-debated disputable categories: chanting (versus other practices), personal (vs. the impersonal or other concepts of God), *smṛti* (vs. *śruti*),[10] *bhakti* (devotion) (vs. the paths of karma [action], *jñāna* [knowledge], or yoga),[11] Krishna (vs. any other deity). To be fair, Staal is just as categorical and equally disputatious: "It is an indisputable fact that the *Bhagavad-gītā* (not to mention the Vedas) does not require such constant chanting" (SSR 93). Prabhupāda counters with a host of proof texts. He argues for a unity of meaning in and privileged access to all "Vedic" (*śruti* and *smṛti*) texts,[12] while saying that Krishna alone is their one ultimate goal, and chanting his

8. It seems that the course was eventually accredited; see SSR 92.

9. For Rahul Peter Das's summary of the use of the term "Vedic" by Prabhupāda, see chapter 1 n. 14. The pamphlet's full title was more lengthy: "The Krishna Consciousness Movement Is the Genuine Vedic Way: A Cogent Discussion between A. C. Bhaktivedanta Swami, Acarya: International Society for Krishna Consciousness, and Dr. J. F. Staal, Professor of Philosophy and South Asian Languages, University of California, Berkeley" (SSR 90–104). The entire idea was Prabhupāda's, as was the instruction to widely distribute it among "educated circles, business men, and foundation authorities" to remove the stigma of hippiedom; see Brahmananada 700414.

10. *Śruti* (hearing) and *smṛti* (remembering) refer to categories of scripture. *Śruti* constitutes the Veda (knowledge or revelation) with its four divisions: the Ṛg, Yajur, Sāma, and Atharva, each divided into *Saṁhitā* (collection), *Brāhmaṇa* (ritual text), *Āraṇyaka* (forest treatise), and *Upaniṣad* (secret doctrine). *Smṛti* are later texts in pursuance of the Veda, though exactly *which* texts differs among the traditions. Gauḍīya theologian Jīva Gosvāmin considers the Purāṇas and Itihāsas (the epics), though technically *smṛti*, as religiously more important than *śruti*; see Das 1998:142–143. For Prabhupāda's view, see Das's comments referred to in the previous note.

11. These are not mutually exclusive categories.

12. Prabhupāda writes to Staal: "*Bhagavad-gītā*, although *smṛti*, is the essence of all Vedic scripture, *sarvopaniṣado gāvaḥ*. It is just like a cow which is delivering the milk, or the essence of all the Vedas and Upaniṣads, and all the *ācāryas*, including Śaṅkarācārya, accept the *Bhagavad-gītā* as such. Therefore you cannot deny the authority of the *Bhagavad-gītā*

names their recommended means of achieving him. Staal, in turn, denies the parity of *smṛti* (here, the Gītā) and *śruti,* and by marshalling his own proof texts, debates Prabhupāda's interpretation of *satataṁ* (always) *kīrtayantaḥ* (chanting) in Gītā 9:14. He also offers his own view, that the "*Gītā* is broad-minded and tolerant of a variety of approaches, although it also stresses one aspect above all others (i.e., *sarva-phala-tyāga* [renunciation of all fruits (of one's work)])" (97).

And so it goes, back and forth, neither submitting. Staal, seeing no end to it, cites Patañjali—"*mahān hi śabdasya prayoga-viṣayaḥ:* For vast is the domain for the use of words." Prabhupāda, too, recognizing the futility of further philosophizing, offers a final, pragmatic, louder-than-words proof: public enthusiasm for recent Krishna chanting in Berkeley and Detroit. The polemic is age-old, debated for centuries by gurus of Prabhupāda's lineage and their Staal-like adversaries,[13] with this further similarity: Vaishnava *bhakti* movements, being largely popular and pietistic, have usually needed to prove their bona fides to the established orthodoxy.[14] And Prabhupāda was no exception. He hoped that the polemical tract would convince its designated recipients (as he had attempted to persuade Staal) that Krishna consciousness was "the genuine Vedic way," and not "another edition of the Hippie movement" (Brahmananda 700414).

Prabhupāda was delighted by the publication of the first in-depth book about ISKCON, *Hare Krishna and the Counterculture* (1974), by another Berkeleyite, J. Stillson Judah,[15] the director of libraries and professor of the history of religions at the Graduate Theological Union. Judah uses a wide selection of primary and secondary literature and interviews with Prabhupāda and the devotees, along with a careful reading of Prabhupāda's books, in a monograph that arguably balances history and theology with sociology better than any other participant-observation field study since.[16] Judah's stated purpose is to acquaint others with the history

---

because it is *smṛti;* that view is *śruti-smṛti-virodhaḥ,* 'in conflict with the *smṛti* and the *śruti,*' as you have correctly said" (SSR 99).

13. The particulars, lying as they do at the heart of Gauḍīya theology, will be scrutinized later.

14. Legitimation was accomplished by methods too numerous to detail here. Promoting "Vedāntisation" and "Sanskritisation" of the *bhakti* religion is but one example; see van Buitenen 1966:30–35. Gauḍīya history is replete with efforts to gain acceptance: political, social, and textual-praxis.

15. Had he known of it, he would have been far less delighted with another title published the same year, Faye Levine's *The Strange World of the Hare Krishnas.* Levine, a journalist who lived in the New York temple for a month, concludes: "There is something inescapably frightening about their altered personalities. In the end, a certain absence of humanity must be noted" (1974:162).

16. We must bear in mind that a publishing date of 1974 means that Judah did not have in hand Prabhupāda's collected letters, conversations, or later dictated writings when preparing his book.

and philosophy of the movement in the context of the devotees' transformation within a culture that is itself changing (Judah 1974:4). For Prabhupāda, Judah's work explicitly presents what the Staal tract could not: an ISKCON freed from (though admittedly populated largely by) hippiedom.[17]

Devotees constitute a new subculture, fashioned from selected elements of the counterculture, combined with the ideals and goals of the devotees' natal religions, all validated by a newly adopted Vaishnavism. From this unlikely brew Judah distills a number of basic truths, one of which Staal had found most perplexing: "Even though the majority of Krishna's devotees had already been following some sort of unitive Eastern discipline, examples already given reveal that one element had been missing—love for a personal deity as the basis of love for all and everything" (173).[18] Judah's multidisciplinary approach traces this truth to its sources: a lack of equal security and satisfaction in impersonal countercultural options; the incapacity of former faiths to offer devotees an experience of God, a larger meaning of life, and close meaningful fellowship;[19] and the ability of Chaitanya's philosophy to synthesize monism and dualism in its presentation of Krishna as the "cosmic deity" and "ocean of bliss": "the Supreme Personality of Godhead" (Judah has adopted Prabhupāda's nomenclature).

Unfortunately for our purposes, the book's strength is also its greatest weakness. It is sympathetic to a fault. Judah's close and extensive association with the movement proves informative, *but* obliging:

> Because my approach to the subject has been sympathetic, I treat the Movement objectively from the standpoint of the devotees' beliefs and their

17. Prabhupāda writes to Judah: "It is my great delight that you have realized how Krishna Consciousness has transformed lives from drug-addicted hippies to loving servants of Krishna and humanity" (Judah 750611). In another letter, he asks permission to publish portions of the book in ISKCON's monthly magazine and to include it with street sales of his own books; see Judah 750603 (rare offers, though they did not materialize; compare his unwillingness to sell a godbrother's book; see Tamal Krishna 1998c:90). Prabhupāda insisted that his secretary carry Judah's book to be cited at important meetings. See his meeting with the mayor of Evanston, IL, 750704rc.chi, or with the press in Mauritius 751002pc.mau. By 1976, when he asks for the book in Auckland and Delhi, it has been left elsewhere, on one occasion in court (presumably as part of an ISKCON defense); see 750607rc.hon.

18. As a later study notes: "Unlike other scholars who wrote in the 1970s, he [Judah] discusses the relationship between the believer and Krishna [as a primary conversion factor]" (Zaidman-Dvir 1994:8). This redeems the Lofland-Stark "Conversion to a Deviant Perspective" model Judah uses, which on its own "explains little about how persons come to experience a transformation in their state of consciousness" (Rochford 1985:55).

19. See table 7, "Reasons Why Hare Krishna Devotees Abandoned Their Former Faith," in Judah 1974:151. See also chapter 1 n. 11.

> life situations without making a critical study of the beliefs themselves. In deference to the devotees I have included little critical discussion of such subjects as the Krishna traditions or beliefs, which they would consider inaccurate as well as objectionable. (9)

Judah is sociologically critical, but merely offers an annotated bibliography in lieu of doctrinal analysis.[20] We are presented the standard Gauḍīya theology and no more. This has merit. The chapters and accompanying charts on ISKCON's historical and literary antecedents and its beliefs, sketched from primary and secondary sources including Prabhupāda's translations and his purports, are accurate and most helpful, and an excellent point of departure. However, the development of Prabhupāda's thought is never investigated.

The ambivalence that Prabhupāda must have felt by being squarely located within the counterculture while laboring to establish ISKCON's bona fides is palpable. Three concurrent though independent ethnographic studies, each employing participant-observation methodology, resulted in doctoral dissertations that confirmed the obvious: ISKCON's umbilical connection with hippiedom was not easily severed. The studies—Gregory Johnson's (Harvard, 1973), Francine J. Daner's (Illinois, 1973, which evolved into *The American Children of Krishna,* published in 1976), and John P. Reis's (Wisconsin-Madison, 1975, with the tantalizing title, "God Is Not Dead, He Has Simply Changed Clothes...")—affirm what Prabhupāda could not help but admit: "the hippies are our best customers. Almost all of our important disciples are recruited from that group" (Gaurasundara 690713).

Johnson's research showcases the San Francisco chapter of ISKCON as a primary, microcosmic group successfully providing what the amorphous Haight-Ashbury counterculture host failed to offer: a coherent, sustainable "alternative community." Reis and Daner note the anomie that pervades the greater society, while Daner makes use of Erik Erikson's concepts of identity and alienation to explain what drives individuals to "revitalization movements" like ISKCON.[21] Nearly all who entered ISKCON

20. Joseph T. O'Connell in a review of Judah's book observes that the decision to omit doctrinal criticism "means that major questions are not posed and treated in the book" (1976b:20). Judah's appreciation for the movement may be measured by his willingness to sponsor ISKCON Berkeley's official affiliation as a graduate institute within the Graduate Theological Union (in marked contrast to Staal's disapproval of an accredited experimental course at UC Berkeley four years earlier). Prabhupāda accepted Judah's offer to teach in the proposed institute (something unexpected considering Judah's "outsider" status), but it never materialized; see 750622(and 25)gc.la.

21. Daner observes "the theme of satiation and revulsion with sense gratification and the permissiveness of our society" that underlies the personal biographies of all her interviewees (1976:104). Daner's research links psychological aspects of conversion to previous revitalization studies: "A revitalization movement is defined as a deliberate, organized, conscious effort by members of a society to construct a more satisfying culture" (Wallace 1956:265). Anthony Wallace in one such study explains a revitalization

had some prior experience with drug use. Johnson identifies members by their drugs of choice.[22] Reis includes a history of the drug movement, and Daner's interviews read like drug-culture autobiographies. While Prabhupāda protested to the contrary, much within the movement's rituals and doctrines "idealized, organized and dogmatized many of the members' previous 'hippie' attitudes" (Johnson, 179).

The social-scientific nature of these studies helps frame their underlying questions, informs their answers, and potentially relativizes their need to seek solutions through analysis of Prabhupāda's thought. Daner views ISKCON as a "forcing house" according to Erving Goffman's total institution model. Her title to chapter 6, "I Am Not This Body," encapsulates a basic ISKCON and very standard "Hindu" tenet: to deny the body as an ultimate identification. While the behavioral changes necessary to arrive at this realization may be voluntary, they are nevertheless adjudged to be "abasements, degradations, and profanations of (the) self" and "(t)he very act of putting one's body in a humiliating position while uttering obeisances is a further assault on the self" (Daner 1976:73, 75).

The second chapter of Johnson's treatise, "A Retreat from Pain or a Search for Meaning?" highlights the deprivation versus cognitive-interpretation debate surrounding conversions. Johnson sees the limitations of the deprivation approach, which views conversion as "merely an act of desperation: it is a willful act of choice" (90). But his examination of doctrine and ideology as a basis for this choice is at best indirect: "the specific permutations of the texts were not stressed; of more importance were the ways in which the doctrine became personally interpreted by the participants in the ceremonies" (32). The consequences of this strategy are debatable. As the temple "leader" ("Tamal was attributed as being the person 'most touched by the grace of Krishna'" [55]), I am frequently cited. Rather than Prabhupāda's books (not one is listed in the bibliography!), I, a recruit of barely half a year, become Johnson's principal doctrinal interpreter.[23]

---

subclass: "'Revivalistic' movements emphasize the institution of customs, values, and even aspects of nature which are thought to have been in the mazeway of previous generations but are not now present" (Wallace 1956:267). Based on this latter statement, J. Frank Kenney further identifies ISKCON as a "*Bengal* revitalization movement," and with good reason. However, Kenney cites an early article of mine as his sole evidence without sufficiently taking into account the fact that it was written at the end of my four-year tenure in India and, I now admit, was slanted to reflect nineteenth-century views many in India still find appealing; see Kenney 1980 and Tamal Krishna 1975.

22. Johnson's study began as part of a larger project of the U.S. Office of Education to examine migrants into Haight-Ashbury. He relates the long-term, transcendentally perspectival "carrier" group of members to the "psychedelic" years of 1968 and 1969; for those joining afterward—the "seeker" group—the movement's ideological and philosophical appeals were secondary to personal transformation.

23. Johnson spoke to Prabhupāda in 1969, but their reported discussion is minimal; see Johnson 1973:38. Daner complains in print (and complained to me several times) of a canceled appointment with Prabhupāda; see Daner 1976:18–19. It sometimes happened

Table 2.1

	Material	Spiritual
Personal	A	D
	Regulated life	A pure devotee's life
Social	B	C
	The social order	The spiritual society

Reis does little more. Although he listed most of Prabhupāda's books then available, a careful reading reveals that all his literary citations are drawn from ISKCON's monthly magazine, its handbook, and secondary literature. This is unsurprising, since his work is "primarily concerned with ISKCON as a sociological phenomenon" (Reis, 5). Only Daner makes direct, though sparing, use of Prabhupāda. She also primarily relies on secondary literature, in this case Dimock and Hopkins (in Singer 1966) and Zaehner (1968), to flesh out her chapter on "Roots in India."[24] As the counterculture faded, social scientists noted its continuity in the proliferation of youthful religious groups. Jonathan F. Moody's dissertation, "Ethics and Counter Culture: An Analysis of the Ethics of Hare Krishna" (Claremont, 1978), diligently systematizes Prabhupāda's ethical teachings to ascertain the role ethics plays in defining the counterculture and what prescriptions it provides for the behavior of believers. He proposes a four-stage ethical development, illustrated as a four-quadrant figure, derived by diagraming the nexus of two sets of polarities (table 2.1).

With the help of textual evidence and interviews, Moody works through a counterclockwise rotation on the chart, from personal-material to the highest ethic, personal-spiritual:

> The key is remembering that the moral life is a process from material to spiritual, from bondage to freedom in service, from regulated to spontaneous devotional service, from an ethic of deed to an ethic of attitude. Any

that Prabhupāda learned later that someone coming to see him had been turned away by mistake without his knowledge; see Satsvarūpa 1980–83 2:173–175. Reis makes no mention of meeting Prabhupāda.

24. Still, her primary and secondary readings pay off, enabling her to identify issues where traditional scholarship and academic scholarship divide. Particularly insightful is her comment that what differentiates Prabhupāda's Gītā from other translations is that his interprets its teachings in the light of the Śrīmad Bhāgavatam; see Daner 1976:27 and n. 13.

given devotee is influenced by both ends of these polarities, and falls in a unique place in the process. (218–219)

An individual's moral growth is measured in each of the four quadrants in terms of discipline, sacrifice, and attitude, but in quadrant "D" ("a pure devotee's life") "ethics is a spontaneous love for Godhead; no rules apply.... Rather, there is an antinomian relationship of direct intuition with the divine" (291). According to Moody, the ethics of Krishna consciousness are defined by a dynamic tension between regulation and spontaneity, reflected in the tension between the authority of the movement as a whole (originating in the person and teachings of Prabhupāda) and individual identity and responsibility (mediated through the local temple and its president). This ethical dynamic—of the legal and antinomian, or of the principled and contextual—is present in any persistent system. It is clearly reflected in the tension that separates the dominant culture from its counterculture.

There are inevitable difficulties in basing social theories on theological concepts, particularly when the latter are deeply embedded in Sanskritic terms unfamiliar to the researcher. "Regulated" and "spontaneous" are translations of two categories of *bhakti-sādhana* (devotional practice): *vaidhī bhakti* (devotion expressed through following laws) and *rāgānuga-bhakti* (devotion expressed by following spontaneous feelings of love). It is one thing to connect institutional injunctions with individual restraint. But to correlate the spontaneity of love of Godhead with the need for individual self-expression (much less a proclivity for countercultural freedoms) risks mistaking the liberated and the bound states, a source of theological confusion that has confounded the tradition since nearly its inception.[25]

Moody's theory is further jeopardized by making the temple in Laguna Beach, California, during the period January 1975 to July 1976 his sole testing site. He is aware of its atypicality: The temple community consists largely of peripheral members who do not live by the demands of the movement (114–115); the community attracts "devotees who are not sufficiently serious" (228); "the assumed order of a Krishna conscious community is often lacking" (235); and "Laguna Beach is not characterized by total conversion. Therefore, the move away from drugs is not firm...and for many the life of the beach does not change" (287).[26]

---

25. The theoretical distinction between the two forms of practice and the discrepancies arising from misapplication of more advanced practices to fulfill worldly desires are repeated themes in Prabhupāda's teachings, especially NOD, which itself has elicited further clarification; see Dhanurdhara 2000. For theory and for controversies of old, see Haberman 1988. Scholars, too, have argued the issue; see Dimock 1989:xvii and O'Connell 1989. For recent confusions in ISKCON, see Tamal Krishna 1997a. For an overview that includes other Vaishnava traditions, see Rosen 1993.

26. This, in striking contrast with Daner's description of the typical ISKCON temple as a "total institution" as Goffman defines it; see Daner 1976:12–13.

Unbeknownst to Moody, the temple president (his most cited interviewee, whose influence in the temple is "dominant") could not make the move away from drugs; he was at the center of a thriving heroin business for which he was later convicted.[27] This significant fact lends Moody's seriously flawed conclusion an unsuspecting irony: "For the devotees live their counter culture ethic and style in the face of the law given the right by the spontaneity that is above the law" (287). It would seem that in juxtaposing ethical polarities, Moody has unwittingly confused devotees belonging to quadrant "A" with those in "D," that is, devotees still needing regulation with those spontaneously devoted. The absence of a "normal" ISKCON temple as a control group proves fatal to his thesis; he has no way of gauging whether the group he is studying is representative of either ISKCON or the counterculture it has theoretically left. Although Moody's study, unlike those of Johnson, Daner, and Reis, holds out the promise of creative engagement with Prabhupāda's thought, in the end its misconceived social hypothesis confuses rather than clarifies Prabhupāda's (i.e., Chaitanya's) ethical system.

ISKCON could not easily divorce itself from the counterculture, even if Daner could declare: "Bhaktivedanta, with the help of his disciples, has successfully transplanted Vedic culture in America with as few errors in transmission as possible. He has made only the most necessary compromises in order to render this essentially Hindu system operable in the West" (Daner 1976:103). If ISKCON was not a new religion, the overall impression created by these four monographs is that it certainly is a new religious movement. This more nuanced understanding prevails among scholars: "While Hare Krishna may not be new in India, it is new in America.... Adherents of the Krishna movement here are not really engaged in the same religious worldview or place in the culture as those in India. So even though there are old themes which are taken up, the product is in some measure new" (Hargrove 1978:258). Perhaps a newer vintage of an old wine in a new bottle.

The label "new religious movement" (NRM), though well intentioned, was particularly troublesome in the face of Prabhupāda's repeated assertion that he did not change anything. ISKCON remains vexed with the label, as the title of a senior disciple's article indicates: "NRM Is a Four-Letter Word: The Language of

27. Moody notes, "The president...found it very difficult to support the opinion of the movement that drugs are demonic; for him, they were the first step in spiritual search" (269). A not uncommon view, but in light of his ongoing complicity, damning. After his second conviction, he pleaded that he had joined ISKCON as an impressionable youth and Prabhupāda had told him to traffic drugs and that it would be "karma-free." In fact, when Prabhupāda was offered this tainted wealth, he replied: "I cannot digest your money (absolve you of such karma)" (communicant who wishes to remain anonymous). Later, he instructed, "We should not accept money if it is earned by sinful sources" (Tamal Krishna 1998c:328).

Oppression" (Mukunda 1995). Inappropriate perhaps, but far less stigmatizing than the four-letter trope it was invented to replace: "cult."

Cult-Controversy Discourse: The Mid-1970s to Mid-1980s

"...then they will hate you,..."

During ISKCON's second decade, the pejorative sense of this originally reverential (L. *cultus,* worship) and later anthropological term was utilized by the American anticult movement and became a formidable propaganda weapon. The cult controversy prioritized ISKCON's self-authenticating efforts. The "cult" tag bore far graver consequences than hippie identification, as a $32.5 million initial judgment against the movement in one high-profile brainwashing case confirms.[28] As the retrospective essays of an ISKCON-sponsored academic conference held in 1985 make clear (Bromley and Shinn 1989), the cult controversy not only dominated media coverage but set the agenda for much of the ISKCON-related scholarship.[29] The anticult movement's dismissal of new religious movements was not primarily based on theological considerations (Beckford 1994:19). The media coverage and the scholarship that grew out of the cult controversy followed suit. If by necessity the spotlight of our survey of such scholarship falls upon ISKCON, leaving Prabhupāda in the shadows, the paucity of interest shown in his actual thought becomes strikingly clear.

According to David G. Bromley, opposition to ISKCON escalated when ISKCON's recruitment focus shifted from countercultural havens like Haight-Ashbury to college campuses and other middle-class youth forums.[30] This direct

28. See Bromley 1989 for an excellent summary and analysis of the Robin George case. As Bromley notes, referencing Shinn who served as an expert witness for the defense, "the essence of the trial was a brainwashing/mind control charge upon which all of the other charges...rested" (268). The case was eventually settled out of court for an undisclosed amount.

Shinn explains the origin of the brainwashing term: Edward Hunter, an American journalist, was the first American to translate the Chinese phrase *hsi nao* (literally "wash the mind") into English as "brainwashing," but it is a 1961 seminal study by Robert Jay Lifton of coercive persuasion of American soldiers in Chinese Communist prison camps that launched its present use; see Shinn 1987:127. Prabhupāda plays with the term ("brain-clearing") and cites Chaitanya's *ceto-darpaṇa-mārjanam* (cleansing the mirror of the mind), a result of chanting the holy name of the Lord; see 761103sb.vrn.

29. See Yokum 1986 for a summary of the ISKCON-sponsored conference proceedings.

30. Recruitment stories taken from these two foci clearly confirm Bromley's theory; see parts 1 and 3 of Tamal Krishna 1984, an autobiographical account of recruitment activities and Prabhupāda's letters in response. The mobile witnessing teams specifically identified by Bromley (258) for intensifying opposition are the subject of part 3; counterculture recruitment the subject of part 1.

challenge to establishment values by groups like ISKCON precipitated the cult scare. Its ideational framework was the subversion myth:

> Subversion mythologies are premised on the existence of a conspiracy. They posit a specific danger and a group associated with it, one or more conspirators who have planned and direct the plot, a set of base impulses that motivate the conspiracy leaders, a manipulative process through which the conspirators involve others in their conspiracy, an imminent danger for the entire society, and a remedial agenda that must be followed if catastrophe is to be avoided. (1989:256)

ISKCON putatively fit this conspiratorial theory, with Prabhupāda, its chief conspirator, employing coercive mind-control techniques, especially a mesmerizing mantra.

J. Gordon Melton, another contributor to the 1985 conference, analyzes ISKCON's response to a climate now turned hostile (Melton 1989:95). In a three-pronged strategy, ISKCON sought legitimation by cultivating the scholarly community, presenting itself as a traditional Indian religious group, and aligning with the burgeoning Indian population residing in North America. The titles of two pamphlets published at this time make clear the patent aim: "The Krishna Consciousness Movement Is Authorized" (40 percent of which is scholarly testimonials, prompting Prabhupāda to refer to it as "the quote book") and "A Request to the Media: Please Don't Lump Us In" (i.e., with the "new" cults; Śubhānanda dāsa 1978).[31] Articles by prominent scholars were also printed in *Back to Godhead,* the movement's monthly magazine, and an important study was commercially published, subtitled and featuring "Five Distinguished Scholars on the Krishna Movement in the West."[32]

Was Prabhupāda directly involved in orchestrating ISKCON's defense? As the movement's chief theologian, "Yes"; again, as the supreme commander of its mission (if these roles may be separated) "Yes." He responds to the charge of "brainwashing" on four occasions within his canonical Śrīmad Bhāgavatam

---

31. Prabhupāda offered a rather novel suggestion regarding this first pamphlet's distribution (the second was published after his demise): "You can send it to important members of the government, businessmen, entertainers, sportsmen, etc. Another device is that you can address it to 'Any Respectable Gentleman, Post Office..., City..., State...'. The postman will then deliver it to some respectable gentleman. Everyone who gets it will think: 'I am a most respectable gentleman because he has given it to me.'" More conventional advice was followed: "The best thing is to find out the customers list to some big magazine like '*Time*' or '*Life*,' and post it to them" (Ramesvara 760112).

32. For articles in *Back to Godhead* magazine, see Cox 1977 and Eck 1979. The "Five Distinguished Scholars" are discussed further on.

commentaries, while at the same time in his more freewheeling lectures and conversations during the period between November 1976 and March 1977, hardly a week passes when the topic is not addressed at least once or twice, often more. What was it that drew his attention at this time?

In a reversal of a case filed by a twenty-three-year-old devotee woman against her mother and a deprogrammer on charges of kidnapping, a New York grand jury instead indicted two local ISKCON leaders for using mind control to unlawfully imprison the woman and an adult male devotee similarly kidnapped.[33] The case attracted national attention. In a signed document, two hundred scholars defended ISKCON as an authentic Indian missionary movement (Melton, 95). As ISKCON's governing body commissioner for the northeastern United States, I recognized that the very survival of our movement was at stake. The theological legitimacy of both our beliefs and praxis was being legally challenged. I conveyed my deep concern to Prabhupāda, who issued (in his biographer's words) "a clarion call to battle against the forces of illusion" (SPL 6:217):

> My dear Tamala Krishna,
>
> Please accept my blessings. I am in receipt of your letter dated 22/10/76, along with pictures, newsclippings, etc.
>
> Regarding the point about whether our movement is bona fide, you can use the following arguments. Bhagavad-gita has got so many editions. Our books are older than the Bible. In India there are millions of Krishna temples. Let the judges and juries read our books and take the opinion of learned scholars and professors. Regarding the second point about the parents' jurisdiction over their children, here are some suggestions: Do the parents like that their children become hippies? Why don't they stop it? Do the parents like their children to become involved in prostitution and intoxication? Why don't they stop this?
>
> They are now feeling the weight of this movement. Formerly they thought these people come and go, but now they see we are staying. Now we have set fire. It will go on, it cannot be stopped. You can bring big, big fire brigades but the fire will act. The brainwash books are already there. Even if they stop (it) externally, internally it will go on. Our first class campaign is book distribution. Go house to house. The real fighting is now. Krishna will give you all protection. So, chant Hare Krishna and fight. (TamalaKrishna 761030)

33. See Bromley 1989 for a summary. For Prabhupāda's response, see Satsvarūpa 1980–83 6:216–218, 266–269.

Not the language of pacifism. ISKCON of the second decade had "staying" power, was no longer a "come and go" amusement. Lines were drawn in a battle for America's youth. ISKCON was to fight with books. *Brainwash* books! Later in the letter, Prabhupāda identified what he believed to be the cause of the conflict: "They are afraid that a different culture is conquering over their culture." That fear was not new, as Melton's survey of century-long American attitudes toward Hinduism demonstrates (1989). The anticult movement had merely reworked a tested subversion myth.

I was in India some months later, serving as Prabhupāda's secretary, when news of the New York Supreme Court's decision was published on the front page of *The Times of India:*

> HARE KRISHNA MOVEMENT IS BONA FIDE RELIGION
>
> Washington, March 18, 1977
>
> The Hare Krishna movement was called a "bona fide religion" yesterday by the New York High Court Justice who threw out two charges against the officials of the movement of "illegal imprisonment" and "attempted extortion".... "The entire and basic issue before the court," said the Justice in dismissing the charges, "is whether the two alleged victims in this case and the defendants will be allowed to practice the religion of their choice and this must be answered with a resounding affirmative." Said Mr. Justice John Leahy: "the Hare Krishna movement is a bona fide religion with roots in India that go back thousands of years. It behooved Merril Kreshower and Edward Shapiro to follow the tenets of that faith and their inalienable right to do so will not be trampled upon...." The Justice said, "The freedom of religion is not to be abridged because it is unconventional in beliefs and practices or because it is approved or disapproved by the mainstream of society or more conventional religions." (SPL6:267)

"My mission is now successful," said Prabhupāda. "In 1965 I went there. This is now recognized after twelve years. I was loitering in the street alone, carrying the books. Nobody cared" (267–268).

If the judgment was legally a landmark decision, the apologetic approach of the "conventional religions" (Christianity and Judaism) regarding ISKCON was not noticeably altered.[34] But the judgment did chasten the anticult invective.

---

34. Massimo Introvigne distinguishes the secular anticult movement's approach from the older Christian countercult coalitions that portrayed cults as Satan's agents; see Introvigne 1997:39. The distinction between religious and secular agendas, however, is often blurred.

It forced the brainwashing ideology to be revamped in favour of psychological rather than physical coercion, a shift to the domain and expertise of clinicians (Bromley, 282).

As the studies of the second decade attest, the cult controversy continued. If (as Prabhupāda asserted) in the first decade "nobody cared," in the second nobody could afford to ignore ISKCON. The hidden advantage, at least in certain studies, is an increased engagement with Prabhupāda's thought. While only one scholar tackles Prabhupāda's theology head on, a number evaluate its importance. Many, however, like Chandralekha P. Singh's dissertation, "Hare Krishna: A Study of the Deviant Career of Hare Krishna Devotees" (New York University, 1981), largely continue to avoid it.

Singh identifies ISKCON's "deviance" as the rejection of Judaeo-Christian ethics and morality and the desired roles and lifestyles of mainstream society. However, Krishna devotee deviancy and subsequent social rejection, discrimination, and exclusion, she argues, are largely a social construction of the "cult" mythology, reinforced by the authority of medical professionals. As a participant-observer, Singh finds none of the supposed harmful psychiatric and medical symptoms, nor truth in the claim that members are "psychologically kidnapped." Rather, she proposes "an *activist* view of converts (converts as 'active seekers, not passive victims') and of conversion as a rational, reflective process" (356).

Singh believes, "The largest contribution of our study in our view is that it offers an in-depth understanding of the Hare Krishna group, *its meaning system*" (368, emphasis added). However, only brief references from two of Prabhupāda's books and a dozen or so citations from the movement's magazine underline this contention. Her survey questions (370–371) do not probe beliefs or religious experiences. According to James S. Gordon, the major limitations of such studies are not so much in their findings and methodology as in their scope and perspective. Questions that need asking first are: "What is the ideal of Krishna Consciousness? How successful is ISKCON in bringing it about in its members? Why is it appealing now to young Westerners? What kinds of experiences—religious as well as psychological and social—do they have?" (1989:250).

According to John Saliba, the Christian and Jewish approach has favored apologetics above dialogue; see Saliba 1989 for a documented history. As recently as 1996, Rabbi A. James Rudin, American Jewish Committee director of interreligious affairs and author of *A Jewish Guide to Interreligious Relations,* was unresponsive to my official request to modify, "Most Hindus consider such cults as Hare Krishna...aberrations from authentic Hinduism" (1996:66).

The need to enlarge the scope of public understanding by contextualizing the movement historically, culturally, and theologically was recognized by Steven Gelberg, ISKCON's academic liaison (who also coordinated the 1985 conference). Gelberg conducted interviews with three historians of religion (A. L. Basham, Thomas Hopkins, and Larry Shinn) and two theologians (Harvey Cox and Shrivatsa Goswami) and commercially published *Hare Krishna, Hare Krishna: Five Distinguished Scholars on the Krishna Movment in the West* (1983).[35] Robert S. Ellwood's foreword sets ISKCON apart from other "new" religions: "Although of recent origin in its present institutional form, it differs from most new religious movements and so-called 'cults' in having clearly definable and highly literary sources in an ancient spiritual tradition, albeit one alien to the Western lands in which it now flourishes" (1983:11).

ISKCON is also distinguished by its popular devotional praxis, conveyed intact:

> For Hare Krishna is unique also in being the only successful transplant, not of Hindu yoga or Vedānta, but of the bhakti or devotionalism which is so life-giving to millions in India, but which until now must have seemed virtually untransplantable. Yet here it is, and—still another uniqueness—practically without the acculturating sea-changes which leave the practice of most other imported religions significantly different from that of the homeland. (12)[36]

The uniqueness of conveyance, or the distinctiveness of Prabhupāda's cultural transplantation, and the authenticity of ISKCON beliefs and praxis are two of the volume's central themes, to which Cox adds a third, namely, familiar elements that should make Krishna consciousness seem less "foreign": a personal God who becomes incarnate and (more in common with pietistic Christianity than liberal Protestantism) the importance of religious feeling—singing, ecstatic dancing—coupled with puritanical virtues and "a reticence to make use of historical-critical approaches to the understanding of a scriptural text" (Cox 1983:31). Emphasis is given to the future life, or the other world, not to transforming the present world into an ideal. Basham sees similarities to eighteenth- and nineteenth-century Puritanism, which also eschewed the pleasures of the "permissive society" (Basham 1983:169). Shinn sketches a further parallel: "Very much as John Wesley

---

35. These are persons familiar with ISKCON. Shinn authored an extensive study that is separately treated. Cox, Hopkins, and Shinn contributed forewords to individual volumes of the official Prabhupāda biography (as did Judah and Robert D. Baird, whose critique of Prabhupāda's thought is examined later in this chapter); see SPL 1–5.

36. For another Gauḍīya Vaishnava missionary attempt, contrasted with Prabhupāda's, that of Baba Premananda Bharati some fifty years earlier, see Carney 1998.

is said to have sung Methodism into England, Chaitanya danced and chanted Vaishnavism into Bengal and even beyond Bengal. And you could say also that Prabhupāda chanted Vaishnavism into America and the western world" (Shinn 1983:85).

Hopkins is most insightful in analyzing Prabhupāda's success. A specialist in devotional Hinduism and the Bhāgavata Purāṇa, Hopkins had studied ISKCON from its inception, had consulted with Prabhupāda, and had made a careful study of the Gauḍīya tradition, especially the life and work of Prabhupāda's predecessor, Ṭhākura Bhaktivinoda.[37] Prabhupāda's mission, Hopkins believes, must be seen not just in terms of the counterculture but as a challenge to the whole intellectual tradition that views the West as the fountainhead of wisdom and value and sees India (and non-Western cultures) as culturally and intellectually inferior. He points out that Prabhupāda inherited "a revitalized and spiritually rich Gauḍīya Vaishnava tradition that had been imbued, by both Bhaktivinoda and Bhaktisiddhānta (his biological son and the *guru* of Prabhupāda), with a spirit of universality and of relevance to the modern world" (Hopkins 1983:127). Concern for fidelity and conveyance is part of this legacy: "The emphasis is not on changing the content of the tradition to make it intelligible to people, but on simply making it available—through translation and publication and other forms of propagation—because it is inherently accessible; it deals with the lives of people in a way that is universal" (126). This universal appeal and egalitarian approach rest upon an orientation toward a personal deity of infinite compassion who is concerned for those suffering in the world. Whereas Cox sees ISKCON as otherworldly, Hopkins thinks otherwise: Prabhupāda sought a practical, worldly-otherworldly balance, though within the activities of the religious institution.

But Prabhupāda's most significant contribution, Hopkins believes, was in introducing the *ritualistic* and *experiential* aspects of Krishna consciousness. Hindu tradition "is not one which emphasizes orthodoxy so much as it does *orthopraxis*, correct practice" (118). Enculturation was the essential agency:

> Bhaktivedanta Swami ... was very, very concerned that the tradition be presented in its fullness, as it became more and more clear that the authentic

37. Hopkins contracted Prabhupāda to teach a course on the Bhagavad Gītā in the spring of 1970 at Franklin and Marshall College; see Hopkins 1983:104. Prabhupāda agreed, "provided nobody shall smoke before me, especially when I take the class" (Brahmananda 690526). Although Hopkins says Prabhupāda canceled because of falling ill in the fall of 1969, Prabhupāda seemed prepared to go ahead with the course, though the cold weather was a concern; see Brahmananda 691210. Five years later Prabhupāda writes his former Boston temple president: "That was a misunderstanding. I am prepared to take the class. So you write the professor. You had told me it was very cold there, otherwise I was ready" (Satsvarūpa 741128).

> tradition was irreplaceable, that the cultural tradition out of which Krishna consciousness came was essential to the purpose and practice of Krishna consciousness, and that any attempt to translate it into purely Western cultural terms might only serve to convolute it. (108)

The experiential dimensions of this cultural transmission in combination with the theoretical frame of Prabhupāda's translations ensure a balance between emotion and intellect, central to the Bhāgavata tradition exemplified by Chaitanya and his followers, who gave a rational, intellectual structure to emotion: "Historically, the real power of the Vaishnava devotional tradition has been in its refusal to separate the intellect and the emotions" (138). Shrivatsa Goswami (the fifth interviewee), a hereditary descendant of an early family of Chaitanya worshippers, concurs: "His practical, experiential approach to the Vaishnava texts was the proper approach" (Shrivatsa 1983:249).

According to Hopkins, Prabhupāda made the tradition itself accessible by making important Vaishnava texts widely available for the first time to Western audiences unfamiliar with the total Indian cultural and theological context. Hopkins finds his commentaries "very traditional," closely in keeping with previous commentators: "Unless you know the tradition you won't realize the extent to which he's representing it.... Bhaktivedanta Swami is not commenting on these texts off the top of his head. He's very strongly rooted in his tradition" (Hopkins 1983:141). Prabhupāda bridges an enormous cultural gap by making the teachings practically applicable, "putting the teaching into a new social, intellectual, and linguistic context so that it becomes as accessible now as the previous commentaries were in their time."

To accomplish this, his translations are often combinations of text and commentary, which draw upon not only the past commentaries but the cumulative tradition as a whole.[38] Expanding the meanings of terms and concepts so that they are relevant to his own devotional community and time has often drawn criticism from Sanskritists, but Hopkins believes it clarifies rather than obscures meanings and is essential for the tradition to endure.[39] Thus the Krishna of the

---

38. See chapter 1 n. 20.

39. Winand Callewaert and Shilanand Hemraj criticise Prabhupāda for "over-interpretation and a lack of acquaintance with Western philosophy inherent in the English language." They cite Antonio De Nicolas (1976:420): "No wonder that works like the *BG as it is*...are even possible in spite of the complete disregard for the Sanskrit language the author says he translates from. Example: *dharmakshetre, kurukshetre* is translated as 'Place of Pilgrimage'" (Callewaert and Hemraj 1983:250). Hopkins, however, defends Prabhupāda's translations including, specifically, "place of pilgrimage" in BG 1:1; see Hopkins 1995:100. Another, minor example is Prabhupāda's translation of *pāvaka* in BG 15:6 as "electricity" ("That abode of Mine is not illumined by the sun or moon, nor by electricity" [BG 1972]).

Bhagavad Gītā, though technically the princely warrior of the Mahābhārata, is the same Krishna for Prabhupāda as the pastoral, playful cowherd of the Bhāgavata Purāṇa.[40] This coheres with the Gauḍīya tradition, and to believe otherwise would affect and thereby fail to convey what Prabhupāda means by "Krishna consciousness." Ultimately, Hopkins says, "[t]he very existence of a genuine Vaishnava movement in the West is compelling evidence of his success as a commentator" (142), a salient observation that he alone makes.

ISKCON's second decade closed with a flurry of important scholarly publications fueled by the "cult" scare, a number of them long-term research projects finally come to fruition. In the research of sociologist E. Burke Rochford Jr., concentrated nearly exclusively upon ISKCON for the past twenty-five years, the American Krishnas are shown to be no longer the "children" of Daner's study. Rochford's ongoing research exposes an ISKCON with all the attendant problems of adulthood.[41] His major work, *Hare Krishna in America* (1985), focuses on recruitment in its broadest sense and particularly as an explanation for conversion. Readers are directed to Gelberg and Judah for an understanding of religious beliefs and the tradition's history. Rochford's interest in ISKCON's theology is mainly tangential. Analyzing ISKCON's changing missionary strategy with reference to resource-mobilization theory, he discloses how the use of public places for proselytizing redefined the terms for the movement's legitimation and, in doing so, affected its core theological ritual—*saṁkīrtana*, ecstatic public chanting.[42]

The first half of the study continues the work of earlier social-science research on recruitment, which examines why some persons, rather than others, join ISKCON. In the later chapters Rochford details the shifting patterns of ISKCON's economy and their permutational effect on the public rituals of chanting, book selling, and fund-raising. Prabhupāda had himself emphasized book distribution, but in the face of mounting public resistance, ISKCON leaders stressed the

---

Monier-Williams's *Dictionary* additionally suggests "pure, clear, bright, shining." Kees W. Bolle translates it as "fire" and considers Prabhupāda's choice "comical," a "disregard for the text"; see Bolle 1979:232–233. Bolle also takes Prabhupāda to task for omitting the important adjective "supreme" when translating *dhāma paramam* as "abode" (though Prabhupāda correctly glosses it, and the translation in the 1983 revised edition reflects this).

40. This contested issue is central to Prabhupāda's theology and will later receive in-depth treatment.

41. Rochford's more recent work is referred to in the next section of this chapter.

42. Larry Shinn makes similar observations (Shinn 1987:110–113) and concludes: "When Prabhupāda linked the mission of preaching the Krishna faith to its economic support and survival, the seeds of conflict with an uninformed, wary, and finally hostile American public had been sown" (119).

financial side of book distribution, often at the expense of missionary goals.[43] This only intensified the crisis of legitimacy, both for the public and among ISKCON's members. Succession controversies following Prabhupāda's demise further aggravated the situation. Rochford argues that ISKCON will find it difficult to move from the institutional status of a sect to that of a church or a denomination when its chief motive for such a change is financial and the movement is publicly perceived as threatening.[44]

Mission and the ritual of *saṁkīrtana* remain the focus in Larry R. Underberg's dissertation, "Analysis of the Rhetoric of ISKCON: An Implicit Theory Perspective" (Pennsylvania State, 1987). Underberg selected ISKCON as a high-visibility social movement whose overt "preaching activities" ideally demonstrate that ISKCON's rhetorical practices exhibit a considerable degree of correspondence to the implicit-communication theory found in its teachings. Unlike in other social-scientific studies, the primary sources of data for his research are the movement's publications, including Prabhupāda's books. As in the other studies, these publications are not referenced for theological explication.

In a fourfold presentation, Underberg pairs ISKCON's objectives in the use of rhetoric with the primary means of their achievement: gaining visibility through public chanting, attracting followers by literature distribution, establishing a communal structure by physical and psychological isolation, and confronting opposition by public denial and private rationalization. These goals are common to many social organizations, religious or otherwise. What illumines Underberg's study is his telling citations from the founder and his followers as proof of the implicit assumptions that underlie proselytizing strategies. These assumptions include those the public finds distasteful, particularly that deception, as a technique of rhetoric, is ethical and permissible.[45] The basic premise

---

43. In a letter to me, Prabhupāda writes, "Regarding *saṁkīrtana* [public chanting] and book distribution, both should go on, but book distribution is more important. It is *bṛhat-kīrtana* [loud chanting, a metaphor borrowed from his own guru, who described the printing press as the *bṛhad-mṛdaṅga*, 'loud drum']" (Tamal Krishna 741023). The shift in emphasis during Prabhupāda's presence from chanting to book selling is sketched in a number of accounts. The centrality of book distribution and missionary objectives, especially under increasing financial pressures, was regularly reinforced by strategic manuals; see for example BBT Sankirtan Books 1993.

44. For the problems inherent in the church-sect typology, see ch. 4 of Wilson 1982.

45. Certain categories of deceptions that are widespread in other organizations so as to be considered almost acceptable are accentuated because of ISKCON's high visibility and alterity. Innocuous duplicity is also cited, including my own embarrassing example of a college "preaching program" conducted under the unlikely title "Hemoglobin Types in Ancient Man." While this almost farcical instance itself is harmless, as part of a pattern of deceit it indicates a serious problem that ISKCON has attempted to address. Aware of its need to practice rhetorical "honesty," ISKCON established ministries for improving

undergirding ISKCON's entire rhetorical theory is also disclosed: the view of a dulled and degraded humanity requiring rescue from the onslaughts of the *kali-yuga*. What is not revealed is the researcher's own implicit belief: Apparently he does not agree that humanity is at the mercy of a hostile environment (the *kali-yuga*), a view no less rhetorically determinate than ISKCON's.

In another attempt to explain the rationale underlying ISKCON conversions and faith maintenance, J. Frank Kenney and Tommy H. Polling, two University of Arkansas researchers, published a psychological monograph, *The Hare Krishna Character Type: A Study of the Sensate Personality* (1986). During eight years of participant-observation, the authors found that the predispositional factors of conversion isolated by previous researchers (Judah, Daner, and Rochford) were indistinguishable from those of preconverts to other new religions.[46] This led them to suspect a hitherto unidentified factor specific to ISKCON, namely, that its lifestyle is reducible to dealing with sensuality and how to eliminate it (37); hence, it is especially suited to a "sensate personality."

To test their hypothesis, Kenney and Polling applied the Meyers-Briggs Type Indicator to Carl Jung's interpretative typology of four modes of apprehending reality (thinking vs. feeling, and sensing vs. intuiting), enhanced by a judging versus perceiving dimension.[47] Of the ninety-three devotees tested, 82 percent were found to be sensing types, 78 percent were thinking types, and 90 percent were judging types, confirming their suspicion that "ISKCON provides its membership thinking and judging mechanisms to control sensate propensities within a religious frame of reference" (153). Devotees' preoccupation with sensate pleasures derived from sights, tastes, sounds, and smells are sublimated through

---

communications and book distribution. However, the textual legacy intertwined with circumstantial pressures may always provide opportunities for dissimulation.

46. The eight preconversion biographical and situational characteristics identified in previous studies are: "a socio-economically advantaged family background; an early socialization process characterized by discord as well as an identity crisis prior to membership in ISKCON; an orientation toward being a world saver; a rejection of parental authority and value system coupled with the need for a strong, male authority substitute; extensive use of drugs prior to joining ISKCON; a tendency to view the material world as devoid of meaning and reality; a vegetarian diet; and a tendency to seek a new self-identity in nontraditional Asian religions" (Kenney and Polling 1986:1).

47. It should be noted that there has been criticism of engaging the Meyers-Briggs Type Indicator to a Jungian framework since it bears no clear relation to the numinous experience Jung considered the basis of religion. After reviewing Kenney and Polling's Krishna findings, David Wulff opines, "In spite of the MBTI's enormous popularity among proponents of analytical psychology, research indicates that what is measured are not Jung's types but basic dimensions of personality that also appear—more clearly identified—on other inventories." Wulff suggests that reinterpreting the MBTI Krishna results along other grounds might yield more fruitful comparisons; see Wulff 1991:458–459.

rituals that are elaborate orchestrations for the senses. Myth and rituals combine to provide devotees with the vicarious sense gratification they crave.[48]

Supplementing these test results, taped interviews also indicate that devotees conform to these findings. Furthermore, owing to my autobiography being the only extensive source of its kind at the time, I have the rare honor of being repeatedly cited as one who "evinces sensate characteristics—primarily, the pursuit of and concern with pleasure in terms of material, sensate enjoyment" (114). But I am in good company: By their reckoning, Prahlāda, child-hero of the Bhāgavata Purāṇa's seventh canto, is also an STJ (sensing-thinking-judging type), though a *controlled* sensate.[49] And, as it turns out, so is Lord Krishna: "From a liturgical perspective, the worship of Krishna is designed to provide the deity with sense pleasure. Krishna is fanned, bathed, dressed in finery, entertained, and above all, fed.... Krishna is, above all, a 'God Who Eats'" (117).[50] Kenney and Polling's analysis has merits: It is logical and internally consistent; it makes "sense." It accurately refers to a central theological maxim of *bhakti:* "Bhakti, or devotional service, means engaging all our senses in the service of the Lord, the Supreme Personality of Godhead, the master of all the senses" (CC 2.19:170).[51]

---

48. [The somewhat awkward phrase "sense gratification" used by Goswami here in this sentence is a phrase that can be found many hundreds of times throughout Prabhupāda's work, and thus it appears in this book several times. The phrase should not be taken literally. Rather, in a general sense, the expression refers to the indulgent worldly life and a life that is selfishly pleasure seeking. More specifically, it refers to a state of being enslaved to all futile attempts to satisfy or gratify one's senses with the fleeting pleasures of this world, which results in the degradation of consciousness.—ed.]

49. According to the authors, Prahlāda is a role model for ISKCON sensates because he evinces five of the eight preconvert characteristics mentioned in n. 46. In addition, Prahlāda exhibits dogmatism, traditionalism, and righteousness (major characteristics of the judging function). He interprets all situations within an absolute true-false dichotomy and expresses no emotion when his demon father, Hiraṇyakaśipu, is "murdered by Krishna" ("Prahlāda is cerebral and cold, lacking both sociability and consideration for others"), indicative of the thinking, not the feeling, function. And finally, Prahlāda is a controlled sensate, characterized by his craving for sense enjoyment, represented by his alter ego (his demonic father), limited and controlled by his devotion to Krishna (102–106). Not surprisingly, the Prahlāda narrative was also used in the Robin George lawsuit to persuade the judge that ISKCON is immoral: Young members are trained to hate and even murder their parents; see Tamal Krishna 1997.

50. He is also a God whose conjugal pastimes, described in the Bhāgavata's tenth canto, are of special interest to the Gauḍīya Vaishnavas. Kenney and Polling view this inherited "erotic mythology" as a means to control ISKCON devotees' otherwise uncontrollable sexual appetites. In fact, the two authors interpret the entire *rasa* theory (see their n. 29) as a control mechanism for the sensate personality; see Kenney and Polling 1979.

51. *hṛṣīkena hṛṣīkeśa-sevanā bhaktir ucyate.* This is the second half of a verse from the *Nārada-pañcarātra,* and it is also cited by Rūpa Gosvāmin in the tradition's definitive *bhakti-rasa* text, *Bhakti-rasāmṛta-sindhu* (1.1:12).

It also identifies the locus of the ritual principle: Controlled sensate activities sacralize sensate propensities.[52] But in making the sensate personality normative for all other ISKCON preconversion and postconversion dispositions, it does raise understandable postmodernist concerns about totalization. And again, one becomes more than wary of the tendency to reduce all aspects of doctrine and praxis to a single "essence." "Krishna symbolizes the ideal of the controlled *sensate*"; *ārātrika* (the ceremony of waving lights before the deity) is a "feast for the *senses*; the guru, "a *sensate* religious symbol mediating the Sacred"; and the devotee, "a *sensate* enjoyer" (Kenney and Polling 1986:155–156, emphasis added). Serious questions arise from such reification. For example, although the authors intend their model to be culturally (American) and denominationally (ISKCON) specific, granting the dissimilarity of preconversion factors across cultures, do the tens of millions of theistic Hindus in India and elsewhere, whose belief and ritual systems approximate ISKCON's, also fit into the categories of this sensate typology?[53] Obviously the intention is not to reduce theistic Hinduism (including ISKCON) to merely a religion of sensate myths and rites providing sublimation for materialistic sense enjoyers. Yet their phenomenological approach is open to such potential confusion.

The cult scare is at the center of Larry D. Shinn's *The Dark Lord: Cult Images of the Hare Krishnas in America* (1987). The title utilizes the double entendre of "dark" as a hermeneutical device to investigate the allurement of the deity Krishna, from both the anticult and devotee perspectives. He tests the anticult thesis against literature, interviews, and ISKCON's current position before offering his own alternative interpretation in topical chapters on the guru, his successors, surrender, faith, the religious life, brainwashing, and deprogramming.[54] He concludes that cult stereotypes when applied to ISKCON are dangerously misleading. Social and psychological studies that stress the unconscious factors of conversion and socialization only add to the anticult rhetoric by depriving devotees of the volitional content of their decisions and actions. For example, in couching a discussion of surrender in the context of the identity theories of Erik Erikson and Erving Goffman, Francine Daner portrays surrender to the guru

---

52. Again, Nārada's instruction is cited, this time from the Bhāgavata Purāṇa 1.5:33: "O good soul, does not a thing, applied therapeutically, cure a disease which was caused by that very same thing?"

53. Kenney and Polling's study of Irish Hare Krishnas resulted in nearly identical findings; see Kenney and Polling 1989.

54. Shinn's preparation is considerable: multiple visits to India as a religious historian to study Krishna *bhakti* traditions, participant-observation including 110 interviews in sixteen ISKCON communities facilitated by ISKCON's scholarly liaison, Gelberg, and extensive contact with the anticult movement, its literature, and attendant scholarly studies.

as "helpless" and "harsh" and alterations in personal appearance and living situation a divestment of one's "identity kit" (Shinn 1987:65). Such studies, Shinn believes, say as much about the researchers as they do about those studied. He repeatedly emphasizes that it is the conscious, cognitive factors that weigh most heavily in the conversion decisions and the still more important conversion *processes*.[55] Most importantly, "[i]f there is a common denominator in these devotee conversions, it is that each convert's quest for meaning was finally satisfied in the specific teaching and stories of the Indian cowherd Krishna" (143). This last point offers hope that Shinn will delve into the Krishna theology central to our actual thesis, and Shinn does not disappoint us.

In his chapter "Why Worship a Blue God?" he uses Clifford Geertz's theory of religious symbols—as "models of" and "models for" the cultures in which they arise—to explain the conceptual and affective dimensions behind "the logic of the dark Lord":[56]

> Prabhupāda's conception of Krishna is thus reflective of (i.e. a model of) the Indian linguistic, cultural, and textual traditions in India pertaining to Hindu "high gods" and yet shapes (i.e. provides a model for) some distinctive conclusions of that heritage (e.g. that the divine and impersonal Brahman is actually the supreme and personal Krishna).... [Moreover,] [s]ymbols shape an adherent's life by inducing in the devotee a distinct set of dispositions (i.e. "moods") and inclinations toward action (i.e. "motivations") that lend an identifiable and usually coherent character to his or her life. (88)

This seminal explanation can serve well in our own effort to interpret Prabhupāda's root metaphor, "Kṛṣṇa, the Supreme Personality of Godhead," and his ubiquitous call to action, "devotional service" (his translation for the term *bhakti*). As primary signifiers of unabashed personal devotionalism, they possess a complementary inner logic. Faith and practice make the moods and motivations they inspire "seem uniquely realistic." Beyond the generic attitude of submission and service suggested by Shinn, "moods" and "motivations" are terms pregnant with meaning, highly assimilable to the theory of devotional aesthetics (*rasa*) so central to Krishna theology.[57]

---

55. He argues for asking "How?" someone converts, not just "Why?" See Shinn 1987:135–143.

56. See Geertz 1966.

57. In aesthetics, the normal meaning of *rasa* is the "taste or character of a work, the feeling or sentiment prevailing in it," whereas Vaishnava aestheticians understand it as "a disposition of the heart or mind, a religious sentiment" (see MMW, s.v. "rasa"). Prabhupāda explains, "The particular loving mood or attitude relished in the exchange

Kim Knott's *My Sweet Lord* (1986), entitled after the popular George Harrison record of 1970, is part of an introductory series meant to acquaint the British public with new religions. Knott's sympathetic view of the movement and its philosophy admittedly is that of the devotees. We get little indication of her own perspective. The sociological and historical analysis is so much from the vantage point of ISKCON that the book could well have been a scholarly ISKCON promotional for Britain. She does well in summarizing the complex theology, though her deceptively simple presentation may on occasion convey something other than what Prabhupāda intends: "The supreme Krishna is not limited by His original form of the flute-playing cowherder. He is using His all-attractive form as a means to win the devotees' hearts, and thus to enliven and enlighten them in their search for truth" (1986:61). Even with further explanation and a helpful footnote, one could still misconstrue this as a distinction between "supreme" Krishna and "cowherder" Krishna, or infer limitation on the former by the latter, neither of which Gauḍīyas would countenance. Undoubtedly the problem is one of language and not of comprehension, but in treatment of core beliefs, semantic precision is essential. Ideally, the philosophy is reproduced with transparent accuracy, as in explaining the particularity of Krishna consciousness against other monotheistic religions:

> The differences are essentially those of practice and nomenclature, the most important being the choice of Krishna himself. Their views on this are expressed most clearly in the phrase 'the supreme personality of Godhead'. To worship Krishna is to worship God, but to worship Him in His most attractive form. In this sense worship of Krishna is both easier and more satisfying than the worship of God in other forms. (25)

As an introductory text, the book succeeds admirably and provides a much-needed balance to the monograph of another British scholar, Angela Burr's *I Am Not My Body: A Study of the International Hare Krishna Sect* (1984). Burr concludes that devotees project the problems of society onto their bodies, which are then manipulated unsuccessfully to affect societal changes and personal transformation. A sample of scholarly dissatisfaction with Burr's thesis is that of the anthropologist Charles Brooks, a long-time ISKCON observer, who accuses Burr of "serious anthropological errors": "First and primary among these is the repeatedly stated position that the symbolic is not real. The second results from an attribution of the author's own ideas to her informants. The third is what I see to be a

---

of love with the Supreme Personality of Godhead is called *rasa*, or mellow" (NOD 151), a subject to be dealt with at length in coming chapters.

misapplication of Mary Douglas's theory concerning the relationship between the physical and social bodies." Brooks further criticizes Burr for her "use of loaded rhetoric and innuendo, and her inattention to factual detail concerning ISKCON and the Indian tradition to which it belongs" (Brooks 1986:148). Nevertheless, Burr's monograph has enjoyed a fair degree of academic use.

I will close this survey of the discourse on the second decade with a review of four separately published thematic essays by historian Robert D. Baird that discuss Prabhupāda's thought on other religions and "ultimacy," karma, "rebirth and the personal God," and the Bhagavad Gītā. Looking back over much of the same terrain we have covered, Baird (1995: 515–516) maintains the need for his assessment, much as I have upheld the need for mine:

> [Most] studies of this movement and of Bhaktivedanta are sociological or anthropological. As a religious thinker, Bhaktivedanta is seldom given careful consideration. By analyzing the sociological context in which ISKCON succeeded in recruiting members, as well as the characteristics of the members themselves, it is possible to avoid considering the possibility that there was something in his system of thought that was compelling to his audience.

Baird deserves a careful review, which, more than the others, requires some theoretical argument, because we share a common interest: tracking Prabhupāda's theological footprints. Of those surveyed, he alone is prepared to consider Prabhupāda first and foremost as a religious thinker, though with this qualification:

> Contributing to this neglect is the fact that Bhaktivedanta did not see himself as a religious thinker. He was not seeking to construct a system of thought.... Nevertheless, Swami Bhaktivedanta does possess a system that had been worked out over several centuries.... [I]t was complete when he arrived in New York at the age of 69 (Baird 1995:515–516).

Well, not exactly complete. My contention is that Prabhupāda was a self-consciously religious thinker and desired that others, particularly scholars, respect him as such.[58] But for now, rather than argue these issues, it is more important that we understand Baird's underlying methodological premise, stated at the outset of his

58. As Baird remarks that Prabhupāda emerged with a philosophy ready-made, Eric Sharpe suggests that Prabhupāda was ignorant of the forces contributing to his success: "He knew little or nothing of the country or the people to whom he had been sent and appears never to have reflected on the sociological and psychological reasons behind his triumph" (Sharpe 1985:142).

Bhagavad Gītā essay, though operable in all the others as well. He explains how his approach differs from Edward Dimock's:[59]

> Dimock sees Bhaktivedanta's interpretation as an authentic interpretation within the Gaudiya Vaishnava tradition. My task, however, in this context, is not merely to see Swami Bhaktivedanta as an authentic proponent of Vaishnavism, but to inquire how he interprets the *Gita*. And it must be assumed that this examination is to be done within the context of academic scholarship and not as part of a devotional commitment. . . .
>
> The historian is interested in learning precisely what the text has to say. He wants to understand everything that might be implied in the words of the text without importing anything that is not actually there. Furthermore, he is interested in understanding the ślokas in their historical setting. Exoteric meaning is his only realm, for the esoteric tradition is closed to him (1986:200–201).

Deferring comments for the moment, I will allow Baird his methodology and accept his "value-free" reading of the text in order to summarize his examination of Prabhupāda's *Gītā As It Is*.

Prabhupāda, Baird reports, expands the text well beyond its meaning, which fills the texts and his purports with the beliefs and practices of Krishna consciousness, including the Vaishnava lifestyle. *Bhakti* alone is excellent, all other yogas are subordinate.[60] The Vaishnava position is always shown to be superior to all other positions, especially that of Advaita Vedānta, which is attacked with regularity and vigor.[61] Prabhupāda feels justified in doing so for he believes Krishna is the source, final author, and goal of all the Vedic literature. The Veda and other texts are used to explain the Gītā, whether they were written before or after, in much the same way that earlier or later passages of the Gītā are used to explain

---

59. For an excerpt from Dimock's foreword to the 1972 edition of *Bhagavad-gītā As It Is*, see the first section of this chapter: "Counterculture Discourse: The Mid-1960s to Mid-1970s."

60. In a conclusion to *Modern Indian Interpreters of the Bhagavadgita*, in which Baird's essay appears, Robert Minor, the editor, notes: "Except for Bhaktivedanta, then, no matter how crucial devotion might be to the *Gita* in the eyes of some interpreters and historians, for the majority of figures discussed in this volume, it ranges from less significant to unimportant" (Minor 1986:226). It would be unlikely that Prabhupāda was not conversant with the thought of these prominent men of his time. In fact, his devotional approach to the Gītā is in deliberate contrast with theirs; see BG preface.

61. The position of nondualism associated with Śaṅkara, which Prabhupāda calls "impersonalism," and which also was attacked by Madhva and Rāmānuja; see chapter 1 nn. 8, 22.

a text, with little concern for the structure of the Gītā as a whole. In other words, "[t]he time line is erased" (213).

Baird continues his account of Prabhupāda's views: Not everyone is equally qualified to interpret, to understand, or to teach the Gītā, and (from Prabhupāda's standpoint) scholars come under particularly heavy criticism as "mental speculators."

> They are also called "mundane wranglers" (BG 4.1), "insignificant" (4.1), "demonic persons" (4.2), "foolish and ignorant" (9.11), and persons who are engaged in "foolish speculation" (10.2), and "speculative reasoning" (13.26). Since these scholars are not surrendered to Krishna, they are not Krishna conscious; they are merely offering their own ideas rather than the truth within the *paramparā* [traditional] system (220).

All those who do not hold to Prabhupāda's position are in error. There is little of the argumentation scholars use when deciding between alternative interpretations. Prabhupāda merely announces what is correct: "a spiritual master within disciplic succession merely declares" (221).

Not a very complimentary portrait but, Baird would say, one that Prabhupāda himself has painted. Nor does the normally tempering presence of other faiths soften Prabhupāda's severe expression. In Baird's essays on religious pluralism and "ultimacy," Prabhupāda is cited for his pungent view of those outside his own *paramparā:* Those who reject Krishna are *asuras,* demoniacs, and products of *kali-yuga;* those worshipping demigods are materialistic and lustful; the *prākṛta-sahajiyās*[62] are debauchees, woman hunters, and smokers of ganja. The Cārvākas[63] are atheists and ignorant; the followers of other Indian philosophical schools are imperfect; Buddhists are condemned as voidists; and even the New York hippies are not as fallen as the advaitin impersonalists, who are envious of the Supreme Personality of Godhead. Baird explains that Advaitins are more harshly censored than others because "[i]t is a general principle that those who attack the Vaishnava position are worse off than those who are merely ignorant of it.... Hence those positions that deny the ultimate supremacy and reality of the personal God are more harshly condemned than those which affirm the ultimate reality of the personal deity, as do Muslims and Christians" (1987:114).

62. A heterodox Vaishnava group whose practice includes ritualized sex; see McDaniel 1989:ch. 4.

63. Another heterodox tradition, named after its founder, who espoused a thoroughgoing materialism.

The principle of isolation also is determinate. Chaitanya advised against the study and criticism of other scriptures and warned about unholy association:

> A careful reading of the many works and commentaries of Bhaktivedanta supports the view that he followed this advice himself. There is little to suggest that he read Māyāvādī commentaries (much less that he studied them), that he read the "Koran," the Christian scriptures or any philosophers or theologians in those traditions.... What he knows about other religions comes largely from references to them in his own texts, from occasional personal contact and interviews with persons of other faiths, from information given by devotees converted from other faiths, and from hearsay. (110)

The members of other faiths, therefore, are ultimately objects of conversion, just as they were for Chaitanya. Greater charity is offered to the founders of religious traditions than toward the later expressions of the traditions. Christians, in particular, are criticized for interpreting the instruction not to "kill" as not to "murder," in order to eat meat—a fault not of ignorance, but of disobedience.

Baird continues on, but by now his approach should be clear. In fairness to Baird (and also to Prabhupāda) he includes ameliorating statements that make Prabhupāda's stance on each issue more nuanced and justifiable, but these are not nearly enough to redeem his otherwise grim depiction. Baird's representation is not baseless; he has taken a hard look at Prabhupāda and cannot conceal his dissatisfaction. However, some flaws in his perception need to be mentioned. There are inaccuracies, as when he suggests that the essential requirement of a Prabhupāda disciple is not an inquiring mind but submission,[64] or that, in Prabhupāda's view, to be a member of another religion is to be bound by matter (1995:518, 537). There is misconstruing, as when he belabors Prabhupāda's criticism of mundane scholarship, not recognizing it as a typical assertion of Vedāntic epistemology meant to break the disciples' faith in other ways of knowing.[65] There is frequent obfuscation, as with Prabhupāda's statement that Vedic animal sacrifice gives an animal new life, followed by Baird's exclamation: Prabhupāda

64. Judah is cited as the source for this understanding of a disciple's nature, but nowhere does he make such a claim. Prabhupāda's view is transparent, as in this translation: "Just try to learn the truth by approaching a spiritual master. Inquire from him submissively" (BG 4:34). For a point-by-point "insider" refutation of Baird and other critiques of the *Bhagavad-gītā As It Is,* see Śivarāma 1998.

65. *Śabda* (verbal testimony) is considered valid over against other *pramāṇas* (means of knowledge) such as *anumāna* (logic or reason) and *pratyakṣa* (sense perception). C. Mackenzie Brown finds Prabhupāda's epistemology solidly traditional—knowledge and moral virtue enjoying an intimate relationship; see Brown (n.d.), section entitled "Valid Means of Knowledge: The *Pramāṇas.*"

believes "that the animal is not actually killed!" (1986:206). There are cases of inadequacy, as in an otherwise accurate summation of Prabhupāda's views on karma and rebirth where Baird presents Krishna as an all-powerful monolithic God, but fails to properly articulate the importance of God's manifold energies, a distinguishing feature of Chaitanya's teaching. All such errors notwithstanding, the partisan emphasis that threads them together betrays a deliberate agenda rooted in the very methodological assumption that undergirds his reviews.

It would seem that there is a fault in the basic premise of Baird's studies. In his opening remarks to his Gītā essay, Baird alerts the reader, "The gulf between Swami Bhaktivedanta's presentation and that of the scholarly exegete is unbridgeable" (1986:200). Dimock has merely circumvented this gulf by crossing at another point, accepting Prabhupāda's Vaishnavism as an authentic bridge. Baird, however, is prepared to examine Prabhupāda's thought only "within the context of academic scholarship and not as part of a devotional commitment." But can these be entirely separated? Is it possible, for example, to isolate Śaṅkara from his sectarian interests, or Rāmānuja and Madhva from theirs? Each is as bound within the fixed parameters of his respective text traditions—of "true meaning," "right interpretation," and "right way to live"—as Prabhupāda is within his.[66] They, too, make absolute claims, issue pungent missives attacking opponents, and are at times dogmatic, exclusivist, and dismissive of "mundane" scholarship. For they speak as founding *ācāryas*, with an unceasing awareness of their mission.[67] Dimock was not merely being charitable. It is an exercise in futility to isolate thinkers from the circumstantial complexity that marks their existence, embedded as it is in history, culture, and language.

Yet Baird insists he "wants to understand everything that might be implied in the words of the text without importing anything that is not actually there" (1986:201). But each translator or commentator (or historian of religion), past or present, brings to his task a host of presuppositions that, though perhaps not as neatly integrated or obvious as Prabhupāda's, nonetheless inform his thought and the manner of its articulation. To claim "scholarly integrity" for any one methodological bias brings into question modernist assumptions as problematic as the premodern view that Baird finds so disturbing in Prabhupāda. Perhaps this is precisely what irks him most: Prabhupāda refused to "attempt, as other modern Indian thinkers, to offer an apologetic presentation so as to make his

---

66. Clooney's comments on reader-oriented literary theory are appropriate here; see chapter 1, "The Approach of This Study."

67. For Prabhupāda's self-perception as a founder-*ācārya*, see Tamal Krishna 1999b. Further treatment will follow in a later chapter.

message more acceptable to the modern mind" (1995:516).[68] If Prabhupāda lacked apologetical character, was premodern, his message was no less "compelling to his audience," stimulating scholars like Judah and Hopkins, who saw him not just as a well-preserved specimen of medieval Chaitanyaism but as an outspoken exponent of a vital, living theology.

In Prabhupāda's absence, his uncompromising stance—the "chopping" technique inherited from his guru[69]—became ameliorated, as Baird sees it, by his disciples' more irenic approach (1988:165). In their own scholarship and openness to other religions, in discovering common cause with the burgeoning Hindu diaspora, and in the shift from public solicitation to congregational support, ISKCON may well have softened its founder's stance in an attempt to realize its promise for the future.

A Discourse of Indifference: The Mid-1980s to the Present

"...and at last they will adore you."

As the cult controversy atrophied, academic interest waned.[70] Scholarship, after all, a growth industry, goes with the "hot" topics. When the brainwashing theory vaporized, interest in recruitment and conversion declined. The market was still flush with the spate of mid-1980s publications, and there was nothing on the level of the cult issue to excite publishers. Scholars also lost the assistance of Gelberg, ISKCON's academic interface, when his funding was abruptly cut off.[71]

Circumstantially, ISKCON was quickly moving out of the public eye. The airports in the United States, a high-visibility venue for proselytizing, were

68. Sharpe, in his review of Western images of the Bhagavad Gītā, agrees: "Unlike some other jet-age gurus, Bhaktivedanta made no conscious concessions to the West, other than the use of English. He admitted no compromises where scriptures were concerned (nor in respect of dress, food or life-style)." And "Swami Bhaktivedanta was uninterested in anything save hammering his message home, and this he did in an utterly uncompromising manner" (1985:142, 144).

69. "Some God-brothers complained that this preaching was a chopping technique and it would not be successful.... For my part I have taken up the policy of my Guru Maharaja—no compromise. All these so-called scholars, scientists, and philosophers who do not accept Krishna are nothing more than rascals, fools, the lowest of mankind, etc." (Karandhara 730227).

70. ISKCON and the anticult movement are now on speaking terms, evidence of the civilizing influence of time and, on the part of both, a critical reevaluation of their own pasts. They take part in joint panels, and ISKCON has published an article by the executive director of the American Family Foundation; see Anūttama 1999 and Langone 1999.

71. Gelberg's funding was directly affected by the departure of one of ISKCON's gurus, a trustee of the Bhaktivedanta Book Trust, which financed his work.

virtually closed to solicitation of funds and, indirectly, distribution of literature by a Supreme Court decision.[72] Street chanting, an early trademark of the movement, was now a weekend activity at best. The movement legally and publicly distanced itself from a leader and his schismatic temple community (New Vrindaban, in West Virginia), after both become implicated in serious illegalities, and thereby shifted some of the cult stigma to its separated branch. Issues such as the threatened closure of England's Bhaktivedanta Manor as a public place of worship, while attracting public attention, indicated the members' osmotic absorption into mainstream society—in this case, the Hindu community. ISKCON was no longer strange, much less dangerous. It was "alternative."[73] Still, there were (and are) reminders that ISKCON was (and is) barely over its growing pains. Skeletons like the child-abuse issue suddenly emerged from the past and threatened to propel the movement once again into an unfavorable limelight. Persistent public interest would inevitably demand fresh scholarship.[74]

The paucity of academic publications on ISKCON during this period must be seen as a clear reflection of public apathy, not "adoration." But the lull in public interest indirectly enabled scholarship to creatively appropriate new interests.[75]

---

72. *International Society for Krishna Consciousness, Inc. v. Lee*, 505 U.S. 672 (1992). The decision involving JFK International, LaGaurdia, and Newark Airports was confined to a restriction on the solicitation of donations, not the distribution of literature or the right to speak to people. Many other airports subsequently banned solicitation. See also Boston 1992.

73. See the title of T. Miller 1995. Robert Towler, director of the British agency INFORM (Information Network Focus on Religious Movements), reports just six inquiries received about ISKCON in 1993, including two from students writing about ISKCON, one from a Catholic newspaper reporter, and another from a person wishing to counsel someone who had just left the movement; see Towler 1995. Figures over the past ten years or so suggest a similar trend. The title of Knott's seminar, "The Many Faces of ISKCON," is itself revealing of ISKCON's changing demographics; see Knott 1999. The picture of ISKCON's early homogeneity, said to be a characteristic of "cults," is entirely effaced by Rochford's extensive ISKCON-authorized survey; see Rochford 1999b. Zaidman-Dvir and Malory Nye both document ISKCON's and the Hindu community's mutual accommodation: "It is the first time in the history of ISKCON in America that followers and supporters are not the representatives of the 'counter culture,' but are an affluent section of American urban middle class population" (Zaidman-Dvir 1994:174). This is even more evident in Nye's study (2001).

74. ISKCON has detailed its own child abuse; see Rochford 1998a and Bharata Shrestha 1998. See Goodstein 1998 for the front-page *New York Times* article that followed. Rochford has been writing a book about family and children in ISKCON. [His book was published in 2007 by New York University Press: *Hare Krishna Transformed*.—ed.]

75. Examples are two doctoral dissertations analyzing the efficacy of mantra chanting: a sociological study contrasting the hare kṛṣṇa mantra with a placebo mantra in terms of the modes of "nature" or *prakṛti* (*sattva, rajas, tamas*) and an ethnomusicological study investigating the performance of *kīrtan* within ISKCON as a primary means for developing human perception, emotion, and action; see Wolf 1999 and Puyang-Martin 1996.

A discourse of "indifference" has within itself, both syntactically and semantically, the potential for "difference." It afforded ISKCON time to proactively recast its own strategy. *ISKCON Review,* a scholarly journal that enjoyed only two issues during Gelberg's brief though productive tenure, reincarnated in 1994, this time published from the United Kingdom as the *ISKCON Communications Journal.* The journal's relocation across the Atlantic and its new editor (Śaunaka Ṛṣi Dāsa) invigorated academic interest in both Europe and, with the demise of Communism, the former Soviet republics.[76] In the natural sciences, ventures conceived under Prabhupāda's tutelage resulted in two international conferences on science and religion and a number of monographs, one of which sparked considerable controversy.[77] Because this period is distinguished by the paucity of published full-length academic studies,[78] our approach to the materials will be synchronic rather than diachronic. Briefly summarizing the activity within these structural groupings—comparative and sundry studies, *ISKCON Review/ Communications Journal,* and scientific research—leads us to expect a change in the climate of academic research as the cult controversy recedes and the focus of scholarship gradually shifts from ISKCON toward Prabhupāda's thought.

As Shinn noted in his conclusion, though ISKCON may remain a marginal movement in the West, it clearly has India as its spiritual home (Shinn 1987:177). If anywhere, it is in India that ISKCON is not only "adored" but legitimized, in ways least expected, as Charles R. Brooks's *The Hare Krishnas in India* (1989) corroborates.[79] While it is a matter of record that "caste," like any sociocultural

---

76. Many studies by Europeans, like those by Americans, are social-scientific assessments of ISKCON inspired by national cult controversies that still smoulder. Quite a few ISKCON devotees in Europe have entered academia and contributed studies on the Gauḍīya tradition to lay a foundation for ISKCON's legitimation in their respective countries. Except in cases of substantially original material, I shall not consider them separately.

77. See Singh and Gomatam 1988 for the papers of the First World Congress on the Synthesis of Science and Religion, and Barker 1986 for a personal account. Monographic subjects include philosophy of science (Thompson 1981), artificial intelligence (Gomatam 1988), cosmography (Thompson 1990, 2000), and evolution (Cremo and Thompson 1993). For a full-length volume documenting response to the controversial volume on evolutionary anomalies, see Cremo 1998.

78. Two I do not include. Nori Muster's *Betrayal of the Spirit,* while a valuable though selective autobiographical account of her institutional disaffection, is not academic and is not about the ISKCON of this final period; see Muster 1997, and for its foreword, see Shinn 1997. K. P. Sinha's *A Critique of A. C. Bhaktivedanta* is a defense against Prabhupāda's judgment of Advaita Vedānta; see Sinha 1997. It is clearly a sectarian polemic rather than an academic study. For its rebuttal, see Surya 1999.

79. "Least expected" by Indologists, other scholars, and so-called traditional Indians; see Brooks 1989:10. Reverse missionizing was essential within Prabhupāda's global strategy; while organization of other regions was entrusted to his zonal secretaries, India was his personal responsibility. Although I was officially the zonal secretary for India (1970–74),

marking, is in fluid tension with the particularities of its cultural, political, and economic imbrication, and that *bhakti* traditions like Chaitanya's have provided spiritual impetus for further mobility,[80] Brooks documents how the interaction of *videśīs* (foreigners) with Indian pilgrims and residents in the Krishna pilgrimage center of Vrindaban has forced the traditional symbolic system to be reconfigured.

The popularity of ISKCON's Krishna-Balaram Temple in Vṛndāvana is unquestionable. It attracts 98 percent of the one-day visitors to the town. Perhaps more striking is its effect on long-term residents: They too have accepted the foreigners as sincere devotees, culturally and spiritually adept at performing prestigious functions traditionally assigned by birth. Brooks's anthropological study offers a "concrete example of how interactional processes can transform symbols which express both the individual and cultural experience of history, mythology, society, language, and behaviour" (Brooks 1989:26).[81] Were it not that the foreigners were actually authentic and competent devotees in the perception of the indigenous Vaishnava population, they could not exercise such influence despite whatever other factors were at work.[82] ISKCON's achievement in India amplifies Thomas Hopkins's testimonial to Prabhupāda's authorial talent: "The very existence of a genuine Vaishnava movement in the West is compelling evidence of his success as a commentator."

Prabhupāda's insistence that the "Vedic" way is the right way for the West is challenged by the results of "The *Gurukula* System: An Enquiry in the Krishna Philosophy," a dissertation by Jai Dayal (Rutgers, 1989). Virtually every practice and principle of education at the *guru-kula* (the guru's residence) finds justification in Prabhupāda's teachings, patterned on the ideal of the child devotee Prahlāda, who exemplified the sense control and submission to guru encapsulated

---

in practice I functioned as Prabhupāda's assistant. From the time of his initial departure to the West, he still spent at least half of his time in India.

80. Brooks discusses the groundbreaking work of M. N. Srinivas and McKim Mariott in revolutionizing the standard conception of "caste"; see Brooks 1989:18–25. For the *bhakti* tradition's effect on the caste system, see, e.g., Hopkins 1966; for Jīva Gosvāmin's view, see Chakrabarty 1985:78–80.

81. For example, Brooks devotes an entire chapter (7) to the "cross-cultural dynamics of mystical emotions," detailing how institutional and experiential considerations led Prabhupāda to emphasize regulated devotional practice (*vaidhī bhakti*) for members of ISKCON, which in turn affected the spontaneous practices (*rāgānugā bhakti*) of local residents (and vice versa).

82. Although no study has been thus far undertaken, the same influence could be demonstrated in the Chaitanya pilgrimage center of Navadvīpa, West Bengal, and in other Indian cities and regions where ISKCON operates. A similar effect might be shown on Prabhupāda's godbrothers and their followers. As in Vṛndāvana, such influence is always mutual.

in a single Bhāgavata Purāṇa verse.[83] Although Western "slaughterhouse" educational models spiritually kill their charges by emphasizing materialism, Dayal finds that the *guru-kula* alternative also fails to achieve its goal of producing good devotees who can spearhead a world revolution in Krishna *bhakti*. Evidence indicates that "as they grow older, the tendency of the students is to become increasingly disinterested in Prabhupāda's way" (235). Admittedly, this is a tentative conclusion. History has not proven Prabhupāda entirely wrong when he said that 50 percent would eventually return to the fold (226).[84] The mounting indictment for child abuse leveled at many former *guru-kula* staff may also help salvage the theoretical system to a degree by placing blame on individual failure. Indeed, the headmaster of the school under study only later admitted to being abusive, unknown to Dayal at that time. To whatever extent this aberration skewed research findings, it certainly interfered in determining whether Prabhupāda's thoughts on education are practical, given the supranormal role of the *guru-kula* teacher in a child's character formation. Core tensions highlight this study—continuity-change, isolation-integration—which begs the question, to what degree must ISKCON compromise Prabhupāda's teachings in order to preserve them?

Prabhupāda prominently figures in A. L. Herman's innovative *Brief Introduction to Hinduism* (1991). Herman's thesis is that religions and philosophies primarily exist for solving human problems, that is, for Hinduism, to offer "the Rx [prescription] for the liberation from suffering." His contention is that the very different solutions to suffering prescribed by Hinduism's three primary expressions—bhaktism, brahminism, and Brahmanism—are best articulated by three modern exponents of each: the *bhakti-yogin* Prabhupāda, the *karma-yogin* Gandhi, and the *jñāna-yogin* Ramana Maharshi. They in turn have ancient roots (again, in parallel) with the Harappans, the Vedas, and the Upanishads.

Setting aside this provocative philosophic-historical hermeneutic, what is Herman's view of Prabhupāda's translation of the Gītā, a text that to Herman epitomizes the synthesis of the three traditions under consideration? Much the same as that of Baird: "good Fundamentalist Krishnaism," complete with

---

83. "Nārada Muni said: A student should practice completely controlling his senses. He should be submissive and should have an attitude of firm friendship for the spiritual master. With a great vow, the *brahmacārī* should live at the *guru-kula*, only for the benefit of the *guru*" (SB 7.12:1).

84. Survey results indicate a large percentage of young adults born to devotee parents continue to identify themselves as devotees of Krishna while rejecting their collective identity as ISKCON members; see Rochford 1999a, 1999b:18 .

scholar bashing and appeals to exclusive authority (Herman 1991:137).[85] Further, Prabhupāda misrepresents *jñāna-yoga* and *karma-yoga* as inferior to or simply climaxing in *bhakti-yoga:* "In arguing that the *Gītā* is ultimately and only a bhakti text, Bhaktivedanta must alter, retranslate, or reinterpret a great number of passages in the *Gītā*...and torture them a bit either by translation or interpretation in order to get them to come out as bhakti passages" (139). As an illustration of how Prabhupāda suffuses with *bhakti* a *jñāna* passage of obviously impersonal denotation, Herman first cites his own *Gītā* translation of 5:17: "Thinking on That [*tat*, a neuter pronoun], merging the Ātman with That, making That the sole aim" (140).[86] Herman protests that unlike Ramana Maharshi, who centers the Bhagavad Gītā on the Supreme *Im*personality of Godhead, Prabhupāda in his commentary on this text sees the personality of Lord Krishna even in the neuter pronoun *tat:* "The Supreme Transcendental Truth is Lord Kṛṣṇa. The whole *Bhagavad-gītā* centers around the declaration of Kṛṣṇa as the Supreme Personality of Godhead." As a matter of record, Prabhupāda glosses *tat* simply as "Supreme"; the "personalist" reading is confined to his commentary.

Again, as with Baird's critique, Herman's objections raise crucial questions: Does the text exist outside of a community of interpretation? By which standards should an interpreter of a tradition be judged? When does a translation cease to be a translation and become an interpretation? Or can a translation ever be anything but an interpretation? And are there limits beyond which a translator should not venture?

A study such as Herman's does not present Prabhupāda and his thought in nearly so favorable a light as, for example, the devotee-edited interviews in the book subtitled "Five Distinguished Scholars on the Krishna Movement in the West." *ISKCON Communications Journal* and its predecessor, *ISKCON Review,* by offering insiders and outsiders a devotee-moderated forum in which to examine and locate Prabhupāda's legacy, more or less assure views on the whole supportive of ISKCON and its founder.

In the *Review's* first issue, the ISKCON theologian Ravīndra Svarūpa Dāsa assures readers that reason and reflection are as much a part of the Gauḍīya Vaishnava tradition as its more widely known emotional side (Ravīndra

85. Baird and Herman offer the identical citation to illustrate Krishna fundamentalism:
In this present day, man is very eager to have one scripture, one God, one religion, and one occupation. So let there be one common scripture for the whole world—*Bhagavad-gītā*. And let there be one God only for the whole world—Śrī Kṛṣṇa. And one *mantra* only—Hare Krishna, Hare Krishna, Krishna Krishna, Hare Hare/Hare Rāma, Hare Rāma, Rāma Rāma, Hare Hare. And let there be one work only—the service of the Supreme Personality of Godhead. (BG 1972:28)

86. *tad-buddhayas tad-ātmānas tan-niṣṭhās tat-parāyaṇāḥ/gacchanty apunar-āvṛttiṁ jñāna-nirdhūta-kalmaṣāḥ.*

Svarūpa 1985b). He attempts to demonstrate that modern historical consciousness, with its normative claims of temporality, change, development, and progress is a product of the mode of passion (*rajo-guṇa*) and represents a relatively recent shift from the preceding paradigm, which was located in the mode of goodness (*sattva-guṇa*) and survived for nearly two millennia, the hierarchical worldview known as the Great Chain of Being (1993a). Ravīndra Svarūpa argues that Prabhupāda did indeed inaugurate a revitalization movement, but that its seemingly premodern, mode-of-goodness worldview, far from being an exotic Indian import, bears striking resemblance to its European counterpart, whose lost cultural heritage Krishna *bhakti* seeks to restore (1995). Despite appearing heavily freighted with culturally conditioned forms, ISKCON exemplifies the nonsectarian flowering of *bhakti*—a progressively dialectical synthesis of karma (as thesis) and *jñāna* (karma's antithesis) (1993b). Note that this is the very same principle, now given a hermeneutical twist, that Herman and others found objectionable.

Ravīndra Svarūpa's use of karma, *jñāna,* and *bhakti* as a typology for the progressive stages of spiritual life is but one effort to subvert the reductionist pigeonholing of ISKCON as a "religion," particularly a "Hindu" religion.[87] The enigmatic question of whether ISKCON is or is not "Hindu" is repeatedly raised in the *Journal* (Rāsamaṇḍala 1994; Flood 1995; Nye 1997; Brzezinski 1998; Hṛdayānanda 1999).[88] Rāsamaṇḍala and Flood agree that Bengali or Gauḍīya Vaishnavism is a far clearer nomenclature; Nye looks at the close alliance of ISKCON and the Hindu community of Great Britain; and Hṛdayānanda dāsa Goswami (Howard Resnick) offers an extensive deconstruction of the term from a Gauḍīya perspective before posing the question, "For whom does Hinduism speak?" He argues "that the modern transformation of the term 'Hindu' into an internal, monistically tilted self-definition for the followers of the Vedas, is problematic for Vaiṣṇavas, and that 'Hinduism' cannot in all respects speak for

---

87. Ravīndra Svarūpa:

> The Western youth who joined ISKCON never thought of themselves as 'converting' to something called 'Hinduism'.... [T]hey did not think that in adopting ISKCON's practices they were plunging into the historically conditioned forms of a particular religious sect. Indeed, they usually did not think of themselves as practicing something called 'a religion' at all. Prabhupāda managed quite compellingly to convey an altogether different vision. (1993b:35–36)

88. It is also at the center of Zaidman-Dvir's (1994) extensive study. She concludes that ISKCON's sectarian form of Hinduism is in constant negotiation with the more ecumenical Hinduism of its diaspora Hindu congregation, leading to organizational modifications within the former and theological modifications among members of the latter, often successfully negotiated through the segregation of space, time, and resources.

Vaiṣṇavism" (51). Still, he acknowledges that there may be an uneasy marriage of the two:

> And yet, we saw that Chaitanya himself, the founder of the Gauḍīya-Vaiṣṇava movement, did accept the term "Hindu" for ordinary dealings with the Muslim rulers. We must keep in mind here the common, contrasting Sanskrit philosophical terms: *vyāvahārika,* "relating to ordinary or mundane affairs, usage, or practice" and *pāramārthika,* "relating to a spiritual object, or to supreme, essential truth." It seems fair to say that according to O'Connell's survey [1973] of sixteenth- to eighteenth-century Gauḍīya Vaiṣṇava literature, the Vaiṣṇava devotees considered themselves Hindu in a *vyāvahārika* sense, but never in a *pāramārthika* sense. Indeed, from the *pāramārthika* viewpoint, "Hindu" is simply another *upādhi,* or worldly designation (51–52).

This explains rather well Prabhupāda's apparent ambivalence illustrated in Brzezinski's thoroughgoing, database analysis of Prabhupāda's statements regarding Hinduism. Brzezinski concludes that despite Prabhupāda's rejection of "normative" Hinduism, his occasional profession of Hindu identity may best be explained by R. C. Zaehner's contention that Hinduism characteristically resists "either/or" approaches, being a religion of "both/and" (1968:45). One may both believe and practice self-consciously much that others equate with Hinduism and at the same time deny altogether one's identification with it.

This sort of ambivalence is further reflected in Prabhupāda's attitude toward other religions. Robert Baird, as I have already noted, finds Prabhupāda intolerant, and so does J. Frank Kenney, who concludes that a meaningful dialogue for a theologically exclusive ISKCON vis-à-vis other religions is impossible.[89] Eight years later Kenney reaffirms ISKCON's intolerance, but in the face of articles by Gelberg and Ravīndra Svarūpa is prepared to reconsider the possibility of ISKCON as a potential dialogue partner, with the caveat that the opinions of one or two intellectuals do not necessarily represent those of the official institution.[90]

Against Baird's contention that Prabhupāda had little direct contact with Christian theology or, if he did, that it had little effect upon him (the view of his official biographer),[91] Peter Schmidt (1999) has documented substantial

89. Kenney bases his interpretation of "tolerance" on Gustav Mensching's sense of "the positive acceptance of other religions as legitimate possibilities for encounter with the Sacred" (Kenney 1982:82).

90. See Kenney 1990, Gelberg 1986, and Ravīndra Svarūpa 1989.

91. See SPL 1:21–26.

influence during Prabhupāda's Calcutta education from the theologically liberal Scottish missionary Dr. W. S. Urquhart. Prabhupāda's view of Christianity, Schmidt argues, was an amalgam of that of his college professor and the attitudes of his predecessors, Bhaktisiddhānta Sarasvatī and Bhaktivinoda Ṭhākura.

That there has been a determined move within ISKCON toward dialogue with people of faith is a matter of record, and an official statement to that effect has appeared in a *Journal* article.[92] This seems to confirm Baird's opinion that Prabhupāda's disciples are likely to adopt his more ameliorating views. It also indicates that selective readings of Prabhupāda's divergent views on any one topic, whether by insiders or outsiders, can facilitate broadly differing interpretations.

A number of scholars have emphasized that Prabhupāda has much to offer other religions. Klaus Klostermaier had somewhat rhetorically asked, "Will India's Past Be America's Future?" (1980). He suggests that European religions have largely ignored the question of consciousness, so central to the Krishna conscious experience, and indicates a further area of experiential neglect in "The Education of Human Emotions: Śrīla Prabhupāda as Spiritual Educator" (1996). Edmund Weber (1997) suggests significant theological contributions Prabhupāda and ISKCON have to offer Christianity, which according to Graham M. Schweig (1998b) are feasible owing to Prabhupāda's openness to diverse religious traditions as forms of *bhakti*.

Others wonder about ISKCON's ability to transmit its essential heritage. Ekkehard Lorenz (n.d.) analyzes the Bhaktivedanta purports from within the context of the commentarial tradition and tackles the question of transmission versus innovation. Finn Madsen (n.d., 2000) examines ISKCON's efforts to institute *varṇāśrama* (the social orders and stages of life) in Scandinavia. Shukavak Dasa (1998) raises the question whether an ISKCON more concerned with the exoteric mode embodied in *vaidha-bhakti-sādhana* can in fact offer the esoteric depth of *rāgānuga-bhakti-sādhana* for which the tradition is principally known. That question leads into Jan Brzezinski's (1996–97) consideration of ISKCON's (and, thereby, Prabhupāda's) relationship to the *paramparā* institution of Gauḍīya Vaishnavism, and to Shukavak's (1999) full-length study of Bhaktivinoda and his encounter with modernity.

Tradition's encounter with modernity is especially evident with regard to the debate over the role and status of female devotees, in which the multivalent weighting of Prabhupāda's statements can have decisive bearing on ISKCON's future (Lipner 1994b:24; Flood 1995:13).[93] Susan J. Palmer (1994) and Kim Knott

92. See Cracknell 1996, Clooney 1996, Trapnell 1998, and Carney 1999. See Śaunaka Ṛṣi dāsa 1999 for ISKCON's official statement.

93. As it does upon the evolving status of the family as a whole; see Rochford 1997.

(1995) have documented ISKCON's difficulties in reconciling traditional models with modern realities.[94] Knott problematizes the issue by juxtaposing the theoretical gender equality of a soul-based theology (in which the feminine divine Rādhā is the exemplar par excellence) with *strī-dharma* (the duty of a woman) understood as having three distinct levels of meaning within the founder's teachings: *bhagavad-dharma* (divine duty), "Vedic" *varṇāśrama-dharma* (the ancient notion of duty based on orders and stages of life), and "Hindu" *varṇāśrama-dharma* (its modern interpretation). Some of Prabhupāda's statements seem blatantly sexist, yet he opened his movement to women. Knott explains:

> Needless to say these complex levels of interpretation have led to many misunderstandings among both commentators and devotees.... The need to balance a commitment to ideals and the wisdom of a spiritual tradition situated in real time and place inevitably elicits mixed messages, those spoken out of an appreciation of ideals and those framed in the experience of the hard realities. It is commendable in the face of this tension that the founder of the Hare Krishna movement made a philosophy and practice available to women that had once been largely closed to them, allowing them effective material equality with men and the opportunity to serve in the same ways *despite* his own cultural background and the ideal prescriptions of his tradition. He acted in accordance with the spirit of *bhagavat-dharma*, in the manner of Chaitanya, and in the specific context of Kali-yuga as it manifested itself in the West. (41)

The tension that arises when the founder's literal reading of the textual tradition confronts "hard realities" is nowhere more pronounced than in issues relating to modern science. Specifically with regard to evolution and cosmography, Prabhupāda makes two primary claims: (1) that life originates from life, not from matter, and (2) that the cosmographic descriptions of the Bhāgavata Purāṇa provide an accurate picture of the universe.[95] Thus, in the face of the televised, much-heralded first Apollo moon-landing expedition, Prabhupāda can calmly pronounce, "They have not landed!"—a sensational media grabber and the immediate cause of his secretary's

94. Palmer's interviews (recorded 1974–76, all in Montreal) are outdated and too minimal to be either current or truly representative; see Sītā 1995.

95. Prabhupāda's views of these exploratory fields permeate his teachings, but are especially the foci of *Easy Journey to Other Planets* ([1960] 1970a); SB fifth canto chs. 16–26 (cosmography); and *Life Comes from Life* (1979; evolution).

apostatic defection.[96] What is seen, after all, does not square with the Bhāgavata depiction: There is only a barren planet. As Mikael Rothstein (1996) and C. Mackenzie Brown (n.d.) both point out, as a theological discourse the confrontation with scientism—the belief in the omnipotence of scientific knowledge and techniques—strengthens belief in traditional notions over against the Darwinian and Copernican bogeys. Rothstein's ingenious comparison of transcendental meditation (TM) with ISKCON traces attitudes toward science to their respective theologies. Monistic TM, based in Advaita Vedānta, is susceptible to syncretism, whereas a highly personalistic ISKCON, based in Vaishnava *bhakti*, is prone to hostility and avoidance, a "negative syncretism" that acts as a self-defining paradigm.

Prabhupāda is keenly aware of the high stakes involved in the "science game." The hierarchical and thoroughly moralized structure of the purāṇic universe, embedded within notions of karma and reincarnation, is threatened by a universe in which chance and randomness, not a purposeful God, are life's defining features. Prabhupāda's two-science model—material and transcendental—is one that his scientifically educated followers have upheld, though have argued with considerably more technical sophistication and far less vitriol. Although extending Prabhupāda's insights linguistically and conceptually, their scholarly interpretation is ultimately "higher dimensional," for as Rothstein concludes, their understanding of the potentials of modern science is framed by Prabhupāda's own clear conviction: There will not be and cannot be any arrival at fundamental metaphysical truth through the mundane scientific process.

What appears, at first sight, to be competing truth claims that have but little in common upon further consideration may be theological and naturalistic accounts sharing rational discourse and questioning, though with quite differently contextualized inquiries.[97] Naturalism does not lack a mythic dimension, nor is theol-

---

96. Prabhupāda was living at the time in a furnished apartment on Baker Street beside Regents Park in London. Prabhupāda's conversation while watching the Apollo mission with his secretary in 1969 is reported by his biographer (SPL 4:70):

> Prabhupāda asked Puruṣottama, "So, what can you see?"
> "They're exploring the moon's surface," he said.
> "So, what is there?"
> "Well, it looks like they have landed inside a crater somewhere, and the ground is sandy with some rocks. Oh, look, they're showing some shadows from some of the rocks that are lying around!"
> "That's all you can see? There are no people? There are no trees? There are no rivers? There are no buildings?"
> "No," Puruṣottama replied. "The moon is barren."
> "They have not landed on the moon," Prabhupāda said emphatically. "This is not the moon."

97. Thus, "[t]he empirical claim of the Hare Krishna movement that meat-eating Americans could not have landed on the moon in 1969, is evidently false in the realm of

ogy devoid of empirical evidence. Their explanations are not methodologically exclusive. Competing narratives can enter into dialogue, provided that a healthy skepticism is balanced against an equal measure of charity. Echoing our survey's original thesis, we are confronted by the same concern for "location," for what we see and how we explain what we see will depend very much on where we stand, or the horizon of our seeing.

Summary and Reflections

After a survey of more than three decades of scholarship on Prabhupāda and ISKCON, a clear pattern emerges. Public perception and its scholarly response have never granted Prabhupāda completely equal franchise. Apart from a few notable exceptions, academic accounting has had difficulty breaking free of the enforced constraints of the binding narratives of counterculture and cult-controversy discourse. In the wake of these powerful narratives, amid a discourse of indifference, Prabhupāda has been only slightly more privileged. Throughout, the preponderance of scholarship from non-Indological specialists has further cemented the perception of ISKCON's hybrid identity.[98] Unless the center of discourse is moved to accommodate a narrative whose terms are amenable to his theology, Prabhupāda's thought will continue to be indirectly treated, to appear fantastic or at best sectarian, or worse still, be entirely ignored. Never a full partner in dialogue, his voice will remain the muted voice of an illegitimate "other."

I find it strange to have to describe as "muted" a voice that rings with revolutionary fervor and whose assertions are punctuated by blunt expressions of moral judgment. Discourses of opposition do tend to heighten invectives and to invest speech with an urgency not otherwise felt. Even without the stimulus of anticult rhetoric, however, Prabhupāda was ready to issue a harsh indictment against a civilization he deemed spiritually bankrupt. The counterculture narrative was hardly one with which he identified. He was *counter*-countercultural and so saw nearly everyone else as an "other." He never perceived himself as a victim or his mission as a mechanism of resistance. He was not weak. Few would be cheered to

historical action, but can be understood and seen to be coherent from within the history of the movement's theology in which the moon is regarded as a pure, sacred space" (Flood 1999:173).

98. One can speculate why this is so. Certainly Advaita Vedānta until recently has attracted Indologists more than theistic brands of Hinduism, as have those exponents of a more modernized Hindu ethos. Chaitanya scholars have been intrigued by the tradition's emphasis on *rāgānuga-bhakti,* which many believe ISKCON does not emphasize. For all, India may be less appealing when she appears on one's doorstep, represented in a sectarian, exclusivist, emotional, often immature, and aggressively missionary form. (I am indebted to Rachel McDermott of Barnard College for her insights in this regard.)

measure progress in terms of derision or hatred, yet Prabhupāda seemed to grow stronger in adversity. Opposition was proof that his message was effective, and indifference was not his friend. He would have scorned "otherness."

Prabhupāda's assessment and mine are inverted. I see the most recent period of indifference as a favorable transition to a more direct engagement with his theology and the earlier periods as clearly abusive and confining. There was a time when it would not have been so, when standing by Prabhupāda's side, I would have seen as he did. My present position is one step removed—a participant-observer like others I have surveyed, with this singular difference: unlike their scholarly constructions, mine seeks to understand Prabhupāda's thought.

Prabhupāda took pleasure in polemical debate. I will resist advocacy of his position beyond attempting to give him fair opportunity to make his case. In arguing on his behalf for a level playing field, I have had to expose methodological and theoretical biases that have checked his thought from being understood, and I have sought to correct innocent historical or philosophical confusions that marred research. But justice must be equitable. The ways in which ISKCON and Prabhupāda have contributed to this occlusion—historically, methodologically, and philosophically—will similarly be bared in the coming chapters.

Academic research struggles to be neutral and objective yet, ironically, often reinforces the very issues its methodology seeks to dispute. This has been the case with ISKCON-related research that has allowed anticult critics to set the agenda of discourse.[99] The media has played an equally defining role, seesawing upward and downward against the weight of public sentiment. At least academic interest added an even-handed sobriety to this highly unstable mix. Considering the desperate nature of the times, when not only philosophies but also lives were at stake, researchers cannot be blamed for deferring debate over Prabhupāda's thought. ISKCON often dwarfed its founder, looming like an overgrown adolescent, confusing, even menacing. By analyzing recruitment and membership characteristics, scholarly assurance calmed a curious and often worried public.

But Prabhupāda the thinker and Prabhupāda the founder are not two different individuals, and scholars could not entirely avoid one while dealing with the other. Theological issues have affected the social-scientific studies, even more so the historical treatments. In fact, the building blocks for a workable theology are already present within the discursive formations surveyed. But unlike Doniger's stone walls in Ireland that required no mortar to hold them together, previous

99. Noting the work of Gordon and Melton, typical of the scholarship surveyed, Thomas Robbins asserts that they "are all concerned to refute the allegations against 'cults' put forward by various activist clinicians; nevertheless, their efforts seem to reinforce the tendency whereby the relevant... issues bearing upon the Hare Krishna movement are defined by the vehement opponents of the movement" (1997:79).

theoretical constructs are in crumbling disorder, ill fitted from the start to house Prabhupāda's thought. If a suitable edifice is to be built, first the discourse narrative must be redefined. We must discover an approach that makes Prabhupāda's theology the locus of our attention, that can negotiate the two worlds out of which Prabhupāda's thought arises—the contemporary and the cumulative tradition—and that juxtaposes their claims and their standards of scholarship without being naive toward their respective presuppositions.

I propose to employ a long-respected Gauḍīya Vaishnava hermeneutic that organizes theological inquiry into three broad divisions: *sambandha* (relationship), *abhidheya* (execution), and *prayojana* (goal).[100] Prabhupāda's explanatory translation to a defining text unpacks the terms' essential meanings:

> The Vedic literatures give information about the living entity's eternal relationship with Kṛṣṇa, which is called *sambandha*. The living entity's understanding of this relationship and his acting accordingly is called *abhidheya*. Returning home, back to Godhead, is the ultimate goal of life and is called *prayojana*. (CC 2.20:124)[101]

Prabhupāda's predecessor, the theologian Bhaktivinoda Ṭhākura, uses these terms to enshrine what he considers the tenets of Chaitanya's theology. He suggests that these terms constitute what is to be ascertained: the object of valid knowledge (*prameya*), which in turn depends on the means of acquiring valid knowledge (*pramāṇa*). Epistemological priority militates in favor of considering the means first, the objects of knowledge thereafter.[102] The great advantage of this schema is

---

100. This threefold hermeneutic is deemed suitable for explaining the Gauḍīya's preferred text, the Bhāgavata Purāṇa; see Jīva Gosvāmin 1986a:150. The six *sandharbhas* (authoritative Gauḍīya texts) themselves are also divided according to this schema. Indeed, the claim is extended to the entirety of "Vedic" literature; see CC 2.20:124–143. Prabhupāda himself used this hermeneutic to analyze the Bhagavad Gītā; see Bhaktivedanta Book Trust 1981. Regarding Prabhupāda's translation of *abhidheya* as "execution," though the term normally conveys the meaning "what is signified," Stuart Elkman notes that Jīva Gosvāmin "qualifies the term with the expression *vidheya-saparyāya*, i.e., 'in the sense of something to be performed'" (Jīva Gosvāmin 1986a:73 n. 2). According to MMW, *saparyā* means "worship, homage, adoration"; specifically, *vidheya-saparyāya* is "worship, devotion, etc. that is to be performed," which is the implication in Prabhupāda's translation of *abhidheya* as "execution." [As I have noted in my introduction, the purpose of this work is to construct a sound foundation on the basis of the meanings given to *sambandha* and *abhidheya* so that further scholarship can help discern Prabhupāda's *prayojana*.—ed.]

101. *veda-śāstra kahe: "sambandha," "abhidheya," "prayojana" kṛṣṇa prāpya, sambandha bhakti, prāptyera sādhana.*

102. The means and its object taken together yield what Bhaktivinoda describes as the tradition's ten foundational "truths" ("Daśa-mūla-tattva"):

> First, *pramāṇa*. (1) The Vedas and all other writings in pursuance of the Vedic version are an authoritative source of true knowledge. Next, the three-fold *prameya*.

the in-house confidence it has enjoyed from Chaitanya's earliest theologians to his most recent exponents. For our purposes it can be organizationally amenable to Prabhupāda's thought, capable of accommodating traditional ideology and the various theological issues culled from our survey of recent scholarship.

Chapter 3 considers *pramāṇa,* the sources of knowledge, by seeking to address these issues of authority: Which sacred texts and commentaries shape Prabhupāda's purports, or commentaries? What historical forces operating outside the Gauḍīya tradition were influential in the early formation of his thought? Is his hermeneutic merely a naive literalism and are his "expanded-text" translations justifiable? How does the *paramparā,* or succession of disciples, function as a "transparent via media" for the transmission of knowledge? Why is Prabhupāda's position as founder-*ācārya* crucial to the conservation of this knowledge system and what are its precedents? How does ISKCON function as a repository and facility for the dissemination of these archives of knowledge? In discussing preservation and transmission, chapter 3 also examines the importance of enculturation and Prabhupāda's creative ability to compress enormous concepts within tightly wrapped *sūtras* that slowly reveal the concepts.

Chapter 4 probes the category of *sambandha* (relationship), exploring the use of "Krishna, the Supreme Personality of Godhead" as the root metaphor of Prabhupāda's theology, simultaneously conveying majesty and intimacy. Its fruitfulness as a translation of the tradition's governing *sūtra* will be measured and contrasted with other past and present Krishna images for its strength to marshal numerous relational models: Krishna's relationships with the living entities, the world, and his own abode and associates, and in turn their relationships with each other. Body-self dualism and the personal-impersonal dialectic are also considered.

In chapter 5 (on *abhidheya,* execution), we learn how Prabhupāda integrated the philosophical concepts of the previous chapter with the affective elements of the *bhakti* process to produce a "living theology." His ubiquitous use of the term "devotional service" (a search produced over nine thousand instances) confirms that the ritual and experiential dimensions, or the affective elements, are at the

---

Sambandha [relationship]: (2) Krishna is the Supreme Personality of Godhead, one without a second. (3) Krishna possesses infinite energies. (4) Living beings are Krishna's separated parts. (5) Certain living beings are engrossed by *māyā,* Krishna's illusory energy. (6) Certain living beings are released from the grasp of *māyā.* (7) All spiritual and material phenomena are simultaneously one with and different from the Lord. (8) Krishna is an ocean of *rasa* (the transcendental bliss that forms the essence of any relationship with the Lord).

Abhidheya [execution]: (9) Devotional service [*bhakti-yoga*] is the means of attaining the final object of spiritual existence.

Prayojana [goal]: (10) Love of Krishna [*prema*] is alone the final object of spiritual existence. (Bhaktivinoda Ṭhākura 1988:45–46)

heart of Krishna *bhakti*. The rationale behind his selective appropriation of key components—chanting, hearing, and sacred image worship to name but three—and his apparent emphasis on *vaidhī bhakti* rather than *rāgānugā* explains how he made devotional service a practical engagement for all. Rather than recommend the path of *rāga* in its traditional sense, his sacralization of a broad range of missionary endeavors as *saṁkīrtana*—a powerful, transformative force enabling one to gradually come face to face with God—is perhaps the outstanding (and certainly the most controversial) feature of his theology. "Warfare" as a modality of mission is explored both for its disquieting and inspiring effects.

Did Prabhupāda alter the traditional understanding of *prayojana*, the goal of love of Krishna (*prema*), or act in fulfilment of Chaitanya's mission by his seeming redefinition of "spontaneity" as manifest preaching enthusiasm rather than internal ecstasy? This would be the task of further research. Here one would seek to determine if these are competing moods or, in fact, outward and inward expressions of the same Krishna *bhakti*, reflecting the exoteric and esoteric nature of Chaitanya's own appearance. Stated in another way, in a tradition that views *bhakti* both as its means and end, to what extent are the words "back to Godhead" world affirming or world denying? Against the nondual liberation of Advaita Vedānta, I would maintain that the Gauḍīya Vaishnava goal of union with the Godhead is interpreted by a hermeneutic of relational models in terms of the theory of *rasa*.

The following chapters are not intended as a rehearsal of Gauḍīya belief, for which good studies already exist.[103] The employment organizationally and substantively of a traditional schema is necessary to evaluate Prabhupāda's contribution, which is the real focus of these chapters. In ways that previous scholarship has to a large extent lacked, these chapters are meant to sensitize us to the many voices of Prabhupāda. The amalgam of past and present in a cumulative tradition is never entirely homogenous. Tensions arise when a self-consciously traditional movement, fixed by the mammoth literary canon of its founder, is confronted by the ever-changing conditions of time, place, and circumstance. I hope that this study will lay the foundation for a future constructive scholarship that, while selecting and exploring questions, acknowledges the theology from which they emerge.

103. See De 1961, A. K. Majumdar 1969, and Kapoor 1976.

3

Sources of Knowledge: Pramāṇa

I PROPOSE, AS discussed above, that we consider Prabhupāda's theology within a traditional schema preferred by such Gauḍīya theologians as Jīva Gosvāmin and Bhaktivinoda Ṭhākura. This schema is necessary because despite his being a prolific member of a commentarial tradition, Prabhupāda has not offered us a ready-made systematic by which to order his thought. The doctrinal loci to be considered within our chosen schema, far from being slavish scholasticized categories incapable of creatively responding to current needs, will allow us to correlate the texts and tradition with the factors that make Prabhupāda's interpretation particular and discrete. A solely text-driven analysis of Prabhupāda's thought that does not recognize its situational character would violate the historicist premise that animated our previous survey, that is, the imbrication of scholarship, society, and culture. Their mutual interplay demands a reflective equilibrium, a "both/and" approach rather than an "either/or" approach, in which the theology Prabhupāda crafted is contextualized in the light of its contemporary setting. We are not, therefore, about to embark on an exercise in traditional epistemology, though what immediately follows provides a sampling of what this would include.[1]

Gauḍīya Vaishnavism, like other systematic perspectives that appeal to Vedic authority, is initially concerned with ascertaining the *pramāṇa,* the means by which knowledge that is certain is acquired, before attempting to determine that which is knowable (*prameya*). In contradistinction to the current aversion toward an absolute, ahistorical vocabulary of any sort, Gauḍīya Vaishnavism, while making a conditional allowance for relative, historically contingent knowledge, insists on the capacity of *valid* knowledge (*pramā*) to reveal and circumscribe the true nature of an object as it actually is. For the Gauḍīyas, *śabda* (from *śabd,* to sound) is "revelation," not just verbal testimony, and ultimately the only source

---

1. Epistemology is the primary concern of the tradition's chief philosopher, Jīva Gosvāmin, in his *Tattva-sandarbha.* For a reliable translation, see Elkman's version (Jīva Gosvāmin 1986b). For a summation of Gauḍīya epistemology, see Chakravarti 1969, ch. 1.

of valid knowledge in which epistemological certainty resides.[2] *Śabda* alone is considered free of the four human defects—misperception (*bhrama*), inattention (*pramāda*), the propensity to cheat (*vipralipsā*), and imperfection of the senses (*karaṇāpāṭava*)—that flaw and invalidate other forms of evidence not confirmed by *śabda*.[3]

While all the Vedāntic schools generally identify *śabda* with *śruti* (the Vedas, especially the Upaniṣads), the Gauḍīyas also include some of the so-called *smṛtis* (the Itihāsas, or epics, and the Purāṇas) and also give these Vedic supplements the same divine status. Their composer Vyāsa, the classifier of the Vedas, is considered a descent of the Godhead.[4] Jīva Gosvāmin argues that because of the decadence of the *kali-yuga*, the Purāṇas are more intelligible and accessible and, in fact, are superior to the Vedas, whose real sense is incomprehensible without them. Among the Purāṇas, the Bhāgavata is considered Vyāsa's final composition, his own commentary on the Vedānta Sūtra, self-validating and superior to all others.[5] As the essence of the Vedas, Purāṇas, and Itihāsas, the Bhāgavata is the ultimate *pramāṇa* and that upon which the entire system of Gauḍīya thought primarily rests.

Prabhupāda religiously adheres to *śabda-pramāṇa*, which he refers to as a deductive process (*avaroha-panthā*, literally, the descending path). The academic project in which this study partakes, however, is more akin to an inductive, "ascending" approach (*āroha-panthā*), wherein inferred conclusions are probable rather than necessary (though, in traditional terms, this opens them to the four human defects, a potentially fatal flaw).[6] To accomplish our immediate task—that

2. Julius Lipner contrasts *śabda* with its nearest Christian equivalent, "scripture" (from *scribere* in Latin): "For Hindus, 'scripture' in its most authoritative form is what has been heard and transmitted orally, not what has been written" (1994a:25).

3. In his *Sarva-savādinī* commentary to *Tattva-sandarbha*, Jīva Gosvāmin lists ten *pramāṇas*, which he then collapses into three: *pratyakṣa* (sense perception), *anumāna* (inference), and *śabda*, before concluding that only the last, *śabda*, is independently reliable in revealing the Absolute. Prabhupāda follows Jīva; see CC 2.6:135P.

4. That Vyāsa is seen as a divine descent allows simultaneously for the Veda having an authored origin and yet having none (*apauruṣeya*). After considering evidence including traditional sources favoring such a view, Thomas B. Coburn concludes: "[Value-neutral critical editing] allows one to affirm, on academic grounds, that the Purāṇas have developed from an early nucleus to their present extent, and it also allows one to affirm (or to deny) that that nucleus was of divine origin, as a matter of personal faith. Similarly, whether Vyāsa be understood as mortal editor, or divine incarnation, is a matter on which academic judgement not only can but must remain silent" (1980:351). Frederick Smith, 1994, concurs.

5. For the superiority of the Purāṇas and among them the Bhāgavata's supremacy as the natural commentary on the Vedānta Sūtra, see Jīva's *Tattva-sandarbha* verses 12–24 (Jīva Gosvāmin 1986b:77–115); for a summary of Jīva's argument, see Chakravarti 1969:8–11.

6. For Prabhupāda's comments, see, for example, 721119bg.hyd.

of attempting to determine the sources of Prabhupāda's thought—we must take seriously all significant influences, even though to do so we may have to depart from, or the influences we discover may ultimately be subsumed under, the tradition's allegiance to *śabda*. This bottom-up rather than top-down construction may at first appear antithetical to *śabda's* ultimacy, but it is in fact congruent with the tradition's own allowance for many *pramāṇas* in final subordination to *śabda*. Structurally and substantively, our approach is in line with Gauḍīya epistemology, though no doubt a creative appropriation of it.

Our task is to identify the provocative, extra-*sampradāya* forces and those operating within the Gauḍīya tradition itself (individual and collective) that are seminal to, if not finally determinative, of Prabhupāda's thought. Because documentation of the early period of Prabhupāda's life is fragmentary and inadequate, the tendency has been toward one-sided and misleading reductions. The particular persons and circumstances of his time, whose often invisible presence nevertheless make themselves felt amid his sacred texts and commentaries and traditional systems, need to be adequately sketched if our theological portrait is to achieve its desired resemblance.

I say "sketched" for in their own right they already have been elaborated upon elsewhere. Here I mainly draw connections to Prabhupāda, direct or otherwise, often missed by previous scholarship, and in so doing anticipate thematic elements to come. This adumbrated history of persons and events focuses, sometimes disproportionately, on new constructions with the understanding that any consequent imbalance adjusts itself against the old. The discussion concludes with a text- and commentary-based analysis incorporating the roles of the disciplic succession, the founder-*ācārya*, and ISKCON in Prabhupāda's theological formulation.

The Influence of Parents and Teachers

The earliest and likely the most influential person in Prabhupāda's life apart from his guru was his father, Gour Mohan De (1849–1930), a Krishna devotee like the generations before him. To him Prabhupāda dedicated his Bhāgavata Purāṇa tenth canto summary study, *Kṛṣṇa, the Supreme Personality of Godhead:*

> A pure devotee of Kṛṣṇa, who raised me as a Kṛṣṇa concious child from the beginning of my life. In my boyhood ages he instructed me how to play the *mṛdanga* [clay drum]. He gave me Rādhā- Kṛṣṇa Vigraha [divine images] to worship, and he gave me Jagannātha-Ratha [a ceremonial chariot] to duly observe the festival as my childhood play. He was kind to me, and I imbibed from him the ideas later on solidified by my spiritual master, the eternal father. (KB 1: v)

We find here ideas elemental to his theology: *kīrtana*, temple worship, festivals. The hagiographical *Śrīla Prabhupāda-līlāmṛta* portrays Gour Mohan's guiding affection and single-minded prayer that his son become a preacher of the Bhāgavata and a servant of Krishna's consort Rādhārāṇī (the ultimate goal of Gauḍīyas)—a portrait substantiated by Prabhupāda's own testimony.[7]

His mother, Rajani (1866?–1912), who passed away in his sixteenth year, was as affectionate and no less prayerful, though her petitions centered more on his worldly well-being. She too hailed from a long-established Gauḍīya Vaishnava lineage, but was not averse to marshalling a broad spectrum of Hindu wisdom for her son's protection.[8] Prabhupāda imbibed her practical nature, her skill in cookery, and, through observing her perform traditional household duties, an abiding faith in the efficacy of the "Vedic" way of life. If Gour Mohan is to be credited for encouraging Prabhupāda's early practice, solidified later through the doctrinal instruction of his guru, it is Rajani who deserves recognition for much of his enculturation vital to both practice and belief. Father and mother, then, were instrumental in what some scholars believe was Prabhupāda's most significant contribution: the introduction of the ritual and experiential aspects of Krishna *bhakti*.[9]

Peter Schmidt has questioned the significance of paternal influence (he is silent about Rajani's role) in Prabhupāda's theological formulations. Schmidt cites a number of discrepancies to justify his claim that Prabhupāda's own testimony does not support the official ISKCON biography's depiction of its founder as one who from his earliest childhood began to develop spiritual insight and authority.[10] Schmidt concedes: "Certain, however, is only Bhaktivedanta Swami's childlike faith native to the common piety of the times and his naive fascination wherever possible for the rituals of his father's religion, the theological meaning of which he did not thoroughly understand."[11] However, the psychological importance of childhood impressions cannot be overestimated. Whether or not

7. See, for example, 750303ar.dal. Not all of Prabhupāda's remembrances of youth agree with the SPL version.

8. As when she would apply a drop of her saliva to his forehead before he would go out to play. "She once offered blood from her breast to one of the demigods with the supplication that Abhay be protected on all sides from danger" (SPL 1:9).

9. Hopkins is one such scholar; see chapter 2, "Cult-Controversy Discourse: The Mid-1970s to Mid-1980s."

10. See Schmidt 1999:103–120. Schmidt is the only scholar to scrutinize Prabhupāda's early history; others merely repeat the version popularized by the official biography.

11. "Fest steht jedoch lediglich Bhaktivedanta Swamis in der Volksfrömmigkeit beheimateter kindlicher Glauben und eine womglich naive Faszination für in ihrer theologischen Bedeutung unverstandene Rituale der väterlichen Religion" (Schmidt, 120).

a child can cognize and articulate the patterns formed in childish play does not determine their significance in later life. Similarly, in theological terms, the supraintellectual fruit of Vaishnava devotion, or *prema,* love for Krishna, is not specifically dependent upon the cultivation of *jñāna* (knowledge).[12] Prabhupāda's Vaishnava faith, the result of his early religio-cultural training (however informal), persevered in the face of a formal British-Christian education under Scottish missionaries. In the devout Vaishnava family of Gour Mohan and Rajani, the "common piety of the times" (Schmidt's "Volksfrömmigkeit") was infused with Krishna *bhakti.* The family regularly went to bathe in the Ganges, fed religious mendicants (from whom they sought the boon of Rādhārāṇī's favor for their son), and held daily *kṛṣṇa-kathā* (recitation of Krishna's pastimes).[13] Beyond the immediacy of their own home, one-fifth of Bengal followed Chaitanya, including most of Calcutta's wealthy, influential families.[14] While Prabhupāda's faith may not be as legendary as hagiography suggests, Schmidt's findings seem to equally undervalue it. Indeed, both extremes appear methodologically related: the official biographer lacked the ease and thoroughness of an electronic InfoBase to access Prabhupāda's corpus, while Schmidt lacked the practitioner/biographer's firsthand knowledge of Prabhupāda's theology and person to guide his InfoBase searches.[15]

---

12. Briefly, as this subject will later be treated at length, on the strength of such statements as SB 1.2:7, Gauḍīya Vaishnavas believe knowledge to be subsumed by and to follow from devotion nondeductively.

13. Prabhupāda's own remembrances confirm each of these activities. In his liberality, Gour Mohan fed anyone dressed in the ochre robes of a renunciant, though Prabhupāda observed that most were beggars and *ganja* smokers; see, e.g., his conversation with me, 760210mw. may.

14. Chakrabarty 1985:385, cites both the census figures of 1881 and 1901 and British and Indian writers to corroborate this statement. Although these census reports are not entirely reliable and do not distinguish the many Gauḍīya Vaishnava sects, the results are more than suggestive.

15. The InfoBase was developed after the official biography's completion. Although Schmidt makes extensive use of the InfoBase, he fails to find, or at least cite, an important autobiographical letter in which Prabhupāda disputes the claim that his devotion, prior to meeting his guru, was naive or ever ordinary (which I found in response to almost irreverent probing on my part). The following excerpt forms an explicit statement of self-understanding characteristic of religious authority, tightly wedding history to theology. Whether Prabhupāda was Krishna conscious throughout his early life is a moot question; that he claimed he was cannot be ignored, especially when Schmidt relies so heavily upon his word:

> So far as I am concerned, I cannot say what I was in my previous life, but one great astrologer calculated that I was previously a physician and my life was sinless. Besides that, to corroborate the statement of Bhagavad-gita *'sucinam srimatam gehe yogabhrasto samjayate'* [*sic*] which means an unfinished *yogi* takes birth in a rich family or born of a suci or pious father. By the grace of Krsna I got these two opportunities in the present life to be born of a pious father and brought up in

Schmidt seems on firmer ground when investigating the influence of the Reverend William Spence Urquhart (1877–1964), a sixth-generation clergyman, professor of philosophy at Scottish Churches' College and later its principal (also editor of the esteemed *Calcutta Review* and the last westerner to be the vice-chancellor of the University of Calcutta). Schmidt and the biography concur in support of Prabhupāda's own recollections of his professor: "The philosophy professor, Dr. W. S. Urquhart, he was very friendly to me, very kind, just like father" (751016mw.dur). "[A] very big philosopher" (740524r2.rom). "A very perfect gentleman. Kind-hearted" (730421mw.la). "Dr. Urquhart was a godly man.... He was very saintly" (770215ed.may). But their agreement ends here. The biographer claims, "Abhay studied the Western philosophers and scientists, yet they held no fascination for him.... The sudden access to the wealth of Western knowledge.... left Abhay untouched" (SPL 1:26). Thus, when Urquhart disputed the theory of karma and reincarnation on the grounds that there was no witness to judge the misdeeds of past lifetimes, Prabhupāda, according to the biographer, "was displeased to hear this criticism, and he knew how to refute it, but being only a student remained silent" (24).

The College Setting and Christian Influences

Schmidt reads the situation differently. His argument, based on Prabhupāda's own admission, is that Prabhupāda was far more interested in his academic studies than in his spiritual practices and at the time had no philosophical reply for his professor.[16] When later in his career he does respond, Urquhart's views, beyond just those on karma and reincarnation, are projected to represent Christianity as a whole. Schmidt demonstrates that Prabhupāda does more than passively hear from his professor; he accepts much of what he learns from him—from a psychology lesson equating women's inferior intelligence with their smaller brain

---

> one of the richest, [most] aristocratic families of Calcutta (Kasinath Mullick).... Although I had immense opportunities to indulge in the four principles of sinful life because I was connected with a very aristocratic family, Krsna always saved me, and throughout my whole life I do not know what is illicit sex, intoxication, meat-eating or gambling. So far as my present life is concerned, I do not remember any part of my life when I was forgetful of Krsna. (Tamal Krsna700621)

16. Schmidt culls the following references in support of his view: "'But at the time we were not so intelligent. We could not answer.' 'But he [Urquhart] had no knowledge of *Bhagavad-gītā*. We also at that time did not know. We were not very interested.' 'Later on these activities [the deity worship of Krishna] were suspended due to my association in the schools and colleges, and I became completely out of practice'" (Schmidt, 114 n. 279). For a further reference, see 710215ba.gor: "and due to my association with college friends, younger days, I lost my faith practically, although I was born in a Vaishnava family."

size, to the mandatory Bible classes where he is taught about Christ and Christ's message.[17] It is particularly with reference to the latter, where Schmidt tackles his primary interest—Prabhupāda's encounter with Christianity, that his argument becomes most compelling.

In his comparative reading of Urquhart and Prabhupāda on the historical and Christological Jesus, Schmidt discovers striking commonalties of thought and language.[18] Both Urquhart and Prabhupāda see Jesus as a great historical personality, an exemplary religious teacher and moral authority whose mission is the salvation of humanity. Again, both strictly reject the use of speculative philosophy, emphasizing faith in and service to a loving God as the only feasible and genuine path to the attainment of eternal life. Stressing doctrinal adherence, neither the professor nor his former student publicly doubts the historical authenticity or divine origin of the biblical Jesus literature.[19] Schmidt highlights their use of identical biblical quotes (John 14:6) and common theological terms ("son of God") as well as patterns of speech ("religionist")[20] to further confirm Urquhart's impact on Prabhupāda's understanding of Jesus. Differences exist where Urquhart's claims violate the boundaries of orthodox Gauḍīya Vaishnava belief (e.g., incarnational uniqueness or the explication of John 14:6).[21]

---

17. Regarding gender, the attitudes of both men might best be described (to borrow from Kim Knott) as "equality-in-difference." Scottish Churches' College was one of the first to introduce coeducation in Calcutta, a cause Urquhart championed; see Dr. Urquhart Farewell Committee 1937:xi–xii. Prabhupāda was the first of his godbrothers to allow celibate female students to reside in his ashrams as *brahmacāriṇīs*, a status of at least theoretical equality.

18. Schmidt's focus is a series of lectures Urquhart delivered before an Indian audience at Scottish Churches' College in 1915 (a year before Prabhupāda's entrance) and published the same year; see Urquhart 1915.

19. Yet Schmidt contradicts himself. Earlier, he states that Prabhupāda "condemned" (*verurteilt*) any changes made to the Bible (Schmidt, 132), only to conclude that he never openly doubted its historical authenticity ("Wie dieser bezweifelt er die historische Echtheit und den göttlichen Ursprung der biblischen Jesusliteratur niemals öffentlich") (147). While Prabhupāda does acknowledge the divine inspiration underlying the Bible's composition, unlike Urquhart, at times he questions its authenticity. On one occasion, he invokes historical criticism to doubt whether all the passages attributed to Jesus were in fact spoken by him (especially in John, and in particular John 14:6: "I am the Way; I am Truth and Life. No one can come to the Father except through me"); see Satsvarūpa691031. Of course, Prabhupāda does not subject his own texts to similar critical scrutiny.

20. "Religionist" is too common a term to be credited solely to Urquhart. Prabhupāda's guru also uses it; see their correspondence in SPL 1:92.

21. The comparativist problem of contrasting the Christian concept of Incarnation to the Hindu concepts of *avatāra* and guru does not trouble Prabhupāda. According to Prabhupāda (see his conversation with me, 770416rc.bom), Bhaktisiddhānta Sarasvatī placed Jesus within the specific category of divine descents classified by Rūpa Gosvāmin as *śaktyāveśa-avatāra*: "Whenever the Lord is present in someone by portions of His various potencies,

If Urquhart's influence upon Prabhupāda were limited to his Christology, it would still be significant. The true measure of his effect, however, can be estimated only against the breadth of Prabhupāda's entire thought, a project that Schmidt acknowledges overreaches the boundaries of his study.[22] When we consider that in addition to the Bible class (a half-hour daily for four years), Urquhart also instructed Prabhupāda in both Indian and Western philosophy for two years, we may expect the consequence of their extensive association to be considerable. Bear in mind Prabhupāda's own remembrances of his favorite professor—"a very perfect gentleman," "godly," "very saintly," "very friendly to me,... just like father"—and the young Prabhupāda's impressionable age, when an active, philosophic mind like his would begin to intellectually formulate the devotional impressions of childhood, and we have the chemistry needed for strong bonding. I am led to hypothesize that beyond its Christian advocacy, the theology of the philosophically rigoros, morally upright reverend was essentially compatible with his student's Vaishnava upbringing and later became the template against which his student-turned-missionary framed the Gauḍīya theology of his guru, Bhaktisiddhānta Sarasvatī.

No doubt this appears to be a large claim, which upon first hearing may cause uneasiness not just among those nurtured on the official biographical account, nor alone the hermeneutically suspicious, but anyone wary of naive comparisons. While all might be reassured were I at once to acknowledge the cultural, historical, and theological differences that mar any proposed congruence, I prefer to reiterate our purpose here. We are seeking clues to the sources of Prabhupāda's exported Vaishnava theology, not launching a full-blown comparison with Urquhart's nineteenth-century liberal Protestantism.[23] We are as unlikely to find one-to-one congruences as to discover total dissimilitude. Both Urquhart and Prabhupāda were far too discerning to allow for either. Their respective ways of being orthodox also rule out the possibility of a pervasively syncretistic mingling. So my claim, especially if softened, is in fact reasonable: Prabhupāda distilled from the hundreds of hours of classes and sermons a sense of what was and was not theologically acceptable to the religious sensibility of the West (of which Urquhart was the archetypal representative), then shaped his theology accordingly.

---

the living entity representing the Lord is called a *śaktyāveśa-avatāra*—that is, an incarnation invested with special power." Others in this same category include Vyāsa, Nārada, and Paraśurāma, and the number is incalculable (*asakya gaṇana*); see CC 2.20:366–373. Prabhupāda's Christology obviously differs from Urquhart's, as does his reading of John 14:6 (see n. 155), wherein he understands Jesus as guru, by which he has in mind something akin to the Hebrew *rabbī* (lit., "my great one"); see 740701lec.mel.

22. See Schmidt, 131.

23. What we actually seek is compatibility. For the valorized leap from "comparison" to "compatibility" specific to Hinduism and Christianity, see Lipner 2000.

When one recalls the harsh criticism that Prabhupāda later meted out both to academics for speculating and to Christians for their nonvegetarian diet,[24] his glowing reminiscence of his professor is striking. Urquhart himself was averse to philosophical speculation, but his diet should have provoked Prabhupāda's censure. That it did not may indicate more than a residual adolescent fealty. Students in those days were often political, even militant, and Prabhupāda was no exception (he rejected his degree in support of Gandhi's noncooperation movement). That his professor was held in great esteem, approaching reverence, requires a deeper understanding.[25]

In a book describing cultural contact and conversion in colonial India, Antony Copley characterizes the student-professor relationship between, among others, the well-known Christian convert Lal Behari Day (1824–94), like Prabhupāda, born to *suvarṇa-vaṇik* Vaishnava parents, and the Reverand Alexander Duff (1806–78), inaugurator of the education-based Scottish Mission to India.[26] Much as Urquhart was to Prabhupāda, Duff was to Day, "a teacher, a friend, and above all, a surrogate father" (Copley 1997:231). Considering that Prabhupāda was not a convert, such appreciative appellations in addition to "godly" and "saintly" are intriguing, the more so when we follow the evolving missionary strategy Copley traces through a series of mid-to-late nineteenth-century Protestant missionary conferences. Ideological strategy, especially in its form eventually bequeathed to early twentieth-century missionaries like Urquhart, is immediately germane to the subject of Prabhupāda's education.

Itinerating ("the dramatic and direct confrontation with Indian religions, by word of mouth, in the bazaar, the mela, the village" [Copley, 14]) failed to bring about large-scale conversions, which increased frustration, thereby gradually persuading missionaries that their future lay in promoting education. Most itinerants were ignorant of Hinduism; educators were much less so. But if there was a shift in strategy by the 1880s, the missionary aim remained unchanged. Duff, who fifty years earlier had anticipated this transformation, had clear objectives from the outset:

> In many ways Duff was driven by a quite terrifyingly simple idea: Mission had to destroy Hinduism and the only means was through the agency of

24. See Baird's review in chapter 2.

25. John Berwick's chapter on the student community in Bengal ca.1870–1922 reveals a highly volatile student body often at odds with their teachers and administrators; see Berwick 1995.

26. Duff founded the General Assembly Institute (popularly known as Duff's Institute) in 1830, which in 1844 reopened as the Institute of the Free Church of Scotland, and in 1908 became the Scottish Churches' College.

> an indigenous, anglicized, Indian elite. Duff did not reject out of hand the alternative strategy of itinerating and vernacularism... but, at this stage, his was the shuddering alternative of an English-medium higher education. (Copley, 221–222)[27]

In 1855, at the first conference held after sixty years of mission in Bengal, Rev. D. Ewart (of the Scottish Mission) voiced the same view, but it was at that time still a minority opinion:

> The aim was to evangelize the pupils, and this could only be achieved with missionaries as teachers. The missionary gained attention 'by imparting useful and eagerly desired knowledge, call it secular if you wish, and follows it up by preaching the gospel to the impressible minds that surround him'.... Such a missionary education... 'has a certain powerful destructive tendency as regard all confidence in the Hindu shastras and all regard to the distinction of caste'. (Ewart 1855, quoted in Copley, 17)

Ewart's and others' hopes for the success rate of conversions through education were not, however, to be realized.[28] By the Allahabad Conference of 1872, educators, though still the minority voice compared with those in favor of itinerating, were prepared to shift the focus from direct evangelism to preparation, to be satisfied, at least for the moment, with moral and social change. Conversion would not be paramount. But ten years later, at the Calcutta Conference of 1882, doubt had again set in. Harking back to Duff's ideas, the Scottish educator J. Wilson declared that Hinduism had not been "killed through its brain," only "scotched" at best. "The hereditary affection of many generations will not let it die" (J. Wilson 1883, quoted in Copley, 25).

Lurking behind this gnawing doubt was "an almost apocalyptic faith that Indian religions were in terminal decline" (Copley, 14). But the many nineteenth-century Hindu reform and revivalist initiatives that reared their heads up high indicated that the multiheaded Hindu serpent was not easily slain. In response, missionary strategy entering the twentieth century veered in another direction—inclusivism. However, as Copley notes in his epilogue, this thinly veiled

27. The following extract from Duff's book, *India and Indian Missions,* leaves little doubt about his vitriolic view of Hinduism: "Of all the systems of false religion ever fabricated by the perverse ingenuity of fallen man, Hinduism is surely the most stupendous.... Of all systems of false religion it is that which seems to embody the largest amount and variety of semblances and counterfeits of divinely revealed facts and doctrines" (Majumdar 1965:155).

28. R. C. Majumdar estimates less than one percent of the total during the whole of the nineteenth century; see Majumdar 1965:155.

inclusivism had worrying continuities with an exclusivist past. Singling out the work of the Scottish missionary scholar J. N. Farquhar (1861–1929), the prophet of fulfilment theology, Copley finds that "at its heart was hiatus rather than 'fulfilment' between Hinduism and Christianity" (251). Farquhar speaks of a disintegrating Hinduism, which "must die in order to live. It must die into Christianity" (Farquhar 1913:51, quoted in Copley, 251).

And Farquhar was not alone. Urquhart, with whom Farquhar had a close working relationship, asserts, "I have no hesitation in saying that such studies as I have been able to make in Indian philosophy have confirmed me in the faith that God has not left Himself without a witness in the characteristic thought of India, that much of it is unconsciously anticipative of Christian thought, and that Jesus Christ will one day be recognized there also as the 'light which lighteth every man that cometh into the world'" (Urquhart 1928:xiii).[29] Not to be outdone, Farquhar concludes his survey of *Modern Religious Movements in India* by declaring, "*Christianity has ruled the(ir) development throughout,*" and "*almost without exception, the methods of work in use in the movements have been borrowed from missions*" (italics in original, (1915) 1998:433, 442).

Lest we think this to be wishful, erstwhile missionary rhetoric, compare that last remark to those of two late twentieth-century commentators, Richard King and Romila Thapar (whom King cites):

> Thus, since the nineteenth century, 'Hinduism' has developed, and is notable for a number of new characteristics, which seem to have arisen in response to Judeo-Christian presuppositions about the nature of religion. This new form of organized or 'syndicated Hinduism': seeks historicity for the incarnations of its deities, encourages the idea of a centrally sacred book, claims monotheism as significant to the worship of deity, acknowledges the authority of the ecclesiastical organization of certain sects as prevailing over all and has supported large-scale missionary work and conversion. (King 1999:104–105, Thapar 1985)

With the advantage of hindsight, our two astute observers substantively confirm (not, of course, in intent) Farquhar's triumphalist assertion. And in so doing, they leave us squarely facing the question: To what extent does their conclusion apply to Prabhupāda?

---

29. Apart from Farquhar and Urquhart, one may also see, for example, Kennedy [1925] 1993. Macnicol's *Indian Theism* ([1915] 1968), a University of Glasgow dissertation, is heavily indebted to Farquhar and moves just as certainly in the direction of his fulfillment theology.

We have seen that Urquhart, Prabhupāda's college mentor, inherited a missionary agenda that, while overtly deferring on conversion, coveted it no less. A liberal English education would instill the distinctive traits of Western culture by training the student's mind, character, and personality. Its utilization as a subterfuge to stamp out "superstition" (i.e., indigenous religions) is barely covert. The multivalency of seemingly "neutral" subjects like English literature has been clearly identified by postcolonial critiques.[30] In fact, the missionaries recognized this themselves: "It is not to be overlooked that the area of what is commonly called English literature is more or less pervaded with the ideas and sentiments of Christianity" (Coles 1858, quoted in Copley, 19).

One need only compare Thapar's "syndicated Hinduism" with ISKCON to estimate how much Prabhupāda "borrowed" (to use a term of Farquhar's). He was, after all, a member of his college's English Society, and recited Keats, Shelley, and others.[31] He sat through hundreds of hours of listening to Urquhart, whose philosophy classes (if his books are any indication) were as unidirectional as his Bible expositions and only slightly less "fulfilment" oriented than Farquhar's.

Now, it would be easy enough to lay all of these cards on the table and surmise that ISKCON is but a Christian-Vaishnava hybrid, making Prabhupāda's fond recollection of his favorite professor the final trump card. Urquhart's theology would then be posited as the template for Prabhupāda's Gauḍīya theology. Or if this contention were too strong, then its softer version—that Urquhart and his theology signalled what Prabhupāda might expect from his future Western audience—would at least be confirmed.

As tempting as the finesse of hybridity may be, the overlapping trajectories of Urquhart and Prabhupāda simply do not coalesce. For either contention to succeed (though we may never be able to decide between them), we will need to examine precisely what it is about Urquhart's teaching that Prabhupāda could have found so compelling and adaptable. We turn therefore to Urquhart's magnum opus, *Pantheism and the Value of Life*, a survey of Indian philosophy (and, more limitedly, Western as well).[32] Like his other, lesser writings, this book was targeted to

---

30. English and its literature became a vehicle for civilizing the colonial subject. "Indeed, literature might be the best complement to ideological transformation.... Literature buys your assent in an almost clandestine way, and therefore it is an excellent instrument for a slow transformation of the mind, for good or for ill, as medicine or as poison, perhaps always a bit of both" (Spivak 1993:137). Indeed, Sara Suleri's study, *The Rhetoric of English India*, demonstrates that the term "English India" is idiomatically broad enough to be historically and linguistically viable in both a colonial and postcolonial setting, and to include imperial and subaltern materials; see Suleri 1992.

31. See SPL 1:22.

32. Here one is reminded that I use interchangeably the culturally specific term "philosophy" along with its sisters "theology" and "religion"; see chapter 1, n. 9.

establish the Christian imperative.[33] Since it was published in 1919, we may confidently assume that it is representative of whatever its author understood and imparted of Indian philosophy at the time of Prabhupāda's instruction. In anticipating Prabhupāda's reaction, we will not project ourselves back to that time, however, for there are reasons to believe Prabhupāda's responses then were at best muted.[34] Instead, we bring the professor into conversation with Prabhupāda, the prolific author and outspoken missionary whose views are matters of public record.

Urquhart's argument is based on the premises that "pantheism" always has been India's paradigmatic intellectual doctrine and pessimism her prevailing evaluation of life—at first sight, an argument one would hardly expect Prabhupāda to find appealing. Still, we have an equal interest in what might register disturbingly on Prabhupāda's Vaishnava faith. In its totalizing engulfment of his own belief, this argument is certain to do just that: to arouse his antipathy. But in its details, there is much he would find to recommend it.

In defining pantheism Urquhart offers a binary formula: "*Nothing is which is not God, and God is everything which is*" (italics in original, 25). His explication exposes the core problem for Vedāntic interpretation:

> A rigorous application of the pantheistic principles compels us to identify God with the whole world or with none of it. If, however, we press the principle that God is *all,* and if especially we retain in our minds the idea that the only complete unity is an abstract unity excluding differences, then we are immediately landed in the extreme of acosmism. If, on the other hand, we press the principle that *all* is God, we cannot avoid the identification of the details of the world, in all their seeming incompleteness and contrariety, with God. (589)

We may note that each Vedāntic interpreter attempts to resolve this dilemma with a pivotal maxim that defines his school.[35] Chaitanya's solution is *acintya-bhedābheda* (inconceivable dualism and nondualism), as Prabhupāda explains, which "establishes everything to be simultaneously one with and different from the Personality of Godhead" (CC 1.1:46P). Śaṅkara's Advaita (nondualism) perhaps best exemplifies the extreme of acosmism, the doctrine that the world is unreal and only God

33. Farquhar is thanked in the preface for his assistance in the preparation of the manuscript for publication. The thesis in its original form earned Urquhart a Ph.D. from the University of Aberdeen.

34. See n. 16 in this chapter.

35. See, for example, chapter 1, n. 8, for Madhva's dualistic solution and n. 22 for Rāmānuja's nondualism of particulars.

is real,[36] though Urquhart claims that pantheism in some form underlies Indian philosophy from the earliest to its most recent expression. Whether the Vaishnava Vedāntic *ācāryas* would agree to be labelled pantheists is extremely doubtful.[37]

Urquhart's binary definition of pantheism is less contentious than Śaṅkara's doctrine. Prabhupāda's twofold description suggests a close parallel:

> The impersonalists think of the Absolute Personality of Godhead in two different ways, as above mentioned [SB 2.10:33–34]. On the one hand they worship the Lord in His *viśva-rūpa,* or all-pervading universal form [*all* is God], and on the other they think of the Lord's unmanifested, indescribable, subtle form [God is *all*]. The theories of pantheism and monism are respectively applicable to these two conceptions of the Supreme as gross and subtle, but both of them are rejected by the learned pure devotees of the Lord because they are aware of the factual position. (SB 2.10:35P)

Would space permit the luxury of extensive parallel citations, the congeniality of the two theologians would be clearer still. About *God and the self,* both postulate that relational intimacy necessitates permanent individuality—a community of nature yet duality of subject and object (Urquhart); a oneness of quality but difference in quantity (Prabhupāda). They share the conviction that denying permanence to either God or the individual strips each of personality, robs them of responsibility, and thereby morality, and ultimately divests life of its most fulfilling relationship. Unity may deliver one from sorrow, but—at the expense of difference—holds no possibility of joy.

About *God and the world,* Urquhart's demand for a God at once immanent (in the world) and transcendent (over it) is not quite met by Prabhupāda's view of an absolute Godhead relatively extended through diverse energies. Here, beneath the surface, their ideas begin to clash. Prabhupāda is uncompromising: pessimism about material existence is a criterion for spiritual advancement (BG 13:8P, 661222cc.ny). Urquhart challenges the pessimistic conception of illusion (*māyā*) that deprives the world and life in it of meaning (605), which denies history and

---

36. The term "acosmism" was coined by Hegel and applied to the philosophy of Spinoza, though many would consider this a misapplication, as Urquhart himself notes (1919:550).

37. Urquhart indirectly admits that the case of Madhva disputes his totalistic paradigm: "He (Madhva) emphasizes duality at the expense of unity; and, as his system thus departs from pure monism and Pantheism, it does not call for special treatment here" (188). Rāmānuja flirts too closely with the identity of beings with Brahman for Urquhart's theistic sensibility; but his emphasis on *viśiṣṭa* (qualified) identity earns him the concessionary label "positive" pantheist; see 185–239. Others have described Rāmānuja as a "panentheist," but Julius Lipner contests this description, more so the label "pantheist"; see Lipner 1986:142, 174 n. 35.

progress in favor of cyclic process (341), which emphasizes determinism and indifference in place of change (647).

About *bhakti*, the Gītā, the Purāṇas, and Krishna, Urquhart continues his indictment. The *bhakti* cults are historicized by him as vague emotional responses to abstract pantheistic overintellectualization, with little ethical or intellectual content of their own. *Bhakti* permits the worshipper to single out without reason a particular god for adoration as supreme and universal. The Gītā's promising theistic teaching of devotion to a personal God, with potential for an ethical transformation of life, is tarnished by fatalism, inaction, and pessimism, which result from pantheistic identity-concepts imported from the Upaniṣads. As for the noble Krishna of the Gītā, the Vishnu and Bhāgavata Purāṇas' erotic and sensual distortions allow their deity to break the bonds of all morality. Consequently, for the worshipper, intensity of feeling becomes everything, and faith alone, independent of conduct, ensures salvation. Urquhart cites H. H. Wilson: "It matters not how atrocious a sinner a man may be... if he die with the words Hari or Kṛishṇa or Rāmā upon his lips and the thought of him in his mind, he may have lived as a monster of iniquity—he is certain of heaven" (Urquhart, 434–435). Even without hearing Prabhupāda's replies, the above digest tells us that Urquhart challenged much that his student must have held sacred, at least subsequently in a more explicit form. Before a response would be forthcoming, further experience, learning, *and* authority were required. But when finally so invested, Prabhupāda would identify the same enemy (impersonalism), champion the same cause (theism), and issue his own challenge: "Krishna is the Supreme Personality of Godhead."

Recalling the liturgical prayer Prabhupāda composed to describe his mission—"You are kindly preaching the message of Lord Caitanya and delivering the Western countries, which are filled with *impersonalism* and *voidism*"[38]—we are looking at a near mirror image of the Scottish professor's missionary strategy. Urquhart's sweeping generalization about Indian pantheism, the cornerstone of his fulfillment theology, is reflected in Prabhupāda's all-embracing depiction of its Western counterpart. Apart from their own doctrines, all others are found wanting. Among these, Śaṅkara's heads a common list that includes, though is not limited to, polytheism, Buddhism, Brahmoism, Vivekananda's neo-Vedānta, and, from the West, the philosophies of Spinoza, Hegel, and Schopenhauer.[39] Indeed,

---

38. See chapter 1, "The Need and Aim of This Study." Apart from their Western expressions, "impersonalism" refers to *māyāvāda*, the doctrine affirming the world to be illusion, while "voidism" specifically refers to its Buddhist parallel.

39. For Prabhupāda's critique of these Western philosophers, see Prabhupāda 1985. Urquhart never criticizes Chaitanya or the Bengal school of Vaishnavism in writing, despite his criticism of particular *bhakti* movements and their leaders, whatever their

under their favorite respective rubrics of pantheism and impersonalism, Urquhart and Prabhupāda are able to dispose of nearly every competing system of thought.

More than a liberal arts education, Prabhupāda received from Urquhart an extended lesson in religious instruction. His virgin faith was tested in the crucible of a century of Protestant mission. There is a certain irony that this melting pot forged a countermissionary of Prabhupāda's steel, a fusion of Bengali Vaishnavism and fulfillment theology. Prabhupāda co-opted the spirit of his Scottish professor's method—a bold philosophical assertion of his religion's superiority. Urquhart's theme of personalism became the cornerstone of Prabhupāda's mission.

Urquhart was for Prabhupāda simultaneously a firsthand example of a zealous overseas missionary and later, in commentaries, an invisible *pūrvapakṣin* (philosophical adversary) with whom to argue. For Urquhart's classes and sermons were meant not only to stimulate but also to disturb. To interpret Prabhupāda's refusal of a baccalaureate degree solely as support for Gandhi's protest of British imperialism is to overlook the possibility that Prabhupāda may also have been registering resentment, however unconsciously, for much in his education, in the only manner he knew how. Proper articulation would await meeting with his guru. Before we come to that, a prelude is in order.

Earlier Vaishnava Teachers in Bengal

The pressures applied by missionary educators were only part of a larger challenge quite unlike any India had faced before. Modernity seeped into all human institutions through a network of channels too numerous to be thwarted. As the principal seat of the British, Bengal was a laboratory for testing modernization alternatives. Although clearly oversimplified, the competing choices are often described as bipartisan. Anglicists—both missionary and administrative—vied to create what Macaulay in his famous Education Minute of 1835 termed "a class of persons, Indian in blood and color, but English in taste, in opinions, in moral and in intellect."[40] Their chief adversaries were the Orientalists, Western Indologists who sought, through using historical-critical methods and promoting the indigenous and the vernacular (particularly Sanskrit), to rescue the "authentic"

---

popularity. Perhaps it was a matter too close to home. Had he done so, Prabhupāda would certainly have remembered him less favorably.

40. Thomas Babington Macaulay (1800–59), British parliamentarian and member of the Supreme Council of India (created by the India Act of 1834). See Majumdar 1965:81–85 for Macaulay's Minute.

Vedic civilization of antiquity from its decadent modern Hindu expression.[41] The offspring of this progenitorial polemic were the *bhadralok* (lit., the "gentility, cultured folk"), the socially privileged, self-consciously superior Bengali intelligentsia.[42] The *bhadralok* took advantage of both factions to fashion its own idea of renaissance in a way that neither protagonist had expected.[43]

Prabhupāda inherited this dramatic legacy. "Renaissance" or "revitalization" implies dissatisfaction with the present and a desire to revive something of the past. Prabhupāda was heir to a revitalized Gauḍīya Vaishnavism, a century of effort by his immediate predecessors to relate their tradition to the modern world. Both Kedarnath Datta, known later as Bhaktivinoda Ṭhākura, and his son Bhaktisiddhānta Sarasvatī (formerly Bimala Prasad, 1874–1937) had to work through many of the same questions Prabhupāda confronted upon reaching the West: "How Vaisnava teachings can be presented to the widest possible audience, how they can be explained to the Western mentality, how new devotees can be brought into the Chaitanya movement, and how the movement can be stabilized to ensure its continuity" (Hopkins 1989:50).[44] It is the evolution of their solutions to these questions that we now trace.

The typically *bhadralok* spectrum of traditionalist/modernist experience that shaped Bhaktivinoda's thought is indicated in the foreword to Shukavak N. Dasa's (1999) definitive biography of the Ṭhākura:

> Raised in a traditional Śākta household in village India, exposed in Calcutta to Western rationalism and Christian devotion, charged by his profession

---

41. For a critique of Orientalism and its colonial and Indological imbrication, see Said 1979, Halbfass 1988, Inden 1990, Breckenridge and van der Veer 1993, and King 1999. David Kopf draws a clear line between modernization and westernization, between Orientalists who favored only modernization and anti-Orientalist Macaulayites who were in favor of both. Richard King, however, offers the more convincing argument that "modernity" is inextricably bound up with the European Enlightenment project and that Orientalists, in their methods, goals, and values, were involved in the Europeanization of the Orient; see Kopf 1969:275–278 and King 1999:87–88.

42. "In essence, bhadralok-mindedness consisted of cultural adaptability and migrational flexibility on the part of mainly the upper-caste Bengali. . . . The synthetic (often syncretic) mentality that resulted from English education was the hallmark of the bhadralok. . . . Contrary to Kipling's much-quoted line, East did meet West in the bhadralok" (Lipner 1999:9–10).

43. Many have noted that "renaissance," as in "Bengal Renaissance," carries a distinct imperialist irony; see Spivak 1993:139. Here I use the term to denote a process of "revitalization," as per Wallace's definition; see chapter 2, n. 55. Kopf 1969:280–289 does so as well.

44. While acknowledging Prabhupāda's personal qualities and the fortuitous conditions in America coinciding with his arrival, Thomas Hopkins credits Prabhupāda's success specifically to the legacy he brought with him from Bengal; see Hopkins 1989.

> as a magistrate to adjudicate British law, and gradually drawn to and then converted to Chaitanya Vaishnavism, Bhaktivinoda had the range of life experience from which a creative synthesis could emerge. (Hopkins 1999:ix)

Drawing largely from Bhaktivinoda's autobiographical *Svalikhita-jīvanī*,[45] Shukavak follows Bhaktivinoda's immersion within Calcutta's *bhadralok*. The luminaries with whom he shared intimacy include his maternal uncle Kashiprasad Ghosh (with whom he lived from his fourteenth to his twentieth year); his college teacher and lifelong friend, Ishwar Chandra Vidyasagar; his Hindu School classmates Keshub Chandra Sen and the Tagores, Satyendranath and Gajendranath, and their brother Dvijendranath (Bhaktivinoda lived for some time at Jorasanko, their home); his literary associates Michael Madhusudhan Datta and Bankim Chandra Chatterjee; the newspaper publisher Sisir Kumar Ghosh; and the American Unitarian Rev. Charles Dall (whose congregation he joined). These names are at the forefront of nineteenth-century India's political, social, and religious upheaval.

The result of their association is visible not only in Bhaktivinoda Ṭhākura's few available early activist speeches and English compositions[46] but more significantly in the novel manner in which he later attempts to construct a bridge for modern educated Indians like himself to access their own tradition. The *bhadralok* audience of his Dinajpur speech (1869), "The Bhagavat: Its Philosophy, Ethics and Theology," could easily identify with the speaker's own spiritual quest, unimpressed as they were by a Chaitanya Vaishnavism that lacked vitality and had become heredity-based and tainted by *sahajiyā* and tantric influences:

> When we were in college, reading the philosophical works of the West and exchanging thoughts with the thinkers of the day, we had a real hatred toward the *Bhagavat*. That great work looked like a repository of wicked and stupid ideas scarcely adapted to the 19th century, and we hated to hear any

45. Written in the form of a lengthy letter to his son Lalita Prasad Datta, the autobiography has been questioned by the followers of Bhaktisiddhānta. In principle, they take exception to Lalita Prasad's criticism of his elder brother Bimala Prasad (Bhaktisiddhānta); see Acyutananda720722. Specifically, they challenge its frank admissions. But Shukavak offers compelling evidence to substantiate its authenticity; see Shukavak 1999:9 n.11. Two other substantial biographies of Bhaktivinoda are Bhakti Pradip Tirtha 1939 and Rūpa Vilāsa 1989.

46. For example, we find him championing the cause of Kulin Brahmin women suffering polygamy (c. 1857), and presenting Rev. Duff with the first volume of his anticipated twelve-volume English epic poem, *The Poriade* (1856:8), describing the wanderings of Porus (King Puru), who allegedly checked Alexander's advance into India. Duff apparently responded with the suggestion that he instead write about the cruelty of the zamindars; see Shukavak 1999:54–55.

> arguments in its favour. With us a volume of Channing, Parker, Emerson or Newman had more weight than the whole lot of the *Vaishnav* works.[47] Greedily we pored over the various commentaries of the Holy Bible and of the labours of the Tattva Bodhini Sabha,[48] containing extracts from the *Upanishads* and the *Vedanta*, but no work of the *Vaishnavs* had any favour with us. (Bhaktivinoda Ṭhākura 1959:6)[49]

His life had become transformed, the Ṭhākura goes on to explain, when a year earlier, having obtained a copy of the *Caitanya Caritāmṛtu*, he was able to "discern the historical position of that Mighty Genius of Nadia," Caitanya, and thereafter read the complete Bhāgavata with Śrīdhara's commentary.[50]

To attract the *bhadralok* to his newfound "Eastern Saviour," Bhaktivinoda made their objections the basis for a critical reassessment of the Bhāgavata. For the *bhadralok*, Krishna had assumed immense religio-political importance as a symbol of cultural and national pride. But the moral life of the Bhāgavata's Krishna appalled not only missionaries like Farquhar and Urquhart but many urbanized Bengalis whose Puritanism was adopted from and rivaled that of Victorian England. Bankim Chandra Chatterjee's *Krishna-caritra*, published in 1884, offered one possible solution: to purge the "historical" Krishna of the Gītā of his later, imagined purāṇic misconduct. While the reconstructed Krishna could now serve as a national hero to rival Christ and the Gospels, much of the tradition, especially its rich purāṇic resource, was jettisoned. Bhaktivinoda, however, chose another approach. Rather than eliminating the "mythology" from Krishna's life, his *Kṛṣṇa-saṁhitā* ((1879) 1998) uses the same critical apparatus to interpret it. Reason prevails, but not at the expense of faith.[51]

---

47. This remark is too close to Macaulay's—"a single shelf of a good European library was worth the whole native literature of India and Arabia"—to be mere coincidence; see above, n. 40. Channing, Parker, and Emerson were prominent nineteenth-century American Unitarians, Newman an English Catholic.

48. An indirect reference to the Brahmo Samaj, by mention of perhaps its most famous early publication.

49. Shukavak 1999:259–282 offers the entire speech in a "Reading Supplement." For the spectrum of opinions about Vaishnavism during this period in Bengal, see Chakrabarty 1985, ch. 22.

50. Śrīdhara Svāmin's fourteenth-century commentary is *Bhāvārtha-dīpikā*.

51. Bankim's *Kṛṣṇa-caritra* is the seminal work for a number of efforts to interpret the life of Krishna for national purposes; for some of these, see B. B. Majumdar 1969:250–265. But Shukavak points out that Majumdar errs in asserting that Bankim was the first Indian scholar to undertake a critical study of Krishna's life. Bhaktivinoda's work preceded his by five years; see Shukavak 1999:126 n. 8. Majumdar mentions that in the second edition of the *Kṛṣṇa-caritra*, Bankim "changed and modified many of his views.... He attributed

Before his *Saṁhitā* directly addresses the topic of Krishna, Bhaktivinoda assures his *bhadralok* readership that they may plausibly reexamine the traditional texts of their ancestors and reappropriate them in ways consistent with modernity. Unlike the *kamala-śraddhās* (persons of "tender faith") whose subjective and parochial literalism comprehends only the narrative level of scripture, the *bhadralok* as *madhyamādhikārīs* (those of middle entitlement or fitness) have the right and obligation to discern the symbolic through critical scholarship.[52]

Traditional exegesis, he says, will not serve the needs of the modern intellectual, because matters of phenomenal knowledge (i.e., purāṇic history and cosmology) are particularly susceptible to rational analysis, even if transcendence is not. Using this hermeneutic, thousands of *yuga*-cycles of Prajāpatis and Manus are compressed into a period of one hundred years (4463–4364 B.C.E.) to conform to an Indian history of some six thousand years, complete with migrating Āryans and Moghul and British rule. The same time frame is linked to a progressive intellectual history encompassing all major texts, which assigns the Bhāgavata, for example, to an anonymous ninth-century Dravidian origin. Finally, religion, culminating in the *mādhurya-rasa* (sentiment of sweetness) promulgated by Chaitanya, is the subject of a third evolutionary analysis, this one employing the *rasa* theory as a heuristic device.

Having introduced a rational basis for considering Vaishnava theology, the *Saṁhitā* proper—281 Sanskrit verses with accompanying Bengali commentary—addresses with continued ingenuity its primary subject. Krishna and his abode's supremacy are ontologically established, his "incarnations" tied to human evolution, his *līlā* framed within a discussion of the limitations of human language, and his destruction of demons metaphorically related to the removal of corresponding obstacles to devotion.

The *Kṛṣṇa-saṁhitā* is arguably Bhaktivinoda's most daring and innovative work, part of a larger attempt to articulate the meaning and identity of his tradition for not only an urban intelligentsia but a universal audience that extended from the Vaishnava population of rural eastern India to an envisioned overseas public. He attempted to popularize the canonical Vaishnava texts through prose, verse, and vernacular commentaries, using his position within society to provide his work with respectability and honor. It is no overstatement to claim that under his guidance, "Vaishnava journalism as well as Gauḍīya Vaishnava organisation

---

the change of opinion to his mature age, greater investigation and more intense thinking" (236–237). According to one of Bhaktivinoda's biographers, the Ṭhākura was the prime instigator; see Rūpa Vilāsa 1989:150–151.

52. There is a third level—the *uttamādhikārīs*, those of the highest qualification—whose understanding is based on pure relishable sentiment, *rasa*. This subject is treated at greater length in Bhaktivinoda's *Jaiva Dharma* (1893) 2001; see also Shukavak 1999, ch. 7.

in Bengal really became meaningful" (Chakrabarty 1985:394). He wrote, translated, edited, or published about a hundred works (many were essays and poems), including works of others, making the tradition's texts and commentaries widely available, and by so doing, simultaneously standardized and publicized the boundaries of Vaishnava orthodoxy.[53] With the help of government surveyors and archaeological maps, he established Chaitanya's birthplace in Māyāpur on the eastern bank of the Ganges, instead of in Navadvīpa, on the western side.[54] He also evangelized from village to village after the style of a British circuit-court judge through a program aptly named *Nama-haṭṭa* (lit., "Marketplace of the Holy Name").[55] He balanced family, professional, and religious duties, exemplifying the exoteric model of *varṇāśrama-dharma,* while in his final years, as a *bābājī,* he exclusively pursued *rāgānuga-bhakti,* the esoteric practices he had elaborated upon and personally cultivated over many years.[56]

The revolutionary element of renaissance that characterized Bhaktivinoda Ṭhākura's mission—a dissatisfaction with the present, a future with the past clearly in mind—was ratcheted up to high gear under Bhaktisiddhānta Sarasvatī's leadership. Indeed the word "revolution" derives from the sense of circular motion, hence, the return of a period of time. The late nineteenth-century notion that knowledgeable Hindus had more to learn about spirituality from their own spiritual masters than from the West was reaffirmed by the choice of the

53. Nevertheless, Bhaktivinoda's talent as a writer has evaded most literary historians, a reason for Banarasinath Bharadvāj (1989) to call him "'the undiscovered literary genius of Bengal'" ((quoted in Devamayī) 1997:69). The influential Sisir Kumar Ghosh referred to Bhaktivinoda in 1888 as the "seventh *gosvāmī*" (quoted in Shukavak 1999:106), a reference to the Six Gosvāmins (Rūpa, Jīva, et al.), Chaitanya's principal theologians, who also excavated and revived holy places and personified pure devotion. Halbfass 1988:218, 336, speaks of Bhaktivinoda's universalism. It appears that his were the first efforts to transfer Chaitanya's teachings to the West, as an appreciative letter from Reinhold Rost of London's India Office attests; see Shukavak 1999:89–92. An English tract, *Sri Caitanya Mahaprabhu, His Life and Precepts,* was dispatched in 1896; see Bhaktivinoda (1896) 1981.

54. A mystical description of the place and related scriptural glorification are presented in *Navadvīpa Dhāma Māhātmya;* see Bhaktivinoda (1890) 1989. As Shukavak notes, however, the location of the birthplace is still hotly contested; see Shukavak 1999: 103–108.

55. For a metaphorical description of the "marketplace" (its personnel, currency of exchange, wares, etc.), see Bhaktivinoda [1891] n.d.; Bhaktivinoda signed this tract as a "sweeper."

56. Bhaktivinoda had fourteen children, but one died at the age of one month. A *bābājī* is the *paramahaṁsa* stage (highest stage) beyond *varṇāśrama-dharma.* For Bhaktivinoda, scientific (*vaijñānika*) *varṇāśrama* is "natural," i.e., based on the psychological makeup and qualifications of the individual. He considered the contemporary caste system, based on birth, its corrupted remnant. Natural *varṇāśrama* stabilizes the conditions for and is sanctified by the practice of *vaidhī bhakti.* This obligatory devotion, when transformed into spontaneous passion, is called *rāga;* see Shukavak 1999, ch. 8.

illiterate, emotional ecstatic Gaurakiśora dāsa Bābājī (c.1830s–1915) as the guru of the learned Bhaktisiddhānta.[57]

Bhaktisiddhānta Sarasvatī as Prabhupāda's Guru

Bhaktisiddhānta Sarasvatī did not undergo Western acculturation and the consequent tensions between traditional faith and modern critical thought that marked Bhaktivinoda's early life. His father's increasing Vaishnava orthodoxy precluded that eventuality. Instead we find him by his father's side—evangelizing, pilgrimaging, proofreading—an eidetic youth vowing lifetime celibacy, known already as Siddhānta Sarasvatī for his mastery of Sanskrit, mathematics, and astrology.[58] Absent are those tempering circumstances of a Christian education, *bhadralok* socialization, and government service that might have constrained his revolutionary spirit, which was as much his nature as a sign of the changing times. If the father's modality often tended toward an accommodating pluralism and theological ingenuity, the son's selective inclusivism and institutional expansion moved more in the direction of an exclusive triumphalism. In fact, the difference in tenor is an indication of their callings: for Bhaktivinoda, the recovery of a tradition; for Bhaktisiddhānta, its consolidation and expansion. Carefully groomed to inherit his father's mantle, he did so with intrepid diligence.

Here, we may do well to rejoin *our* Prabhupāda (for Bhaktisiddhānta Sarasvatī was also addressed as Prabhupāda by his disciples)[59] to learn exactly what it was that impressed him most about his guru. He quickly found out just how uncompromising and challenging Bhaktisiddhānta could be. As a skeptical young

57. Gaurkiśora and Bhaktivinoda shared an intimate friendship and mutual connection to the revered Jagannātha dāsa Bābājī of Vraja and Navadvīpa. Gaurkiśora considered Bhaktivinoda his *śikṣā*-guru, while Bhaktivinoda took *bābājī*-initiation from Gaurkiśora in 1908; see Rūpa Vilāsa 1989:228–229. About Gaurkiśora dāsa Bābājī it is said: "Although he wore his begging bowl as a hat, did his worship in an outhouse, and would beat with an umbrella Vaishnavas who wanted initiation from him, he was greatly respected by the Vaishnava community for his detachment and devotion" (McDaniel 1989:53). For further biographical information on both Jagannātha dāsa Bābājī and Gaurkiśora dāsa Bābājī, see Haridāsa 1941 (date of 465 Gaurabda in original publication—denoting the Bengali calendar year) and Karṇāmṛta 1990.

58. In recognition of his writing and publishing many important astrological treatises, he was offered a chair in astronomy at the University of Calcutta by the vice-chancellor, Sir Asutosh Mukhopadhay, but declined. There are a number of excellent devotional biographies that detail his life; see Bhaktikusum Sraman 1983, Rūpa Vilāsa 1988, and [Devamayī dāsī] 1997.

59. See chapter 1 n. 5. I have drawn the following paragraphs describing Bhaktisiddhānta from Prabhupāda's statements after a search of the Bhaktivedanta VedaBase for "my Guru Mahārāja," then corroborated them in biographical accounts.

Gandhian and a married manager of a pharmaceutical laboratory, he had to be dragged to their first meeting in 1922, so disillusioned was he with the usual "holy men" his father entertained, only to hear the guru deprecate his nationalist sympathies and in their stead recommend that as an English speaker he go to foreign countries to preach the gospel of Caitanya (SSR 296–297).[60] Perhaps because their meetings were so few, each made an indelible impression.[61] Certain themes his guru emphasized repeatedly surface in Prabhupāda's remembrances, merge with Prabhupāda's character, and get projected into his own activities. Above all, the subversive image of the revolutionary again comes to mind: Bhaktisiddhānta, at war with *māyā* (illusion).

Battle occurs on many fronts, with the following targets in the line of Bhaktisiddhānta's direct fire: the *smārta* Brahmins and caste *gosvāmins,* for insisting that birth alone makes them, not the Vaishnavas, qualified as priests and *ācāryas;* the *māyāvādins,* for considering as *māyā* the Lord's form, his abode, and his personal service; Bhāgavata reciters and temple priests who use the sacred for business and are said to have less dignity than an honest street sweeper; the *sahajiyās,* for being devotional imitators; and most secluded *bābājīs,* famed for their renunciation, for secretly coveting worldly pleasure. If to this list are added all false gurus, yogis, *avatāras,* and all their followers, together they constitute a "society of cheaters and the cheated."[62] Little wonder that Bhaktisiddhānta was so feared, even hated.[63]

---

60. When the freedom fighter Netaji Subhash Chandra Bose (a former classmate of Prabhupāda's and the secretary of Urquhart's Philosophy Club) asked Bhaktisiddhānta Sarasvatī not to thwart the nationalist movement, Bhaktisiddhānta invoked the colonialist metaphor of the effeminate Bengali as an apolitical dodge. According to Prabhupāda, Bose was told: "For your national propaganda you require very strong men, but these people are very weak. You can see. They are very skinny. So don't put your glance upon them. Let them eat something and chant Hare Krishna" (741021sb.may; SPL 1:76).

61. Prabhupāda writes, "I was only with my Guru Maharaja four or five times" (Satadhanya720220), then later asserts, "not more than ten times" (750203mw.haw). Other obvious ways he would have had Bhaktisiddhānta's association are through his guru's writings and by conversing with his guru's other disciples.

62. For a translation of his lengthy 1911 essay on Brahmins vis-à-vis Vaishnavas, see Bhaktisiddhānta 1999. Of the priestly business, he said: "śālagrāma-dvārā bādām bhāṅga" ("The priests are taking the *śālagrāma* Deity as a stone for cracking nuts"). His "A Hundred Warnings..." is an essay against Sahajiyāism, which appeared serially in *Sajjana-Toṣaṇī* in 1916–17; for a translation, see Bhaktisiddhānta 1993. Describing the dangers of *bābājī* seclusion, he wrote: *"duṣṭa man! tumi kiser vaiṣṇaba? / pratiṣṭhār tare, nirjaner ghare/taba 'hari nām' kebal kaitaba"* ("My dear mind, what kind of Vaishnava are you? Simply for false prestige and a material reputation you sit in a solitary place and pretend to chant Hare Krishna, but this is all cheating") (Bhaktisiddhānta 1998:verse 1).

63. Bhaktisiddhānta claimed that many of these parties collaborated to attempt his murder; see 690207ba.la. On another occasion, he and his followers were stoned while

At the heart of this severe critique is his concern to stabilize the tradition by cementing its boundaries against proliferative heteropraxes. Each condemnation is an instance of defining Vaishnava orthodoxy as he and his predecessors understand it. Each censure treats of a substantive issue, which, had he not responded as he did, would have radically changed the direction of the movement. A specific example should elucidate the matter in two ways: his criticism of the very popular Radharaman Charan Das for suppressing the audible chanting of Hare Krishna with his own rhyming *kīrtan,* and his criticism of the same Radharaman for dressing one of his followers as Rādhā's friend, Lalitā.[64]

Against these delimiting moves, Bhaktisiddhānta's indictment of an exclusory, caste-based status quo paves the way for Prabhupāda's global mission, the sort of universal religion anticipated in the Bhāgavata.[65] Vaishnava *bhakti* affords one brahminical status automatically, perfection potentially in one lifetime.[66]

---

circumambulating Navadvīpa. During a similar circumambulation of Vṛndāvana in 1932, the seven principal temples shut their doors to him.

64. There are said to be two faults in the rhyme *bhaja nitāi gaur rādhe śyām / japa hare kṛṣṇa hare rām,* viz. *siddhānta-virodha* (opposing conclusion) and *rasābhāsa* (conflicting *rasas*). The heterodox *sakhibhekīs* dress and worship an ordinary soul as an eternal associate of the Lord; see Haberman 1988, ch. 6, for the historical antecedent to the debate. For the biographies of Radharaman Charan Das and his follower Jayagopala Bhattacharya, see Kapoor 1993 and 1995, respectively.

65. "Two main points stand out in (a) description of the religion of the Bhāgavata*:* the almost complete break with the traditional religious ceremonies based on the Vedas, and the absence of the qualifications based on birth and status that restricted participation in orthodox ceremonies" (Hopkins 1966:11).

66. Prabhupāda explains Bhaktisiddhānta's argument for awarding Vaishnavas brahminical status: "Regarding the validity of the brahminical status as we accept it, because in the present age there is no observance of the Garbhadhana ceremony, even a person born in brahmana family is not considered a brahmana, he is called dvijabandhu or unqualified son of a brahmana. Under the circumstances, the conclusion is that the whole population is now sudra, as it is stated kalau sudra sambhava. So for sudras there is no initiation according to the Vedic system, but according to the Pancaratrika system initiation is offered to a person who is inclined to take Krsna consciousness.

During my Guru Maharaja's time, even [when] a person was coming from a brahmana family, he was initiated according to the pancaratrika system taking him to be a sudra. So the birthright brahmanism is not applicable at the present moment. The sacred thread inaugurated by my Guru Maharaja according to pancaratrika system and Hari-bhakti-vilasa by Srila Sanatana Goswami must continue. It does not matter whether the priestly class accepts it or not. When my Guru Maharaja Bhaktisiddhanta Sarasvati Goswami Prabhupada introduced this system, it was protested even by His inner circle of Godbrothers or friends. Of course He had actually no Godbrothers, but there were many disciples of Bhaktivinoda Thakura who were considered as Godbrothers who protested against this action of my Guru Maharaja, but He didn't care for it.

Actually one who takes to chanting Hare Krsna Mantra offenselessly immediately becomes situated transcendentally and therefore he has no need of being initiated with sacred thread, but Guru Maharaja introduced this sacred thread because a Vaisnava was

Preaching is focused in large cities, with the emphasis not on reclusive *bhajan* or seeing God, but on working in such a way that God will see you. In the spirit of *yukta-vairāgya* (balanced renunciation), the true follower of Rūpa Gosvāmin (a *rūpānāga* Vaishnava) does not live under a tree dressed only in a loincloth. Everything—palatial buildings, automobiles, radios, and especially printing presses (the *bṛhad-mṛdaṅga*, or "big drum"), as well as mixing with kings and politicians and preaching overseas—should be utilized to please Krishna, hence, must not be renounced.[67]

In place of the looser-knit, far-flung congregation of his father, Bhaktisiddhānta Sarasvatī established the Gauḍīya Maṭh, eventually a well-ordered missionary army of *brahmacārins* (celibate students) based in sixty-four temple-ashrams and led by eighteen *saṁnyāsin* disciples with himself as its head.[68] He established four presses, from which he reedited and published his father's huge literary corpus, matched by his own equally large output, a Bengali daily newspaper, and fortnightly journals in Bengali, Oriya, Assamese, Hindi, and English.

Prabhupāda had only slight though meaningful opportunities to actively participate in this broad mission during Bhaktisiddhānta's lifetime: he helped raise funds to establish temples in Allahabad and Bombay and occasionally contributed to the *Harmonist*, the English fortnightly.[69] But his time would come.

---

being mistaken as belonging to the material caste. To accept a Vaisnava in [a] material caste system is hellish consideration [naraki buddhi]. Therefore, to save the general populace from being offender to a Vaisnava, He persistently introduced this sacred thread ceremony and we must follow His footsteps" (Acyutananda700114).

67. "[A]*nāsaktasya viṣayān yathārham upayuñjataḥ / nirbandhaḥ kṛṣṇa-sambandhe yuktaṁ vairāgyam ucyate*": "When one is not attached to anything, but at the same time accepts everything in relation to Kṛṣṇa, one is rightly situated above possessiveness" (Rūpa Gosvāmin, *Bhakti-rasāmṛta-sindhu*, 1.2.255, quoted in A. C. Bhaktivedanta 1989:318).

68. By accepting *saṁnyāsa* instead of the traditional Gauḍīya *bābājī-veśa* (dress) as his father and his guru had done, Bhaktisiddhānta was both deferring to their superiority and exemplifying his father's teaching that a preacher work within the parameters of *varṇāśrama-dharma*. Again breaking with tradition, he modelled his *saṁnyāsa* upon the Rāmānujaite *tridaṇḍi-svāmin* rather than the Śaṅkarācārya *eka-daṇḍin*, by retaining the *śikhā* (tuft of hair) and Brahmin's thread as signs of eternal service to the guru and the Godhead. Interestingly, Prabhupāda, with the same stated intention as Bhaktisiddhānta—to establish *daiva* (divine)-*varṇāśrama*—would initially favor *gṛhasthas* (married couples) over *saṁnyāsins* and *brahmacārins* for preaching; see 710329bg.bom.

69. We may note a verse Prabhupāda penned that caught his guru's attention, apparently for so aptly encapsulating their mission. Thereafter Bhaktisiddhānta ordered the *Harmonist* editor to publish whatever he wrote (SPL 1:81–6):

Absolute is sentient
Thou hast proved,
Impersonal calamity
Thou has moved.

"He will do everything when there is need," the guru reportedly told Prabhupāda's *saṁnyāsin* godbrothers when they recommended he assume the presidency of the Bombay center (730921r2.bom).

Prabhupāda was keenly aware that his family duties prevented him from serving his guru like the *brahmacārin* and *saṁnyāsin* disciples. In what was to be their final exchange, he inquired how he might best serve. Bhaktisiddhānta replied:

> I am fully confident that you can explain in English our thoughts and arguments to the people who are not conversant with the languages of other members. This will do much good to yourself as well as your audience. I have every hope that you can turn yourself [into] a very good English preacher if you serve the mission to inculcate the novel impression to the people in general and philosophers of [*sic*] modern age and religiosity. (Prabhupāda 1994:9)[70]

Prabhupāda immediately recognized this to be the same instruction he had received at their first meeting. Referring to this letter as the order that defined his mission, he comments: "We should take up the words from the spiritual master as our life and soul. We should try to carry out the instruction, the specific instruction of the spiritual master, very rigidly, without caring for our personal benefit or loss" (681209db.la).[71]

Prabhupāda as Authoritative Commentator

Bhaktisiddhānta specifically encouraged writing and publishing.[72] Prabhupāda's early efforts began in 1944 with the publication of *Back to Godhead* magazine and culminated in the three volumes of the *Śrīmad-Bhāgavatam* first canto in 1962–65.[73]

---

70. Letter dated December 3, 1936, from Puri. Bhaktisiddhānta died on January 1, 1937.

71. Prabhupāda is paraphrasing part of a commentary to the *Gītā* 2:41 by Viśvanātha Cakravartī Ṭhākura; see Bhūrijana 1997:40–41 for a translation of the commentary and its significance for Prabhupāda's mission.

72. Prabhupāda often referred to a meeting in which his guru advised him that building a large temple in Calcutta had caused quarreling among the members about use of the rooms; if Prabhupāda ever got money, it would be better to spend it for printing books; see, e.g., 750620a2.la.

73. All the volumes of *Back to Godhead* (BTG) published in India intermittently from 1944 to 1960 (along with two issues of the Hindi edition from 1958) have been made available by the Bhaktivedanta Archives; see Prabhupāda 1994. Distribution was both local and international. Prabhupāda also assumed the editorship and wrote extensively in Bengali for the *Gauḍīya Patrikā* and *Sajjana-toṣaṇī* magazines, each under the auspices of an individual godbrother's separate institution; see Prabhupāda 1992a for an English

In the West, the *Bhāgavatam* and other literary work remained a preoccupation, no matter how busy or occasionally unwell he might be. The "family business," as he called it, of producing books always weighed foremost in his mind. The daunting task of transplanting an entire cummulative tradition depended entirely upon his ability to establish its canonical literature.

When we peer into his purports, we witness his engagement with the very issues that we observed Bhaktivinoda and Bhaktisiddhānta wrestle with, issues that affect presentation, expansion, and preservation. As we might expect, Prabhupāda's stance vis-à-vis the tradition is remarkably similar to his guru's: institutionally, creatively flexible; theologically, dogmatically conservative. The guru's and disciple's dissimilitude is largely due to differences in time, place, and circumstance, factors crucial to an understanding of Prabhupāda's contribution. To isolate what is unique in Prabhupāda's work we must first identify his textual sources.

His fidelity to Bhaktisiddhānta is immediately apparent by "unzipping the purports" of his books, a text-critical task and the title of an in-house study (unpublished) by Ekkehard Lorenz (n.d.). In attempting to resolve European translators' problems for the Bhaktivedanta Book Trust, Lorenz sought recourse in the original sources Prabhupāda used when translating the Bhāgavata, which were many. Above all, his findings confirm the extent of Bhaktisiddhānta's influence in Prabhupāda's work. This is particularly obvious from the end of the fourth canto onward, where Prabhupāda relies primarily on Bhaktisiddhānta's *Gauḍīya Bhāṣya,* a twelve-volume Bhāgavata edition in Bengali script that includes the Sanskrit commentaries of Viśvanātha Cakravartī and Madhva, along with Bhaktisiddhānta's two Bengali commentaries.[74] Prabhupāda cites the same texts and commentaries referenced by his guru and, starting from the fifth canto, includes translations of his guru's chapter summaries.

To compile the first and second cantos, Prabhupāda used an eight-commentary Sanskrit edition with Hindi texts; here, his purports explicitly cite Jīva most often, followed by Viśvanātha and, to a lesser extent, Śrīdhara.[75] For the third

---

translation of many *Gauḍīya Patrikā* articles. An extensive manuscript of his English translation of and commentary on the *Gītā* was stolen in 1948; see SPL 1:135. His first published book, *Easy Journey to Other Planets,* appeared in 1960.

74. Viśvanātha Cakravartī Ṭhākura (1626–1708), one of the foremost Gauḍīya Vaishnava *ācāryas,* completed his commentary, *Sārārtha-darśinī,* in 1704. Madhva's commentary is known as the *Bhāgavata-tātparya-nirṇaya.* Bhaktisiddhānta's commentaries are *Ananta-gopāla-tathya* (consisting largely of citations from previous commentators) and *Sindhu-vaibhava-vivṛti* (his own exegesis); see Bhaktisiddhānta 1962.

75. See Nitya-svarupa Brahmachari. 1907. Jīva Gosvāmin's commentary is entitled, *Krama-sandarbha.*

canto Prabhupāda made use of a Gita Press edition with Devanāgarī verses and reproduced verbatim many of its English-text translations and footnotes.[76] These multiple sources provoke some to question whether a modest grasp of Sanskrit made Prabhupāda seek vernacular alternatives whenever possible. Had a Bengali edition been available, then he would have used it for the first and second cantos just as he did from the end of the fourth canto onward, or for that matter, as he used the English Gita Press edition for the third. But surely Prabhupāda was aware of his guru's *Gauḍīya Bhāṣya* edition before 1972, when he received a copy from his American Sanskrit editor. By the late 1920s, the *Gauḍīya Bhāṣya* was the standard text used in all the Gauḍīya Maṭhas that Prabhupāda at first visited, then lectured in, and, especially after retirement from business, occasionally lived in.

I am not persuaded, as Lorenz's findings seem to imply, that Prabhupāda lacked a thorough knowledge of Sanskrit, or alternatively, that he felt handicapped by English, nor that the subtleties of Vaishnava theology at times eluded him. Admittedly, I have not had to help translators untangle knotty inaccuracies and ambiguities. The more generous explanation is that the Sanskrit commentaries were used to produce the first and second cantos when Prabhupāda had little else other than translation work to occupy his time. Once ISKCON began to expand, Bengali commentaries facilitated translation done under severe time constraints, a factor that Lorenz recognizes could have led to shortcuts and miscues. It is unlikely that an assembly of learned *saṁnyāsins* would have awarded the title "Bhaktivedānta" to a somewhat inept traditional scholar, nor would they, individually, have made a less qualified householder godbrother the editor of various publications.

Unlike his sources for the Bhāgavata, the sources for Prabhupāda's other principal works are more certain. His *Bhagavad-gītā As It Is* is heavily indebted to the commentary of Baladeva Vidyābhūṣana, to whom it is dedicated. His commentary to the *Caitanya Caritāmṛta* is mainly a translation of those by Bhaktivinoda and Bhaktisiddhānta, to which he repeatedly refers. His summary of Rūpa Gosvāmin's classic *Bhakti-rasāmṛta-sindhu* is just that, a summary, as the title page makes clear. And, *Kṛṣṇa, the Supreme Personality of Godhead* incorporates the commentary of Sanātana Gosvāmin.[77] With the exception of the last, Prabhupāda signals his sources. Nevertheless, as Lorenz notes, despite extensive use of his guru's Gauḍīya Maṭha Bhāgavata, Prabhupāda never mentions it anywhere (though he does formally dedicate the work to him).

---

76. See Goswami and Sastri 1971.

77. Baladeva Vidyābhūṣaṇa's eighteenth-century *Gītā* commentary is *Gītā-bhūṣaṇa-bhāṣya*. Bhaktivinoda's commentary to the *Caitanya Caritāmṛta* is the *Amṛta-pravāha-bhāṣya;* that of Bhaktisiddhānta, *Anubhāṣya*. Rūpa's elder brother Sanātana Gosvāmin (traditionally, 1488–1588) wrote a commentary to the Bhāgavata's tenth canto entitled *Vaishnava-toṣaṇī*.

This may lead one to wonder: Was Prabhupāda worried that an obvious dependence on his guru's work would diminish his own prestige? Or that it might connect his readers to his guru's organization, the Gauḍīya Maṭha, rather than to ISKCON? These suggestions cannot be rejected out of hand. They remind us that scripture is for Prabhupāda the principal means of defining his institution (as much as the institution becomes for his followers a means to define scripture). When the founder of an institution is also the primary interpreter of its texts, scripture and institution are inextricably connected, informing us, as does one well-chosen title, of the interwoven nature of "Authority, Anxiety, and Canon" (Patton 1994). Whoever controls the texts wields immense power.

Pedigree is always crucial. At the start of his *Gītā* commentary, Prabhupāda lists his genealogical descent: He is the thirty-second spiritual master in an unbroken line that begins with Krishna.[78] Viewed as such by his followers, his dictated writing can take on prophetic proportions. Although Prabhupāda's purports are methodical reflections drawn chiefly from the works of previous commentators, to the devoted reader they may appear to be a prophetic recovery of a deposit of ancient wisdom—what has been described as "lost contacts with the hidden powers of life" (Wach 1944:348). A characteristic of the guru system is that the guru repeats his predecessors' message, which ultimately is understood to be the message of the divinity, a channelling Prabhupāda refers to as "the mystery of the disciplic succession." This allows Prabhupāda to state: "there is no difference between hearing directly from Krishna and hearing directly from Krishna via a bona fide spiritual master" (1989:861).

Prabhupāda's silence regarding certain sources may be understood as an instantiation of the basic attitude toward knowledge in Indian philosophical thought. In the commentarial tradition, texts and their exegesis are bequeathed to the latest member of the disciplic succession as communitarian wealth. There is no notion of intellectual property. The theological deposit is a disciple's prime inheritance, to be increased through further expository development. As Eliot Deutsch explains, "The tradition text simultaneously *is* a kind of authorless truth (as embodying *śruti*) and becomes something new with each vital engagement with it" (1988:170). While it may be true, as J. N. Mohanty asserts in his entry on "Indian Philosophy" in the *Encyclopedia Britannica,* that if "one is to be counted as a great master (*ācārya*) one has to write a commentary (*bhāṣya*) on the *sūtras* of the *darśana* concerned" (quoted in Deutsch, 171), this is primarily accomplished through *appropriation* (or, as is partly the case with Prabhupāda, through the

78. "For an understanding of the Vedas, one must have God for a guru, or someone who has God for a guru" (Sheridan 1992:120). For a critical historical overview of the lineage, see Deadwyler 1992.

very act of translation). As Deutsch observes: "The content of appropriation is the stuff of personal identity.... Appropriation is a creative retaining and shaping of a content that is made one's own. It is not a passive receptivity, but a dynamic engagement: What is appropriated gets changed in the act of changing the bearer of it" (172). In Prabhupāda's mind, translating or even excising an already translated text is not unethical, for the text tradition is a type of public domain. For example, in a further study (n.d.), Lorenz documents how Prabhupāda's anti-impersonalist rhetoric is often directed against the very persons whose English translations he usurps. S. Radhakrishnan is a favorite unnamed *māyāvādin* target, though his Gītā translations ([1948] 1995) appear to have been adapted for use in Prabhupāda's Macmillan edition. Yet Prabhupāda dismissed the charge of plagiarism raised by one of his English editors, claiming that the Gītā's teachings are Krishna's words, not another's:

> 'Just copy the verses from some other translation,' he tells me, discarding the whole matter with a wave of his hand. 'The verses aren't important. There are so many translations, more or less accurate, and the Sanskrit is always there.[79] It's my purports that are important. Concentrate on the purports. There are so many nonsense purports like Radhakrishnan's and Gandhi's and Nikhilananda's. What is lacking are these Vaishnava purports in the preaching line of Caitanya Mahaprabhu. That is what is lacking in English. That is what is lacking in the world'. (Hayagriva 1985:210)

The purports mark Prabhupāda's most distinct theological contribution. According to Lorenz, their content far exceeds the parallel commentaries of his predecessors in three areas: impersonalism, sex and women, and the guru.[80] Although other categories might equally suggest themselves, that 89 percent of what Prabhupāda writes about the spiritual master's position and qualifications is not found in earlier commentaries is significant. He is laboring to define and establish not only his own authority but also the principle of disciplic succession, the dynamic agency responsible for transmitting the tradition.

---

79. Here it must be borne in mind that Prabhupāda had already translated all the verses (twice, if we recall the theft of his previous manuscript; see n. 73 above). His instruction to "just copy the verses" was meant to avoid necessitating his constant consultation.

80. Lorenz bases this conclusion on a sample of data gathered from the Gītā and the Bhāgavata's second canto. Of course, statistical data of this sort always run the risk of being influenced by the selection of questions. The topic "embodied existence," for example, while a pervasive subject in Prabhupāda's purports, is also likely to receive far less attention from previous commentators.

While a commentator must retain a healthy respect for the previous commentators, the present and future audiences' special needs require a creative appropriation of scriptural authority, a matter more dependent on personal realization than ancestral legitimacy. Prabhupāda discusses his own commentarial ethic:

> Personal realization does not mean that one should, out of vanity, attempt to show one's own learning by trying to surpass the previous *ācārya*. He must have full confidence in the previous *ācārya*, and at the same time he must realize the subject matter so nicely that he can present the matter for the particular circumstances in a suitable manner. *The original purpose of the text must be maintained* [italics in original]. No obscure meaning should be screwed out of it, yet it should be presented in an interesting manner for the understanding of the audience. (Prabhupāda 1987:202)

That "interesting manner" goes far beyond rhetorical flourishes. Much of Prabhupāda's commentary is motivated by the usual surface irregularities in the text—odd phrasings, unusual syntax or vocabulary—and details of characters' backgrounds, motivations, and so on. Theological or homiletic interpretation, or equally, cultural transmission, particularly occurs in those purports whose elasticity far exceeds the texts. Clearly, Prabhupāda is laboring not merely to translate the text. His is the task of translating an entire tradition.

To Prabhupāda, the main texts themselves suggest a hierarchy to be followed in their order of study. They are classified from the general to the specific according to the degree to which they address views singular to the tradition. Thus, the Bhagavad Gītā, whose doctrinal tolerance allows for a semantic range commodious even to opposing schools of thought, expresses its far-ranging and multilayered concerns concisely enough to be recommended as foundational reading. For Chaitanya theologians, in addition to supporting many key beliefs, the Krishna-centred Gītā allows the Godhead's incomprehensible power and majesty to be conflated with the deity of intimacy, Krishna.[81]

The ascendancy of the Gītā for Chaitanyaites of the nineteenth and twentieth centuries parallels its rise as a symbol of a reified "Hinduism" serving the diverse intentions of those within and outside India.[82] Earlier on, from within the tradition, Jīva and Krishnadāsa are the first to cite the Gītā regularly, though commentaries are not produced until those of Viśvanātha Cakravartī and Baladeva Vidyābhūṣaṇa in the seventeenth and eighteenth centuries, respectively,

---

81. For the Gītā's significance to the Chaitanya tradition, see especially Schweig 2001.

82. For the Gītā and reified "Hinduism," see Minor 1995.

to be glossed in Bhaktivinoda's commentaries a century later.[83] While the Gītā is increasingly used by Bhaktisiddhānta and his followers, it assumes preeminent proselytical and pedagogical value only when the mission comes West with Prabhupāda.[84]

By Prabhupāda's reasoning, the Gītā's philosophizing, along with Rūpa Gosvāmin's aesthetic, *Bhakti-rasāmṛta-sindhu* (made available in Prabhupāda's comprehensive summary, *The Nectar of Devotion* [1982a]), is preparatory to that paramount pan-Vaishnava text, the Bhāgavata Purāṇa. These, along with a multiplicity of pre-Chaitanya and *gosvāmin* texts, are woven into the fabric of the tradition's definitive work, the *Caitanya Caritāmṛta*. Again, it is their increasing specificity in terms of the tradition's goals that suggests their sequential order, even if there is much about their explanation—Prabhupāda's commentary—that does not. For while his purports resonate with the "level" of the texts, they reiterate basic concepts as well.

The timetable of Prabhupāda's translation shows these essential texts completed, at least in partial or summary form, by 1970.[85] Six years later, in a letter to his institution's minister for higher education, he outlines a formal program of credentialled study:

> I have also suggested for the GBC's consideration, that we introduce a system of examinations for the devotees to take. Sometimes there is criticism that our men are not sufficiently learned, especially the *brāhmaṇas*. Of course second initiation[86] does not depend upon passing an examination. How one has moulded his life—chanting, attending *ārātrīka*, etc., these are essential. Still, *brāhmaṇa* means *paṇḍita*. Therefore I am suggesting examinations. "Bhakti-śāśtrī"—(for all *brāhmaṇas*) based on Bhagavad-gītā, Śrī Īśopaniṣad, Nectar of Devotion, Nectar of Instruction, and all the small

---

83. See O'Connell 1995.

84. Though a number of Bhaktisiddhānta's followers have produced Gītā commentaries, in my occasional visits to their ashrams I have never noticed the sort of formal study ISKCON makes of the Gītā, i.e., daily classes, study guides, etc. For study guides, see Prabhupāda's own analysis in Bhaktivedanta Book Trust 1981; for other examples, see Jagadīśa 1986 and Bhūrijana 1997. For a correspondence course, see the advertisement in *BTG*.

85. This includes the first two cantos and a two-volume summary of the tenth canto of the *Bhāgavatam*, plus a summary of the *Caitanya Caritāmṛta*. From 1970 on, literary productivity slowed only slightly due to the demands of an expanding institution. Prabhupāda still continued on average to produce three volumes of the *Bhāgavatam* per year and, during a two-year period, a seventeen-volume edition of *Caitanya Caritāmṛta*.

86. Second initiation indicates the awarding of *brāhmaṇa* status beyond the consideration of birth.

> paperbacks.[87] "Bhakti-vaibhāva"—the above plus first six cantos of *Śrīmad Bhāgavatam.*[88] "Bhaktivedanta"—the above plus cantos 7–12 of *Śrīmad Bhāgavatam.* "Bhakti-sarvabhauma"—the above plus *Caitanya-caritāmṛta.* These titles can correspond to entrance, BA, MA, Ph.D. So just consider how to organize this Institute. (Svarūpa Dāmodara761001)[89]

This hierarchy of study makes sense only when the texts are understood to offer a progressive revelation of the tradition's ultimate aim—*prema,* love for Krishna. Still, a book as sophisticated as Rūpa's devotional aesthetic, even in its summary (*The Nectar of Devotion*), is hardly elementary, and one should note that each successive examination in the above schema includes the texts of earlier ones. Their study is to be continued. Nevertheless, to incorporate Rūpa's work within the "entrance" list of titles may best be explained as an instance of Prabhupāda's talent for making the complex and difficult seem deceptively simple.

Summary and Reflections

I have traced Prabhupāda's birth and upbringing, his college education, and his discipleship through sketches of his father and mother, professor, and guru. Like a confluence of three rivers (*triveṇī:* the Ganges, Sarasvatī, and Yamunā), their collective parental influence unites to support his task (though the professor's presence, like the Sarasvatī, usually goes unnoticed).[90] Only by adding to this the limitless fount of a lifetime's experience (the minutiae of circumstances with regard to marriage, a business career, two world wars, etc.) can we arrive at an approximation of all the sources of his knowledge. My purpose, however, is not to produce a comprehensive biography. Rather, I have identified the main currents that feed into the theological stream of his thought. So prepared, we are now ready to follow his theology as it eddies about, flowing to and fro, shaping itself around an audience isolated geographically, culturally, and linguistically from the tradition's origins.

---

87. *The Nectar of Instruction* is a translation of and commentary on Rūpa Gosvāmin's *Upadeśāmṛta.* The "paperbacks" are produced largely from Prabhupāda's lectures.

88. *Śrīmad* ("beautiful" or "glorious") *Bhāgavatam,* another name for the Bhāgavata Purāṇa.

89. The immediate origin of this system is Bhaktisiddhānta, who introduced an entrance exam called "Bhakti-śāstrī" in 1919 and an "Ācārya" exam later; see Bhaktikusum Sraman 1983:365. Although "Bhakti-śāstrī" examinations were held during Prabhupāda's time, the system was not strictly enforced. Nevertheless, members of ISKCON study the texts according to this progression.

90. Traditionally, the three rivers are said to merge in the North Indian city of Prayāga (now Allahabad), the Sarasvatī at present invisible; see CC 2.18:222P.

4

Krishna, the Supreme Personality of Godhead: Sambandha

CHAITANYA'S FIRST THEOLOGIANS were systematicians, ever conscious that theirs was the task of formulating and authenticating the teachings of their inspired master for a newly founded movement.[1] Prabhupāda's responsibility was similar. Like the *gosvāmins,* he believed that his writing would be the theological support for generations of faithful to come.[2] His mission was time-bound: He was sixty-nine upon arrival in America, with failing health.[3] Therefore, as discussed above, there is a deliberate plan in the selection of literature that he chose to translate. His strategy is keyed to gradation, to progressively unpacking the theology by prioritizing the texts, and to wrapping enormous concepts in tight, deceptively simple packaging.

As culturally apart as Prabhupāda's audience is from that of Chaitanya and the *gosvāmins,* their heterogeneous memberships include common elements. Without my intending to oversimplify the parallels, we can note definite similarities. There is what the tradition considers *the* essential metaphysical misconception. A number in both audiences, irrespective of their terms of reference, locate ultimate reality in the neuter monistic principle underlying the universe,

1. The movement was "newly founded" in the sense of it being given a specific doctrinal shape by Chaitanya and the *gosvāmins.* The existence of Vaishnavism in Bengal prior to Chaitanya is clear. Whether Chaitanya possessed a philosophy of his own or merely inspired the *gosvāmins* to articulate one is a moot point here; for discussion, see De 1961:111–119.

2. His exemplary character and dedication to the cause are more pertinent to the subject of the next chapter.

3. His diary kept during the ocean crossing to America marks his first heart attack. There are no entries from August 25–31, 1965, save this cryptic message on the last day: "Passed over a great crisis of the struggle for life and death. A separate statement has to be written on this crisis area" (Prabhupāda 1995). A second attack in June 1967 and subsequent hospitalization are described in SPL 3:127–140. Further heart palpitations occurred in my presence during August 1970.

Brahman in Indian thought—a *nirviśeṣa,* or formless, attributeless state most commonly identified with Śaṅkara's philosophy, which Prabupāda calls "impersonalism." To the Gauḍīyas, any path, however potentially liberating, unable to find its way beyond such impersonalism becomes gridlocked.

Caught in this impenetrable snarl of traffic are not only Advaita Vedāntins but travelers of any stripe, other than those seeking a highly personal theistic destination. This would include Buddhists. While their influence in Bengal at the time of Chaitanya had waned, they were still prominent in Orissa.[4] And Kṛṣṇadāsa records their conversion by Chaitanya during his tour of South India (CC 2.9:47–62). Buddhism in the West was already on the rise by the time Prabhupāda arrived in America, and it appealed across and beyond religious boundaries.[5]

Other competing notions also vie for allegiance in Chaitanya's and Prabhupāda's audiences. In addition to the Islamic, Śaiva, Śākta, Nyāya, and Vaishnava adherents in Bengal (the Hindu sections often infused with sensual tantric teachings), Chaitanya encountered various philosophic positions during his extensive travels: Vaishnavas, Mīmāṁsākas, Sākhyas, Pātañjalas, and followers of the Purāṇas and Āgamas.[6]

Prabhupāda's audience, if anything, is still more diverse. It includes Christians, Hindus, Jews, Muslims, atheists, hedonists, and practitioners of Eastern and Western religious derivatives in such plentiful combinations as to offer, as one observer terms it, "what religion has come to mean in America: the spiritual smorgasbord... 'religion à la carte'" (Hatcher 1999:42). The bewildering array of theological diversity and conflict in the Christian faith alone that marked an intense period of experimentation starting in the mid-twentieth century has led another observer to pronounce the resultant unprecedented pluralism of belief systems a "shattered spectrum" (Kliever 1981). Add to this heady mix a worldwide proliferation of persuasions met with during his fourteen globe-trotting expeditions, and we can appreciate what Prabhupāda faces.

---

4. Bengali-Orissan Buddhism was primarily tantric. Vīrabhadra, the son of Chaitanya's chief associate, Nityānanda, is said to have converted twenty-five hundred Buddhist renunciants (men and women) in Kardaha, Bengal. Large numbers also became Chaitanya's followers in Orissa, though their thought retained much that was distinctly Buddhist; see Kennedy [1925] 1993:11–12, 69–71 and Chatterjee 1983:145–146. See also n. 6 below. The Gauḍīya Vaishnava attitude toward Buddhism has been primarily hostile; historically, Buddhists are portrayed as objects of conversion. However, there is real potential for Buddhist-Vaishnava dialogue; see, for example, Tamal Krishna 1998b.

5. A voluminous literature chronicles the rise of Buddhism in America; for a most accessible history, see Fields 1992.

6. As a strategy, Chaitanya's touring and its hagiographic portrayal are part of a larger phenomenon: the medieval renouncer as *digvijāyī* ("conqueror of the quarters"); see Sax 2000.

As many as are the similarities, the cultural divide that separates Prabhupāda's audience from Chaitanya's is oceanic. There is little to compare to the utter strangeness of an elderly Vaishnava *sādhu* in 1965 walking down New York's Fifth Avenue, or to his orthodoxy contrasted with a drug-maddened San Francisco Grateful Dead concert at which he chanted two years later, or, a few years after, to the incomprehension of the Florida state policemen investigating "the torture of two young children" and instead discovering the sanctified images of Rādhā and Krishna "flamed" by the sacred *ārātrika* lamp. These are but a few of innumerable examples. Whatever differences Chaitanya encountered, and as fundamentally different as Hindu society may have been, say, from its Muslim rulers,[7] Prabhupāda's otherness is worlds apart. This vast divide, the striking foreignness that separates Prabhupāda from his host community, is a pivotal methodological determinant when considering Prabhupāda's theology.

Of course, to speak of "Prabhupāda's theology" may in one sense be a misnomer, for his is supposed to be the normative system of thought crafted some five centuries earlier by Chaitanya's *gosvāmin* followers. This was the consensus among scholars we surveyed and Prabhupāda's own opinion as well.[8] Yet I dare to disagree. Why? I make for Prabhupāda no maverick claim of doctrinal inventiveness. Vedānta traditions eschew the notion of theological originality. Nevertheless, that the basic Gauḍīya Vaishnava system of thought enshrined five centuries ago can still be spoken of as normative is to be credited not only to the resilient craft of its original chief architects but to their descendants as resourceful preservationists. And preservation is rarely a passive receptivity. Appropriation within a commentarial tradition, as we have learned, "is a creative retaining and shaping of a content that is made one's own" (Deutsch 1988:172). In Prabhupāda's case, to engage the text as part of a larger project of cultural transmission is to mine its rich repository of customs, values, and so on, so that it may now produce a living theology in the West and around the world.

Still, Prabhupāda has been credited at best with theological fidelity, as if conveying intact the entire cumulative tradition to a radically foreign host involved little creative theologizing! Baird and Sharpe, for example, both judged that Prabhupāda is not a self-conscious religious thinker—that his philosophy was ready-made or that he was woefully ignorant of the forces that propelled him to success.[9] For them, his uncompromising doctrinal loyalties border on intolerance, for others, on insensitivity and misapplication, as when Daner or Burr

7. There were substantial differences; see R. C. Majumdar 1973.

8. Refer to chapter 2, particularly to the comments of Dimock and Hopkins.

9. See chapter 2 n. 58.

found within ISKCON instances of social or psychological aberration.[10] And there have been silent voices—cautious, taciturn, and mostly Indological—whose reticence seems to question even his theological fidelity.[11]

In all its various appearances, the tendency to deny Prabhupāda full agency has thus far been traced to the binding narratives (i.e., countercultural, cult-controversy, and indifference) that shaped ISKCON-related discourse. To determine the exact nature and extent of his contribution, the lacuna in past research—a lack of focus on his thought—must be made up for by a careful inspection of his dictated writings. Our corpus-based study should be twin anchored: on the one hand, to Prabhupāda's current interlocutors: the devotee, general, and academic audiences; on the other, to theological antecedents like the seminal *Sandarbha* texts of Jīva Gosvāmin, the *Caitanya Caritāmṛta* of Kṛṣṇadāsa Kavirāja, and the more recent work of Bhaktivinoda and Bhaktisiddhānta. This present-past contextualization, with special attention given to his creative organization of the theology and his presentation of its arguments (the bread and butter, so to speak, of any theologian), while not demonstrating outright doctrinal originality, will at the least expose certain of his strengths (or weaknesses) as an inspired exegete.

We shall keep to the broad schema already underway: After the identification of the chief sources of Prabhupāda's knowledge (*pramāṇa*), the object of this knowledge (*prameya*) now becomes our principal concern.

The Relationship with Krishna as Sambandha

Sambandha is a technical term in rhetoric indicating the topic under discussion. As a *prameya*, or object of valid knowledge, it is that to which a formal argument concludes. The opening aphorisms of the Vedānta Sūtra, therefore, announce the *sambandha*, Brahman: Now, therefore, inquiry should be made about Brahman. It is that from which everything emanates (1.1:1, 2).[12] It remains for each Vedānta tradition to explicate this Brahman, or ultimate reality, according to its particular vision. For Chaitanya and his followers, Brahman is the divinity of Krishna.

The Gauḍīya position notwithstanding, the enigmatic figure of Krishna can be an elusive subject. Scholarship—whether by practitioner

10. Refer to chapter 2.

11. One conclusion of our earlier survey is that the primary reviewers of Prabhupāda's work are not Indologists, but social scientists lacking in South Asian expertise.

12. *athāto brahmajijñāsā* ||1|| *janmādyasya yataḥ* ||2||.

or nonpractitioner[13]—has long debated over Krishna, or more accurately, the Krishnas.[14] Each group has dueled in a respective intellectual arena—the former circumscribed by theology and all that empowers it, the latter by text criticism and archaeological finds—both often sharing the same evidence. While we may resist debating the "historical" Krishna, his emergence as the Godhead warrants a brief excursus.

By "historical" Krishna I mean a twofold sense, inextricably entwined, of Krishna's actual presence within world history and the study of his developing role as an object of worship. When the same textual, epigraphic, and plastic-art data is used to substantiate both interests, the theologized belief in Krishna's "human" historicity may be no more of a conjecture than is the hypothetical phasing of an evolving religious awareness of him.[15]

Thus the ambivalent question: How "old" is Krishna? Friedhelm Hardy, translating Jan Gonda (1960:52), warns us against any reductionist "attempts to arrive at the hypothetical ur-*form* of a deity, and to explain from it the partial aspects of its character, which are known from history, in terms of an evolutionary development" (1983:18). Scholarship, it seems, has been unable to resist this urge. One common reckoning is that "ur-Krishna" coalesces with his "ancestors": ur-Vedic Vishnu and Nārāyaṇa of the Brāhmaṇas, his evolutes Vāsudeva-Krishna of the Bhāgavatas, the Purāṇic Krishna-Gopāla, the Pāñcarātric *vyūhas,* and all the *avatāras* to at last stand fully erect as the deified amalgam, "Synthetic-Krishna," survivor of an arduous process of natural selection.

This is not meant to make light of past scholarship, earnest and extensive as it is, but to recognize the difficulties in reconstructing the origin of a particular deity when the evidence for his early history, according to one recent study, is

13. Although the terms "practitioner" and "nonpractitioner" are not commonly used when speaking of types of scholarship, I am not satisfied with the alternatives. "Insider" and "outsider" are problematic; see chapter 1 n. 13. Similarly, "believer" and "nonbeliever" are no less troublesome, i.e., one may believe but not practice. "Practitioner," however, generally implies a greater commitment.

14. According to Suvira Jaiswal, the "Krishnas" have commanded attention as no other Indian deity. She lists scholarly treatments by many eminent Indologists from the past two centuries; see Jaiswal 1981:62–63. David Kinsley makes a similarly large claim for devotee scholarship: Krishna's history is nearly synonymous with the history of Hindu devotionalism; see Kinsley 1975:57. If recent and forthcoming publications are any indication, interest is not waning; see Asha Goswami's *The Krishna Legend: A New Perspective* (2001), Freda Matchett's *Krishna: Lord or Avatāra?* (2001), Edwin Bryant's *Krishna: A Sourcebook* (2007), and Guy Beck's *Alternative Krishnas* (2005).

15. See, e.g., B. B. Majumdar 1969 and Rayachaudhuri 1975; both attempt to establish Krishna as a real, historical person.

isolated items traceable to only fourteen sources: eight literary and six archaeological.[16] More than mere humility prompts such disclaimers as

> We do not intend—or pretend—to give definitive answers on the multiple problems raised by the scanty evidence. We will only try to let a little more light enter into the obscurities of the maze by putting some order in the arrangement of the materials . . . of what for us is to remain necessarily a very incomplete image of the formation and evolution of the Krishna story. (Preciado-Solis 1984:35)

One must acknowledge the human limitations implicit in attempting to divine matters that may remain an ultimate mystery, hidden as they are in so distant a past. Perhaps, as Alf Hiltebeitel half jokes, paraphrasing V. S. Sukthankar, editor of the Poona critical edition of the Mahābhārata: "Krishna is the *Paramātmā*—the Supreme Lord—who is 'winking' at all of these scholars who struggle to figure him out" (1992:52).

Krishna may also wink at practitioner scholarship that exalts with absolute certainty its chosen form of the divinity above all others. The principal Vaishnava sects do not agree on a single supreme persona (as opposed to distinguishable Godhead). Śrī Vaishnavas favor Vishnu-Nārāyaṇa, Mādhvas exalt Vishnu, while those following Nimbārka, Vallabha, and Chaitanya favor Krishna, each persona being associated with his divine consort(s). Instead of there being a gradual apotheosis, each group argues without vacillation or contradiction for its chosen deity's simultaneous presence within history and transcendence over it, and all seek to verify their particular deity's ultimate status with textual citations.

For Gauḍīya Vaishnavas, "Krishna," rather than Brahman or Vishnu-Nārāyaṇa, is the *bhagavat-tattva* (the ultimate principle, "God"), and as such is the *sambandha*. I will specify exactly which "Krishna" Gauḍīyas worship. Besides the Godhead's nature, *sambandha's* connotative sense signifies the Godhead's actions and the Godhead's infinite energies as they relate with each other, subjects treated in a manner unique to this school under the axiomatic principle of *acintya-bhedābheda* (inconceivable difference and nondifference simultaneously).

It may be helpful to locate *sambandha* within the tradition's chief tenets by a glance at the thumbnail sketch by Prabhupāda's predecessor Bhaktivinoda, who sent it to Western scholars in 1896:

> [After declaring the Vedas and Purāṇas the only acceptable evidence for matters of spirit] (1) Hari (the Almighty) is one without a second. (2) He is

---

16. Evidence includes material from the Chāndogya Upaniṣad, the Nirukta, Pāṇini, Buddhist and Jain texts, Meghasthenes, and Patañjali, which consists largely of names of Krishna and his relations, and of tribes, a sect, and locations, plus episodes associated with Krishna's life; see Preciado-Solis 1984: table 1 for a summary.

> always vested with infinite power. (3) He is an ocean of *Rasa* [loving sentiment]. (4) The soul is his *Vibhinnangsha* or separated part. (5) Certain souls are engrossed by *Prakriti* or His illusionary energy. (6) Certain souls are released from the grasp of *Prakriti*. (7) All spiritual and material phenomena are *Vedavedprakash* [divinely endorsed manifestations] of Hari, the Almighty. (8) Bhakti is the only means of attaining the final object of spiritual existence. (9) *Prem* [love] in Krishna is alone the final object of spiritual existence. ([1896] 1981:23–24)[17]

In this list, items one through seven constitute the *sambandha*, our present concern. Eight, *abhidheya* (the means), and nine, *prayojana* (the goal), await consideration.

Where in Gauḍīya literature is *sambandha* specifically theologized? The topic is of sufficient breadth to occupy Jīva Gosvāmin entirely for three of his six *Sandarbhas*.[18] Coverage in Kṛṣṇadāsa's biographical *Caitanya Caritāmṛta* is especially concentrated in two of the chapters (2.20–21) that form part of Chaitanya's teachings to Sanātana Gosvāmin, though Kṛṣṇadāsa traverses much of the same ground as Jīva, whose work and person he had on hand to consult.[19] Kṛṣṇadāsa claims to have composed this work under the direct order and inspiration of Sanātana's deity, Śrī Madana-mohana,[20] whom Gauḍīya Vaishnavas believe grants *sambandha-jñāna* (knowledge of *sambandha*).[21]

---

17. Bhaktivinoda elaborates upon each of these tenets for half of the forty-seven-page tract and in other writings often employs them to organize his theology. Elsewhere, he speaks of these nine items, along with Veda *pramāṇa*, as the ten tenets of faith, *daśa-mūla* (ten roots), alluding to a medicinal preparation of the same name made from ten tuberous roots, a tonic with universal application. His essay *Daśa-mūla-tattva* is exclusively devoted to their explication; see Bhaktivinoda 2000.

18. The three are *Bhagavat, Paramātmā,* and *Kṛṣṇa Sandarbhas*. For reliable editions of the *Sandarbhas*, see Purīdāsa Mahāśaya (Jīva Gosvāmin 1951), Śyāmalāla Gosvāmī (Jīva Gosvāmin 1915), and Cinmaya Chatterjee (Jīva Gosvāmin 1986b). For the most comprehensive English summary, see De 1961:254–421. Two works are seminal to Jīva's *Sandarbhas:* for Sanātana Gosvāmin's *Bṛhad-bhāgavatāmṛta*, see the Gopīparāṇadhana Dāsa edition (2001–2) and for Rūpa Gosvāmin's *Laghu-bhāgavatāmṛta*, see the Haribhakta Dāsa edition (1989).

19. For the critically annotated English translation of the *Caitanya Caritāmṛta* with an extensive introduction to the text, the Chaitanya movement, and its theology, and an exhaustive bibliography, see the Dimock-Stewart edition (Kṛṣṇadāsa Kavirāja 1999). Unlike Prabhupāda's translation, two sequential numbering systems are employed to distinguish the verses from other quoted texts. Unless otherwise noted, my references will be to Prabhupāda's edition and numeration.

20. See CC 1.8:73–80.

21. See Prabhupāda's purport to CC 1.1:47.

Baladeva Vidyābhūṣana in his *Govinda-bhāṣya* commentary on the Vedānta-sūtra and elsewhere throughout his voluminous writing, but most specifically in *Prameya-ratnāvalī*, expounds upon nine tenets, from which Bhaktivinoda's nine postulates certainly derive.[22] This cumulative movement starting with Jīva's purely theological Sanskrit treatment and Kṛṣṇadāsa's slightly later vernacular theological narrative eventually reaches what is arguably its most succinct formulation: Prabhupāda's *mahāvākya*, or "great utterance," to which we now turn.

Prabhupāda's English Mahāvākya Phrase

For Prabhupāda, the wide range of topics that come under the umbrella of *sambandha* is commanded by one axiomatic truth: *Krishna is the Supreme Personality of Godhead.*[23] This is Prabhupāda's *mahāvākya*, his "great saying" that informs the entire content of his thought, which would radically change without it. As a semantic time-release device, it is deployed throughout his already prioritized texts as a gradual disclosure of reality.

Nowhere are Prabhupāda's pedagogical skills more in demand than in making the otherwise abstruse Gauḍīya Vaishnava ontology comprehensible.[24] Much of this burden is shouldered by formulaic assertions, foremost among them his *mahāvākya: Krishna is the Supreme Personality of Godhead.*[25] As the key to decoding the network of relationships clustered under the umbrella of *sambandha*, the

---

22. Their lists of nine differ, for as many have noted (e.g., Dasgupta [1922] 1975, De 1961), Baladeva is more closely aligned with Madhva's thought than are other Gauḍīya theologians. For reliable editions of Baladeva's *Govinda-bhāṣya*, see the Bhaktisrirupa Siddhanta Gosvami edition (Baladeva 1968–70); for his *Prameya-ratnāvalī*, see the Śaśibhūṣaṇa dāsa edition (Baladeva n.d.).

23. The *mahāvākya* usually appears without the verb "is," though without changes of sense; thus: *Krishna, the Supreme Personality of Godhead.* I use the two versions interchangeably.

24. Here our study is of "logos" (words and ideas), though it would be of considerable value to study Prabhupāda's use of "icons" (images and ideas) to present Gauḍīya theology. For example, see the dust jacket to his Bhāgavata first canto, devised to pictorially summarize the entire ontology, or for that matter any of his lavishly illustrated books.

25. Two others—"devotional service" and "Krishna consciousness"—are, like the *mahāvākya*, overarching signifiers of a *prameya*, or object of valid knoweldge, their scope large enough to require their own chapters. Of course, to speak of these terms individually is purely theoretical. They never function in isolation, though their segregation is heuristically efficacious. Analysis of them is not intended as a comprehensive theory of language vis-à-vis Prabhupāda's thought, but rather as an acknowledgment that every discourse warrants semiotic study.

mahāvākya is ubiquitously used as both a pedagogical tool and a methodological controlling device.

For the uninitiated, *Krishna, the Supreme Personality of Godhead* can be a striking combination of words—ponderous, inelegant, and off-putting, perhaps explaining why scholarship to date has failed to identify this metaphysical nomenclature as a mirror image of the tradition's key interpretative strategy. The necessity of a unitary semantic thesis, whatever it may be, is common to all Indian schools of thought (Mumme 1992:69–70). With at least one good interpretative device, apparently contradictory passages can be brought into conformity with the canon. Not only does this allow a work such as the Bhagavad Gītā to be seen as a single, unified text but it then allows all the canonical texts to appear as a simultaneous revelation that supports a single meaning and even anticipates all future development and change (*ekārthatva* in Vedānta).[26]

Pivotal *mahāvākyas* are found across many traditions. They are given unquestionable importance by Śaṅkara. Indeed, "Śaṅkara bases the whole of his doctrine upon the 'great sayings' (*mahāvākyāni*) of the *Upaniṣads*" (De Smet 1953:10). This is not hyperbole. For Advaita Vedānta, the success of any theory of meaning depends on its relative success in explaining the meaning of its *mahāvākyas* (Potter 1970:59).[27]

Why does Śaṅkara give such importance to the *mahāvākyas*? Plainly, because "*Brahmajñāna* [knowledge of Brahman, ultimate reality] . . . is produced as soon as the exact meaning of the 'great sayings' (*mahāvākyāni*) of the *śruti* is thoroughly grasped" (De Smet, 123). *Śruti*, or the Vedic revelation, is the only *pramāṇa* of *brahmajñāna* (169), and within *śruti* "the passages directly [i.e., primarily and independently] authoritative, according to him, are the 'great sayings' (*mahāvākyāni*)" (203). Thus, the *mahāvākyas* alone truly conduce to "the Veda's end" (literally, Vedānta).[28]

Mahāvākyas are not the exclusive tool of Advaita Vedānta. Rāmānuja also has his hermeneutic *mahāvākyas*, though he gives them slightly less authority.[29] Amid the vast firmament of a tradition's authoritative texts, a *mahāvākya's*

26. A common notion among Vedāntins, as De Smet notes with regard to Śaṅkara: "The whole *śruti* has one meaning throughout, a postulate without which the whole fabric of the *Vedānta* would crumble away" (1953:205).

27. Many treatments of Śaṅkara's thought explicate his chosen *mahāvākyas*. Preeminent among the few that theorize about his use of *mahāvākyas* is De Smet 1953; see also Murty 1959:68–87.

28. In classifying the *mahāvākyas* as the primary Vedic passages (because they are assertive statements that convey knowledge of Brahman), Śaṅkara dethrones the *codanas* (rules for the performance of sacrifice), considered by the master of exegesis Jaimini as the true *śabda pramāṇa;* see the discussion in De Smet 198–208.

29. See Lipner 1986:82, 165 n. 8.

luminosity outshines that of all others, as it encapsulates the tradition's inner core, the purport of its beliefs: "[Once] the recurrent dominant theme, in other words *purport* [*tātparya*] is discovered... in terms of it all scriptural statements can be interrelated (*samanvaya*) and a consistent doctrine developed out of them. *Purport*, therefore, provides the clue, the aperçu, of scripture" (Murty 1959:80). One means of determining whether *Krishna, the Supreme Personality of Godhead* is the "purport of purports" in Prabhupāda's system is to observe the panoply of concepts that it subsumes. Let us therefore view the traditional ontology in its barest skeletal form, articulated in Prabhupāda's conceptual terminology, but following the order of its treatment in Jīva Gosvāmin's *Sandarbhas*.[30] This is standard Gauḍīya Vaishnava theology, and Prabhupāda accepts it all. His detailed argumentation, while original insofar as it confronts his specific audiences, will be evaluated more profitably in terms of topics we discuss later. While I need go into little detail here, this summation will serve us well as a convenient précis of Gauḍīya ontology and enable us to be well informed of all that is implied when the *mahāvākya* is mentioned.

As will be obvious, unlike many other translators, Prabhupāda does not shy away from rendering technical terms in English.[31] While his choices may be questioned, the result is reader friendly. Prabhupāda's conviction is that his providing familiar handles with which to grasp difficult concepts, even if they are clumsy or approximate, is preferable to the reader's struggling to grasp both the concepts *and* the language. That the efficacy of his rationale may be gauged, I include in parentheses the original Sanskrit terms so that one may attempt to judge how far he succeeds.

Let us digress, though, to consider the implications of Prabhupāda's reliance on a Sanskrit canon to shape his message. Today, those using Sanskrit unreflectively have come under increasing criticism for their participation in a discourse that continues to oppress others. The role of Sanskrit in constructing inequality by the monopolization of access to Sanskrit learning is unmistakable. In fact, instead of a singular idea of inequality, one must speak of "inequalities"—gender, ethnos, race, and so on—constructed in diverse ways. In the article "Deep Orientalism?" Sheldon Pollock urges that we seek the roots of social power beyond the Raj by pointing us to precolonial India and its ideologically rich Sanskritic tradition. The "biogenetic map of inequality" created by such semantic distinctions as

30. See n. 18 above. The subject matter is also treated by Kṛṣṇadāsa in CC 2.20–21. Fine treatments of the subject are available in a number of surveys of Gauḍīya thought; e.g., see Chakravarti 1969 and Kapoor 1976.

31. Dimock, for example, when translating the CC, chooses not to translate most technical terminology. He believes that to do so "is to water down the force of an idea or the subtlety of a complex insight"; see Kṛṣṇadāsa Kavirāja 1999:xxix.

ārya/anārya (*ārya* meaning "noble") amounted to a "pre-form of racism" in early India. There is a prohibition of knowledge and radical censorship for *śūdra*s and all who are not twice-born (Pollock 1993:107–108). Thus certain socioeconomic relations of dominance are set up with transcendent legitimacy. Traditional India itself is an agent of inequality.

Pollock also interrogates the notion of *adhikāra,* the discussion within Vedic ritual texts of determining "qualification" or "right" to participate, as a "fulcrum of inequality in *vaidika* India." Inequality in these contexts has three characteristics: it restricts literacy; it creates communities of the despised; and the fact that such a discussion takes place at all indicates a conscious awareness of the need to legitimize the asymmetry that characterized it (109–110). The many responses to inequality within the larger tradition, among Buddhists and various sectarian movements, are further evidence of this last. Such movements by their nature were subversive of hierarchy.

Bhakti as taught in the Bhāgavata represents almost a complete break with Vedic sacrifice and with the necessity of suitable qualification by birth (a requirement for Vedic ceremonies). As Hopkins argues, "The extension of salvation, through devotion, to Śūdras and even to the lower unclean castes indicates a definite attempt to bring members of these groups into the *bhakti* movement, and one would suspect that they made up a large part of its mass support." The leadership, though, probably came from outside the lower classes, from "devoted ascetics whose learning and prestige gave the movement its structure" (1966:21, 22).

This upper-caste leadership had to find a way to legitimize subversion. The most plausible solution was Sanskritization of the texts.[32] J. A. B. van Buitenen explains:

> I should like to suggest that in the archaism of the *Bhāgavata* we have the expression of the same concern. The Krishna legend has to *sound* Vedic because it *was* Vedic. There is a similar reaching back to the most ancient sources—however imperfectly known—to make the old foundation support the new edifice. Here Sanskritization once more takes a linguistic form. Writing in Sanskrit was not enough; to the faithful the supremacy of Krishna was hardly in doubt, but the high-sounding language (which often must have been unintelligible) gave appropriate notice of its Vedic orthodoxy. (1966:38)

---

32. "Sanskritization, then, refers to a process in the Indian civilization in which a person or a group consciously relates himself or itself to an accepted notion of true and ancient ideology and conduct" (van Buitenen 1966:35).

Subversion and legitimation are coordinately present in Chaitanya and his early followers' movement, a membership that cuts across class boundaries yet is led by learned, highborn ascetics whose canonical writings are mostly in Sanskrit. More recently, Bhaktivinoda did much to modernize the tradition, but Sanskritization as a larger project of legitimizing the present by promoting the past remained at the center of his work[33]—as it did for his son Bhaktisiddhānta and as it also did for Prabhupāda.

Although historically Gauḍīya Vaishnavism has undercut the hierarchical power structures of society in many ways, nevertheless it has left itself open to criticism for disregarding the potentially oppressive role of the Sanskritic tradition. Inequalities persist today because their basis is in some ways foundational. For an international movement like ISKCON, the problems are by no means limited to the "Dalits" ("the oppressed") of India. This subject warrants further discussion in the chapter that follows.

We will now embark on an overview of Gauḍīya theology as part of deliberating upon the *mahāvākya*. Although the inadequacy of any summarized account must be assumed, this exercise will at least indicate, through the degree of *coherence* and *scope*, the *mahāvākya's* ability to assemble related ideological categories. Once the *mahāvākya's* importance for conceptual clarity and comprehensive ordering is registered and, further, when its origins are traced and its nature and uses (*fertility*) are theorized,[34] Prabhupāda's significant and original contribution in making the phrase *Krishna is the Supreme Personality of Godhead* his *mahāvākya* should become clear. Now, the résumé of *sambandha*.[35]

The *mahāvākya's* predicative element, "the Supreme Personality of Godhead," encompasses a nested, tripartite model[36] of ultimate reality as Brahman, Paramātman, and Bhagavān, while still claiming that reality is nondual, or one

33. For a discussion specifically of Sanskritization with reference to other reformers among the Bengali *bhadralok*, see Lipner 1999:12–14.

34. *Coherence, scope,* and *fertility* are terms borrowed from Ian Barbour, who proposes them (along with *agreement with data*) as categories by which to assess beliefs within a paradigm community, scientific or religious (though each applies the criteria somewhat differently). *Coherence* indicates "consistency with other accepted beliefs [and] insures the continuity of the paradigm community." Their *scope* is the degree to which "religious beliefs can contribute to a coherent world view and comprehensive metaphysics." *Fertility* demonstrates, on the personal level, that "religious beliefs can be judged by their power to effect personal transformation" (Barbour 1990:38–39).

35. Thorough point-by-point referencing of this highly condensed survey would prove more extensive than the résumé itself. Other than key verses often cited by the tradition, references generally are to those broad sections of Prabhupāda's writing wherein detailed coverage is available.

36. The word "model" is used throughout this chapter in the sense of "an archetypal image or pattern"; see OED, s.v. "model." In other words, within the Gauḍīya tradition, it is

without equal (*advaya-jñāna-tattva*).[37] The impersonal Brahman, or supreme reality, devoid of variety, is Krishna's bodily effulgence in which perfected *jñānins* (knowers) merge their individuality,[38] while the Supersoul (*paramātman*), the goal of yogic meditation, is Krishna's localized expansion present within the hearts of all living beings.[39] Brahman is merely the undifferentiated (*nirviśeṣa*) or unqualified state (*nirguṇa*) of Bhagavān, the supreme Lord, while Paramātmā is Bhagavān's differentiated and qualified state partially manifest. Brahman realization is the experience of Krishna's eternity feature (*sat*); *paramātmā* realization is the experience of eternal knowledge (*sat-cit*). But realization of *bhagavān* through devotional service (*bhakti*) is the experience of all the transcendental features of the Supreme Personality of Godhead: eternity, knowledge, and bliss (*sat, cit,* and *ānanda*) in a discernible form (*vigraha*).[40] Krishna, *bhagavān,* and the Supreme Personality of Godhead are thus indicators of ultimate reality in its fullest sense.

The Three Ultimate Spiritual Energies

Bhagavān's ultimacy rests upon the function of his infinite energies (*śaktis*), which in their actions and their relationships with him are inconceivably simultaneously one with and different from him (*acintya-bhedābheda*), hence characteristic of the school's distinctive theological vision. These energies, or potencies, are grouped within three principal categories.[41] The spiritual energy (*cit-* or *svarūpa-śakti*) is Krishna's own internal (*antaraṅga*) potency active in the spiritual world; the material energy (*māyā-śakti*) is his external (*bahiraṅga*) potency active in the material world; and the living entity (*jīva-śakti*) is his marginal (*taṭastha*) potency, located on the border line between the other two. To speak of the Supreme Personality of Godhead is to assume the actions of these multiple potencies. Hence, a brief description of their functions is in order.

The spiritual energy of the Supreme Personality of Godhead is again threefold:[42] (1) The potency by which he maintains his own and all other existence

---

not the likeness or resemblance of another thing, but something that itself has ontological status.

37. The entire discussion of *sambandha* is based on explicating this paraphrase of SB 1.2:11.

38. See BG 14:27; *Śrī Īśopaniṣad* 15 and 16 (Prabhupāda [1969] 1982b); CC 2.20:159.

39. See SB 2 ch. 2; CC 2.20:161.

40. See CC 1 ch. 2.

41. This distinctive theory of *śaktis* is based on the Viṣṇu Purāṇa 6.7:61; for its explanation, see CC 2.6:154–156. See also BG 7:4–5.

42. Again, the Viṣṇu Purāṇa is the basis of this theory—1.12:69; for a discussion of this verse and the subjects of this paragraph, see CC 1 ch. 4.

is called *saṁdhinī-śakti.* This energy manifests as Krishna's form and attributes, his abode (*dhāman*) and eternal associates (*parikaras*), and the entire spiritual sky (*paravyoman*) of countless spiritual planets (*vaikuṇṭha,* lit., "without anxiety"). "Form," "associates," "planets," and other descriptions that resemble phenomenal terms actually do not imply embodiment within matter. Even when Krishna and his associates descend into this world, their bodies are eternal (*nitya*) manifestations of *saṁdhinī-śakti.* (2) The potency by which he understands himself and causes others to know him is called *samvit-śakti.* Such cognition is fruitful only when enlightened by the third and highest aspect of the spiritual potency, (3) *hlādinī-śakti,* by which Krishna enjoys spiritual bliss (*ānanda*) and causes his devotees to enjoy the same. *Hlādinī-śakti,* the "pleasure potency," when personified, is known as Śrīmatī Rādhārāṇī, Krishna's divine consort and counterpart. As Krishna is the origin of all other forms of the Godhead, similarly, Rādhārāṇī is the ultimate source of all divine energies. The two are actually one in identity, but they appear separately to enjoy loving pastimes (*līlā*) *that resemble but are not to be confused with mundane conjugality.*[43] The essence of the *hlādinī* potency is love of Godhead (*prema*), whose essence is ecstatic emotion (*bhāva*), which, when developed to the ultimate degree, becomes *mahābhāva.* Śrīmatī Rādhārāṇī is this most intensified form of pure love for Krishna (*mahābhāva-svarūpa*). Thus she and Krishna together are the highest form of the divinity, who is the *sambandha.*

Contrasted with the model of the world of spiritual energy is its perverted reflection, the material world, domain of the divinity's material energy (*māyā-śakti*), whose connection to the Godhead, albeit external or indirect, ensures that this world is real though temporary (but never, as Śaṅkara insists, an illusion). The creation of the material world(s) is not ex nihilo, nor does inert matter (*prakṛti*) independently evolve. Creation through material nature proceeds at each stage with the active involvement of the Supreme Personality of Godhead, who descends in his *paramātmā* feature as the three *puruṣa* "incarnations."

The process of creation is described in richly metaphoric language.[44] Reclining in the Causal Ocean (*virajā*) between the spiritual and material worlds, the Supreme Personality of Godhead Krishna in his expansion as Kāraṇodakaśāyī Vishnu (lit., Vishnu, who reposes on the Causal Ocean) exhales through his bodily pores the seeds of unlimited universes (*brahmāṇḍas*). Vishnu's glance

43. This two-in-one identity is the basis of the tradition's Chaitanya theology—that he is the combined form of Rādhā and Krishna; for an elaborate explication of this theory, again see CC 1 ch. 4.

44. As one of the ten primary topics of a *mahā-purāṇa* (SB 12.7:9–10), "creation" (*sarga*) in its various phases is discussed throughout the Bhāgavata. However, for a single comprehensive description, see CC 2 ch. 20.

(his divine halo, Śambhu [Śiva])[45] impregnates the womb of the material nature (Śiva's consort, *māyā-śakti* personified) with the living entities that had remained within Vishnu after the previous universal dissolution (*pralaya*). The living entities' combined residual karma, ripe for fruition, along with the time factor (*kāla*), destabilizes the three modes (*guṇas*) of material nature—goodness, passion, and ignorance (*sattva, rajas, tamas*), and this produces the total material energy (*hiraṇmaya-mahat-tattva*), whose evolution as discrete elements enlarges the seedlike universes.

Krishna's second Vishnu expansion, the Personality of Godhead Garbhodakaśāyī Vishnu (aptly named, since *garbha* means "womb"), separately enters each of these universes and takes the unborn living entities with him. Finding only darkness and emptiness, he half fills the universe with his own perspiration,[46] lies upon this water, and produces from his navel the lotus birthplace of Brahmā, the universe's first progenitor, and engineer of the heavenly (*svarga*), hellish (*naraka*), and earthly (*bhūrloka*) planetary systems. Krishna's third Vishnu expansion, the Personality of Godhead Kṣīrodakaśāyī Vishnu (lit., Vishnu who lies on the Milk Ocean), finally enters each living and nonliving entity as the Supersoul (*paramātman*), their indwelling maintainer.

As a spirit soul (*ātman*),[47] the living entity (*jīva*) is qualitatively one with, but quantitatively different from, the Supreme Personality of Godhead, in keeping with the school's *acintya-bhedābheda* maxim.[48] Like the Godhead, the individual soul is eternal, full of knowledge, and bliss. However, the soul is not infinite or all pervasive. As an eternally discrete part of the supreme whole, or Personality of Godhead, the living entity shares a symptom of the Godhead, consciousness, but whereas the Godhead's consciousness extends everywhere, the living entity's is limited to its body. Consciousness distinguishes the individual soul from dull matter. But unlike the Godhead, the infinitesimal soul is prone to material nature's influence—hence, the soul's marginal position (*taṭastha*).

---

45. Within Vaishnava theology, Śiva and Brahmā are cast as chief gods, nevertheless subordinate to Vishnu/Krishna, though Śiva (Vishnu's divine halo) is nearly equal to Krishna. His position is like yogurt compared to milk; see *Brahma-saṁhitā* 5:8 and 45.

46. One ordinarily perspires because of excessive bodily heat, so this is an image of the Godhead exerting himself in the activity of creation, an act that nevertheless may be considered his "play" (*līlā*) rather than work, though "play" does not convey its full import.

47. Prabhupāda's choice of terms often shows a clear debt to his colonial education. Examples are his translations of *ātman* as "soul" (though he uses "self" interchangeably) and of *avatāra* as "incarnation." For the latter, see n. 53 below.

48. The characteristics of the immortal soul are described in the BG 2:11–30.

From a time immemorial (*anādi*),[49] forgetful (*avidyā*) of its constitutional position as the eternal servant of the Supreme Personality of Godhead, the conditioned soul searches different universes for a happiness separate from the Godhead's. In each lifetime, the conditioned soul is provided a material body from among the 8.4 million "species"[50] in which to enjoy sense gratification, but also repeatedly suffers birth, death, disease, and old age (*saṁsāra*). This seemingly endless transmigration ends with the revival, through the grace of devotional service (*bhakti*), of the soul's dormant Krishna consciousness. Freed from the conditioning of actions (karma) performed under false bodily identification and the rebirths that are their consequence, the liberated soul returns home, back to Godhead.

My précis has now laid out the attendant associations to the predicative element "the Supreme Personality of Godhead," but it would be incomplete without at least a mention of the Godhead's numerous forms, expansions, and plenary portions (*aṁśa*).[51] Broadly, in three groups, they are *svayaṁ-rūpa, tad-ekātmā,* and *āveśa*.[52] "Incarnations" of the Supreme Personality of Godhead within the material world include the *puruṣa-avatāras* (the three Vishnus), *manvantara-avatāras*

---

49. These words, "from a time immemorial," begin a discussion of the soul's transmigration. They touched off a major controversy in ISKCON about the origin of the soul. The majority of Prabhupāda's statements explain that before coming to the material world the soul originally took part in Krishna's pastimes. Other statements seem to say otherwise. The disputants' positions ("fall" and "no fall") are argued in the light of Prabhupāda's and the previous *ācāryas'* interpretations of relevant texts. More than anywhere else, this is one area where Prabhupāda's exegesis seems to border on doctrinal novelty. For the "fall" position (the official ISKCON view), see Hṛdayānanda et al. 1996. For the "no-fall" position, see Satya Nārāyaṇa and Kuṇḍalī 1994. For a framing of the issue, see Tamal Krishna 1997a.

50. Prabhupāda reads this literally, though his use of the word "species" is not in conformity with modern systems of classification. The number 8.4 million is derived from the Viṣṇu Purāṇa: "There are 900,000 species living in the water. There are also 2,000,000 nonmoving living entities, such as trees and plants. There are also 1,100,000 species of insects and reptiles, and there are 1,000,000 species of birds. As far as quadrupeds are concerned, there are 3,000,000 varieties, and there are 400,000 human species" (CC 2.19:138P). Transmigration is discussed in BG 15:7–11 and SB 3 ch. 31.

51. Compare Prabhupāda's translation of *aṁśa* as "plenary portion" with the definition of the OED, s.v. "plenary": "with full power or authority."

52. *Svayaṁ-rūpa* is the original form of Krishna as a cowherd in Vṛndāvana. The *tad-ekātma-rūpa* forms are the *caturvyūha,* the four manifestations of the Supreme Personality of Godhead as Vāsudeva, Saṁkarṣaṇa, Pradyumna, and Aniruddha, and their expansions, who include the various categories of *avatāras* except, within the category of *āveśa-rūpa,* the *śaktyāveśa-avatāras.* These last are personalities especially possessing a particular power of the Godhead: Nārada with *bhakti-śakti* (the energy of devotion), Paraśurāma with *vīrya-śakti* (the energy of heroism), etc.; see CC 2 ch. 20. For a schematic understanding of the entire subject, one may consult Tony Stewart's helpful chart, "The Avatāra System," in the CC Dimock-Stewart edition (Kṛṣṇadāsa Kavirāja 1999).

(one for each period of Manu, or seventy-one *mahā-yugas*), *guṇa-avatāras* (Brahmā, Vishnu, Śiva), and *śaktyāveśa-avatāras* (Nārada, Paraśurāma, Sanaka, etc.).[53]

To the degree that it is appropriate to speak of any manifestation of the Supreme Personality of Godhead in relative terms, the extent to which these numerous forms manifest "opulence" (*aiśvarya*, majesty) and sweetness (*mādhurya*) determines their differences, hierarchy, and the devotees whom they attract. Models of Godhead are ultimately relational. Deity and devotee relish a particular loving exchange or "mellow" (*rasa*).[54] Krishna himself is no exception: he is perfect (*pūrṇa*) in Dvārakā, more perfect (*pūrṇatara*) in Mathurā, most perfect (*pūrṇatama*) in Vṛndāvana—appraised in terms of the sweetness of his and his devotees' love.[55]

This most perfect form, Krishna-Gopāla of Vṛndāvana, the cynosure of Gauḍīya Vaishnava devotion, is the *mahāvākya's* ultimate subject, the complement to the predicative "the Supreme Personality of Godhead." Possessor of infinite potencies, infinite attributes, the cause of all causes, the deity in whom all expansions and "incarnations" are simultaneously present, Krishna of Vṛndāvana is a divine cowherd boy whose transcendental form and dress nevertheless appear humanlike. Garlanded with forest flowers, he plays a flute, his eyes blooming like lotus petals, his head bedecked with a peacock-feathered crown, and his adolescent threefold-bending figure tinged with the hue of blue clouds.[56]

Krishna's planet Goloka (lit., place of cows, but also known as Gokula, Śvetadvīpa, Vraja, or Vṛndāvana) is situated in the spiritual sky, "above" those allocated to his expansions, "incarnations," and their respective associates. Its superiority is not locational (for there is an identical replica, equally spiritual, upon earth). Rather, its superiority owes to its unsurpassed opulence and

---

53. Rather than translate *avatāra* as "descent," Prabhupāda appears to ignore the etymological meaning of "incarnation" (from the Latin participle *incarnatus,* invested with flesh). For example, when translating the key verse describing Krishna's birth (BG 4:6), he glosses the verb *sambhavāmi* (from *sambhū:* to be born or produced from, or exist) as, "I do incarnate," yet indicates by his translation of the verse a wholly other meaning, i.e., "I still appear in every millennium in My original transcendental form." His commentary emphasizes, "He appears exactly in His eternal body, uncontaminated by this material world." Whether *avatāra* and incarnation are conceptually, linguistically, or religiously synonymous is highly dubious; see Lipner 1996.

54. Prabhupāda asserts, "But as we have seen our spiritual master translate this word *rasa* into 'mellow,' we shall follow in his footsteps and translate the word in that way" (NOD 151).

55. See CC 2.20:399–401, which cites Rūpa Gosvāmin's *Bhakti-rasāmṛta-sindhu* (1945) 2.1:221–223.

56. This description is drawn from the *Brahma-saṁhitā* 5:30–31, trans. Bhaktisiddhānta Sarasvatī ([1932] 1985). (The translation attributed to him was, in fact, done by two of his disciples; the English commentary is based on Bhaktivinoda's and Jīva Gosvāmin's commentaries.)

sweetness. Specifically, the preponderance of sweetness (*mādhurya*) provides the idyllic background for Krishna's rustic pastimes. The land (*cintāmaṇi*), the trees (*kalpataru*), and the cows (*kāmadhenu*) fulfill all desires. The water is ambrosia, each word a song, every step a dance.[57]

Krishna (i.e., Krishna-Gopāla) never ventures out of Vṛndāvana. When he seems to, as when he slays the evil Kaṁsa during his advent upon earth, it is actually his expansion Vāsudeva-Krishna, the son of Vasudeva and Devakī, who goes to Mathurā and later to Dvārakā and becomes Arjuna's charioteer at Kurukṣetra. If he appears to leave, if the residents of Vṛndāvana suffer his separation (*vipralambha*), he yet resides in their hearts, and even at times before their eyes, in a form unmanifest (*aprakaṭa*) to mortal vision.[58]

Krishna is bound to Vṛndāvana by the unparalleled love of its inhabitants, a love free of awe and reverence. The knowledge that their son is the Supreme Personality of Godhead inhibits Vasudeva and Devakī from feeling purely parental affection for Vāsudeva-Krishna. The childhood antics of Vṛndāvana-Krishna are reserved instead for the cowherd king and queen, Nanda and Yaśodā, who refuse, under the "illusion" of Krishna's mystic potency (*yoga-māyā*), to believe him to be other than their small child. The cows he tends, the friends (*sakhas*) he wrestles with, the cowherd maidens (*gopīs*) who share his love in hidden bowers almost never sense that their dearest is the Supreme Personality of Godhead. Vṛndāvana's incomparable opulence as the scene of Krishna's pastimes (*līlā-mādhurya*, especially his dancing with the *gopīs*), of his devotees' love (*prema-mādhurya*), of his flute song (*veṇu-mādhurya*), and of his form (*rūpa-mādhurya*) is irresistibly sweetened as nowhere else by the presence of the pleasure potency personified (*hlādinī-śakti*), Śrīmatī Rādhārāṇī.[59]

I conclude my synopsis of *sambandha* with this captivating vision of Vṛndāvana-Krishna fresh within our purview. The nexus of subject and predicate—of forest-frolicking Krishna in tandem with the majestic opulence of the Supreme Personality of Godhead—is the secret of the *mahāvākya's* strength. By its very presence, expressed or merely understood, it causes the diverse topics under the heading of *sambandha* to cohere into recognizable ontological order. I have not evaluated the sense of this order, but only demonstrated its scope and dependence on the *mahāvākya*, which appears at every juncture as the binding, cohesive agent. I shall theorize more extensively about the *mahāvākya's* function, but

---

57. See *Brahma-saṁhitā* 5:29, 56.

58. See the opening pages of the KB chapter entitled "Uddhava Visits Vṛndāvana."

59. These four sweet features, coming as they do at the end of a list of Krishna's sixty-four qualities, are said to be unique to Krishna and are not found in any of the other forms of Godhead; see NOD chaps. 21–22.

first I need to determine its pedigree, for nowhere does Prabhupāda outrightly state: "This is my 'great utterance.'" Nor, on his behalf, has anyone else done so.

There is a more obvious choice. Chaitanya criticizes Śaṅkara for substituting "*tat tvam asi*" ("you are that") in place of what Chaitanya considers the true Vedic *mahāvākya*, the *praṇava* (*oṁ*) (CC 1.7:128–30). Prabhupāda concurs: "Only *oṁkāra* [pronouncing the syllable *oṁ*] is the *mahāvākya*" (1.7:128P). Such an absolute delimitation seems to shut out competitors. *Oṁ* has all the simplicity and grace that *Krishna the Supreme Personality of Godhead* lacks.

But context, as always, is crucial. Chaitanya is addressing his critique to an assembly of *saṁnyāsin* followers of Śaṅkara in Vārāṇasī (Benares). As students of the Vedas, they are well aware of the syllabic primacy of *oṁkāra*.[60] Chaitanya's purpose is to gradually induce them to chant Krishna's name (which they finally do) (1.7:149) by persuading them, first, of Krishna's identity with *oṁkāra*, and then, of Krishna's denotation throughout the Vedas (1.7:131). His strategy is to attract them from impersonal Brahman to Krishna via the *praṇava*. Projecting into the present, Prabhupāda explains elsewhere that today's "impersonalist has a tendency to place more emphasis on *omkara* and less on the Personality of Godhead, Sri Krishna . . . one may chant *omkara* and achieve impersonal realization. But we are Vaishnavas and we are seeking the supreme perfection. Therefore we are chanting the supreme name—Krishna" (letter to Nandarāṇī n.d.). This observation, beyond its current value, is historically relevant, for *oṁkāra*, despite its prestige, rarely has been activated as a Gauḍīya *mahāvākya*.[61] Grandiose as it is, *Krishna the Supreme Personality of Godhead*, at least tentatively, appears a better candidate. Prabhupāda may not have specifically referred to it as his *mahāvākya*, but Śaṅkara also did not attach the official label "*mahāvākya*" to his chosen dicta.[62]

Deeper Theological Implications

Our *mahāvākya* has a worthy etymological history. "Godhead," a Middle English term with a long theological past, enjoyed currency among the colonial missionaries. Though we do not find it used by Prabhupāda's Scottish professor (he preferred "God"), Urquhart repeatedly spoke of God's "personality." Hindus responding to the Christian imperative, particularly those using English as a medium, appropriated

60. See Prabhupāda's lengthy purport to CC 1.7:128 for numerous text citations that substantiate *oṁkāra's* primacy.

61. In fact, Chaitanya's and Prabhupāda's assertions merely underscore the singularly intertraditional respect accorded the *praṇava* as expressive of the highest truth; see, for example, Beck [1993] 1995.

62. I am indebted to Dr. Jacqueline Hirst for pointing this out.

as much missionary language as Hindu theology would accommodate and more. There is evidence that Bhaktivinoda chose the phrase "The Personality of Godhead" for the title of one of his early English works.[63] Bhaktisiddhānta makes use of the following variants: "the Transcendental Personality of Godhead" (Rūpa Vilāsa 1988:95); "the Personality of the Transcendental Absolute (Purushottama)" (Bhaktisiddhānta 1985:17); and, "Kṛṣṇa is Supreme Godhead" (Bhaktisiddhānta 1933:xvi).[64] Clearly, in its several syntactic possibilities, *Krishna, the Supreme Personality of Godhead* can be found in the English writings of Prabhupāda's predecessors and contemporaries alike. Not, however, with the frequency that Prabhupāda employs it: *Krishna, the (Supreme) Personality of Godhead* appears no less than 7,926 times in the course of his teachings.[65]

To account for such exploitation we must trace the phrase's deeper, semantic history to its textual source. *Puruṣottama,* the name in the Gītā by which Arjuna thrice addresses Krishna in the vocative and after whom the Gītā's fifteenth chapter, "*Puruṣottama-yoga,*" is named, is a likely place to begin. Prabhupāda glosses *Puruṣottama* as "Supreme Person" (8:1), "greatest of all persons" (10:15), and "best of personalities" (11:3). Only when it appears in the accusative case as Krishna's own self-description does Prabhupāda finally scan "the Supreme Personality of Godhead" (15.19).[66] Each offers a nuanced context to argue for the supremacy of Krishna above all other understandings of the Godhead: 8:1, wherein Krishna is approached as the supreme authority; 10:15, when introducing Krishna's divine representations by which he pervades the worlds (*vibhūti*); 11:3, when requesting Krishna for a theophanic display of universal magnitude (*viśvarūpa*); and 15:19, wherein Krishna declares himself the final object of perfect knowledge.

Vaishnavas reading these Gītā passages find support for a belief in Krishna as the Godhead. Not so others who privilege, for example, the theophanic form or even formlessness over and above Krishna's humanlike form. Apart from these alternatives, multiple readings raise again the equally intriguing question of *multiple* Krishnas. Is the divine charioteer of Arjuna really the highest Vaishnava expression of the all-pervasive, self-manifest, transcendent, and changeless

---

63. Shukavak describes it as an English prose work of 1871 mentioned only in ISKCON publications; see 1999:285. But it is mentioned along with a date of 1883 in a 1950 preface (well before ISKCON's formation) to one of Bhaktivinoda's English works; see Bhakti Prajnan Keshab [1950] 1981:B.

64. The first variant is from a conversation with Prof. Albert E. Suthers of Ohio State University in 1929, the second from a lecture on the birth anniversary of Bhaktivinoda, 1933.

65. See chapter 1 n. 16, regarding how this figure was obtained.

66. Compare Zaehner's ([1969] 1973:359) no less cumbersome translation of *Puruṣottama:* "Person [All-] Sublime."

Godhead? From the Gauḍīya Vaishnava perspective, Vāsudeva-Krishna, as well as Nārāyaṇa, Vishnu, and all the *avatāras,* originate in the Gauḍīya's most cherished deity, the flute-playing cowherd of Vṛndāvana, youthful Krishna-Gopāla, beloved of the *gopīs.* The Gītā's use of the name *Puruṣottama,* however, no matter how it is glossed, makes none of this transparently clear. If the phrase *Krishna, the Supreme Personality of Godhead* is a *mahāvākya,* and hence is definitive, its source must be elsewhere.

Bhagavān is a term whose taxonomic value emerges with the multiple deities it predicates and has perhaps a closer affinity to Prabhupāda's *mahāvākya* than *Puruṣottama.*[67] One who possesses *bhaga*—fortune, excellence, majesty, loveliness, and so on (traditionally reckoned as sixfold: full wealth, strength, fame, beauty, knowledge, and renunciation)[68]—is designated as *bhagavān.* The term is derived from the root *bhaj* (to serve, honor, revere, love, adore), as are *bhakti* and *bhāgavata,* or *bhakta* (one who belongs to *bhagavān,* i.e., the devotee). The root *bhaj* also means "to share," which indicates reciprocity between *bhagavān* and *bhakta.*[69] *Bhagavān* appears in twenty-three verses of the Gītā: whenever Krishna is about to speak (*śrī-bhagavān uvāca*) and twice in the vocative when addressed by Arjuna.

Comparing the rendering of *bhagavān* in two of Prabhupāda's Gītā editions is revealing. The earlier, Macmillan version, reading "The Blessed Lord said," is changed without fail in the revised edition published after his demise to "The Supreme Personality of Godhead said." We are at once suspicious (as have been many), but it should be recalled that Prabhupāda, after translating the Gītā, considered the verse translations less important than his commentary and permitted his original English editor to adapt translations done by others.[70] That this appears to be what happened is borne out by consulting the Radhakrishnan and Zaehner editions available to Prabhupāda's editor, both of which read, "The

---

67. Graham Schweig briefly reflects on Prabhupāda's translation of the Sanskrit word *bhagavān* as "the Supreme Personality of Godhead," noting the profuse application of this phrase throughout his writing; see Schweig 1998b:106–107.

68. See the Viṣṇu Purāṇa 6.5:47.

69. Jaiswal interprets other, earlier meanings of these terms to prove their original association with Nārāyaṇa and that he, not Vāsudeva-Krishna, was the original *bhagavān* of the *bhāgavata* worshippers; see Jaiswal 1981:37 onward.

70. See chapter 3 n. 79. As might be expected, revisions to this and other volumes of Prabhupāda's translations have caused consternation among some of his followers, who have mounted a campaign to have them reversed; see, e.g., Madhudvisa 1999. For the official ISKCON justification of the revisions, *Responsible Publishing,* see Bhaktivedanta Book Trust (BBT) 1998 and BBTedit.com.

Blessed Lord said."[71] The editor obviously preferred this to the more archaic-sounding alternative.

Prabhupāda seems to consider them interchangeable, as both are able to counteract an impersonalism he strongly opposes. He writes:

> The Māyāvādī atheists also interpret the *Bhagavad-gītā*. In every verse of *Śrīmad Bhagavad-gītā* it is clearly stated that Kṛṣṇa is the Supreme Personality of Godhead. In every verse Vyāsadeva says, *śrī-bhagavān uvāca*, "the Supreme Personality of Godhead said," or "the Blessed Lord said." It is clearly stated that the Blessed Lord is the Supreme Person, but Māyāvādī atheists still try to prove that the Absolute Truth is impersonal. (CC 2.6:132P)

Elsewhere, he is unequivocal:

> In the Gita Press edition, you will see "*paramātmā*." They never say Krishna. They're so much afraid that "If I say 'Krishna', He will at once capture me." You see? [*Prabhupāda chuckles.*] So, in a different way—"*parabrahman*," "*Chaitanya*"—like this, so many impersonal ways they will say. But that is not required. *Bhagavān uvāca* means Supreme Personality of Godhead, Krishna. Sometimes they say, "Blessed Lord" said. No. Why [do] you say [that]? The Supreme Personality of Godhead Krishna said.... (700307lec.la)

If any doubt remains, Prabhupāda's original Gītā manuscript is available. In it, he unfailingly renders *śrī bhagavān uvāca* as "The Supreme Personality of Godhead said."[72]

It appears that we are very close to locating the Sanskritic basis of Prabhupāda's *mahāvākya*. Still, as Friedhelm Hardy observes, the notion of *bhagavān*, "a single, all-powerful, eternal, personal and loving God," is not deity specific, at least to outside observers: "That means, the concept itself is an empty slot, to be filled by concrete characteristics which then make up a specific Bhagavān-figure who serves as (the one and only) God to a given group of people" ([1988] 1990:79). This poses a problem, as even among Vaishnavas *bhagavān* has diverse referents

71. See Radhakrishnan [1948] 1993 and Zaehner [1969] 1973.

72. In my personal communication of March 21, 2001, with Jayadvaita Swami, the editor of the revised edition, he explained that the only exceptions to "The Supreme Personality of Godhead said" read "The Personality of Godhead said." He added that the manuscript for the first six Gītā chapters is either typed by Prabhupāda or retyped from his original. The last twelve chapters are transcribed from his audiotaped dictation, which was not preserved. The manuscripts are with the Bhaktivedanta Archives, a division of the BBT.

(e.g., Vishnu, Nārāyaṇa, etc.). The appellation can also extend to powerful devotees and sages like Nārada, though their status is clearly different.[73]

To encapsulate the tradition's essential position, the Sanskritic equivalent of Prabhupāda's English *mahāvākya* must link Krishna and *bhagavān* unambiguously. The Mīmāṁsaka or exegetical demand that a *mahāvākya* serve a single purpose is achieved when the parts of a *mahāvākya* share three prerequisites: "*ākāṅkṣā* (mutual expectancy), *yogyatā* (compatibility) and *sannidhi* (proximity)" (Subrahmanyam 1990:42).[74] As an instance of the first, the single word "Krishna" evokes the questions "Krishna what?" or "Krishna or who?" just as the word *bhagavān* gives rise to the question "Which *bhagavān*?" In any case, a word or words are required to complete the sense (*ākāṅkṣā*). "Compatibility" refers to "the potency of some contiguous word to satisfy this want," while "proximity" "is spatial in written words and temporal in spoken words. It must belong to the words, because, otherwise, we could not know which words should be construed together to form a sentence" (De Smet 1953:259). Some suggest a fourth prerequisite: *tātparya-jñāna*, knowledge of the intention of the speaker or writer.[75]

The Bhāgavata Purāṇa offers precisely the unambiguous linkage we are seeking. After a list of the principal *avatāras*, a half verse identified by Jīva Gosvāmin as the governing *sūtra* of this foremost literature of the tradition asserts: *ete cāṁśa-kalāḥ puṁsaḥ kṛṣṇas tu bhagavān svayam* ("All these are the portions and fractions of the portions of the *puruṣa*, but Kṛṣṇa is *bhagavān* himself") (SB 1.3:28).[76]

Krishnas tu bhagavān svayam is the ideal juxtaposition we are searching for. Jīva carefully defends it against potential doubts. If it is argued that *bhagavān* (i.e., Vishnu/Nārāyaṇa) has manifested as Krishna, he cites a grammatical rule that a predicate should not precede its subject, as, unlike the subject, it is unknown to the reader.[77] Krishna is the known subject, *bhagavān* the unknown predicate, not vice

73. See, e.g., SB 1.13:38.

74. Under this cited rule, a single sentence or an entire discourse can be qualified as a *mahāvākya*. Mīmāṁsā is a philosophical tradition of "Enquiry" or exegesis largely based on Jaimini's (*Pūrva-*) *Mīmāṁsā Sūtra*. The Vedānta Sūtra clearly exhibits a thorough acquaintance with its principles and methods of exegesis (De Smet 1953:198).

75. De Smet refers to the *Vedāntaparibhāṣā* of Dharmarāja Adhvarīndra (sixteenth century) when mentioning this fourth condition (actually, he combines *ākāṅkṣā* and *yogyatā*); see De Smet 1953:258–259.

76. *Puṁsaḥ* refers to the *puruṣa*, the cosmic person from whom the universes come. Earlier (SB 1.3:1–5), *bhagavān* has been described as the source of both the primal and the secondary *puruṣa*, the latter in turn described as the source of all the *avatāras*. For a discussion of 1.3:28 as the governing *sūtra*, see Jīva Gosvāmin's *Kṛṣṇa-sandarbha* (1986b) 28–29. Also see CC 1.2:67–90.

77. *anuvādam anuktvā tu na vidheyam udīrayet* (Mammaṭa's *Kāvyaprakāśa*).

versa.[78] *Svayam* ("oneself" or "in person") adds further emphasis, to distinguish Krishna from other *bhagavān* figures. To the objection that Krishna is among the aforementioned list of *avatāras* and therefore cannot be the *avatārin* (the source of the *avatāras*), a Mīmāṁsā rule weights a later statement (in this case, 1.3:28) more than an earlier one (1.3:23).[79] When Krishna does appear as an *avatāra,* it is principally to favor his associates with the wonder of his *līlā,* beginning with his birth, and only secondarily to remove the burden of the world.[80] The particle *tu,* by its position, ensures that there be no confusion about Krishna's unique status. Understood as "but," *tu* distinguishes Krishna from both the *puruṣa* and all the *avatāras.* It also has the force of *eva* ("indeed" or "certainly") and emphasizes the primacy of Krishna compared with the Godhead*ness* of Nārāyaṇa, Vishnu, and others, which is relative (*guṇībhūta*).

To Jīva Gosvāmin, the unambiguous force of this verse is definitive. It is the *paribhāṣā-sūtra* that governs how all that follows is to be interpreted.[81] Stated only once and never to be repeated in context,[82] the *paribhāṣā's* certainty connects apparently unrelated facts and arguments, restricting what would otherwise be unrestricted to a specific interpretation. Summarizing Jīva, S. K. De is worth quoting *in extenso* for he indicates just how central to the tradition this authoritative statement is:

> It is thus a Mahāvākya or a great proposition, like the phrase *tat tvam asi;* and the proper śāstric method would be to explain every other proposition, which appears inconsistent or contradictory, in the light of the

---

78. That is, the statement does not read, *bhagavāṁs tu kṛṣṇaḥ svayam.* Kṛṣṇadāsa further explains that had Krishna been only a portion and Nārāyaṇa the Godhead himself, the statement would have read: "Nārāyaṇa is the source of the *avatāras, bhagavān* himself; he is [now] Krishna"; see CC 1.2:84–85.

79. Jīva further points out that unlike the list's other *avatāras,* even in the earlier verse (1.3:23) Krishna (together with his brother Balarāma) is referred to as *bhagavān.* For an opposing view, that this single statement (1.3:28) fails to supersede those that present Krishna as a portion or portion of the portion of the Godhead, see for example, Sheth 1982. He derives this view from his more comprehensive thesis that traces Krishna's gradual divinization through the Harivaṁśa, Viṣṇu Purāṇa, and Bhāgavata (1984).

80. "Secondarily" because it does not behoove the Godhead himself to perform what his *avatāras* can easily accomplish, namely, the removal of the earth's burden. He does so as a secondary function through the *aṁśa-kalāḥ,* the *avatāras* who are his parts and fractions of his parts and who are all present within the *avatārin* Godhead when he descends; see CC 1.4:7–13.

81. According to the grammarian Pāṇini: "a rule or maxim that teaches the proper interpretation or application of other rules" (MMW, s.v. "paribhāṣā").

82. A *paribhāṣā* appears only once: *paribhāṣā ca sakād eva paṭhyate śāstre, na tv abhyāsena: Kṛṣṇa-sandarbha, anuccheda* 29 (Jīva Gosvāmin 1986b).

> significance of such a Mahāvākya. It is also maintained that this Paribhāṣā statement not only controls all other *Bhāgavata* texts but also conflicting texts in other Purāṇas, which must be interpreted in such a way as not to appear inconsistent with it. The reason for this is that the *Bhāgavata,* as already demonstrated in the previous Sandarbhas, is the most authentic and infallible scripture, superseding the authority of every other śāstra (*sarva-śāstropamardaka*), and this particular śruti or Mahāvākya occurs in that work purposely to determine the highest spiritual truth (*paramārtha-vastu-paratva*) in a definite and indisputable manner. It is like the emphatic and indisputable command of a king to his followers, and it has been repeatedly utilised as such, for reconciling conflicts, by authoritative commentators like Śrīdhara-svāmin. (1961:321)

Clearly, this is the origin of Prabhupāda's *mahāvākya.* While the English *mahāvākya* lacks an equivalent for the particle "*tu,*" contextual positioning normally compensates for the loss of its explicative value. Although on occasion his English translation of *kṛṣṇas tu bhagavān svayam* varies slightly, the sense is always the same: Krishna's supremacy is absolute and unambiguous. He is "the Supreme Personality of Godhead."

As a borrowing of inherited linguistic figures and images from Sanskrit (and English, if we recall the variants employed by his predecessors), the *mahāvākya's* Sanskrit-English correspondence is intentional. With strength to marshal a multitude of theistic models, "Krishna, the Supreme Personality of Godhead" is a deliberate effort at identification with the tradition's "root metaphor."[83] I will show that the term "metaphor" has limited value in conceptualizing Prabhupāda's thought, so here I use it restrictedly. As Paul Ricoeur argues, "Root metaphors assemble and scatter. They assemble subordinate images together and they scatter concepts at a higher level. They are the dominant metaphors capable of both engendering and organizing a network" (1976:64, quoted in McFague).

Prabhupāda's *mahāvākya* is the interpretative linchpin that governs his thought. While he cites over three hundred times the Sanskritic original *kṛṣṇas tu bhagavān svayam,* and then usually to confirm Krishna's ontological primacy,[84] he intones its ubiquitous English translation with a mantralike intensity, and with good reason. For it serves a second, broad, no less important function. For Prabhupāda, the *mahāvākya's* value is not only explanatory (as a controlling device), it is revelatory. Faith in Krishna as the Absolute Truth is instilled by the presence within the *mahāvākya* of Krishna's holy name and also by the *mahāvākya's*

---

83. I am borrowing the term "root metaphor" from Stephen C. Pepper (1942).

84. See, e.g., SB 2.10:7P or 3.2:15P.

semantic range. The former depends upon the theological-ontological principle that Krishna and his name are identical in all respects,[85] while the latter's breadth has already been indicated in my résumé of *sambandha*.

Before Prabhupāda, the *mahāvākya* functions solely as the *paribhāṣā-sūtra*. To repeat, for his predecessors—Bhāgavata commentators all the way back to Śrīdhara—"it is like the emphatic and indisputable command of a king to his followers." The simile is appropriate: In days of old a monarch's authority was such that a single word was law itself. Similarly, *kṛṣṇas tu bhagavān svayam* controls the entire Bhāgavata yet appears just once. It occurs five times in Kṛṣṇadāsa's theobiographical "summa," the *Caitanya Caritāmṛta*,[86] and only somewhat more often in later works. But that was yesterday; today, monarchy is under siege. Compared with the past, Prabhupāda's English *mahāvākya*, like royal proclamations, is delivered to audiences that are not at all convinced of its authority. Unlike royal statements, however, it cannot afford to vacillate. As the foundation of the tradition's "magisterium," there is no retreating. Rather, to ensure its sovereignty, the *mahāvākya* is reiterated with such frequency. And it directly partakes in all forms of discourse in a manner no *paribhāṣā* would.

Technically, a *paribhāṣā* is mentioned only once. But *Krishna, the Supreme Personality of Godhead* repeatedly asserts itself.[87] In this sense it functions as a mantra, understood in the broadest sense, which reveals itself the more it is recited. Harvey P. Alper explains: "[T]he *mahāvākyas*, at least in some regards, are mantras: They are verses from the Veda; they are objects of repeated meditation; they are instruments of liberation; they are slogans enunciating the truth" (1989b:388). Prabhupāda is the first to exploit the *mahāvākya's* pedagogical value beyond its status as a *paribhāṣā*. He imports the full cognitive content of the *paribhāṣā* and harnesses it to the equally versatile and perhaps, for his purposes, more effective vehicle of mantra.

---

85. See particularly the citation from Padma Purāṇa in CC 2.17:133. We shall look at this topic in depth in the next chapter. For a comprehensive compilation of Prabhupāda's instructions about the holy name, see Prabhupāda's *Śrī Nāmāmṛta* (1982d). The wider application of this tenet may be judged by its presence within multiple religio-cultural traditions; cf. the Hebrew/Jewish and Sant for example.

86. CC 1.2:67, 1.5:79, 2.9:143, 2.20:156, 2.25:134; it is quoted in 2.23:67 as part of another verse.

87. For Prabhupāda's use of repetition as a pedagogical tool, see Bhūrijana 1997:178–179. Śaṅkara offers extended argumentation for the necessity of repetition (*abhyāsa*); see De Smet 1953:162–163.

The Question of Translation

To the Gauḍīyas, mantras are linguistic instruments whose success owes to their inherent meaningfulness, a view by no means universally accepted. Both within the tradition and in nonpractitioner scholarship there is a divergence in the Vedāntic attitude regarding mantras that parallels the divergence in attitude toward *mahāvākyas*. Again, Alper explains:

> For those who believe [mantras] are really linguistic instruments, aligning themselves with Bhartṛhari and Maṇḍana,[88] they work because they lead to the understanding, albeit deep, extraordinary understanding. For those who believe they are nonlinguistic, aligning themselves with the tradition of mystic ineffability, they work 'magically', by occasioning a 'leap', an ultimately inexplicable transformation of one's way of being in the world. (1989b:388–389)

Those in the latter group, who consider mantras alinguistic phenomena, consider them also untranslatable, "like the nattering of infants and madmen, like the patterned song of birds" (Alper 1989a:11).[89] Clearly, they would not categorize the Gauḍīya *mahāvākya* as a mantra, in either its Sanskritic or translated form. Even among those who would, some might consider the translation—*any* translation—as *only* a step down in creativity, and one that involves an inevitable loss in semantic value.[90] Thus the question: Does Prabhupāda's translation of the *mahāvākya* distort and thereby diminish its meaning? Or does it accelerate it?

I am not questioning here the authority of vernacular translation, an issue practically as old as any tradition that has debated it; nor the linguisticality of mantras and, hence, the status of their translation. Neither by this discussion am I positing an alternative to the all-important Hare Krishna *mahāmantra,* which Prabhupāda did *not* translate.[91] In attempting to assess Prabhupāda's contribution, I am probing whether the work of translation can ever be merely a change

---

88. Gauḍīya Vaishnavas part ways with these early grammarians over a number of important issues; see the discussion of Gauḍīya views in Beck [1993] 1995.

89. Frits Staal, for one, argues that mantras are alinguistic "bits and pieces from the Vedas put to ritual use" (1989); see Alper's discussion (1989a:10–14) and his working bibliography (1989b). Alper, while disagreeing, admits Staal's position is not easily refuted.

90. Generally, translation today is considered important and creative, prompting the term "transcreation"; see, e.g., the title to Ashok Kumar Malhotra's *Transcreation of the Bhagavad Gītā* (1999). Such creativity can lead, at times, to a loss of the original meaning; see Clooney 2000.

91. At least he did not translate it for ritual use. He did, however, explain the *mahāmantra's* general meaning as: "O my Lord, O energy of the Lord, please engage me in Your service!"

of language, or is the translator inevitably a transformer, an interpreter in the light of ever-new circumstances? For an audience so different from Chaitanya's, as much as Prabhupāda disclaims originality, by necessity his role is likely to be a creative one. And though, again, he might deny it, if he extends the function of the tradition's *mahāvākya* even limitedly, in one sense he is the creator of a new mantra.[92]

This sort of creativity is not of the degree of, say, Vivekananda or S. Radhakrishnan, a selective distillation and appropriation that Brian Hatcher, with both appreciation and skepticism, describes as "eclectic." Hatcher has in mind not the patterns and processes of historical change denoted by "syncretism," "but a particular method of change—a method based on conscious selection—and the systems of criteria and classification that may (or may not) guide this method" (1999:8). S. K. De (1961) affixes nearly the same definition to what he sees as the *gosvāmins'* eclectic penchant for a wide, though highly selective, citation of texts to support their views, a method to which Prabhupāda also adheres. But creativity, eclectic or otherwise, implies more than following one's predecessors. In common with Hatcher's view of the two aforementioned Hindu reformers, there is in Prabhupāda the spirit of the "poet," where "the root meaning of *poesis* is 'the act of creating'. Poets are the ones who come along from time to time and by redescribing our world, re-create it for us... give us a new set of metaphors through which to view our world and our experiences" (1999:166). For many in his audience, Prabhupāda is the "maker of new words, the shaper of new languages" (Rorty 1989:20, quoted in Hatcher)—the harbinger of a new order.

Like Hatcher, Janet Soskice speaks of such visionaries in much the same light: "The great divine and the great poet have this in common: both use metaphor to say that which can be said in no other way but which, once said, can be recognized by many" (1985:153). But in contrast to Hatcher's remarks that poets redescribe and re-create our world using a new set of metaphors, and in response to Paul Ricoeur's (1977) language of redescription (which Hatcher may well have had in mind), Soskice prefers that metaphors describe something new and unique: "The point deserves emphasis—redescription, however radical, is always *re*-description. The interesting thing about metaphor, or at least about some metaphors, is that they are used not to redescribe but to disclose for the first time" (89).

Soskice's observations on the meaningfulness of metaphor in religious language are richly suggestive of ways in which to understand Prabhupāda's

---

For his more extended explanation, see SSR 146–148. For explanations by previous *ācāryas*, see Bhakti Dayita 1982 and Rohiṇī Kumār 1984.

92. Although traditions characteristically believe in a fixed number of mantras, Alper believes an infinity of new mantras may be created (1989a:6 n.).

mahāvākya. Undoubtedly, there is a fundamental difference in foci. She is speaking of metaphor grounded upon Christian assumptions, and I am speaking of Prabhupāda's *literality* in terms of iconic Hinduism. Soskice reminds us that the literal-metaphorical distinction is one of *usages,* not of states of affairs (i.e., that there are two or more ways of expressing the same state of affairs).[93] Still, the differences can be stark.

Julius Lipner has drawn our attention to this distinction in the method of Śaṅkara. As an exegete, Śaṅkara gives primacy to the literal interpretation of scripture and resorts to figurative usage only when the literal does not apply. Such, for him, is the case in Gītā 13:13: "With hands and feet everywhere, eyes, heads and mouths everywhere, / With hearing everywhere, It stands in the world enveloping all."[94] Coming as it does between verses that describe Brahman apophatically or negatively, "[t]he verse affirms the existence of Brahman ... by figuratively ascribing to Brahman the sense-organs and limbs of living beings.... In other words, Śaṅkara is making the point that for 13.13 to work, its proper context as metaphor must be understood" (Lipner 1989:180).

Not so for Prabhupāda. In his purport to the same verse, he interprets it as a literal description of the Supersoul (*paramātman*):

> As the sun exists diffusing its unlimited rays, so does the Supersoul, or Supreme Personality of Godhead. He exists in His all-pervading form, and in Him exist all the individual living entities, beginning from the first great teacher, Brahmā, down to the small ants. There are unlimited heads, legs, hands and eyes, and unlimited living entities. All are existing in and on the Supersoul. Therefore the Supersoul is all-pervading. (BG 13:14)[95]

Such naked literalism provokes one to wonder whether Sockice's theory of language is relevant in any way to Prabhupāda's thought. Would it not be better to look to theories within the Indic traditions, rich as they are with language theory from earliest times? Yes, it would, were we dealing with the Sanskritic version of our *mahāvākya*. Then we would be more inclined to agree with André Padoux's remark: "I, for one, have no doubt that mantras as they exist in actual fact (that is, in the area of Indian civilization) can be properly explained and understood only within the Indian tradition" (1989:296–297). But our English-language mantra is clearly transcultural, developed for export with an international clientele in mind.

93. For Soskice's discussion of the literal-metaphorical distinction, see Soskice 1985 ch. 5.

94. Translation by Lipner.

95. Prabhupāda's translation includes an opening verse omitted in many MSS; hence, the difference in numeration.

Prabhupāda's Root Metaphor

When we speak of the *mahāvākya* as metaphorical, we do so in the way that Ricoeur speaks of root metaphors: as open ended and gathering numerous subordinate images. But this should not hide the fact that its fundamental sense is to be literally understood. The *mahāvākya* ontologically refers with full cognitive value to Krishna as the Supreme Personality of Godhead—not alinguistically like the "patterned song of birds." Soskice's theorizing is appealing because it can help us to understand how Prabhupāda's *mahāvākya*, like metaphors, crosses boundaries by depicting reality in a strikingly original way. Specifically, where her comments pertain to referentiality and contextualization, we will find actual common ground.

"Krishna, the Supreme Personality of Godhead" does more than merely extend previous conceptions of God. For most, it offers a disclosure of a new kind. Even superficially the *mahāvākya's* surface tension—if nothing else, its wordiness—makes us stumble over its unconventional pattern and forces us to speak of an unfamiliar subject in a still more unfamiliar way. But like a metaphor, it is the *mahāvākya's* semantic rather than syntactic content that primarily contributes to a radical discontinuity. A metaphor is needed not just to invigorate a tired term, but when conventional understandings preclude ontological novelty. It is more than, as some have suggested, "a matter of teaching an old word new tricks" or "a happy and revitalizing, even if bigamous, second marriage" (Goodman 1968:69, 73). Prabhupāda's *mahāvākya* points to a radically different understanding. At first, this may not be obvious, for the individual terms can be defined with the help of an ordinary dictionary. However, as "the locus of the metaphor is not the word but the complete speech act" (Soskice, 68), so the English *mahāvākya* functions only when understood in complete contexts of speech. It arises from contact between the Gauḍīya Vaishnava tradition and multiple communities of reception. And it involves at least three linguistic communities: Sanskrit, Bengali, and English (many more, if translations of his English *mahāvākya* are considered).

In its Sanskritic form the *mahāvākya* is embedded within a text (the Bhāgavata) that heralded a near-democratic ethic that scorned wealth and status.[96] With its pivotal *paribhāṣā-sūtra, kṛṣṇas tu bhagavān svayam,* which sets Krishna above all other deities, the very same text became in the hands of Gauḍīya theologians a bulwark of theological orthodoxy. Not that social liberality and religious orthodoxy are necessarily incompatible, but the point is that the text, along with its key *sūtra,* has always polarized throughout its history.

96. See Ingalls 1966 and Hopkins 1966.

The present is no exception. Transplanting the tradition's root metaphor into alien soil has only made it all the more revolutionary. To Prabhupāda's first unacculturated Western audiences, Krishna is *not* the Supreme Personality of Godhead. He may be a Hindu deity and, as such, a marvellous item of exotica, but he is not *God*. Prabhupāda's early lectures test the waters for Krishna. Prabhupāda reaches out to his listeners more as a teacher than a preacher, his voice nevertheless urgent, palpably expectant. In time, as his mission picks up steam, his voice becomes more confident, more emphatic and commanding. Throughout it all, one hears the *mahāvākya*, pressed into repeated service, a staccato utterance—challenging.

Mahāvākyas, unlike certain other speech acts (metaphors or whatever), may possess agency.[97] But as linguistic instruments, they can and should be linked to theories of reference. Our postmodern sensibilities make it uncomfortable for us to hear that a word's "meaning" determines how a speaker uses it "to refer." This takes no account of the role played by the speaker, or of the fact that the speaker belongs to a community of interest, which in turn is bound to a tradition of interpretation. As Soskice reminds us, "it is not words which refer, but speakers using words *who* refer." She notes, "reference is determined by speakers in contexts of use, and not simply by individual speakers but by communities of speakers whose language provides access to the states and relations which are of interest to them" (132).

We know what Prabhupāda's early audiences do not: that the *mahāvākya* is a distillation of text and orality with a lengthy medieval and colonial past. Prabhupāda shares with his forebears the descriptive vocabulary articulating their experience, which in turn has become his, and he now hopes to share it with others. This hope also obliges him to assimilate or at least acquaint himself with the vocabulary of his audience's linguistic community, because theories of reference point as much ahead to the hearer as to the speaker, as well as behind to those who have spoken before.

Prabhupāda's *mahāvākya* conceals a host of linguistic theological affiliations that are neither reducible to nor equivalent to the denotation of the English term "God," a term that, in consideration of the training he received from Urquhart, Prabhupāda might have been expected to use. Clearly, "English education also familiarized the Indian with ways of seeing, techniques of translation, or modes of representation that came to be accepted as 'natural'" (Niranjana 1990:778,

97. My purpose here is to speak of referentiality, not to resolve whether a *mahāvākya* mantra is or is not a speech act, or to what extent it possesses inherent power or is empowered outside itself.

quoted in R. King).[98] Deliberately choosing an alternative term, Prabhupāda and his Gauḍīya preceptors departed from British missionary ideology by raising the ante on the term's ideological purchase. They wanted an English equivalent to *bhagavān* that, when tied to the specific referent they had in mind (Krishna), would be sufficiently suggestive and amenable to their theological needs.

It takes little to imagine what those needs were. One common representation that needed their immediate response was the promotion of Indian philosophy and culture as a reified entity, "Hinduism," essentially couched in the Advaita Vedāntic terms envisioned by Vivekananda and Radhakrishnan. In an essay entitled "Scholars Deluded,"[99] Prabhupāda summons his *mahāvākya* to neutralize Radhakrishnan's (following) comment to the Gītā 9:34:[100] "It is not the personal Kṛṣṇa to whom we have to give ourselves up utterly but the unborn, beginningless, eternal who speaks through (Kṛṣṇa)." Prabhupāda's *mahāvākya*, "Krishna, the Supreme Personality of Godhead," simultaneously challenges this widespread perception of the Absolute as ineffable and impersonal and for Western audiences whose focus has been the Abrahamic God paints an unmistakably different face on the Godhead.

Protecting Krishna's Intimate Līlās

The *mahāvākya* is also intended to correct perceived misconceptions about Krishna's character. Unaware of Krishna's overarching majestic potentialities, what are others to make of this rustic, flute-playing god? The occasional hint of his divinity appears as a mere ornament in his playful Vṛndāvana pastimes—crucial, but a foil. He seems capricious, especially his amours, a fertile field for orthodox theologizing and heterodox imitation, and no less as grist for deprecation. *The Betrayal of Krishna: Vicissitudes of a Great Myth* announces one recent disapproving title.[101] Its author's purpose, David Haberman informs us, is "to cleanse Krishna of his dirty associations with Braj—and that means most particularly with Radha—and restore him to the pristine state of the *Bhagavad-Gita*" (1994a:87). Few subjects seem to vex outside representations, as does Vṛndāvana-Krishna. Christian missionaries, Orientalists, Hindu reformers, the Krishna-Christ debaters, and

98. See, e.g., nn.47 and 54 above.

99. The essay carried over to two issues of *BTG*: vol. 3, nos. 13 and 14 1958; see *"Back to Godhead"* 1994:149, 150, 156.

100. *man-manā bhava mad-bhakto mad-yājī māṁ namaskuru / mām evaiṣyasi yuktvaivam ātmānaṁ mat-parāyaṇaḥ* (BG 9:34).

101. See Chaitanya 1991. (This twentieth-century author is not to be confused with the fifteenth-century Bengali mystic.)

figures like Bankim Chandra Chatterjee—promoting the varying agendas of colonial discourse—feel a communal discomfort. As Haberman concludes, "all have one thing in common: they finally agree that Krishna-Gopal of Braj is a false form of divinity" (105). At best, as Prabhupāda's initial audiences thought, Krishna is exotic, but not *God.*

Colonial representations cannot be ignored, especially when they address the subject central to Prabhupāda's thought. In fact, Prabhupāda's *mahāvākya* is intended to defend Krishna-Gopāla and his seemingly human proclivities against these outspoken critics. Expunging the Vṛndāvana *līlā* is not an option. Instead, he consistently qualifies Krishna's humanlike propensities with the predicative "the Supreme Personality of Godhead."

A case in point is Prabhupāda's handling of the Bhāgavata Purāṇa's tenth canto. Conducting a search restricted to the Vṛndāvana episodes that deal with Krishna-Gopāla, one finds the predicate occurring over two hundred times in Prabhupāda's early summary treatment, and double that in his later verse-by-verse translation and commentary (though the latter covers less than a third of the earlier summarized chapters).[102] The effect is to amply remind the reader of Krishna's divinity, but not so much as to overwhelm the sense of Krishna's sweetness.[103]

The original Bhāgavata tenth canto narration achieves a similar balance by breaking the narrative flow with Parīkṣit's intermittent questions and Śuka's answers, and often employing reverential terms such as *bhagavān.* A primary example is found in the opening verse to the *Rāsalīlā-pañcādhyayī,* the five chapters (29–33) describing Krishna and the *gopīs'* famed play of the *rāsa* dance.[104] Śukadeva begins informing the audience, *bhagavān api:* it is the Deity who turns his mind "toward loving affairs" (*rantum*) and this will be accomplished

102. There are ninety chapters in the Bhāgavata's tenth canto. If the two describing Krishna's message delivered by Uddhava to the *gopīs* are included, forty take place in Vṛndāvana. Prabhupāda's summary, which weaves together the verses and previous commentaries, is of all ninety. His verse-by-verse translation and commentary, owing to his demise, stopped at chapter 13. (His disciples thereafter completed the translation of cantos 10–12.)

103. An interesting contrast in strategies is provided by the summary of the Vṛndāvana episodes by the pioneer of Krishna Vaishnavism in America, Baba Premanand Bharati, whom I mentioned earlier. Notice especially the choice of the predicate in his title, *Sree Krishna, the Lord of Love* (1904). The book's two parts distinctly separate theology and narrative pastimes, the latter omitting the Vāsudeva-Krishna period entirely. Bharati's strategy is to have the reader first absorb the initial theological lessons, and afterward be free to relish the sweetness of the "Lord of Love."

104. On the theological implications of the Rāsalīlā episode for Gauḍīya Vaishnavas, complete with a poetic translation of all five chapters, see Schweig 1998a. [For the vastly evolved version of this work to which Goswami refers, see Schweig 2005a—ed.]

through his "internal potency" (*yoga-māyā*).[105] Shortly thereafter, hearing that the amorous and passionate love of the cowherd maidens freed them of all material attachments, Parīkṣit asks: "O sage, the *gopīs* knew Kṛṣṇa only as their lover, not as the Supreme Absolute Truth [*brahmatayā*]. So how could these girls, their minds caught up in the waves of the modes of nature, free themselves from material attachment?"[106] To which Śuka replies: "You should not be so astonished by Kṛṣṇa, the unborn master of all masters of mystic power, the Supreme Personality of Godhead, for, after all, the entire world is liberated by him."[107] Prabhupāda's *mahāvākya* strengthens such responses and does so with utmost economy. While Rādhā, his personified pleasure potency, is not directly named in the Bhāgavata, the divinity of Krishna's foremost lover is also ensured, not only through Prabhupāda's theologizing but by prefixing her name with the reverential *Śrīmatī* whenever she is mentioned in his commentary, *rāṇī* (queen) adding further majesty. Thus he used "Śrīmatī Rādhārāṇī" instead of "Rādhā" or "Rādhikā."

This contrast—between the embraceable, forest-ensconced deity of sweetness and the awesomely opulent Godhead—is the tension upon which Prabhupāda's *mahāvākya* trades. Depending upon the context, it seesaws between the two. When eternal pastimes (*līlā*) are its focus, or when the text speaks of Krishna's practical and personal involvement in a devotee's life, the stress is on "Krishna"; when divine attributes or divine functions are its concern, it stresses "the Supreme Personality of Godhead."[108] As one moves to the foreground, the other retreats. But this back-and-forth motion goes nearly unnoticed. The two are so intimately united that neither is ever really absent. Their union is so well established, their presence in Prabhupāda's writings so ubiquitous, that when either is literally absent, the other is automatically understood.

One is reminded that the Mīmāṁsā demand that a *mahāvākya* serve a single purpose is achieved when its parts share three prerequisites: *ākāṅkṣā* (mutual expectancy), *yogyatā* (compatibility), and *sannidhi* (proximity). Or as Soskice

---

105. *bhagavān api tā rātrīḥ śāradotphulla-mallikāḥ / vīkṣya rantuṁ manaścakre yoga-māyām upāśritaḥ* // SB 10.29:1.

106. *kṛṣṇaṁ viduḥ paraṁ kāntaṁ na tu brahmatayā mune / guṇa-pravāhoparamas tāsāṁ guṇadhiyāṁ katham* // SB 10.29:12.

107. *na caivaṁ vismayaḥ kāryo bhavatā bhagavaty aje / yogeśvareśvare kṛṣṇe yata etad vimucyate* // SB 10.29:16.

108. In discussing Krishna's *līlā* and his involvement in the life of a devotee, Prabhupāda often uses simply "Krishna" without appending "the Supreme Personality of Godhead"; see Prabhupāda's summarized "science of *bhakti-yoga*," *The Nectar of Devotion*. Yet he invokes "the Supreme Personality of Godhead," usually without directly mentioning "Krishna," during Chaitanya's instruction to Sanātana Gosvāmin on the subjects of *śakti* and *avatāra*; see CC 2 ch. 20.

suggests about metaphor: "a form of language use with a unity of subject-matter and which yet draws upon two (or more) sets of associations, and does so, characteristically, by involving the consideration of a model or models" (49).[109] When "Krishna" and the English equivalent to *bhagavān* are juxtaposed, each is strengthened in a way that neither on its own would be. To say "Krishna is the Supreme Personality of Godhead" is to bring together the host of associations and related models affiliated with the *mahāvākya's* two primary elements, while nevertheless speaking of only one true subject. It offers, as Soskice would have it, "two ideas for one."

Prabhupāda has effected a marriage of the two that leaves little scope for either doubting Krishna's divinity or puzzling over the divinity's vagueness. In doing so, he has been unable to avoid what Soskice and others, including Radhakrishnan, would judge to be a naive realism—an unsupportable one-to-one coherence between description and reality.[110] Bimal Krishna Matilal, at the outset of his study of classical Indian theories of knowledge, however, has seriously questioned whether such judgment of any well-reasoned perception is fair:

> Naïve realism is not really naïve. To describe a philosophic doctrine as naïve is at best misleading and at worst false. We may however understand the expression 'Naïve Realism' as a proper name rather than a descriptive phrase. To avoid anomaly, some philosophers have suggested the expression 'Direct Realism'.... We may be better advised to omit the term 'naïve'. (1986:1)

My intention here is to provide a sense of how Prabhupāda's thought is likely to be interpreted by different communities. It is not my purpose to determine the exact status of Prabhupāda's theological position. I merely wish to sound a cautionary note against the facile labeling of a system of thought that has philosophical sophistication and has been ably defended, at least within India, during centuries of debate.

In advocating a position of critical realism, Soskice joins others such as Sallie McFague and Ian Barbour in accepting that metaphors and models can be reality depicting as long as they do not claim to be exhaustively descriptive.

---

109. Soskice distinguishes metaphor from model: "model and metaphor, though different categories and not to be—as frequently they are by theologians—equated, are closely linked; the latter is what we have when we speak on the basis of the former" (1985:55). See n. 36 above for my use of "model."

110. I include Radhakrishnan here based on his view of Vaishnavism as conceptually limited. Madhva, for example, is criticized for transferring the distinctions of this world to the kingdom of God; see Minor 1988:40.

For McFague (1982), a metaphorical theology will be "open-ended," "tentative," "indirect," "iconoclastic"—demythologizing, by breaking the hold of idolatrous literalism. For Soskice, a model or metaphor's "vagueness" is particularly vital to extending its meaning and possibly its life, and to ensuring against it degrading itself by "vulgar anthropomorphism" (1985:149).

As Soskice herself acknowledges, any view, including these, is tied to the experiences of a particular linguistic community with its history of shared assumptions. In the above views, for example, one senses that it is the biblical heritage warning against worship of images that "makes it not only possible but necessary that in our stammering after a transcendent God we must speak, for the most part, metaphorically or not at all" (1985:140). Ian Barbour concurs: "The biblical prohibition of graven images or 'any likeness' (Exodus 20:4) is both a rejection of idolatry and an acknowledgement that God cannot be adequately represented in visual imagery" (1990:45)—nor, by extension, in literary description.[111]

How are we to understand this in the light of Pāñcarātra theology?[112] Vaishnava praxis is entwined with this theology, which asserts: A mantra designates a deity, and a deity has tangible form. In fact, "Deities have three forms (*mūrti*): as personifications (*devatāmūrti*); as symbolic diagrams (*yantramūrti*); and as sound (*mantramūrti*)" (Gupta 1989:230).[113] In Pāñcarātra, there is no hedging about their correspondence—deity: mantra: form (1:1:1).

In speaking of *mūrti,* Sanjukta Gupta is not speaking here of "likeness." In *Darśan,* Diana Eck draws the following definitions of *mūrti* from Apte's Sanskrit-English lexicon: "anything which has definite shape and limits," "a form, body, figure," "an embodiment, incarnation, manifestation." She concludes, "the *mūrti* is more than a likeness; it is the deity itself taken 'form'" (Eck 1985:38).

Many find such an alliance of "form" and "spirit" profoundly troubling, which could explain why some feel a discomfort with Gauḍīya theology generally and

---

111. On Gauḍīya Vaishnava theology of image worship in the context of the general Jewish prohibition against idolatry, see Kṛṣṇa-Kṣetra 2001.

112. An early sect devoted to Vishnu that initiated members from all social groups and both genders. The sect's Āgamas (texts concerned with specifying ritual procedures) contributed to standardizing the worship of sacred images and the recitation of mantras. The Pāñcarātra (and the movement connected with it) is difficult to date, but its antiquity can be judged by its close association with the *puruṣa-sūkta* of the ur-Veda; see Dasgupta [1922] 1975 3:12.

113. *Mūrtis* may also have multiple "lives." Their interesting "biographies" contained in Davis 1997 illustrate how their ontological status is valorized by the interpretive communities with which they come in contact. For a discussion of Vaishnava understandings of *mūrti,* see Narayanan 1996.

with Prabhupāda's *mahāvākya* specifically. Prabhupāda's disciple Ravīndra Svarūpa Dāsa helps to focus the issue:

> This sort of concrete depiction of God, of course, leads critics, whether of Western or Eastern extraction, to charge those who uphold it with projecting mundane ideas onto spiritual nature. Our response is to assert that Kṛṣṇa's form is not anthropomorphic; rather, the human body is theomorphic, modelled on the veritable spiritual form of God. But the other side balks at the notion of "spiritual form" or "spiritual body." The idea strikes them as an oxymoron. They have been habituated in understanding spirit as something in abstraction from, or in opposition to, what is concrete and specific—as something remote, in particular, from the body and its senses. (1985a:77)

This is not the place to launch a comparative theory of the history of religions or any other discipline. If it were, however, then a good place to begin is for present scholarship to give up its role of cultural agency in deprivileging concrete theism as idolatry. As Joanne Waghorne remarks, "It is not enough to say simply that a Judeo-Christian heritage made the study of 'idols' difficult. The axioms and methods of both disciplines [anthropology and history of religions] have been as intellectually iconoclastic as any hammer in the hand of an image-smashing prophet" (1985:2).

Whether depiction of the deity takes "shape" in sacred image or sacred sound or written word, the embodiment of divinity in India has in many traditions been literally understood. Without such an understanding, the appeal of the many Gauḍīya Vaishnava models would not be the same. Krishna's multiple roles in Vṛndāvana as friend, son, and lover, and his numerous other relationships through his expansions, including the overseer Supersoul of all conditioned souls, compare favorably with and also extend McFague's "God as mother, lover, and friend of the world as God's body."[114] Using her terms, Prabhupāda's models are "open-ended," but they are not "tentative," "indirect," "iconoclastic." Their literality, their "vulgar anthropomorphism" (Soskice), is at the core of their relational quality. Krishna's father and mother and his particular cowherd friends and lovers are roles for the faithful aspirant to emulate—not to become.[115] Individuality is preserved. In the "drama" of *bhakti* the scripting is open ended, but the parts

---

114. These are the basic relational models developed in McFague 1988.

115. Prabhupāda explains: "As it is an offense to consider oneself to be Krishna, so it is offensive to consider oneself to be Yaśodā, Nanda or any other associate of the Lord" (NOD 206).

of Krishna and of his devotee are not roles discarded when the curtain comes down. It is "a drama on which the curtain never falls; the Vraja-līlā is eternal" (Haberman 1988:37).

These favored models, embellished, as Soskice suggests, "by the glosses of generations," constitute the world specific to Prabhupāda's Gauḍīya tradition of interpretation. Their richly descriptive vocabulary, tied as it is to sacred texts and the faithful's experiences, is neither arbitrary nor dispensable. As McFague acknowledges, "Since theological models are hierarchically ordered and interrelated, changes in subordinate models have the potential both of enhancing and endangering the status of the root metaphor" (1982:110). This is a critically important comment, for if the root metaphor of a religion is lost, so is the religion.

Summary and Reflections

I have labored long over this discussion of Prabhupāda's *mahāvākya*, "Krishna, the Supreme Personality of Godhead." Its working hypothesis has been that mining Prabhupāda's root metaphor would help make known the content and nature of his theological contribution in terms of the tradition's principal subject, Krishna. It is hoped that such a focus has been suggestive of the integrity and ontological scope of Prabhupāda's system of thought.

As expected, it is not in outright doctrinal originality that Prabhupāda makes his mark, but through creativity in the area of preservation and transmission. His genius is in appropriation, a creative retaining and reshaping, ensuring that the latter both guarantees and extends the former. His predecessors had used the *mahāvākya's* Sanskritic equivalent to assemble subordinate images, citing it on occasion, but when not, still allowing its hidden strength to reconcile contradictions and guide their arguments. Recognizing its untapped potential, Prabhupāda steps up the *mahāvākya's* utility through translation and by constant repetition, and harnesses its mantralike force. The resultant revelation communicates ultimate reality in a manner that uniquely bridges the Gauḍīya tradition and its newly found audiences. This is a considerable achievement.

With his chief ontological assumption that Krishna is the Supreme Personality of Godhead in place, we are ready to consider some of the transformative practices of Prabhupāda's living theology. To speak of Krishna, the Supreme Personality of Godhead (*bhagavān*), is to speak of his devotee (*bhāgavata* or *bhakta*) and devotional service (*bhakti*), the means by which one comes to love Krishna. It is here, in his implementation of the principles of *bhakti*, devotional service—where the full range of customs and values are culturally transmitted—that Prabhupāda has been credited with making his most obvious and innovative theological contribution.

5

Bhakti, Devotional Service: Abhidheya

THE MODERN THEORIZATION of *bhakti,* predicated on the definition "devotion to a personal deity," appears tailored to complement Prabhupāda's *mahāvākya,* "Krishna, the Supreme Personality of Godhead." *Bhakti* as *abhidheya* (in a formal argument, the "means" by which it proceeds) is here the means of gaining Krishna.[1] The second *prameya,* or object of valid knowledge within our traditional tripartite schema (*sambandha-abhidheya-prayojana*), *bhakti* as *abhidheya* is the process linking the *sambandha,* "Krishna," to the ultimate goal, the *prayojana,* "Krishna consciousness" or Krishna *prema.*[2]

The connections go beyond the procedural formalities of textual argument. The close linguistic and theological affinity between *bhakti* and the *bhāgavata* (a term signifying both deity and the devotee) invariably means that to speak of one leads to speaking of the other. Having just deliberated on the *sambandha,* "Krishna, the Supreme Personality of Godhead," exploring the range of subjects denoted by *abhidheya*—*bhakti's* characteristics and the modes and functions of its execution—follows naturally.

Our interest, of course, is Prabhupāda's share in the discussion. If, as is often the claim, Hindu tradition "is not one which emphasizes orthodoxy so much as it does *orthopraxis,* correct practice" (Hopkins 1983:118), Prabhupāda is less likely to

1. Prabhupāda translates *abhidheya* with the sense of "activity in relationship to the Lord" (CC 1.7:146P), though the term normally conveys the meaning "what is signified." Stuart Elkman notes that Jīva Gosvāmin "qualifies the term with the expression *vidheya-saparyāya,* i.e., 'in the sense of something to be performed'" (Jīva Gosvāmin 1986a:73 n. 2). According to MMW, *saparyā* means "worship, homage, adoration"; specifically, *vidheya-saparyāya* is "worship, devotion, etc. that is to be performed," which is the implication in Prabhupāda's translation of *abhidheya* as "activity in relationship to the Lord."

2. See CC 2.20:124–125. Chaitanya offers Sanātana Gosvāmin an overview of *bhakti:* see CC 2 ch. 22. *Prema,* the *prayojana,* is normally translated as "love" or "affection." "Krishna consciousness," while by no means a translation of *prema,* is suggestive of the *prayojana's* specific connotations within Prabhupāda's theology. It must be the subject of further research.

make original contributions in the praxis-rich area of *abhidheya* than we saw him make in the realm of *sambandha*.

We may be surprised. As doctrinally conservative as Prabhupāda is, I predict that to ensure the success of his mission he will be forced by the cultural divide that separates his audience from the Chaitanya tradition to take theological risks in the province of *abhidheya* that he would not have dared to in the sphere of *sambandha*. Historically, in the larger picture, this would be in keeping with the spirit of *bhakti* in the movements it shaped. We had occasion to briefly compare Chaitanya's audience with Prabhupāda's. For either audience, *bhakti*, unless subversive to authority, would not have been as accessible as it proved to be. At the same time, as Frederick Smith has noted, "one of the interesting characteristics of *bhakti* doctrine and movements is an ambiguity, bred of a corresponding tension, between embracing the past and breaking away from it" (1998:22). I anticipate that Prabhupāda will exploit "tradition as a modality of change" (Waldman 1986) for all its ambiguity. In doing so, we may expect him to forge a future by legitimizing a reenvisioned past while simultaneously subverting it.

Influence of Pan-Indic Conceptions of Bhakti

To properly locate Prabhupāda's expression of Chaitanyaite *bhakti*, it may help to first have a sense, however general, of some issues important to scholars within the broad sweep of *bhakti's* pan-Indic influence, which bear on Chaitanya Vaishnavism and Prabhupāda's own particular conception of *bhakti*. Karen Prentiss's work, *The Embodiment of Bhakti* (1999), provides certain thematic categories useful for our purposes.[3] As with any other subject of study, separating out scholarly constructions is easier said than done. This immediately beomes apparent when we look at our opening definition of *bhakti*—"devotion to a personal deity"—a meaning popular even today and, to repeat, one easily linked to Prabhuapāda's *mahāvākya*.[4] Its monotheism bespeaks communities with shared interests—nineteenth- and early twentieth-century Orientalist scholars and Christian missionaries—who viewed monotheism historically as the ultimate religious development and crafted their definition of *bhakti* accordingly. "Fulfilment" theologians like Prabhupāda's professor, W. S. Urquhart, considered *bhakti* as at best nascent monotheism.[5] But many appreciated the "*bhakti* movement" as one of reform, heightened feelings,

3. Prentiss offers an excellent overview of current and past trends in *bhakti* scholarship in her introduction and in part 1 of her book.

4. For current examples of this pervasive phrase, see Prentiss 1999:215 n. 22; for its approximation in English-language dictionary entries, see 213 n.1.

5. See chapter 3.

and social mobility, on a parallel with Protestant Christianity.[6] For others, *bhakti's* monotheism amplified their sense of ancestry, already prefigured in Indo-European language connections. In short, whether explained as modern sectarian reform or ancient idea, borrowed from outside or indigenous to India, the definition "devotion to a personal deity" enjoyed the peculiar cross-cultural ambiguity of defining *bhakti's* monotheism while at the same time serving its European observers as a means of self-understanding and self-presentation.[7]

In addition to its monotheism, the definition's Orientalist agenda privileges an image of God with attributes (*saguṇa*) and possibly betrays a Vaishnava bias. This representation is strongly criticized as artificial and exclusionary by Krishna Sharma, author of *Bhakti and the Bhakti Movement* (1987). Her thesis is to be noted if for no other reason than the importance, in a negative sense, assigned to Chaitanya Vaishnavism.[8] Why, she asks, must *bhakti* be treated as "a specific religious mode…[as] a belief and an attachment to a personal God" (1987:ix)? Rejecting this monolithic approach as a modern construction of Western Indologists, she argues for a more generic definition hospitable to diverse *bhakti* movements and their devotees. In fact, the accommodation Sharma seeks is now a reality. Current scholarship both locates *bhakti* within regional contexts and acknowledges the validity of approaches to a God without attributes (*nirguṇa*).

Still, some scholars find an inherent contradiction, theoretically and practically, between the terms *bhakti* and *nirguṇa*.[9] While the *saguṇa-nirguṇa* distinction in recent *bhakti* scholarship may have replaced the more unitary Orientalist definition, not all scholars agree that it is helpful or well founded. A. K. Ramanujan observes:

> All devotional poetry plays on the tension between *saguṇa* and *nirguṇa*, the lord as person and the lord as principle. If he were entirely a person, he would not be divine, and if he were entirely a principle, a godhead, one could not make poems about him.… It is not either/or, but both/and;

6. Harvey Cox's and Larry Shinn's descriptions of ISKCON indicate that *bhakti's* Protestant image is alive and still healthy; see chapter two.

7. Halbfass 1988 is still the most trusted reference on the dynamic nature of the encounter between India and Europe.

8. A *saguṇa*, monotheistic representation could equally apply to Śaiva-*bhakti*, as in time it did. But this took place later, after a Vaishnava-based definition of *bhakti* was already well established; see Sharma 1987:201–254 for detailed argumentation.

9. On the contradictory nature of *bhakti* and *nirguṇa*, see the chapters by Staal and O'Flaherty in Schomer and McLeod 1987. The entire volume indicates the extent of current scholarship focused on just one *nirguṇa* tradition. Not that the *nirguṇa-saguṇa* distinction was entirely lacking among Orientalists; see Prentiss 1999:21 and n. 23.

myth, *bhakti*, and poetry would be impossible without the presence of both attitudes. (1984:212, quoted in Prentiss)[10]

Our previous chapter's findings certainly seem to confirm this. The correlative terms *saguṇa* and *nirguṇa* are yet another way to explain the tension in "Krishna, the Supreme Personality of Godhead." In Prabhupāda's words, "The Lord is *saguṇa* by His own internal potency, but at the same time He is *nirguṇa*, since He is not in touch with the material energy" (SB 3.7:2P).[11]

Here, a word again to remind us of our purpose: We are looking at these scholarly representations of *bhakti* for the ways in which they intersect Chaitanya Vaishnava understandings, particularly Prabhupāda's *bhakti* perspective. A questionable element in Sharma's attempt to unravel the *saguṇa-nirguṇa* conundrum is to assign paradigmatic importance to Chaitanya and his school of Vaishnavism. "No other religious tradition," she contends, "is so vehemently opposed to the ideology *of advaita-vāda* and its impersonal conception of God. In no other religion, is the antipathy to the path of *jñāna* so noticeable, and dependence on mere emotion and faith, so complete" (1987:255). And, she adds, ISKCON has maintained this legacy, never compromising the personal aspect of the deity Krishna (263–264 n. 4). In her view, Orientalists beginning with H. H. Wilson chose the particular beliefs and practices of the Vaishnavas of Bengal as the archetype for constructing their universalized definition of *bhakti*.[12]

Wilson was one of the first Western scholars to characterize *bhakti* in terms of unfettered emotionalism, a view that is no longer so generalized, but even today finds support, judging by Sharma's specific comment about Chaitanya Vaishnavas. The lingering stigma of unbridled emotionalism is evidenced in Prabhupāda's ongoing censure of heterodox *sahajiyā* groups for their flamboyant disregard of orthodox injunctions. His title "Bhaktivedānta" indicates the tradition's conscious need to counterbalance piety with scholarship.

As Prentiss notes, Orientalist critiques missed the tension that *bhakti* traditions maintain between emotion and intellection, the latter grounding the former

10. For another example of scholarship that objects to the either/or, hierarchically dichotomous casting of *nirguṇa* over *saguṇa*, see Anantanand Rambachan 2001.

11. The ambivalence inherent in describing the Supreme in both/and terms as *saguṇa* and *nirguṇa* is apparent in many Upaniṣads; see, for example, Prabhupāda's translation of and commentary on text 5 of Īśopaniṣad.

12. See Sharma 1987:255–279. While she makes an intriguing claim, assessing its veracity will take us beyond the scope of this study. If one were to pursue it, one might begin by questioning whether other Vaishnava traditions were not equally opposed to Advaitic monism. Or conversely, in what ways Chaitanya Vaishnava theology accommodates it. S. K. De, for one, offers reasons why Chaitanya could not have been as anti-Śaṅkara as depicted by his biographer Kṛṣṇadāsa; see De 1961:151 n. 1.

in thoughtful, conscious reflection (1999:20). Orthodox Chaitanyaite texts, for example, value intellection in determining eligibility (*adhikāra*) for *bhakti*, as here (Kṛṣṇadāsa citing Rūpa Gosvāmin in CC 2.22:67): "One who is expert in logic and in understanding the revealed scriptures, and who always has firm conviction and deep faith that is not blind, is to be considered a topmost devotee in devotional service."[13] The performance (*sādhana*) of *bhakti* is to be cultivated over time. The spontaneous outflow of emotion that results is rarely achieved without arduous practice.

Yet early scholars of comparative religion like Rudolf Otto and Nathan Söderblom denied that *bhakti* involved conscious effort and was a *sādhana* of rigorous practices. As David Haberman points out, Otto, in his enthusiasm to find parallels with Christianity (1929:7), depicted Hindu *bhakti* as offering a salvation "not attained as a reward of our own works, but as a gift of grace, by a saving power above" (quoted in Haberman 1988:62). In Otto's view, to speak of *bhakti* as a *means* was out of the question. Söderblom's definition (1931:104–105) integrates many of the representations of *bhakti* current at the time: "a new path of salvation which does not consist in works, offering, or the exploits of ascesis, nor in knowledge and insight, but in faith, devotion, love towards a living personal deity or savior... Salvation... which is *unmerited, not acquired, but given*" (quoted in Haberman 1988:63, emphasis Haberman's).[14]

Bhakti as *abhidheya*, as a means, went unnoticed by the many influenced by such opinions. Had their comparative project been more linguistically based, they would have recognized that the means and the end of *bhakti* share a common derivational origin, which makes them inseparable. *Sādhana* is the means to attain the *sādhya*, that which is to be attained. Both are derived from the Sanskrit root *sādh*, to accomplish or to attain the goal, to bring something to perfection. Many scholars not only failed to comprehend *bhakti* as a *means* but they seemed equally unaware that for a lot of *bhakti* traditions, it is also the *end*.[15]

---

13. This description of the *uttama-bhakta* (highest devotee) is a citation from Rūpa's *Bhakti-rasāmṛta-sindhu* 1.2:17 (CC). It is followed by descriptions of the *madhyama-adhikārī* (devotee whose eligibility is "second class") and the *kaniṣṭha* ("neophyte" devotee). Knowledge of scripture is a prime determinant of *adhikāra*.

14. "Grace," i.e., God himself as the "means," suggests the "monkey-cat" debate over *bhakti* vs. *prapatti*, which captures the relative importance of "faith" over "works" in the Śrī Vaishnava community; see Fortshoefel and Mumme 1999.

15. Because in the stage of conditioned life *bhakti* is considered eternal though nonmanifest, "means" is really only the attempt to make manifest what is already there; see BRS 1.2:2, cited in CC 2.22:105: *kṛti-sādhyā bhavet sādhya-bhāvā sā sādhanābhidhā / nitya-siddhasya bhāvasya prākaṭyaṁ hṛdi sādhyatā* ("When transcendental devotional service, by which love for Krishna is attained, is executed by the senses, it is called *sādhana-bhakti*, or the regulative discharge of devotional service. Such devotion eternally

The freedom from social and temporal constraints that *bhakti* in some ways affirms was often misinterpreted as moral transgression, though in some cases conflation was warranted. Bengal was rife with sects who, while affiliated to the Chaitanya movement, endorsed heterodox practices. Here it will do no harm to recall Prabhupāda's professor citing H. H. Wilson: "It matters not how atrocious a sinner a man may be... if he die with the words Hari or Kṛishṇa or Rāmā upon his lips and the thought of him in his mind, he may have lived as a monster of iniquity—he is certain of heaven" (Urquhart 1919:434–435). Prabhupāda's and his predecessors' stinging critique of the *sahajiyās*, over against whom Chaitanyaite orthodoxy was measured, must be read in the light of such comments.

In Sharma's view, the imbalance between emotion and intellection among the followers of Chaitanya (which then influenced subsequent understandings of *bhakti*) is traceable to their decision to support their master's mood by basing their theology upon aesthetics, the theory of *rasa*, rather than upon Vedānta, as other Vaishnavas did.[16] Of course, Chaitanya Vaishnavas argue that their theology is Vedānta based, since they accept the Bhāgavata as the natural commentary on the Brahmasūtra.[17] Nevertheless, Sharma is right that emotion is for Chaitanyaites the highest approach to Krishna. Their reality is "a universe of feelings" (Klostermaier 1988).[18] Some would argue that positing Vedānta as normative ideology is as hegemonic as the definition of *bhakti* she seeks to reform. In particular, the implication of her emphasis on the monistic Vedāntic tradition is to privilege a characterization of the emotional complex as the agency of *saṁsāric* transmission that leads to bondage, not liberation. The mind, the ego,

---

exists within the heart of every living entity. The awakening of this eternal devotion is the potentiality of devotional service in practice").

16. See Sharma's extensive "Note A—Bhakti as a Rasa" (1987:283–295). Hers is merely a recent incarnation of an older, eighteenth-century argument, also based on the belief in the authority of the *prasthānatraya* of Vedānta (i.e., the Brahmasūtra, Upaniṣads, and the Bhagavad Gītā), that questioned the legitimacy of Chaitanya Vaishnavism as an independent *sampradāya* because it lacked a Brahmasūtra commentary of its own. To satisfy critics, Baladeva Vidyābhūṣaṇa wrote a formal Chaitanyaite commentary to the Brahmasūtra. For a detailed discussion of this debate, see Jīva Gosvāmin 1986a:25–50 and Wright and Wright 1993. In any case, Sharma's view is questionable. As Edward Dimock notes, "It was impossible for Chaitanya, as it is impossible for any educated man in India today, to escape the influence of the great Sanskrit theological and philosophical tradition; he did not attempt any exception to the rule that one must connect one's thought or system to that of the Vedic and Upaniṣadic tradition in order to have it accepted as authoritative" (1966:72).

17. See chapter 2.

18. Elsewhere Klostermaier remarks, "Chaitanya not only re-instated feeling as a valid way to liberation but developed a hierarchy of feelings—creating in the process a new elite based on feelings rather than on knowledge or on possessions" (1980:97).

the senses—all become suspect. Chaitanya Vaishnava aesthetics, however, entail a positive attitude toward the empirical personality; the aim is the sublimation of emotions, not their elimination.[19]

Given the emotional bent of Chaitanya, or at least his *gosvāmin* followers, we should not be surprised that they sought canonical validation primarily in the Bhāgavata Purāṇa to authenticate their unique approach to *bhakti*. Here was a book that (1) centered *bhakti* on Krishna; (2) presented *bhakti* as a venerable, ancient teaching whose origins predated Krishna's appearance; and (3) established Krishna's life as the cynosure of *bhakti* (Matchett 1993:96). Scholarly examination does not invalidate these Bhāgavata claims. Scholars are largely in agreement that the Bhāgavata's "emotional" Krishna *bhakti* represents a gradual development from a more "intellectual" *bhakti*, whose tacit origins are noticeable, if terms such as *śraddhā* (faith) are considered, in the ur-Veda and Upaniṣads, but which found full expression in the Bhagavad Gītā. As John Brockington has emphasized, the Gītā is only a partial indication of how *bhakti* is indebted to the epics, even if they originally were heroic poems rather than devotionally inspired literature and the Gītā is an interpolation in the Mahābhārata, as he argues elsewhere (1997).

> It is no exaggeration to state that without the two Sanskrit epics, and especially the *Rāmāyaṇa*, the *bhakti* movement could not exist in the form in which we know it. They have provided the source and the continuing inspiration of so many of its most important figures. Not merely are they so familiar in some version to virtually every Hindu that they are part of his or her basic world-view, but they are also the soil in which the flourishing growth of the *bhakti* tradition has taken root and been nurtured (2005).

Along the way, folk religions and non-Vedic worship, but especially the South Indian Āḷvārs, made contributions essential to an "emotional" *bhakti* that did not depend upon earlier notions of karma, *jñāna*, yoga, *dharma*, and *yajña* (sacrifice).[20] Actually, it reworked them.

---

19. For a discussion of how the normative valorization of Vedānta resisted "emotional" *bhakti*, see Hardy 1983:13–17. While offering a concise discussion of Rūpa Gosvāmin's application of *bhakti* as a *rasa*, David Haberman contrasts Rūpa's view of the liberating nature of emotions to Abhinavagupta's aesthetic (tenth century), derived ultimately from the monistic teaching of Vedānta; see Haberman 1988:30–39. For a thorough treatment of Rūpa's aesthetic and its indebtedness to Bhoja (eleventh century) rather than Abhinava, see Delmonico 1990.

20. This line of argument is most clearly drawn by Hardy 1983. Shrivatsa Goswami 1983:205–219 draws a similar line. F. Smith 1998 traces the development of the Bhāgavata's *bhakti* from Vedic and Upaniṣadic origins. See also J. Miller 1993.

Rūpa Gosvāmin's Conception of Bhakti

Bhakti's superiority comes to be defined over against these contending notions. They and the representations of *bhakti* we have looked at thus far—monotheism, *saguṇa-nirguṇa*, emotional-intellectual—crystallize dialectically as the *paribhāṣā-sūtra* of Rūpa Gosvāmin's *Bhakti-rasāmṛta-sindhu*, the Chaitanya Vaishnava tradition's preeminent *bhakti* thesis:[21] "When first-class devotional service develops, one must be devoid of all material desires, knowledge obtained by monistic philosophy, and fruitive action. The devotee must constantly serve Kṛṣṇa favorably, as Kṛṣṇa desires."[22] Prabhupāda's translation of this pivotal verse and his discussion in *The Nectar of Devotion* (his summary study of Rūpa's thesis) directly launches us into the heart of our chapter by circumscribing what Prabhupāda means by *bhakti*.

As we might expect, the definition promotes the form of monotheism we have come to identify with Prabhupāda's *mahāvākya*. *Bhakti's* object is solely Krishna. But Krishna must be understood as the Supreme Personality of Godhead, inclusive of the host of associations discussed above. Prabhupāda's perspective on *bhakti* is therefore quite wide, incorporating Krishna's expansions, abode, paraphernalia, devotees, and so on. And it moves within the spectrum of contrasts from majesty to intimacy upon which his *mahāvākya* trades. Vṛndāvana-Krishna's sweetness and the awesome opulence of the Godhead are always in tension in Prabhupāda's *bhakti* conception.

Prabhupāda unpacks the key concepts of Rūpa's definition. *Bhakti* is "cultivation" (*anuśīlana*), repeated and devoted service, following the predecessor teachers (*ācāryas*). Prabhupāda stresses that *bhakti* is always active and that all activities performed with body, mind, or speech must be in relationship to Krishna. Those that are not should be avoided. Activities that please Krishna and that are performed with a favorable attitude (the twofold sense of the term *ānukūlyena*) are truly *bhakti*. Such activity should be devoid of any other motive or desire (*anyābhilāṣa-śūnya*) and *jñāna-karmādy-anāvṛtam:* must not be covered or obscured by the processes of *jñāna*, karma, and so on (i.e., yoga, *yajña* [sacrifice], or *vairāgya* [renunciation]). Here, *jñāna* indicates "philosophical speculation" leading to "a conclusion of voidism or impersonalism," while karma alludes to all "fruitive activities"—Vedic rituals or, for that matter, any work unfavorable

21. For the BRS with the commentaries of Jīva Gosvāmin, Mukunda dāsa Gosvāmin, and Viśvanātha Cakravartin, see the Haridāsa Dāsa edition (1945). An English translation with extensive notes on these commentaries has been completed through the "eastern division" of the text; see the Bon edition (1965). David Haberman did a complete English translation, *The Bhaktirasamrtasindhu of Rupa Goswami* (2002).

22. *anyābhilāṣitā śūnyaṁ jñāna-karmādy anāvṛtam | ānukūlyena kṛṣṇānuśīlanaṁ bhaktir uttamā* || BRS 1.1:11 cited in CC 2.19:167. For Prabhupāda's discussion, see NOD xxi–xxiv.

to *bhakti* (NOD xxiv). The argument here is not against *jñāna* or karma, but for *bhakti's* superiority.[23] In sum, Prabhupāda's explanation of Rūpa's definitive text, in keeping with Gauḍīya thought, presents *bhakti* as independent of and superior to all other modes of worship.[24]

As a manifestation of Krishna's internal pleasure potency (*hlādinī-śakti*), *bhakti* is innately present in the living entity (*jīva*), whose nature, at least qualitatively, is like Krishna's: loving and blissful. When the living entity receives initiation from a spiritual master and begins to practice serving Krishna, the influence of Krishna's internal potency descends through the disciplic succession (*guru-paramparā*). *Bhakti,* dormant until then, is awakened, and thereby ignorance is dispelled.[25] Although Krishna's pleasure is the sole motive for performing *bhakti,* the *bhakta,* the servant of Krishna, also shares this bliss.

The entire *bhakti* process is compared to the growth of a garden "creeper" (*bhakti-latā*). Starting as a seed planted in the heart by the guru through instructions and initiation, regularly watered by the practice of hearing and chanting Krishna's names and glories, the creeper grows until it pierces the walls of the universe, enters the realm of Krishna's abode, and at last takes shelter of the desire tree, Krishna, and produces the fruit of love for Krishna (*prema-bhakti*). When the ripened fruit falls, the devotee gardener with great bliss tastes the juice of the fruit of love and becomes eternally happy.[26] This is considered the highest perfection of life, dwarfing the four standard aims (*puruṣārthas*) of human existence: discharge of duty (*dharma*), economic gain (*artha*), fulfillment of desire (*kāma*), and liberation (*mokṣa*). *Bhakti* is thus the means and the end, the living being's natural function and highest duty (*para-dharma*). It conduces to the supreme pleasure of both the deity and the devotee.

This clear idea of what Prabhupāda understands by "*bhakti*" differs little thus far from the Chaitanya Vaishnava notion. What then specifically characterizes Prabhupāda's contribution? As with the *mahāvākya,* translation is the fulcrum from which his initiative springs. For Prabhupāda, translating "*bhakti*" is no mere intellectual or academic exercise—it has a practical goal: to engage people with a living spiritual tradition. When searching the semantic register of *bhakti*

---

23. For the Chaitanyaite view of *bhakti* in relationship to *jñāna* and karma, see the discussion in A. K. Majumdar 1969:334–337.

24. Baird's and Herman's criticisms of Prabhupāda for privileging *bhakti* above other yogas should thus be understood as a critique of the orthodox Chaitanya Vaishnava view of *bhakti* rather than of Prabhupāda per se; see chapter 2.

25. For textual confirmation of *bhakti* as an eternal function of the living being, see n. 15.

26. On *bhakti* as a "garden creeper," see Chaitanya's teachings to Rūpa Gosvāmin, CC 2.19:151–164. Extending the metaphor, the devotional creeper is to be fenced off and protected against weeds and wild animals—offenses (*aparādha*) that hinder *bhakti's* development.

for an English equivalent, Prabhupāda is unlikely to select any of E. Washburn Hopkins's suggested synonyms: "It interchanges with all words of deep affection, *prīti, bhāva, rāga, sneha*" (Hopkins 1911:738). These are elevated states of devotion, which the vast majority of devotees may aspire to, but rarely obtain.[27] On the ground, for the neophyte practitioner and among his followers in general, *sevā* is the term that most closely approximates the semantic value Prabhupāda seeks: in a word, "service." This accords with Jīva Gosvāmin's understanding: *Sevā* is said to be the meaning of *bhaj, bhakti's* root. Being its essential characteristic, *sevā* is synonymous with *bhakti*.[28]

The Relationship of Service to Bhakti

For Prabhupāda, *bhakti* cannot be reduced to an emotional state: "Without activity, consciousness alone cannot help us" (NOD xxi). This explains why he does not seize upon the most likely translation for *bhakti*, "devotion." "Devotion" does not necessarily indicate activity. But the binary expression, "devotional service," does.[29] In translating *bhakti* as "devotional service," Prabhupāda's first stress is on activity as service, then on devotion's affective dimensions.

"Devotional service" is a phrase whose ubiquitous presence surpasses the *mahāvākya*.[30] Yet one rarely sees it used by others. The singular coincidence I am aware of occurs in an article by Frederick Smith (1998:27). Intrigued by the exact correspondence, I wrote to Smith, who replied that given his orientation in the Vallabha *sampradāya*, he was probably using the phrase "devotional service to Krishna" as either a translation or explanation for the word *sevā* as Vallabhācārya uses it. According to Vallabha, the essence of Krishna *bhakti* is *sevā*, so by extension "devotional service" also refers to *bhakti*.[31] Considering the close affinity between Vallabha (1479–1531) and Chaitanya, the coincidence is unsurprising.[32]

---

27. For these transcendental features of *prema-bhakti*, see Chaitanya's teachings to Sanātana, CC 2.23:42–43.

28. See Jīva Gosvāmin's *Bhakti-sandarbha*, section 215 (1962). Other synonyms include "worship," "homage," "reverence," "devotion" (MMW, s.v. "sevā").

29. Prentiss's brief history of "bhakti as devotion" is helpful, especially her mention of Charles Hallisey's effort to invest the term with the sense of conscious activity of agents; see Prentiss 1999:22–24.

30. The phrase "devotional service" appeared in the VedaBase 9,172 times.

31. Personal communication with Frederick Smith, October 22, 2001.

32. The *śuddhādvaita* (purified nondualism) school of thought founded by Vallabhācārya "purifies" or "corrects" Śaṅkara's monism by demonstrating that *māyā* is a dependent energy of Brahman (understood as Krishna), and that the *jīva*, while one with Brahman,

Graham Schweig finds in Prabhupāda's thought another, less obvious synonym for *bhakti* in the word *dharma*, normally understood as "religion," "law," or "duty":

> *Dharma* is explained as the essential irreducible quality of the living being, which is *service*.[33] This ontological sense of the word *dharma* as "service" is related to the translation of the important word *bhakti* as "devotional service": When a person's natural inborn quality of service is transformed back into one's original manifestation of service to God, this is called *bhakti*. (Schweig 1998b:96)

Aligning *bhakti* with *dharma* proclaims its universal nature.

Of course, by defining *dharma* as "service," Prabhupāda aligns himself with other modern exponents of Hindu universalism: Swami Vivekānanda, Sri Aurobindo, and Gandhi. On the strength of the Gītā's *karma-yoga* teachings, all three advocate service in a spirit of detachment. Gandhi, for example, having understood the religious significance of service from the childhood influences of his mother and the Vaishnava stories and songs he heard, links service to *yajña* and *mokṣa*.[34] In Gandhi's hands the *Gītā* is transformed into a manual for social service and reform: We serve the Lord by serving others in whom the Lord dwells.

Prabhupāda, however, is extremely critical of appropriating for any purpose or person(s) what he believes rightfully belongs to Krishna. In a letter to Gandhi at the time of India's independence, Prabhupāda introduces himself as Gandhi's "unknown friend" (the letter has a prophetic quality in that it warns Gandhi of an inglorious, untimely death).[35] Prabhupāda candidly tells Gandhi that his services to the causes of independence, Hindu-Muslim unity, and the Harijans have been in vain. Some three decades later, in a conversation with an Indian social worker at which I was present,[36] Prabhupāda, now on his deathbed, was just as relentless: Where does the Gītā say that, "service to humanity is service to God?" *Sevā*, he explains, is offered to a superior. *Dayā* (mercy) is offered to an inferior. *Bhāgavata-sevā* and *jībera-dayā* have different objects: Service is to be offered to Krishna, mercy to the living entity. In the same conversation, Prabhupāda reproaches Vivekananda for confusing the two. Vivekananda's

---

has a relationship with, and hence is different from, Brahman. Revelation is by an act of grace, so Vallabha's system is also known as *Puṣṭi-mārga*, the "path of [nourishing] grace."

33. See Prabhupāda's BG introduction, 18–20.

34. See Jordens 1998, particularly ch. 14, "The Passion to Serve."

35. See Mahatma Gandhi 470712.

36. The social worker was H. S. Dwivedi of Adarsh Seva Sanga of Pohri District, M.P.; see 770424me.bom. See also Tamal Krishna 1998c:14–15.

welfare service slogan, *daridra-nārāyaṇa* (poor Nārāyaṇa) *sevā*, is a misnomer. "How can Nārāyaṇa be *daridra*?" Prabhupāda indignantly demands. The subtext of both letter and conversation are the same: the futility of misdirected service. Satisfying Krishna with the fruits of one's labor alone guarantees detachment, success, and ultimate liberation.[37]

Clearly, Prabhupāda reads the Gītā as a purely *bhakti* text. He often translates *karma-yoga* as "devotional service," "work in devotion," or "action in Kṛṣṇa consciousness"[38] with the conviction that work performed in a spirit of detachment and offered to Krishna will turn into *bhakti*. In this, he is indebted to Baladeva's commentary. Unlike Viśvanātha, a Gītā commentator whom Prabhupāda also follows, Baladeva equates *karma-yoga* with *bhakti-yoga* because one leads to the other.[39] Prabhupāda asserts, "Service for the cause of the Lord is called *karma-yoga* or *buddhi-yoga*, or in plain words, devotional service to the Lord" (BG 2:51P). Prabhupāda further predicates his Gītā reading upon the Chaitanyaite truism, "It is the living entity's constitutional position to be an eternal servant of Kṛṣṇa."[40] In this way, by predisposing to *bhakti* all service done for Krishna, Prabhupāda assures that even the beginner's actions are liberating, an advantage *karma-yoga* cannot offer by Chaitanyaite reckoning.

Another strategy of Prabhupāda's, a rather unlikely one, is to rehabilitate the fading institution of *varṇāśrama-dharma*, India's social and occupational divisions, in keeping with the notion that such *dharma* is liberating if connected to the "Supreme Personality of Godhead."[41] Chaitanya, in fact, considers it external (*bāhya*) to pure *bhakti* (CC 2.8:59) and Rūpa Gosvāmin concurs: it is not a *bhaktyaṅga*, a limb or part of *bhakti* (BRS 246).[42] Still, Bhaktivinoda accords this institution the status of a secondary function of *bhakti* (*gauṇa-dharma*),

---

37. On another occasion, in response to the altruistic appeal *mānava-sevā* is *mādhava-sevā* (service to man is service to God), Prabhupāda counters with an opposite reading: Service to God is service to man; see SSR 182–184. He goes on to unabashedly claim that ISKCON's *saṁkīrtana* festivals in Hyderabad, Delhi, and Calcutta, respectively, have ended a two-year drought in Andhra Pradesh (1972), the war with Pakistan (1971), and the Naxalite (Communist) movement in Calcutta.

38. These phrases occur throughout BG.

39. See Bhūrijana 1997:xxiii–xxiv. Joseph O'Connell points out that while the Gītā is a text closely bound to issues of social duty, Viśvanātha's commentary tends to disassociate work (*karma-yoga*) from public service; *karma-yoga* is distinguished from, though aligned with, *bhakti*. In this, Viśvanātha follows Chaitanya's biographer Kṛṣṇadāsa; see O'Connell 1976a.

40. *jīber "svarūp" hay kṛṣṇer "nitya-dās,"* CC 2.20:108.

41. See SB 1.2:8 and 13. Compare to concepts of *dharma* in broader South Asian contexts; see, e.g., the essays in O'Flaherty and Derrett 1978.

42. On his tour of South India, Chaitanya encounters the Tattvavādin Vaishnavas of Uḍipī, followers of Madhva, who maintain that executing *varṇāśrama-dharma* for Krishna leads

supportive of primary *bhakti* activities.[43] For Prabhupāda, its divisions provide his disciples with the necessary peace and stability to serve Krishna. In the name of *daiva*(divine)-*varṇāśrama*, ISKCON members can justifiably involve themselves in seemingly worldly matters and still derive the benefits of detached action.

In sum, by translating *bhakti* as "devotional service," Prabhupāda infuses *bhakti* with a sense of activity aligned first to the notion of duty and ultimately to the notion of love. "Devotional service" is dialogic, as it points to a partnership. It is "participatory," as *bhaj*, the Sanskrit root of *bhakti*, implies. *Bhakti* is relational, joining *bhakta* and *bhagavān*. A devotee is fulfilled only through devotional service, but Krishna, the Supreme Personality of Godhead, is already complete. Nevertheless, by accepting his devotee's loving service, Krishna becomes still more complete. The Godhead is dynamic, capable of being affected by the interplay of his energies. "Devotional service" is thus a handmaiden to the *mahāvākya*. Devotee, devotional energy, and object of devotion are bound in a tight compact.

By emphasizing "service" Prabhupāda will also decipher the affective dimensions of the *gosvāmins'* elaborate *bhakti* theology. Emotion is central to Rūpa Gosvāmin's aesthetic theory, particularly when characterizing devotional perfection—the stages of *bhāva-bhakti* ("devotional service in ecstasy") and *prema-bhakti* ("devotional service in love of God")—*bhakti's* ultimate goal. Here, because our focus is the stage of *sādhana-bhakti* ("devotional service in practice"), we are primarily concerned with the means for achieving the goal. This chapter concentrates on *vaidhī* (rule-directed) *sādhana-bhakti*, and unless otherwise noted, this is what I am referring to when speaking of *sādhana*. It is the stage of devotional service when "spontaneity" or "passion" (*rāga*) is not yet attained, when service is performed under the guidance of the spiritual master according to the regulative principles of revealed scripture. The final stages of *bhakti* are subjects deserving further research.

Prabhupāda's achievements from the viewpoint of this chapter are particularly tangible. Examining the activities conducted under the rubric of "devotional service" demonstrates, more than any linguistic theories can, the distinctness of Prabhupāda's *bhakti* conception. To this end, we must set apart his translations and commentaries, which largely reproduce the tradition, from the novel and practical manner by which he breathes new life into it. *Bhakti*, after all, is especially about praxis. Practices more than mirror theory. As the dynamic attribute of a living theology, they extend it. Examining some of the prominent innovations

---

to attainment of Vaikuṇṭha (heaven). Chaitanya disagrees; the goal is attaining love of the Godhead, achievable through hearing and chanting Krishna's glories; see CC 2.9:245–278.

43. See Bhaktivinoda [1886] 1983, ch. 2.

Prabhupāda effects through his creative application of the texts should, in fact, help clarify his contribution to theoretical interpretation.

Circumstances favor Prabhupāda's creativity even more than they did that of his predecessors. His Western audiences' radical discontinuity with Indian cultural forms in general, and specifically with Chaitanya Vaishnava orthopraxis, necessitated original solutions that neither Bhaktivinoda nor Bhaktisiddhānta needed to consider. During their times, practitioners were often devout and learned. Many were renunciants. Bhaktivinoda in later life and Gaurakiśora were *bābājīs*, and Bhaktisiddhānta and his principal disciples were primarily *saṁnyāsins*. Sense control, if challenging, was not a stumbling block. By comparison, most in Prabhupāda's audiences lacked the requisite piety, at least in traditional terms, to follow the basic principles of sense control. Yet Prabhupāda did not relax his demands. Disciples were expected to refrain from nonvegetarian food, gambling, intoxication, and illicit sex—the pillars of "sense gratification." This was seemingly impossible for most in his audience, for whom sensual pleasure was life's prime purpose.

Yet Prabhupāda could confidently declare his process easy: singing, dancing, feasting. Reduced to its simplest formula, devotional service does not require the gymnastic rigors of *haṭha-yoga*, the intellectual acumen of *jñāna*, the ritual purity of *yajña*, or the asceticism of *saṁnyāsa*. A well-known verse fragment from the *Nārada Pañcarātra* that supports *bhakti* as actively sense affirming helps explain Prabhupāda's confidence: "*Bhakti*, or devotional service, means engaging all our senses in the service of the Lord, the Supreme Personality of Godhead, the master of all the senses."[44] Turning to its own advantage the Gītā's warning that the senses are the royal path to bondage,[45] this aphorism instead mandates their *proper* use. Devotional service in practice (*sādhana-bhakti*) is further defined as realizable specifically by the senses, not by *bhāva*, the ecstatic emotion it arouses.[46]

Krishna is always to be remembered and never to be forgotten. This simple order and prohibition are the essence of all regulative principles and the primary concern of the guru on behalf of the disciple.[47] Prabhupāda defines his own task

---

44. Cited by Rūpa Gosvāmin in BRS 1.1:12 to support his definition of *bhakti*. Also quoted in CC 2.19:170, from which this translation is taken. In regard to *bhakti* as a sense-affirming activity, one may refer to Kenney and Polling's research on the ISKCON devotee character type as a "sensate personality" reviewed in chapter 1.

45. See BG 2.59–63.

46. *Bhakti* is *kṛti-sādhyā*, realizable or executed by exertion or activity, hence by the senses; see the definition of *sādhana-bhakti* in n. 15 above. See also De 1961:173.

47. This essential injunction, applicable to all, irrespective of *varṇa* and *āśrama*, caste and occupation, is established by a Padma Purāṇa verse cited by Rūpa Gosvāmin in BRS 1.2:8. It also appears in Kṛṣṇadāsa's CC 2.22:113: *smartavyaḥ satata viṣṇur vismartavyo na*

in this connection: "It is the duty of the *ācārya,* the spiritual master, to find the ways and means for his disciple to fix his mind on Kṛṣṇa" (NOD 21). Here, amid these "ways and means," where resourcefulness matters most, Prabhupāda is also likely to be most original.

Rūpa Goswāmin's Five Principal Practices of Bhakti

For Prabhupāda's contributions to be significant, they should be made in those areas of devotional service that Rūpa Gosvāmin considers essential to the practice of *sādhana-bhakti,* essential in that they are the most expedient means to achieve the goal of Krishna-*prema.* Within Rūpa's list of sixty-four items of *vaidhī sādhana-bhakti,* five in particular are so potent, he says, that "even without faith in them, a person who is offenseless can experience dormant love of Kṛṣṇa simply by being a little connected with them" (BRS 1.2:238, cited in CC 2.22:133). Because they can awaken *bhāva,* the preliminary stage of *prema,* these five practices are most important: (1) associating with devotees, (2) chanting the Lord's holy name, (3) hearing the Bhāgavata Purāṇa, (4) residing in Mathurā, and (5) worshipping the consecrated image of the deity.[48]

Beyond their immediate heuristic value, they provide a programmatic blueprint of essential ISKCON praxis. If needed, I shall stretch their boundaries ever so slightly so that we do not miss what is most novel and representative about Prabhupāda's approach. Rather than narrowly focusing as in the previous chapter, a wider angle will allow us to record the diversity of his contribution. The treatment will be more descriptive than theoretical, as the implications of Prabhupāda's involvement are sufficiently clear to require little argument. We will consider each of the five principal practices in turn, first as it is traditionally understood, then by noting Prabhupāda's contribution.

---

jātucit | sarve vidhi-niṣedhāḥ syur etayor eva kiṁkarāḥ || ("Kṛṣṇa is the origin of Lord Viṣṇu [*sic*]. He should always be remembered and never forgotten at any time. All the rules and prohibitions mentioned in the *śāstras* should be the servants of these two principles").

48. This is the order in its most succinct expression, CC 2.22:128: *sādhu-saṅga, nāma-kīrtana, bhāgavata-śravaṇa | mathurā-vāsa, śrī-mūrtir śraddhāya sevana.* For these practices' original order, see BRS 1.2:90–92. For Prabhupāda's discussion, see NOD ch. 13. The list of sixty-four items originally appears in the *Hari-bhakti-vilāsa,* a text on *ācāra* (conduct), traditionally attributed to Sanātana Gosvāmin, but most likely a cooperative effort with Gopāla Bhaṭṭa Gosvāmin; on its authorship, see De 1961:136–143. An appraisal of Prabhupāda's contribution could also be made in terms of the widely known nine types of *bhakti* mentioned in SB 7.5:23: "hearing, chanting," etc.

(1) Association with Devotees: Sādhu-Saṅga

Rūpa specifies association with a devotee who is *sajātīyāśaye snigdhe,* which Prabhupāda translates as "endowed with similar type of affection for the Lord." Rather than an anthropological reference to endogamous groups or subcastes, "*sa-jātīya*" (from *jan,* to be born) in Chaitanyaite hermeneutics connotes a devotional relationship with Krishna shared by a group of devotees (for example, among the *gopīs,* those who personally attend Rādhārāṇī). In the realm of *sādhana-bhakti,* we have the two practitioners of Bhaktivinoda's *Jaiva Dharma* who are advised to seek association with respective gurus whose affection for Krishna is similar to their own. Elsewhere Rūpa explains that association with devotees of a similar mentality allows for revealing the mind and inquiring confidentially (*guhyam ākhyāti pṛcchati*).[49]

Rūpa also specifies that "one should associate with the devotees who are more advanced than oneself" (*sādhau saṅgaḥ svato vare*), which Prabhupāda further glosses as "a pure devotee" (NOD 110) and "the spiritual master" (CC 2.22:131P), and whom Rūpa describes as manifesting *bhāva,* ecstatic emotions (BRS 1.2:241). This may pose a problem. Other than Prabhuapāda, who in ISKCON can offer such association? Looking outside can be risky. Prabhupāda repeatedly warns against association with his godbrothers for fear their instructions will differ from his.[50] Prabhupāda's only solution is to expand the semantic range of Rūpa's definition to include as worthy association anyone strictly following his instructions, or potentially, all the members of ISKCON. *Sa-jātīya* can then be broadly interpreted to include devotees sharing similar services, the same spirit of the mission, or a similar intense desire for Krishna consciousness, and, when they are sufficiently elevated, "a similar type of affection for the Lord."

In Prabhupāda's view, a growing movement like ISKCON "require[s] thousands of spiritual masters to preach all over the world" (660817le.ny). There is no need to import them from India: "Anyone following the order of Lord Chaitanya under the guidance of His bona fide representative can become a spiritual master and I wish that in my absence all my disciples become the bona fide spiritual master to spread Krishna consciousness throughout the whole world" (Madhusūdana 671102). Lest his disciples be considered unworthy, he further clarifies:

> Generally the spiritual master comes from the group of eternal associates of the Lord; but anyone who follows the principles of such ever-liberated persons is as good as one in the above mentioned group. . . . A person who

49. See *Upadeśāmṛta* 4, translated by Prabhupāda as *The Nectar of Instruction* (1975).

50. "So it is better not to mix with my Godbrothers very intimately because instead of inspiring our students and disciples they may sometimes pollute them" (Rūpānuga 740428).

> is a liberated *ācārya* and *guru* cannot commit any mistake, but there are persons who are less qualified or not liberated, but still can act as *guru* and *ācārya* by strictly following the disciplic succession. (Janārdana 680426)

Nevertheless, one wonders whether this fillip to guruship favors quantity over quality. We must recall that Rūpa singled out five practices for their particular ability to deliver *bhāva,* the culmination of the *bhakti* process. Unless Prabhupāda's advent and ISKCON's formation has wrought a new, still more benevolent dispensation, without a leap of faith it is difficult to see how ISKCON members can cross the chasm from *sādhana-bhakti* to *bhāva-bhakti*. Where is the advanced association needed to lead them across? Again, we come to the hermeneutical bridge that Prabhupāda constructed, his liberal interpretation of *sādhu-saṅga,* and his faith that in time his followers will become *bhāva-bhaktas,* pure devotees, and spiritual masters in their own right who offer spiritually elevated, Krishna-conscious association as Rūpa originally intended. Larry Shinn observes that ISKCON and its members' vitality depends on this: "the movement will fare well precisely to the extent that the leaders adhere to the spiritual practices taught by Prabhupāda and have achieved the kinds of levels of spiritual advancement that come with those practices" (1983:100).[51]

There are obvious reasons for the difference between Rūpa's original Sanskrit dictum, which advocates a specific type and level of association, and Prabhupāda's approach, which pins its hope on the transformative power of *bhakti*. For a start, the daunting task Prabhupāda faces in the Western world, with "not a single devotee of Krishna!"[52] At least none who are yet manifest. To remedy this situation he labors to create the environment necessary to arouse *bhakti,* by producing what he calls "authorized" translations of the Gītā and Bhāgavata and by establishing ISKCON, whose articles of incorporation reveal his thinking: "(c) To bring the members of the Society together with each other and nearer to Kṛṣṇa, the prime entity; thus to develop the idea within the members, and humanity at large, that each soul is part and parcel of the quality of Godhead (Kṛṣṇa)" (SPL 2:133). He keeps the common denominators low: an all-inclusive audience (ISKCON

51. After Prabhupāda's demise, there was considerable debate about the level of advancement of ISKCON's senior members. The fall of prominent gurus has led to a steady exodus of members, some seeking pure association from gurus of the Gauḍīya Maṭh or other Chaitanyaite followers, others claiming Prabhupāda alone as ISKCON's sole guru. In response, ISKCON continues to hone its understanding of the guru. A plethora of papers, books, and websites commend respective positions. For positions in ISKCON, a place to begin a search is the archives of http://chakra.org; for other views, http://vnn.org.

52. Prabhupāda repeatedly makes this claim, e.g., to the organizers of India's famed Gita Press; see 710216cc.gor. Blame for the absence of Krishna devotion in the West is directed at unauthorized Gītā translations "creating havoc in the matter of understanding Krishna."

members and humanity at large) and a fundamental, though elementary aim (awareness of the soul's qualitative oneness with the Godhead). In speaking of "humanity at large," Prabhupāda claims for Krishna devotion the same universality that his predecessors championed. They prepared Chaitanyaite *bhakti* to take its place on the world stage. Then history so favored him that for twelve years the stage was his to perform on. Prabhupāda translated the drama they scripted for a multinational, multilingual, multiracial cast and targeted an audience as diverse as any the Bhāgavata foresees: "Kirāta, Hūṇa, Āndhra, Pulinda, Pulkaśa, Ābhīra, Śumbha, Yavana, members of the Khasa races and even others addicted to sinful acts can be purified by taking shelter of the devotees of the Lord, due to His being the supreme power" (SB 2.4:18).[53] In the wake of this Bhāgavata promise, Chaitanya presages universal deliverance: "In every town and village, the chanting of My name will be heard."[54] *Sādhu-saṅga,* association with devotees, is extended like a lifeline to the entire population of this age. Still, it was left to Prabhupāda to make good these assurances. For this, he had to adjust the institutional formulas of Bhaktisiddhānta's Gauḍīya Maṭh.[55]

His guru's missionaries were most often renunciants (those customarily accepted as *sādhus* in India), and they operated against the background of a supportive Indian culture. We have already seen how Prabhupāda expanded the category of *sādhu*. Further, unlike his predecessors, though in keeping with the spirit of *bhakti* in pan-Indian religious history, Prabhupāda also gave women a vital role in his mission, a role they have been able to reclaim only after many struggles.[56] As Frederick Smith points out, "In Sanskrit grammar, *bhakti* is feminine, just as *yoga, dharma,* and *yajna* are masculine. Not just grammatically, however, but substantially, did the rise of *bhakti*... redress the imbalance of the masculine and feminine forces in (official) Indian religion" (Smith 1998:30). Prabhupāda established women's ashrams, gave women *gāyatrī* mantra initiation, made them priests in his temples, and counted many of them among his best preachers. In addition to noting the many ways women contributed, Prabhupāda credited his

---

53. Although some of these races had Indian origins, Prabhupāda locates them outside India: Hūṇas in East Germany and Russia, Pulindas in Greece, Ābhīras stretching from Pakistan to the Arab world, Yavanas in Turkey, and Khasadeśins in Mongolia and China.

54. *Chaitanya-bhāgavata, Antya* 4.126: *pṛthibīte āche jata nagarādi grām | sarbatra pracār haibe mor nām ||*. In a conversation with me, B. R. Śrīdhara (Prabhupāda's senior godbrother) appreciatively admitted that before Prabhupāda established ISKCON, the disciples of Bhaktisiddhānta read this statement in pious wonderment, unable to imagine it ever being fulfilled.

55. For a summary of Bhaktisiddhānta's mission, see chapter 2.

56. See Knott 1995 and Viśākhā et al. 2000. For a history of prominent women of the past in Chaitanya Vaishnavism, see Brzezinski 1995.

movement's success to their magnetic presence amidst the men, nearly all of whom, he reasoned, would not have otherwise stayed.[57]

Endeavors such as this creatively borrowed elements from Prabhupāda's host culture that enabled his followers to successfully operate, even if to do so meant some breaking with tradition.[58] Another example is the role of the guru vis-à-vis ISKCON's ultimate managing authority, the Governing Body Commission (GBC), a move Bhaktisiddhānta anticipated, but which his disciples were unable to effect.[59] Whereas in India the guru traditionally is autocratic, Prabhupāda introduced the GBC as an overarching organizational structure under which gurus must function. This acts as a system of checks and balances, as does its number of members (nearly thirty). While alleviating much of what may happen when someone becomes the sole immediate presence of the divine will, the GBC's overriding managerial authority at times can seem an institutional intrusion into the spiritual line. Especially when compared with previous textual commentaries, Prabhupāda's purports consistently stress the guru's authority.[60]

After forming ISKCON, Prabhupāda rarely associated with his godbrothers. Hence his disciples, while in his presence, had little opportunity to observe his interaction with peers. This lack of positive example may have contributed to their own difficulties in adjusting to such relationships when they themselves became gurus. Instead, they witnessed Prabhupāda's pained and at times harsh response to being deprecated by some godbrothers who considered his managing the complexities of ISKCON as *karma-yoga,* not *bhakti*. Traditionally, Chaitanya Vaishnava *saṁnyāsins* did not, for example, arrange and perform weddings, oversee farming communities, or manage millions of dollars. In spite of being offered the comforts that came with a successful mission, Prabhupāda's life remained regulated by the spiritual practices that were long his habit, further tempered by the self-imposed rigors of his mission. Still, at least in appearance, his way of life was a far cry from Chaitanya's and even Bhaktisiddhānta's, who both considerably stretched traditional limits. Although rankled by his godbrothers' criticism, Prabhupāda resolutely operated under a principle well known to Chaitanyaites: *yukta-vairāgya* (balanced renunciation). Rūpa enunciates: "When one is not attached to anything, but at the same time accepts everything in relation to Kṛṣṇa, one is rightly situated above possessiveness.... [O]ne who rejects

57. Cf. Bhūrijana 1997:250, and a phone conversation with me on October 30, 2001.

58. Elsewhere I have discussed Prabhupāda and ISKCON's wrestle with culture, borrowing from H. Richard Niebuhr's *Christ and Culture*; see Tamal Krishna 2001.

59. For Prabhupāda's view of the Gauḍīya Maṭh's failure to form a GBC, see his letter to Rūpānuga 740428.

60. Lorenz finds in Prabhupāda's purports 89 percent about the guru that is not in previous commentaries; see my chapter 3.

everything without knowledge of its relationship to Kṛṣṇa is not as complete in his renunciation" (BRS 1.2:255–256, cited in CC 2.23:105P).[61] Flexibility in application is the key to an understanding of Prabhupāda's ethic, as he explains:

> It is not necessary that the rules and regulations followed in India be exactly the same as those in Europe, America and other Western countries. Simply imitating without effect is called *niyamāgraha*. Not following the regulative principles, but instead living extravagantly, is also called *niyamāgraha*. The word *niyama* means "regulative principles," and *āgraha* means "eagerness." The word *agraha* means "not to accept." We should not follow regulative principles without an effect, nor should we fail to accept the regulative principles. What is required is a special technique according to country, time and candidate. (CC 2.23:105P)

Prabhupāda reasoned that a proper arrangement for *sādhus* (understood in the widest sense as devotees from all walks of life) would ensure their *saṅga* (association). He encouraged his disciples to wed, build communities, and start businesses, all as a way of promoting constant *sādhu-saṅga*. Because Rūpa's stipulations for the success of *bhakti* include "abandoning the association of nondevotees" (*saṅga-tyāga*) (*Upadeśāmṛta* v. 3), Prabhupāda hoped that ISKCON would provide its members with their entire needs. His approach above all was practical. "We are not spreading a religion," he remarked. "We are spreading a culture."[62] "Cultural conquest," more than a missionary slogan, understood broadly as a total process of spiritualizing activity and its results, was Prabhupāda's way of building a society of devotees.[63]

(2) *Collectively Praising the Divine Names: Nāma-Saṁkīrtana*

Rūpa Gosvāmin's second principle is *nāma-saṁkīrtana,* traditionally understood as the congregational chanting of Krishna's holy names. Grammatically, *saṁkīrtana* is the compound *samyañc* (complete) and *kīrtana* (glorification or description).

---

61. Regarding criticism, Prabhupāda writes, "All along my godbrothers gave me only depression, repression, compression, but I continued strong in my duty" (Gurudāsa 720829). See also CC 2 final endnote.

62. Spoken by Prabhupāda to Bhūrijana Dāsa, as told to me in a phone conversation in November 2001.

63. The transition away from monastic ashram life that has characterized ISKCON demographics since Prabhupāda's demise has often meant that devotee association now occurs in the context of family life, though the temples and festivals continue to function in an essential way; see Rochford 1995 and 1998b and Rochford's personal communication, August 27, 2001.

Rūpa seems to include in his use of the term a single individual's glorification of the name as long as the act is full, that is, loud as opposed to soft or silent repetition (*japa*). He cites the *vīṇā*-playing *bhakti* saint (Nārada) whose singing induces in listeners a detachment from all material enjoyment, a symptom of *bhāva*. But Jīva Gosvāmin defines *saṁkīrtana* as *kīrtana* performed by a number of persons.[64]

Because the theology of the holy name is central to Chaitanya Vaishnavism, all its theologians have lent their weight to its explication.[65] According to Chaitanya (in the first of eight verses considered his sole written legacy), chanting Krishna's name is the most efficacious of all devotional practices:

> Glory to the Śrī Kṛṣṇa *saṁkīrtana,* which cleanses the heart of all the dust accumulated for years and extinguishes the fire of conditional life, of repeated birth and death. This *saṁkīrtana* movement is the prime benediction for humanity at large because it spreads the rays of the benediction moon. It is the life of all transcendental knowledge. It increases the ocean of transcendental bliss, and it enables us to fully taste the nectar for which we are always anxious.[66]

Rūpa and Krishnadāsa both cite the Padma Purāṇa to establish that Krishna and his name are identical:

> The holy name of Kṛṣṇa is transcendentally blissful. It bestows all spiritual benedictions, for it is Kṛṣṇa Himself, the reservoir of all pleasure. Kṛṣṇa's name is complete, and it is the form of all transcendental mellows. It is not a material name under any condition, and it is no less powerful than Kṛṣṇa Himself. Since Kṛṣṇa's name is not contaminated by the material qualities, there is no question of its being involved with *māyā.* Kṛṣṇa's name is always liberated and spiritual; it is never conditioned by the laws of material nature. This is because the name of Kṛṣṇa and Kṛṣṇa Himself are identical. (BRS 1.2:233, cited in CC 2.17:133)

Chaitanyaites give special emphasis to the *mahā*-(great) *mantra:* Hare Krishna, Hare Krishna, Krishna Krishna, Hare Hare, Hare Rama, Hare Rama, Rama Rama,

---

64. See Kapoor 1976:190.

65. For a comprehensive compilation of Prabhupāda's instructions on the holy name, see *Śrī Nāmāmṛta* (1982d).

66. The *Śikṣāṣṭakam* in its entirety is cited at the conclusion of Prabhupāda's Bhāgavatam introduction and recited as part of the daily liturgy in some ISKCON temples. A more literal translation can be found in CC 3 ch. 20.

Hare Hare.[67] It can be chanted by anyone, in any place or condition, at any time (CC 3.20:18). Chanting the holy names awards the benefits achieved with difficulty in past ages by yogic meditation, Vedic sacrifice, and temple worship (SB 12.3:52). Indeed, chanting the holy names is the most important item of devotional service and completes all others (CC 2.15:107).[68] In keeping with Krishna's ontological primacy, it is said that chanting thrice the *Viṣṇu-sahasranāma* (a Vaishnava prayer consisting of one thousand names of Vishnu) is equal to chanting once the name of Krishna.[69] Moreover, while other holy names award liberation, only Krishna's name imparts Krishna-*prema* or Krishna consciousness.

The ultimate purposes of Chaitanya's *saṁkīrtana* mission are to experience and to freely distribute Krishna-*prema*. But *prema* is not easily achieved. Although the physical act of uttering a sixteen-syllable mantra is relatively simple, *prema* arises only in response to invoking the *pure* name (*śuddha-nāma*) of Krishna. For this to occur, the consciousness must first be cleansed of the karmic "dirt" accumulated over countless lifetimes, a process arduous enough to warrant considerable theologizing.[70] There are three stages of chanting: "the offensive stage, the liberated stage, and the actual platform of love of Godhead" (690610sb.nv). Offenses to the name (*nāmāparādha*) must be avoided before a "semblance" (*nāmābhāsa*) of the pure name can be chanted. Auspicious as the clearing stage, *nāmābhāsa*, is—it awards liberation from all sinful reactions—Chaitanyaites consider it only preparatory to the third and final stage of chanting, which produces Krishna-*prema*.[71]

For Prabhupāda, however, the task is more basic. His immediate concern is to get his audiences to chant. This accomplished, he is confident that Krishna's name will do the rest. Not surprisingly, music plays an important role.

---

67. Chaitanyaites commonly refer to two texts in which the *mahāmantra* appears: the Kalisantaraṇa Upaniṣad and the Brahmāṇḍa Purāṇa (Uttara-khaṇḍa 6:55).

68. In a commentary to Rūpa Gosvāmin's BRS 1.2:230, Viśvanātha compares chanting the holy name to other acts of *bhakti*. According to Viśvanātha, of the sixty-four items of devotional service, hearing (*śravaṇa*), chanting (*kīrtana*), and remembering (*smaraṇa*) are primary. Of these, *kīrtana* is again primary. And among *kīrtanas*, the chanting of Krishna's holy names (*nāma*) is most effective—more so than chanting about his form (*rūpa*), qualities (*guṇa*), or pastimes (*līlā*); see edition of B. H. Bon Mahārāj, Rūpa Gosvāmin 1965:229.

69. Rūpa Gosvāmin in his *Laghu-bhāgavatāmṛta* 1.5:354 and Krishnadāsa in CC 2.9:33 substantiate this claim, citing the Brahmāṇḍa Purāṇa. Prabhupāda adds that chanting Rāma's name thrice equals chanting Krishna's name once; see CC 2.9:33P.

70. On theologizing the chanting of the holy name, see particularly Bhaktivinoda's *Hari-nāma-cintāmaṇi* ([1900] 1990).

71. Liberation vis-à-vis *prema* would be central to the larger discussion of *prayojana*. A list of ten offenses to the holy name from the Padma Purāṇa is cited by commentators in BRS 1.2:119–120; for Prabhupāda's translation and brief discussion, see NOD 72 and CC 1.8:24P.

Among the various *bhakti* traditions, the marriage of music and devotion has long been an effective method of presenting and transmitting the mood, or *rasa*, of divine love. We may recall Larry Shinn's comment: "Very much as John Wesley is said to have sung Methodism into England... Prabhupāda chanted Vaishnavism into America and the Western world," and Allen Ginsberg's words, "He and his children sang the first summer through in Tompkins Park."[72] Ginsberg was only the first celebrity to help Prabhupāda popularize the chanting. The psychedelic California bands in 1967, the Broadway musical *Hair* in 1968, and especially George Harrison's release of the devotees' hit single, "The Hare Krishna Mantra," in 1969, with Harrison on organ and bass, and Harrison's own hit, "My Sweet Lord"—made "Hare Krishna" a household word.[73] Technology and Prabhupada's globalization allowed him to popularize his message like no other *bhakti* saint before him.

According to the Indic musicologist Guy Beck, the source of the popular Hare Krishna melodies in Harrison's recordings and in *Hair* is not Bengali *kīrtana*, but tunes Prabhupāda brought from Vraja Vṛndāvana (Beck 1998:136). Beck credits Prabhupāda with overcoming cultural barriers that had made *bhakti* vocal music, unlike Indian instrumental music, largely unknown and unappreciated. An accomplished *kīrtana* musician and singer, even without formal training, Prabhupāda "achieved a firm place within the Bhakti tradition solely on the merit of his contribution to Vaishnava music" (126). Beck isolates Prabhupāda's particular musical contribution: "The genius of Śrīla Prabhupāda is witnessed in his limitation of rhythms to one, so that while the melodic structure may vary widely... the steady rhythm maintains a fixed identity-point for the devotees and listening audiences" (132).

The need for simplification also determines the musical repertoire. In an extensive study of ISKCON *kīrtana* (including *bhajans*, devotional songs), Mi Puyang-Martin observes, "Linguistic knowledge and skill clearly are of secondary importance to faith, attitude, and effort in *bhakti* practice." She goes on to note that the "linguistic barrier of ISKCON devotees is the major cause of the loss of sections of the Vaishnava music repertory" (Puyang-Martin 1996:213, 217). Martin does not ascribe inferior status to or make negative value judgments about the "reduced"

---

72. For Shinn and Ginsberg, see chapter 2.

73. Even at George Harrison's death, the news media continued to associate him with Krishna's name, playing "My Sweet Lord," which ends with the *mahāmantra*, and recounting, among other incidents, a failed, attempted murder, when George called on Krishna's name to ward off the danger. His song "My Sweet Lord," reissued shortly after his death, briefly topped the charts. The memorial services held at ISKCON temples worldwide, an honor reserved for highly respected devotees, is a measure of ISKCON's profound gratitude for Harrison's many services to the mission. See also the tribute paid him in BTG January–February 2002. Harrison discusses how the chanting affected his life in Prabhupāda 1982a.

repertory, since the worship-ritual function, religious significance, and the time and effort spent on music *are* retained. Besides compensating for his disciples' linguistic handicap, Prabhupāda chose to limit the repertory to enhance the importance of selected songs and understate the need for becoming musically accomplished. Linguistic limitations did not prevent Prabhupāda from expecting disciples to try to master a textual corpus replete with Sanskrit technicalities. Had he felt it necessary, he could just as easily have stressed traditional music proficiency. Rather, the few dozen songs he translated and personally recorded circumscribe the range of Vaishnava theology and emotions he wished his disciples to assimilate.[74]

Prabhupāda's guru, Bhaktisiddhānta, is said to have allowed his disciples to sing off key and out of time and to have disallowed the use of the harmonium as an accompanying instrument so as to focus attention on the holy name. Both gurus' strategies reinforce *kīrtana,* and in the larger sense, *bhakti's* transcendent character. Moreover, delimiting the traditional *kīrtana* repertoire is in keeping with Prabhupāda's policy of vernacularism (a common feature of *bhakti* movements), which encouraged creative local appropriations of the tradition. While Prabhupāda's devotional songs are greatly appreciated, their style is rarely duplicated. The proliferation of *kīrtana* and *bhajan* recordings today, original in language, composition, and instrumentation, indicates that for a tradition to survive, it inevitably must adapt.[75] As Martin concludes, having learned elements of Indian language, music, and ritual practice, his followers "have transformed them conceptually and technically into forms that are more easily understood and produced by devotees of Western background" (291).

As Prabhupāda limited the *kīrtana* repertoire, he also minimized individual vows of *japa* (soft, repeated chanting of the *mahāmantra,* usually counted on a *mala,* or rosary of 108 beads). Haridāsa Ṭhākura, appointed by Chaitanya as the *nāmācārya* (preceptor of chanting the holy name), is said to have chanted three hundred thousand names daily. Chaitanyaites are normally expected to chant sixty-four "rounds" (one round being 108 repetitions of the sixteen names of the *mahāmantra*)—only a third of Haridāsa's vow, though an act that can take five to seven hours. Prabhupāda soon found such rigorous discipline beyond his disciples' reach and reduced the vow to sixteen rounds (Hayagriva 1985:63). This decision had profound ramifications, for it freed his disciples for other engagements. In effect, it set ISKCON's future course. In keeping with Bhaktisiddhānta's priorities, ISKCON devotees were to be *goṣṭhānandīs,* those taking pleasure in expanding the fellowship of devotees, not *bhajanānandīs,* those primarily interested in their own deliverance.

---

74. On Prabhupāda depreciating the need for musical expertise, see 690610sb.nv.

75. ISKCON *kīrtana* recordings are available through ISKCON-related websites and "The Hare Krishna Bazaar" in *Back to Godhead* magazine.

Haridāsa recommends chanting aloud (*ucca saṁkīrtana*) to deliver not only the chanter but others who cannot recite the name, such as trees (CC 3.3:68–72). Bhaktisiddhānta seizes upon this notion to create a metaphor for the printing press—*bṛhat-mṛdaṅga,* the big drum—and Prabhupāda follows his lead. Publishing and distributing books are *bṛhat-kīrtana*—bigger, more compassionate, than any other form of *kīrtana,* a path his disciples can easily tread. This propagational aspect of *saṁkīrtana* compounds its sacred significance. Much as a yogic discipline controls the mind and senses, preaching allows even less qualified devotees a means to purify their existence. Preachers are doubly benefited, blessed for the good they do themselves and again for the good they do others. Prabhupāda believes their *kīrtans* "impress spiritual ecstasy in the hearts of the people" (Mukunda 720208). To be able to impart spiritual ecstasy would imply that his preachers are advanced devotees imbued with special potency by loud chanting of Krishna's name. Kṛṣṇadāsa confirms: "The fundamental religious system in the age of Kali is the chanting of the holy name of Kṛṣṇa. Unless empowered by Kṛṣṇa, one cannot propagate the *saṁkīrtana* movement" (CC 3.7:11). What comes to mind when considering Prabhupāda's use of the term *saṁkīrtana,* therefore, is its public dimension, more reminiscent of the street processions organized by Chaitanya and his followers than their indoor *kīrtanas.* Prabhupāda speaks of the "*saṁkīrtana* movement" or "*saṁkīrtana* street chanting," and of the "*saṁkīrtana yajña*" as the recommended sacrifice for this age. A "*saṁkīrtana* festival" takes place whenever a "*saṁkīrtana* party" or a "*saṁkīrtana* group" "loudly performs *saṁkīrtana* congregationally."

Suggestive of Chaitanya's ongoing mission, the term possesses a referential breadth in ISKCON so wide-ranging in its associations that at times one must strain to make the connections. Burke Rochford has traced the undulating patterns of ISKCON's *saṁkīrtana* activities as they metamorphosed from street chanting to book distribution to diverse initiatives of fundraising.[76] *Saṁkīrtana* has become a catchword to sacralize any conceivable act that may fortify ISKCON and thus contribute, however indirectly, to Krishna's glory. Consequently, even the steadiest in their credulity may have some doubts about the rightful limits of interpretation within the parameters of Rūpa Gosvāmin's original meaning.

What redeems such hermeneutics is the sincere spirit of service that underwrites them. Prabhupāda deeply instilled the mood of *sevā,* service, in ISKCON's *saṁkīrtana* ethos. By his reasoning, to the degree that the mood of *sevā* increases, Krishna becomes the center of one's life and one's efforts to inspire Krishna consciousness in others. Advancement in Krishna consciousness directly relates to absorption in both aspects of *kīrtana.* Chanting and distributing the holy name

76. Rochford's *Hare Krishna in America* is discussed in chapter 2.

are mutually nurturant. Thus, however unrelated to *kīrtana* certain activities may appear, the selfless devotion with which they are performed allows them, at least theologically, to be broadly subsumed under the *saṁkīrtana* movement.

(3) Hearing the Bhāgavata Purāṇa: Bhāgavata-Śravaṇa

The third of Rūpa Gosvāmin's principal practices of devotional service relates to hearing the Bhāgavata Purāṇa: "One should taste the meaning of *Śrīmad-Bhāgavatam* in the association of pure devotees."[77] "Taste" plays upon the Bhāgavata's metaphorical self-description (SB 1.1:3) as the mature fruit of the desire tree of Vedic literature, whose already nectarean juice (*rasa*) is further sweetened by Śuka's recitation (in Sanskrit the *śuka* is a parrot, the bite of whose red beak sweetens fruit). Rūpa advises that one "taste" the Bhāgavata's *bhakti-rasa* in association with *rasikas,* experts knowledgeable in the art of drinking this elixir.

As with prior mandates, the problem of levels of association again surfaces. What qualifications make one a *rasika*? Being a "pure devotee," Prabhupāda replies. And what makes the recipient of such association, the listener or reader, qualified? One must "throw out, just like garbage, the fruitive results of ritualistic ceremonies, economic development and becoming one with the Supreme (or salvation)" (NOD 110)—*dharma, artha, kāma,* and *mokṣa*—that is, the results of *yajñas* and yogas other than *bhakti* must be rejected. When it comes to hearing topics of the Bhāgavata's tenth canto, such as Krishna's *rāsa* dance with the *gopīs,* Prabhupāda raises the bar: "Spontaneous attraction" is required.

The *rasikas* include the actual Bhāgavata speakers (or commentators) like Śuka and those who follow him in the disciplic succession.[78] The metaphor of the ripened fruit of the Vedic tree of knowledge is again invoked. Carefully picked and handed down from a person on a higher branch to a person on a lower branch (each representing a link in the chain of gurus), the Bhāgavata fruit, full of *bhakti-rasa,* arrives on the ground unbroken. Ideally, the Bhāgavata should be heard "from the mouth of a self-realised person called *bhāgavatam*" (NOD 105)—a "pure devotee."

---

77. *Śrīmad-bhāgavatārthānām āsvādo rasikaiḥ saha,* BRS 1.2:91, cited in CC 2.22:131.

78. Prabhupāda advises that one not hear from professional Bhāgavata reciters who lack taste for *bhakti* and are not in the disciplic succession. "One should also avoid those who are averse to Lord Vishnu and His devotees, those who are Māyāvādīs, those who offend the chanting of the Hare Krishna *mantra,* those who simply dress as Vaishnavas or so-called *gosvāmīs,* and those who make a business by selling Vedic *mantras* and reciting *Śrīmad-Bhāgavatam* to maintain their families" (CC 2.22:131P).

Reality is often otherwise. I recall my own experience as an uninitiated novice in San Francisco holding forth from the Bhāgavata. My utter unfitness was in glaring contrast to the *bhāgavatam* ideal. On a walk the next morning, I obliquely indicated my unworthiness to Prabhupāda by asking whether there were any pure devotees in the world other than him. "At least seventy-five," he replied matter of factly, that being the combined number of novices and initiates in ISKCON at the time (Tamal Krishna 1984:25). Thomas Hopkins has it right: "No one ever seriously expected to reach his level, and yet he never set that level so far beyond where people were that they would view it as unattainable" (Hopkins 1983:129). Prabhupāda expected his disciples to become *rasikas,* pure devotees qualified by knowledge and conduct to taste and discourse on the Bhāgavata.

The extraordinary length of Prabhupāda's Bhāgavata edition—over sixteen thousand pages in all—results from the fact that in addition to his English translation and expanded "purport" he included the text both in Devanāgarī script and romanized transliteration, along with word-for-word glosses. The academic approval he hoped this would garner cannot be measured in terms of sales to university libraries, considerable as they may be, by dedicated bands of disciples.[79] In actual use, scholars and students have found its inordinate length off-putting.

If the somewhat self-serving motive of having an elaborate edition has backfired, the big edition has been of immense value as an in-house pedagogical tool. Prabhupāda structured its presentation to train his disciples in Bhāgavata discourse in a manner reminiscent of a Bengali *ṭol,* or native school, in which Sanskrit and related subjects are studied. Preceding his Bhāgavata lecture each morning, disciples would responsively read the Sanskrit text aloud one word at a time, then line by line repeatedly, for five to ten times, with different students leading, followed by the glosses and translation read once responsively, and at last Prabhupāda's purport. This method continues today and, while it cannot replace formal Sanskrit training, it does provide devotees insight into the text that they would not ordinarily have through simple translation.

The books are lavishly illustrated. Again, Prabhupāda's entrepreneurial talent is not to be discounted. Along with his own press and publishing house, he created an art department to provide paintings for his books (and temples), an idea he likely picked up from the popular Gita Press publications. There is, of course, a rich interconnected history of Krishna art and literature.[80] But Prabhupāda's immediate predecessors, despite their publishing zeal, apparently saw no

79. The figure of sixteen thousand pages is based on the most recent eighteen-volume edition including indices. The final six were volumes completed by his disciples. Subsidies keep the sizable edition affordable.

80. See Archer n.d. and Banerjee 1978.

advantage in what would have substantially increased costs. Their successor was catering to a far more affluent audience, though to attribute Prabhupāda's enthusiasm for the lavish productions solely to monetary gain is unfair. Compared to traditional, artistically more stylized presentations of Krishna (e.g., Kangra period art), which he feared would be misunderstood by Westerners as "mythological," he directed his artists to a "realism" in the oil-paint medium that he believed more truly represented the "realism" of Chaitanya Vaishnava theology (Ram das Abhiram n.d.:156–157). Paintings appeal aesthetically and are an especially powerful didactic means precisely because they provide both delight and instruction. Prabhupāda is to be credited with this insight, for translating a strange, complex world and its ideas into the realm of enjoyable intelligibility.[81]

In that he made the Bhāgavata so widely available, Prabhupāda's achievement has to be seen as unique. Even considering their subsidization, in terms of sheer numbers, the quantity of literature distributed is unprecedented: an estimated 440 million books and magazines in nearly one hundred languages and dialects.[82] Thomas Hopkins reflects on the significance:

> What few English translations there were of the *Bhāgavata Purāṇa* and the *Caitanya Caritāmṛta* were barely adequate and were very hard to get hold of.... Bhaktivedanta Swami has really made these and other major texts of the Vaishnava tradition accessible in a way that they were never before, and so he's made the tradition itself accessible to the West. This is an important achievement (Hopkins 1983:140).

Similar acclaim is not always forthcoming. The recent Harvard Oriental Series publication of the Dimock-Stewart edition of the *Caitanya Caritāmṛta* follows twenty-five years after Prabhupāda's edition. What Dimock and Stewart's introduction says about Prabhupāda's CC is equally relevant to his Bhāgavata translation:

> The commentary, called here a "purport," is lengthy and used as a vehicle to lay the foundations of basic Gauḍīya teachings aimed at an audience with little or no background in the history of the movement, but who might be inclined to join the group. In this sense, Prabhupāda's translation is very much a vehicle to proselytize—much as the text has been since its initial writing—only to a foreign, rather than local audience; this

---

81. For Prabhupāda's instructions on the value and use of art in education and book publishing, and for detailed instructions to artists, see Prabhupāda 1992b, s.v., "art." For a pictorial survey of ISKCON art, see Ganga 1990.

82. Inclusive of the years 1965–2001. Personal communication, January 31, 2002, with Māyāpur Śaśi Dāsa, editor of the *World Saṁkīrtana Newsletter*.

> is further evidenced by the somewhat unusual methods of distribution which frequently depend on selling copies to people transiting airports, attending large sporting and musical events, and frequenting other social gatherings.... Except for studies of the contemporary Vaishnava communities, the text is not generally cited in academic writing (Kṛṣṇadāsa Kavirāja1999:75–76).

The tone is somewhat dismissive. The implication is that proselytizing somehow diminishes the edition's literary worth, even while it is admitted that the tradition has always used the text in this way. We should recall that the text tradition militates strongly in favor of a particular hermeneutic and reader ethic, neither of which is disinterested.[83] When Prabhupāda's purport has a proselytical slant, so usually does the text. Many have questioned ISKCON's choice of venues and methods of marketing Prabhupāda's books, but here the objection is given a new twist.[84] In the Bhāgavata's case, after its initial printing, only the first two cantos of subsequent print runs were mass distributed, their subject matter being considered more basic than the later cantos. Dimock and Stewart's critique raises the question whether the temple or classroom is sacred space, while an airport or rock concert is not. That Kṛṣṇadāsa's biography of Chaitanya in the first place was written in Bengali (albeit in a heavily Sanskritic Bengali) rather than Sanskrit is a decision that favored accessibility.[85] Monopolizing knowledge by controlling its access can be a form of intellectual imperialism, a neobrahmanical elitism.

Bhakti movements are celebrated for overcoming establishment barriers that inhibit access to privileged knowledge. Equally so, they are known for constructing new barriers of their own. When he ordered the Bhāgavata to be widely distributed, Prabhupāda seems to have defied both hegemonic centers of power. This is especially true of his trilogy, *Kṛṣṇa,* a summary of the Bhāgavata's tenth canto that includes Krishna's *rāsa* dance with the *gopīs.* A well-defined reader's code to the Bhāgavata prescribes right ways of reading, lest Krishna's humanlike acts be misunderstood as worldly. Prabhupāda issues numerous warnings not to approach the tenth canto pastimes until Krishna's role as the Supreme

---

83. See chapter 1 of this work, particularly Clooney's comments.

84. See Rochford 1985 ch. 7, "Airports and Public Places." For the record, in its second printing the CC was not sold in public venues; instead its evangelizing strength was applied to upgrading the devotion of the faithful. This is consistent with its placement as the consummate text in the hierarchy of Prabhupāda's system of study; see chapter 2.

85. O'Connell speaks of "tales of disagreement among the Vṛndāvana Gosvāmins over the pros and cons of making accessible in Bengali the more esoteric and sensitive teachings of the Gosvāmins." It seems that though Jīva was not in favor, Kṛṣṇadāsa's view prevailed; see O'Connell (n.d.).

Personality of Godhead is understood from the previous nine.[86] It requires "spontaneous attraction," he adds. But his *Kṛṣṇa* book strategy flies in the face of such prohibitions, because it invites everyone, irrespective of qualification, to read Krishna's intimate pastimes. George Harrison financed the first printing and penned the foreword, which concluded, "All you need is love (Krishna)."

What made Prabhupāda, normally conservative, transgress such prohibitions? Obviously, time is a factor. He felt uncertain about living long enough to complete all the prior cantos. Krishna's tenth canto pastimes are "the *summum bonum*" of the Bhāgavata.[87] Devoid of them, it is no more than an elaborate setting deprived of its priceless jewel. Believing in the Bhāgavata's supreme efficacy and bearing in mind Rūpa's words that "one should taste the meaning of *Śrīmad-Bhāgavatam* in the association of pure devotees," Prabhupāda went out on a limb and filled the lacuna created by his readers' deficiencies by himself becoming their associate. His skillful retelling of Krishna's pastimes compensates for his readers' lack of knowledge and practice. By its innocence and unobtrusive though essential background materials, it enables them to relish intimate pastimes free of undue sensuality. It is a decision in which compassion seems to have overruled law.[88]

(4) Residing in a Holy Place: Mathurā-Vāsa

We have already covered some of the theological ground needed to appreciate the next of Rūpa Gosvāmin's main principles of devotional service: "residence in Mathurā-*maṇḍala*." The *maṇḍala*, or circle, of the Mathurā district encompasses the entire area of Vraja, inclusive of Vṛndāvana, where Krishna performs his pastimes. The idyllic, pastoral landscape of Vṛndāvana is a cherished setting, supportive in its sweetness (*mādhurya*) of Krishna's flute song, his form, his pastimes, and his devotees' love.

Chaitanya's *gosvāmin* followers, who erected the principal temples and shrines around which the present town of Vṛndāvana has developed, continued the work of their master by recovering Vṛndāvana's sacred sites forgotten over time. They also created an equally impressive sacred literature to further "reveal" Krishna's pastimes and the places associated with them. The life and literature of Vṛndāvana

86. See, e.g., SB 2.2:12P.

87. "The *summum bonum*" appears as a subtitle to the tenth canto in Prabhupāda's edition of SB.

88. For a vivid testimony to the effectiveness of Prabhupāda's *Kṛṣṇa* book strategy, see for example the compelling story of its reading to an elderly mother nearing death in Keśava Bhāratī 1999.

is thus suffused with remembrances of Krishna, made all the more vivid over the centuries by resident devotee ascetics and countless pilgrims.[89]

Vṛndāvana's geography is mapped on three levels. Charles Brooks explains:

> Not only does the word Vrindaban refer to the town located in the cultural and linguistic region of Braj situated on the banks of the Jumna River in present-day Uttar Pradesh, considered to be the location of Krishna's childhood and adolescence, but Vrindaban also is the celestial realm where Krishna eternally conducts his transcendental lilas. Additionally, the ideal state of mind which is properly the goal of every Krishna bhakta is also called Vrindaban. The essential attribute of all these conceptualizations is the presence of the god Krishna and his retinue (1989:27).

S. K. De clarifies: for Chaitanyaites "there is a mystical interlapping of the infinite and the finite, of the phenomenal and the transcendental" (De 1961:335). The celestial may appear to be phenomenal but in fact is not; it only makes its appearance in the phenomenal world.[90]

Nevertheless, the infirmity, disease, and death that one sees in Vṛndāvana can prove confounding. Prabhupāda attempts to sort out one disciple's confusion: "This is not Goloka Vṛndāvana. This Vṛndāvana is a replica, and therefore nondifferent, but because it's manifest in the material universe, the laws of material nature are working here." Present-day Vṛndāvana's apparent squalor is "Krishna's covering. Vṛndāvana appears this way to drive away the atheists and impersonalists, just as New York attracts them.... Vṛndāvana hides herself from a materialist.... It is a question of consciousness. The real Vṛndāvana is there in your own heart, hiding herself from you" (Wheeler 1990:49–53).

The notion of an internal landscape, the locus of mystical experience,[91] is at the heart, literally and figuratively, of Chaitanyaite *sādhana*, particularly

---

89. Chaitanya instructed Sanātana Gosvāmin to excavate lost places of pilgrimage (*lupta-tīrtha*), inaugurate Vṛndāvana temple worship, compile and propagate *bhakti* literature, and establish ideal Vaishnava behavior; see CC 2.23:103–104. For a suggestive overview of the extensive literature detailing the Vraja region and its environs, see Rosen 1992b. Rosen lists scholarly studies, of which Entwistle 1987 is perhaps the most definitive, and separately, ISKCON-related works. See Rūpa Gosvāmin's *Mathurā Māhātmya* (n.d.) for scriptural citations supporting Mathurā's glories. "The continuing creation of Vraja" is the theme of a 1994 conference held in Vraja; see Case 1994.

90. For more on the difference-in-oneness of terrestrial-celestial Vraja, see the chapters by Gelberg, Kapoor, and Brooks in Rosen 1992a. For Jīva Gosvāmin on the subject, see his *Gopāla-campū*, ch. 1, translated by Brzezinski (1992), included as part of Rosen 1992a. Also see Corcoran 1995.

91. "The locus of mystical experience": see the title of Gelberg 1992.

rāgānuga-sādhana. Within the practitioners' minds and hearts, through devotional contemplation, they synthesize the sensorial impressions of earthly Vṛndāvana with the textual descriptions of celestial Vṛndāvana. With practice, the *bhāvas*, or emotions, associated with Vṛndāvana can then be invoked and sustained anywhere, independent of physical "place."[92] Prabhupāda believed the same could be achieved by *vaidha sādhana:* "wherever you remain, if you are fully absorbed in your transcendental work in Krishna consciousness, that place is eternally Vrindaban. It is the consciousness that creates Vrindaban" (Jadurani 670909). This has obvious implications for devotees who may be unable to physically reside in Mathurā, as Rūpa prescribes.

But Prabhupāda also acknowledged the value of physical pilgrimage and made elaborate provisions for devotees to reside in Vṛndāvana.[93] After all, Vṛndāvana is a place where every particle of dust is considered divine, where the spiritual merit accrued in any devotional act is magnified a thousandfold. It is a place, sweet and beautiful, whose mere remembrance, not to speak of actual residence there, evokes *bhāva*.

Our survey of ISKCON-related scholarship included Charles Brooks's study of the effect of ISKCON's presence in Vṛndāvana. Arguably, Vṛndāvana's increased popularity as a sacred site is tied to ISKCON's expanding mission. Brooks offers evidence of the success of Prabhupāda's reverse missionary strategy:

> Today the presence of ISKCON in Vrindaban is obvious even to people who visit for only a few hours. The temple is visited by practically every pilgrim, and many residents go there regularly. Most well-known or well-to-do Indians stay at the guest house because of its reputation for having the best facilities in town (1989:97).

Prabhupāda initially envisioned an "American house . . . for study and promulgation of the Goswami literatures all over the world" (Sripada Nirpen Babu 670427). The Krishna-Balaram Temple complex he eventually constructed and opened in 1975, apart from attracting local residents and pilgrims, serves as the primary base for the second half of ISKCON's annual Māyāpur-Vṛndāvana festival, held in conjunction with the celebration of Chaitanya's advent day (Gaura-pūrṇimā, according to the lunar calendar, generally in March).[94] There is both a *guru-kula* for Indian and foreign boys and an institute for higher education.

---

92. Gelberg 1992 briefly raises this point.

93. Haberman 1994b is a fine account of Vraja pilgrimage.

94. The date coincides with the Vraja festival of Holi, a riotous festival in which colored powders and liquids are thrown and sprayed in remembrance of a similar pastime of Krishna and the *gopīs;* see Marriott 1966.

The escalation of pilgrims visiting Māyāpur, West Bengal, is even more dramatic. After Bhaktivinoda constructed Chaitanya's birth-site temple (Yogapīṭha), Bhaktisiddhānta, his disciples, and theirs built temples that now line the tiny Gangetic peninsula. As the person who purchased ISKCON's original parcel of land in Māyāpur, in 1971, I have seen the number of pilgrims attending the advent-day festival swell from barely a thousand to numbers approaching a million. On an ordinary weekend, there are not less than fifty thousand. For nearly all, the hundred-acre ISKCON world headquarters is the main attraction. Still to be built is the *adbhut mandir* (wondrous temple) that Nityānanda is said to have described to Jīva Gosvāmin,[95] which Prabhupāda conceived of as a domed hundred-meter-high structure incorporating a "Vedic" planetarium.

Chaitanyaites consider Navadvīpa-Māyāpur identical to Mathurā-Vṛndāvana. Hence, Rūpa's advice to reside in Mathurā is equally applicable to Navadvīpa, and, by extension, to New Vṛndāvana (in West Virginia), New Navadvīpa (Hawaii), New Jagannātha Purī (San Francisco), or for that matter, any temple or place where Krishna or Chaitanya is worshipped. Prabhupāda wrote to the founding organizer of New Vṛndāvana: "We should always know that Vrindaban is not localized in a particular area, but that wherever Krishna is, Vrindaban is automatically there" (Kirtanānanda 680523). Later, he said, "Actually, everywhere, wherever Krishna is being glorified, that is Vrindaban" (Kirtanānanda 721027).[96]

Included in ISKCON's original articles of incorporation is this: "To erect for the members and for society at large, a holy place of transcendental pastimes, dedicated to the Personality of Kṛṣṇa" (SPL 2:133). Prabhupāda attempted to realize this objective on three levels: through his centers (especially those like New Vṛndāvana), his books (especially the *Kṛṣṇa* book), and his charisma—a perceived presence as an eternal resident of Vraja. Through these he wished to extend the jurisdiction of Mathurā-Vṛndāvana terrestrially, celestially, and contemplatively over the far-flung regions of his travels.

---

95. See Mahānidhi 1996:264. To view the present and future of ISKCON at Māyāpur, go to http://www.mayapur.org. The founding of ISKCON's temples in Vṛndāvana, Māyāpur, and Mumbai is the subject of SPL 5.

96. For Prabhupāda's initial visit to New Vṛndāvana and many of his founding instructions, see Hayagriva 1985: chs. 16 and 18. On the tensions involved in establishing New Vṛndāvana as a traditional pilgrimage site while accommodating modernity, see Michael 1989.

(5) Serving the Sacred Image: Śrī-Mūrti Sevana

We now come to Rūpa Gosvāmin's fifth main principle of devotional service: "One should have full faith and love in worshipping the lotus feet of the Deity (*mūrti*, or form of the Lord)."[97] Rūpa provides his own verse to illustrate this:

> My dear friend, if you still have any desire to enjoy the company of your friends within this material world, then don't look upon the form of Kṛṣṇa, who is standing on the bank of Keśī-ghāṭa [a bathing place in Vṛndāvana]. He is known as Govinda, and His eyes are very enchanting. He is playing upon His flute, and on His head there is a peacock feather. And His whole body is illuminated by the moonlight in the sky. (BRS 1.2:239, trans. NOD 109)

"Govinda" especially designates the deity Rūpa established in a grand temple at Vṛndāvana, who was later removed to Jaipur in Rajasthan.[98] As Sanātana Gosvāmin's deity, Madanamohana, is said to grant *sambandha-jñāna*, Rūpa's Govindadeva (and Rūpa's instructions) offers *abhidheya*, the opportunity to serve.[99]

In his commentary on Rūpa's verse, Jīva Gosvāmin informs us that praising by way of reproof is a rhetorical device known as *aprastuta-praśaṁsā*. Rūpa's real intention is to eulogize the deity Govinda of Vṛndāvana. Seeing or serving him makes one "detached from all worldly attraction" (*virakti*, one of the nine ensuing circumstances [*anubhāvas*] attendant on *bhāva*).[100] Summarizing another commentator (Mukundadāsa), Svāmī Bon, a godbrother of Prabhupāda's, asserts:

> The very fact that one has come to Vṛndābana bespeaks one's great fortune; and having come to Vṛndābana if one should see Lord Govinda and

---

97. *śraddhā viśeṣataḥ prītiḥ śrī-mūrter aṅghri-sevane*, BRS 1.2:90, cited by Kṛṣṇadāsa in CC 2.22:130. For *mūrti*, see the discussion in the previous chapter.

98. On the history, architecture, etc. of the Govindadeva Temple, see Case 1996.

99. See CC 1.1:47P. I wish to confirm this with a personal testimony. In 1972, residing with Prabhupāda in the Govindadeva Temple in Jaipur, I sought refuge at the feet of Govindadeva and, after crossing what seemed at the time to be insurmountable obstacles, was initiated into *saṁnyāsa* in the deity's presence; see SPL 5:45–49.

100. The nine *anubhāvas* of *bhāva-bhakti* (BRS 1.3:25–61) are discussed in NOD ch. 18. *Virakti* is the superior stage of *vairāgya*, dispassion or renunciation, which Patañjali defines as "the sign of mastery over craving for sensuous objects"; see T. Miller 1995:32, 93. At the stage of *virakti* there is a complete absence of craving (*vitṛṣṇā*), equivalent to Patañjali's *vaśikāra* (perfect subjugation); see Karambelkar n.d.:26–36. Hence there is no need to forcibly separate from the objects of sense pleasure. For Rūpa, true *vairāgya* is that in which all worldly objects are enjoyed without attachment, in relationship to Krishna; see above, the citation from BRS 1.2:255–256.

> thereby lose all attachments for worldly relations, this significantly establishes the possibility of awakening of bhāva-bhakti in one who will see Lord Govinda's mūrti. (Rūpa Gosvāmin 1965:241)

Translated into everyday life, Prabhupāda advises householders to establish the worship of the *mūrti,* or deity form of Krishna, in the home. "This will save everyone from such unwanted activities as going to clubs, cinemas and dancing parties, and smoking, drinking, etc. All such nonsense will be forgotten if one stresses the worship of the Deities at home" (NOD 109).

The *arcā-mūrti,* or sacred image, fuses form to spirit in Vaishnava theology. The highly personalized conception of Krishna that is the trademark of Chaitanya Vaishnavism is given concrete shape, and Krishna's devotee is provided tangible access through the agency of the *arcā-mūrti.* The Lord's external manifestation in the temple, like his internal presence in the devotee's heart, is an expansion of Krishna meant to deliver his devotee. Worship of the Lord's consecrated, three-dimensional image epitomizes *sādhana-bhakti,* a practice performed with one's senses to a Lord who is eminently accessible.[101]

A major textual authority for Vaishnava image worship is the Vaishnava Saṁhitās, also known as the Pāñcarātra Āgamas. Important as their technical details are, Chaitanya Vaishnavas look to their favored text, the Bhāgavata Purāṇa, to provide the basis for the *attitudes* that define the ritual procedures of temple worship. The Bhāgavata's socially liberal outlook extends the possibility of temple worship to all, irrespective of birth.

Like his guru, Bhaktisiddhānta, Prabhupāda was outspokenly critical of birth as the basis for brahminical status and its incumbent duty, the right to perform worship in the temple.[102] Their position dramatically differed from that observed during the time of Chaitanya, who himself maintained caste restrictions when it came to certain social norms related to *arcana,* the ritual worship of deities. Followers of Chaitanya like the Muslim-born Haridāsa as well as Rūpa and Sanātana, Brahmins expelled from Hindu society for associating with Muslims, did not enter the temple of Jagannātha in Purī.[103] No such caste barriers, of course, applied to the most essential item of *bhakti,* chanting Krishna's names.

---

101. For discussion of divine accessibility, see Carman 1994.

102. For their argument on awarding Vaishnavas brahminical status irrespective of birth, see chapter 3 n. 66. Because for Chaitanyaites the Bhāgavata supplants the Vedas in importance, a non-*brāhmaṇa's* right to study the Veda is not an especially contested issue.

103. See CC 2.1:63.

Prabhupāda, his guru, and before them Bhaktivinoda challenged the notion that privileged birth is the basis for *arcana*. The background of nearly all of Prabhupāda's disciples, unlike Bhaktisiddhānta's followers, was non-Indian, non-brahminical, and non-Vaishnava. If Prabhupāda wished to institute temple worship, then importing Indian Brahmins was not in his mind an option. This would deprive his disciples of the essential benefits of personal *sevā* to the Lord.

Women were another factor. They did not serve as priests in Bhaktisiddhānta's temples, nor were there women's ashrams. Prabhupāda parted ways with his guru's institution by authorizing them to serve as temple priests, with one exception: In ISKCON's temples in India, as a concession to local custom, no doubt to gain legitimation, only men worship the deities. Bhaktisiddhānta made a similar concession. Despite his severe criticism of Brahmin elitism, he had only Brahmin-born disciples perform *pūjā* (worship) in Māyāpur.[104]

Prabhupāda was keenly aware that he was taking risks by authorizing neophytes to worship deities, and he tried as far as possible to standardize the system.[105] Jīva Gosvāmin, commenting on Rūpa's warning against *sevāparādha* (offenses while worshipping), lists sixty-nine prohibitions, nearly half from the Āgamas, the remaining from the Varāha Purāṇa; Prabhupāda carefully lists them in his *Nectar of Devotion*.[106] Still, on a trip to Australia, at the time of leaving Sydney, he prayed before the Rādhā-Krishna *mūrtis:* "I am leaving You in the hands of the mlecchas [uncivilized]. I cannot take the responsibility. You please guide these boys and girls and give them the intelligence to worship You very nicely" (SPL 4:206; Kurma 1999:84). Hopkins's observation in this regard is particularly apt: "The one thing that I remember, the thing that I am constantly struck with, was the total confidence with which Bhaktivedanta Swami had people doing things.... His confidence, however, was not in others or in himself exactly, but in Krishna" (Hopkins 1983:133–134). It is likely that Prabhupāda's confidence is primarily based upon his faith in the efficacy of chanting the Hare Krishna *mahāmantra*. Immediately following the injunction to avoid offenses, Rūpa asserts that one who takes complete refuge in Lord Hari is absolved of all offenses. Moreover, "even when a person becomes an offender to the Supreme Personality of Godhead Himself, he can still be delivered by taking shelter of the holy names of the Lord" (BRS 1.2:119–120, NOD 72). Bolstered by this conviction,

104. The contested issue of Chaitanya's birthplace may have been one factor that influenced his decision; see chapter 3 n. 54. Conceding slightly to the conservative Brahmins of Navadvīpa would have won him support for Māyāpur as the actual birthplace.

105. For ISKCON's temple worship with respect to the Chaitanya tradition, see Valpey 2004. Under the supervision of Valpey (Krishna-kṣetra Dāsa), ISKCON published a detailed worship manual; see GBC Deity Worship Research Group 1995.

106. See BRS 1.2:118 with commentary and NOD ch. 8.

Prabhupāda could take risks. But Rūpa goes on to say that the offender to the Lord's holy names "has no chance of being delivered," unless of course the offenses cease. ISKCON devotees often recite daily the ten offenses to be avoided when chanting the holy names.[107]

Additionally, they sing two prayers to Nṛsiṁhadeva, the half man, half lion *avatāra*. One of them is a verse from the *Daśāvatāra-stotra* of Jayadeva's famed *Gītagovinda*.[108] Jayadeva's verse was first introduced by Prabhupāda at the time of an illness (SPL 3:128–129), the other later for the overall protection of ISKCON. Nṛsiṁhadeva removes obstacles, including offenses, on the path of one's devotion. Nṛsiṁha's protective love is like that of an enraged lion sensing danger to its cubs, and his fierce form is a dreadful visage for those harboring enmity toward his devotees. Compared with his worship in Gauḍīya Maṭh temples, in ISKCON he has assumed a place of uncommon importance, equally popular with children, *saṁnyāsins*, and anyone feeling vulnerable. In Prabhupāda's mind, Nṛsiṁha's prominence is justified, because preachers have to face dangers and impediments all over the world and require special protection. There are large deities of Nṛsiṁhadeva installed in Māyāpur, New Vṛndāvana, and Germany.[109]

The awe-inspiring nature of Nṛsiṁha worship is in marked contrast to the inviting intimacy of Rādhā-Krishna *sevā* and may explain in part its muted role in normal Chaitanyaite praxis, which strives to diminish awe and reverence. Kṛṣṇadāsa has Krishna declare, "Knowing My opulences, the whole world looks upon Me with awe and veneration. But devotion made feeble by such reverence does not attract Me" (CC 1.3:16). In spite of this statement, those following the path of *vaidhī bhakti* are enjoined to first worship Rādhā-Krishna in a manner befitting Lakṣmī-Nārāyaṇa, their more majestic expansions. More intimate Rādhā-Krishna *sevā* must wait until one has reached the level of spontaneous devotion.[110]

The Chaitanya Vaishnavas' fixation on Krishna does not appear to have dissuaded Prabhupāda from establishing other deities, even though their majestic features inspire more veneration than intimacy. Rāma, along with his companions

---

107. For the ten offenses to the holy names, see references in the previous note. Bhaktivinoda suggests how each offense may be remedied; see his *Śrī Hari-nāma-cintāmaṇi* ([1900] 1990).

108. For a translation of Jayadeva's *stotra*, see B. Miller 1977:70–71. For the man-lion *avatāra* story, prayers, and theology, especially from a Chaitanya Vaishnava perspective, see Rosen 1994.

109. It should be noted that all three Nṛsiṁha deities were installed after Prabhupāda's demise. Alhough Prabhupāda never prohibited this, during his lifetime public Nṛsiṁha worship was confined to altar photos and prayers.

110. See Madhusūdana 690124.

Sītā, Lakṣmaṇa, and Hanumān, though not perhaps as awesome as Nṛsiṁhadeva, is another ISKCON favorite. Perhaps this is a concession to his popularity among the large Hindu congregations whose financial strength ISKCON often depends on. Prabhupāda recognized that all visitors to ISKCON temples are not necessarily Krishna *bhaktas,* but so long as they remained within the fold of Vaishnava devotion, he facilitated their worship.[111] Other than pecuniary interests seem to motivate Prabhupāda's decision to locate Rāma, the ideal king, near Washington, D.C. More clearly concessionary to the Hindu communities are the Rāma deities in Mumbai and Letchmore Heath, England. In Washington and Mumbai, however, Rādhā-Krishna occupy the ontologically superior central altar (Sītā-Rāma, as per Chaitanyaite belief their *avatāras,* stand to their side; in England their altar is side by side with Rādhā-Krishna's). In fact, this is the case with any *mūrti* other than Rādhā-Krishna in almost all ISKCON Rādhā-Krishna temples (Atlanta and New Mayapur, France, are examples of exceptions).

The most prominent exception is Vṛndāvana, where Krishna and Balarāma's centrality commemorates the divine brothers' pastimes in days of yore, said to have occurred in the neighborhood where the temple stands. There is yet another reason for this particular exception. For those unfamiliar with Chaitanyaite theology (and this includes most pilgrims, many of whom, while Vaishnava, may not know such details), Prabhupāda wished to emphasize that Krishna-Balarāma are identical to Chaitanya-Nityānanda, whose *mūrtis* stand on an altar to their right. (Rādhā-Krishna are to their left.)

The importance Prabhupāda gives Nityānanda *in terms of temple worship* is unique, at least compared with his immediate Chaitanyaite predecessors. All are in accord with the traditional view: "The sacred biographies of Chaitanya repeatedly treat Nityānanda (or Nityānanda and Advaita Ācārya) as next to Chaitanya in divine status and effective influence in propagating Krishna-Chaitanya bhakti in Bengal" (O'Connell n.d.). This notwithstanding, Nityānanda is not part of the single altar in most of Bhaktisiddhānta's Gauḍīya Maṭhs, which usually have deities of Rādhā-Krishna and Chaitanya to express their theological identity. Often, when the Chaitanya deity occupies its own altar, it is joined by a *mūrti* of Gadādhara. In keeping with the Chaitanyaite propensity to link Chaitanya's associates to their counterparts in Krishna's *līlā,* Gadādhara is considered the descent of Krishna's internal pleasure potency.[112] Thus Bhaktivinoda worshipped

---

111. Chaitanya often made such accommodation, e.g., his praise of Murāri Gupta, a Rāma *bhakta;* see CC 2.15:137–157.

112. Nityānanda's counterpart is Balarāma, Krishna's elder brother, which makes it socially unacceptable for Nityānanda to occupy the same altar as his younger brother, Krishna, when Krishna is with Rādhā. In CC 1.1:41 Kṛṣṇadāsa describes Gadādhara as *nija-śakti* (internal, i.e., one's own potency) which is, in 1.10:15, *lakṣmī-rūpā;* Prabhupāda translates

Gaura (Chaitanya)-Gadādhara, simultaneously seeing them as Rādhā-Krishna.[113] Both altar models differ significantly from Prabhupāda's. The only altar where he established Chaitanya-Rādhā-Krishna is in Kolkata (Calcutta). There is none with Gaura-Gadādhara.

With Rādhā-Krishna on a separate altar, Gaura-Nitai (Chaitanya-Nityānanda) is Prabhupāda's deity of choice. How are we to account for this difference? Concealed in this legitimate question is one of still greater magnitude: What precisely is Prabhupāda's relationship with Krishna? The answer has special consequences for *rāgānuga-sādhana*. Do Prabhupāda's wide-scale promotion of Gaura-Nitai worship and the centrality of the Krishna-Balarāma altar in the town Prabhupāda called "home" indicate his belief that he enjoyed an eternal identity as a *gopa*, or cowherd boy in fraternity with Krishna? Or in a tradition that emphasizes conjugal love (*śṛṅgāra*), does his usual arrangement of altars indicate his belief that his own eternal form or nature (*svarūpa*) was a *gopī*-associate of Rādhā-Krishna? Prabhupāda made no definite pronouncement beyond saying, "The spiritual master is always considered either one of the confidential associates of Śrīmatī Rādhārāṇī or a manifested representation of Śrīla Nityānanda Prabhu" (CC 1.1:46P). To enter the already turgid waters that swirl about this issue is to add one more voice to the dissonance.

What is unequivocally acknowledged and theologically supportable is that Prabhupāda's mission was empowered by Nityānanda. For a mission with an outreach as broad as ISKCON's, Prabhupāda's choice of a profoundly merciful deity is easily understandable. Anyone present at Prabhupāda's arrival in ISKCON's Atlanta temple in 1975 will recall how, speaking to devotees assembled before the large Gaura-Nitai deities installed there, he declared: "*Parama karuṇa, pahū dui jana*. Two Lords, Nitāi-Gauracandra, Nityānanda Prabhu and Śrī Chaitanya Mahāprabhu, they are very kind, you see? They have appeared just to reclaim the fallen souls of this age. So they are more kind than Krishna" (750228ar.al).

---

this as "incarnation of the pleasure potency of Lord Kṛṣṇa." In his purport to the latter verse, Prabhupāda cites the authoritative *Gaura-gaṇoddeśa-dīpikā* (1987:147–153) of Kavikarṇapūra, which identifies Gadādhara as Vṛndāvaneśvarī, Rādhārāṇī. Kṛṣṇadāsa further on, in CC 3.7:144, describes Gadādhara's mood (*bhāva*) toward Chaitanya as submissive like Rukmiṇīdevī's, Krishna's chief queen in Dvārakā. Conjectures concerning Gadādhara's identity turn on the differences between Rādhā's unsubmissive mood compared with Rukmiṇī's submissiveness. The distinction did not seem to trouble Prabhupāda, at least not in his cryptic response to my direct, albeit neophyte, questioning. He replies, "Sri Gadadhara is [the] expansion [of] Radharani" (Tamal Krishna 700527).

113. The "Gaura-Govinda-Ārati" song of Bhaktivinoda, after beginning, "As I behold the wondrous *ārati* of my Lords, Gaura and Gadādhara, I enter into the mood of Their existence previous to appearing in Nadīyā (their Vṛndāvana-līlā as Śrī Śrī Rādhā-Krishna)," proceeds to describe the loving pastimes of Rādhā-Krishna; see Bhaktivinoda's *Gītāvalī* ([1893] 1994)

Thereupon Prabhupāda broke down weeping, unable to continue. While Krishna demands that a devotee first surrender (BG 18:66), Nityānanda and Chaitanya make no preconditions for their mercy, a leniency reflected in the less rigorous *arcana* standards for their worship. Gaura-Nitai deities have made their way into such unlikely places as Kabul, Kosovo, Canton, and the Congo.

The bestowal of mercy explains why, for Prabhupāda, deity worship is as much about mission as it is about the purification of the individual worshipper. The famous Krishna deity of paradigmatic grace is Jagannātha, who annually comes out from his temple in Jagannātha Purī to be processionally pulled by teeming multitudes, irrespective of their ritual impurity, in a festival known as Rathayātrā (chariot procession). Prabhupāda conducted this festival on a childlike scale under his father's tutelage. Although from earliest times Jagannātha is known for accepting bodily service from (indeed, is said to be in a kinship relationship with) the *daityas,* who are of tribal origin, the Purī temple forbids ISKCON foreigners, as non-Hindus, to enter. In Prabhupāda's estimation, this is part of Jagannātha's ongoing *līlā,* his gracious desire to go "public" by granting his *darśan* the world over.[114] Consequently, Jagannātha's Western "discovery" by an unsuspecting devotee at an India imports shop in San Francisco and his subsequent elevation from curious craft figurine to full-blown juggernaut can be seen as a modern version of the "appearance" stories common to many famous deities.[115]

Apart from the car festival, Jagannātha is equally famous for the foods prepared and offered to him fifty-six times daily, which he ritually consumes and transmutes into *prasāda. Prasāda* conduces to the devotees' highest welfare, imbued as it is with divine power and grace. Indeed, Chaitanya's biographers delight in proclaiming the excellence of *prasāda* and spare no detail in describing its intricate preparation and the sumptuous feasts partaken of by the master and his companions. Little wonder then that distribution of *prasāda* became a hallmark of Prabhupāda's mission and the "secret weapon" in his preaching arsenal. ISKCON, a "kitchen religion," has shaped itself to the cultural landscapes

114. On all details of the car or chariot festival, see Mahapatra 1994. For a discussion of caste relationships and the worship of Jagannātha, see Marglin 1999. For a dramatic retelling of the deity's and temple's history, see Tamal Krishna 1985. A personal memoir from 1973: My meeting with Indian prime minister Indira Gandhi in New Delhi began by her pointing with some satisfaction to a front-page newspaper headline reading: "ISKCON's Rath Rivals Nelson's Column" (a towering monument in memory of Lord Nelson in London's Trafalgar Square).

115. See SPL 3, the chapter entitled "New Jagannātha Purī." See also Hayagriva 1985: ch. 8. Many of Vṛndāvana's most famous deities are thought to have miraculously disclosed their presence and were then uncovered (Rūpa's Govindadeva is just one example), strengthening the claim of their divinity and enhancing the prestige of those credited with their discovery.

it encounters, from hippie-inspired "Love Feasts" to the programmatic relief for the destitute ("Food for Life") to a chain of Govinda's restaurants. Beyond the sacramental potency of *prasāda*, Prabhupāda is to be credited for recognizing its universal appeal as an instrument of mission.

Concluding Reflections

The five principal practices of devotional service are "so potent that a small attachment to any of these five items can arouse devotional ecstasy (*bhāva-bhakti*) even in a neophyte" (NOD 109). They are the primary means (*abhidheya*) to realize the soul's relationship (*sambandha*) with Krishna, the Supreme Personality of Godhead. Strong faith is not a prerequisite—this, in the light of Rūpa's earlier statement that *bhāva-bhakti* is very rare (*sudurlabhā*) (NOD 14, BRS 1.1:35). In Viśvanātha Cakravartī's opinion, Krishna hesitates to bestow *bhāva-bhakti* because it portends *prema*, by which he is irresistibly controlled. Even if we accept the additional authority that commentators give Rūpa's text—that for these five practices to be fully effective, practitioners must not commit offense to the deity, the holy name, or the Vaishnavas (no small achievement in itself)[116]—the five principles seem especially concessive. Normally for *bhāva-bhakti* to develop, one's sincerity must be proven by an arduous course of spiritual practices starting with *śraddhā* (faith), followed by *sādhu-saṅga* (association with devotees), *bhajana-kriyā* (devotional practices commencing with initiation), *anartha-nivṛtti* (diminishing of unwanted habits), and *niṣṭhā* (firm faith), and culminating in *ruci* (taste) and *āsakti* (attachment to Krishna).[117] The contrast with these seven phases leading to *bhāva-bhakti* make the five main practices seem all the more wonderful. And perhaps it also makes sense of Prabhupāda's optimism: The potency of the five can compensate for his followers' otherwise insurmountable disqualification.

But his confidence has its limits. We see this particularly in his treatment of *rāganuga-bhakti*. In Rūpa's schema, the stage of devotional service in practice, *sādhana*, can be either "rule-governed" (*vaidha bhakti-sādhana*) or "impassioned," that is, "spontaneous" (*rāgānugā-bhakti-sādhana*). They are parallel modes, both paths leading to *bhāva-bhakti*. Obligation and love, however, are very different motivations, and so too the *bhāvas* that arise as a result of each. In an early communication with me, Prabhupāda explains the distinctive destinations of respective practitioners:

> Regarding your second question: what determines whether a devotee goes to a Vaikuṇṭha planet or to Goloka Vṛndāvana? Those devotees who

---

116. See commentaries of Jīva, Mukundadāsa, and Viśvanātha (Rūpa Gosvāmin 1945), BRS 1.2:238.

117. See BRS 1.4:15–16, cited in CC 2.23:14–15. See also NOD 146.

> are following *vidhi mārg* are meant for going to Vaikuṇṭha planets and those who are following *rāga mārg* are meant for going to Krishnaloka. It is generally [*sic*] that the followers of Lord Chaitanya are going to Goloka Vṛndāvana (Tamal Krishna 700621).

We know Prabhupāda's preference. In keeping with the Chaitanya tradition, both his *mahāvākya* and the ways in which he facilitates the five most potent practices of devotional service lead in the direction of Vṛndāvana, a destination, he makes clear, that is achievable only by *rāgānuga-bhakti*. Why, then, in a chapter dedicated to *bhakti* as "means" (*abhidheya*) have I only touched lightly on *rāgānuga-bhakti*?

I alluded to the reason earlier: The strictures of *vaidhī bhakti* provide discernible limits within which Prabhupāda can take risks. We have seen how he stretches boundaries, searches for porosity, and flexes postulates to enhance *bhakti's* already eminent accessibility. While this does not represent outright doctrinal inventiveness, it exhibits the sort of creativity we have come to associate with preservation and transmission, taken up a level, beyond what he creatively does with *sambandha*. He accommodates his audiences' varied backgrounds, interests, and commitments. Their heterogeneity is an impetus to creatively theologize what might otherwise be formulaic assertions. He does all of this with a calm optimism, a confidence, however, that appears to be lacking when it comes to *rāgānuga-bhakti*.

Finally, the affective dimensions of *rāgānuga-bhakti*, and the liberative state that follows, remain unexplored, unexamined, and unexplicated in the way they deserve. This is not because of any theological fuzziness on Rūpa's or Prabhupāda's part. *Rāgānuga-bhakti* is unquestionably a *sādhana*. Its displacement is more a matter of *emphasis* than an ideological break with tradition, an emphasis, I believe, that is in accord with Prabhupāda's, and which places it outside easy reach. Prabhupāda often makes it appear as though *rāgānuga-bhakti* is not the "means" (*abhidheya*), but instead part of the "goal" (*prayojana*). This would help account for the perception, common among scholars, that members of ISKCON do not practice *rāgānuga-bhakti*. The consequences bear directly on "Krishna consciousness," a fluid phrase defining both the existential state in which devotional service is performed and simultaneously the *prema*-filled experience that is its goal. I hope that this study will not only inspire exploration and explication of the richness of *rāgānuga-bhakti*, but further, from Prabhupada's living theology explored here, provide some foundation for continued work on the building of a theology of Krishna *bhakti*.

Conclusion:
Prema, Purest Love: Prayojana

Graham M. Schweig

The Uncontainable Nature of Prema

After writing the first five chapters of his doctoral thesis but before completing its conclusion, Tamal Krishna Goswami suddenly departed from this world. His doctoral mentor, Julius Lipner, attests to Goswami's intention to write a concluding chapter, which would have continued the thematic momentum built into the topics of the penultimate and final chapters—*sambandha* and *abhidheya*. Lipner explains in his introductory words to the edited thesis mentioned earlier in this book's introduction that Goswami "had constructed an impressive edifice for . . . the last chapter—an analysis of *prema*, or love, as the *prayojana*, or goal, of Krishna consciousness from the Gauḍīya point of view." Without such a conclusion, this third and final phase, *prayojana*, remained largely unaddressed.

The absence of a focused discussion on *prema* from the trajectory of Goswami's first five chapters is notable. Likely, Goswami's plans for the publication of his work would have included an expansion of the concluding portion of the thesis into a full chapter on the subject, which would have completed the third and final phase of his theological analysis. I make no pretense to offer here what Goswami would have written; rather, my intention in these concluding words is to complete the framing of Goswami's work begun in this book's introduction, reflecting on *prema* as the *prayojana* of Prabhupāda's living theology.

That Goswami's departure occurred at the point when he was just about to complete his dissertation, when also he was about to embark on a discussion of *prema*, the ultimate goal of Krishna *bhakti*, points to an important aspect of the subject of *prema*. A certain irony arises when Goswami, in the final phase of his life, missed writing about the final phase of *bhakti*. And again, it is telling that

Goswami, during his last pilgrimage to holy places in India, was in the process of writing a chapter entitled, "Dying the Good Death: The Transfigurative Power of Bhakti." Moreover, confirming my own experience, close friends and colleagues with whom Goswami was in contact during his final weeks report that his comments just prior to leaving for Mayapur were unusual, uncharacteristic, as if he had been anticipating that this would be his last pilgrimage to India. He would be visiting not only the movement's world headquarters, but its most sacred location, the land Goswami himself had acquired for ISKCON several decades earlier and where, as per his instructions in his last will and testament, his remains would be entombed. It is as if his Lord were drawing Goswami closer, through the holiest place on earth that celebrates supreme love in the person of Chaitanya.

The events and factors surrounding Goswami's death certainly call attention to a life immersed in *bhakti*. But what specifically stands out is how, for the *bhakta*, *prema* becomes *transfigurative*, to use Goswami's word: how *bhakti* transforms the life of the *bhakta* into something more beautiful and more elevated, which points to the uncontainable experience of a love so pure, so intense, and so intimately connected with the divine that it ultimately becomes impossible for the *bhakta* to remain in this world. Thus death itself, for the *bhakta*, becomes a welcomed phase of life, a passageway through which the *bhakta* attains a divinely endowed eternal life. Of course, it would be absurd to make any judgment of Goswami with regard to his after-death destination or the level of his personal achievements for salvation, and that is hardly what is being said here. Put simply, the coincidence of Goswami's departure just before he was to write about love and death resonates with the idea that *prema* ultimately cannot be contained within the physical body.

I can take this idea of the uncontainable character of *prema* even further. A discussion on *prema*, or a description of *prema*, ultimately becomes impossible, as even language cannot contain it. As the *Bhakti Sūtra* says, "Indescribable is the essential nature of purest love, *prema*."[1] But this is one task of theology, which is precisely to describe that which is normally indescribable. At the same time, theology respects its subject and the revelational sources on which it is based as something that will always remain hidden because of its unfathomable depth and its infinite breadth. The Chaitanya school of Vaishnavism most essentially preoccupies itself with the subject matter of "purest love," or *prema*. It is, very simply, a theology of love. The constant and unending striving to understand and describe this love and its divine revelation has produced one of the most prolific and sophisticated theological traditions of the world.[2]

---

1. No. 51: *anirvacanīyaṁ prema-svarūpam.*

2. Among the many religious traditions in Hinduism, and even among all in India, Klaus K. Klostermaier suggests that "Perhaps the most subtle and detailed system of gradual ascent to God by means of love has been developed in the Caitanya school of Vaiṣṇavism" (1972:765).

Because the indescribability of *prema* is a recurring theme in the works of the tradition, theologians of the tradition want to avoid reducing this ultimate, most exalted and perfect but rarely attained state of love for the divine to something less than what it is, precisely because it is always, in the end, uncontainable: "A person in whose heart *prema* for and from Krishna has been awakened, such a person's speech, action, and manner cannot be understood, even by a realized and knowledgeable soul" (CC 2.23.39). Yet the seven stages, to which Goswami has referred briefly in the last chapter, through which the *bhakta* must evolve before reaching *prema* are carefully enunciated:

> In the beginning there is faith (*śraddhā*);
> from there one comes together with exalted souls (*sādhu-saṅga*);
> now the initiatory rites are performed for offering the heart (*bhajana-kriyā*);
> then the desires for fleeting useless things cease (*anartha-nivṛtti*);
> then one becomes firmly situated in faith (*niṣṭhā*);
> from there one begins to experience a divine pleasure (*ruci*);
> then one develops intense loving attachment (*āsakti*);
> from there one develops a very deep love (*bhāva*);
> and from there one awakens fully to the deepest and purest love (*prema*).
> Of the *sādhakas* in whom *prema* exists,
> it becomes manifest in the progression of these stages of *prema*. (CC 2.23.14-15)

In these stages to *prema,* one can observe a certain progressive strengthening and intensification of the *bhakta's* love in the practice of *bhakti,* which is especially noticeable in the last four stages. Once a *bhakta* reaches *prema,* or awakens to *prema,* the *bhakta* encounters seven stages within *prema* itself, stages that lead up to a state that finds *prema* utterly uncontainable:

> Purest love (*prema*) has its different stages,
> which progressively increase in intensity:
> tender love in *prema* (*sneha*),
> bold love in *prema* (*māna*),
> affectionate love in *prema* (*praṇaya*),
> passionate love in *prema* (*rāga*),
> deeply passionate love in *prema* (*anurāga*),
> very deep love in *prema* (*bhāva*), and
> deepest and uncontainable love in *prema* (*mahābhāva*). (CC 2.23.42)

When *bhakti* evolves into the greater stages of intensity and intimacy in love for the divine, the *bhakta* is one who both simultaneously contains and becomes unable to contain such a heart brimming over with *prema.* Despite its uncontainable nature, the *Bhakti Sūtra* of Nārada says: "Prema is manifest even in whoever can become a vessel to contain it."[3] The continuously experienced tension between God's presence and God's absence everywhere and in everything increases to such a degree that what moves the *bhakta* at such a deep level of the heart also eventually bursts into the outer world of the *bhakta*.

The word *mahābhāva*, meaning "deepest and uncontainable love in *prema*," deserves further attention. It is a compound that most simply and directly means "great [*mahā*] feeling [*bhāva*]." But in this theological context, the two words in the compound have significant resonances and connotations that are important for understanding its meaning. On the one hand, the prefixed word *mahā-*, taken adjectivally, indicates the great or even superlative depth of *bhāva*. On the other hand, the word *mahā* can mean "abundant" or "sacrifice," both words that can point to the uncontainableness of *bhāva*. Additionally, it is important to note that the word *bhāva*, or "feeling," is related to and derivative of the word *bhava*, or "being."[4] The former is an intensified grammatical form of the latter, and thus *bhāva* is commensurately an intensified state of "being," or *bhava*, in which an abundance of feeling overflows from the depths of one's very being into an uncontainable and boundless love.

The compound term *mahābhāva* is most directly associated with the incomparable love that Rādhā has for Krishna, even to the point of exceeding Krishna's love for Rādhā, which then in turn manifests in the person of Chaitanya, who is the very embodiment of Rādhā's incomparable and uncontainable love. Both senses of the greatest depth and the greatest overflowing of the heart's love are the connotative meaning of the term, which most powerfully supersedes all other meanings. Chaitanya's biographies, especially the *Caitanya Caritāmṛta*, relate many instances of Chaitanya's deepest inner communion with the divine when experiencing Krishna's presence and his most intensive and utterly uncontainable eruptions of longing and loving madness when feeling Krishna's absence. Thus *mahābhāva* is technically an extremely rare form of *prema*, virtually reserved only for Krishna's consort, Rādhā, and the *avatāra* of Chaitanya, who embodies the love between Rādhā and Krishna.

Chaitanya's exhibition of this deepest and most uncontainable love in *prema* can be compared to the uncontainable fountainlike eruptions of the geothermal waters from a hot spring, or geyser. Just as the hot waters from deep below the

---

3. *Bhakti Sūtra*, No. 53: *prakāśyate kvāpi pātre.*

4. Note that the difference between the two words *bhāva* and *bhava* is the first "a": the former is the vowel "*ā*" (an *a* with a macron, pronounced like the *a* in the English word "yacht") and the latter is the *a* without a diacritic mark (pronouned like the *a* in the English word "about").

earth's surface must stream up beyond the surface of the earth in an abundant fountain, similarly, Chaitanya, the *avatāra* of Krishna who assumes the form of a *bhakta*, exhibits this highest and rarely attainable form of *prema*, *mahābhāva*. However, for *bhaktas* coming in the lineage of the Chaitanya *sampradāya* there is the opportunity to bathe in the pool of water formed by the spray coming from the effusive geyserlike waters of *mahābhāva prema* rising from the deepest and most uncontainable devotion of Chaitanya.[5] This constitutes an exceptional form of grace for *bhaktas* of the Chaitanya school, a grace demonstrated and recognized by a more private mantra invoking Krishna's descent as Chaitanya, along with his principal associates, which is recited just prior to the sect's central meditational practice of the multiple recitations of the divine names in the form of the widely known and most powerful *mahāmantra*.[6]

The tradition draws from the model devotee who himself could not contain in his body all the love at this highest stage of *prema*, which he experienced and expressed in various ways. Chaitanya is the paradigmatic *bhakta*, known as the ecstatic mystic who could not contain his meditation on the divine names of Krishna merely within the arena of a home or a temple. He was uncontrollably moved by an intense and boundless love to sing and dance in the streets. He was often overwhelmed by the power of *prema* that he experienced when sounding the divine names of Rādhā and Krishna. Chaitanya's most important biography contains a stream of descriptions of instances in which he would faint, undergo seizures, and even experience total bodily disfigurations due to the *prema* in which he was immersed and unable to contain. The person of Chaitanya is the very paradigmatic embodiment of the perfect *bhakta* who helplessly drowns in the ocean of boundless love. Thus the bodily disfigurations of Chaitanya symbolize the uncontainable nature of *prema*.

A theology of Krishna *bhakti* must deal with the paradox of divine love: how it can move and be revealed in language and persons thoroughly and powerfully, and yet also become utterly uncontainable in either verbal expression or physical

---

5. Steven Rosen has directed my attention to a "volcano metaphor," conceived by a twentieth-century teacher of Chaitanya Vaishnavism, Swami B. R. Śrīdhara, to express this uncontainable state of *prema*. The metaphor appears in the Swami's Sanskrit poem "*Prema Dhāma Stotram*," specifically presented in verses 54 and 55, and it is quoted in his poetic rendering of Chaitanya's life, *The Golden Volcano of Divine Love* (1984). The image of a volcano, however, is not necessarily a positive one, while *mahābhāva* not only is positive but is the ultimate and most exalted state in *prema-bhakti*. Therefore the metaphor of a geyser seems more fitting, as it allows for positive imagery, such as the attractive image of bathing in its waters. Indeed, no one desires to bathe in hot lava. People run away from volcanoes, while they run toward geysers.

6. The *mantra* recited prior to the chanting of the *mahāmantra* is the *pañcatattva mantra*, which is worded: *śrī kṛṣṇa caitanya prabhu nityānanda* | *śrī advaita gadādhara śrīvāsādi gaura-bhakta-vṛnda* ||.

embodiment. This paradox is reflected in the Chaitanya Vaishnava school's metaphysical doctrine of *acintya-bhedābheda*, which, put simply, means that the divine is distinct from everything in existence and yet amazingly not distinct from anything existing at one and the same time. Indeed, this doctrine directly mirrors the *bhakta's* experience. For example, so intense was Chaitanya's experience of *prema* for Krishna that he would also experience visions in both wakeful and dream states. When Rādhā and Krishna appeared before Chaitanya, he would swiftly run toward them, and when they vanished or went away, it drove him to such an intensive level of *prema* that it resembled a kind of madness. The more Chaitanya experienced the presence (*abheda*) of Rādhā and Krishna, the more intensely he would experience the excruciating pain of their absence (*bheda*). And the more he would feel their absence the more he would anticipate the intense experience of joyously coming into their presence yet again. This dialectic of experiencing the ever-increasing intensity of the absence and presence of the divine brings the *bhakta* into a state of loving passion, even to the point of loving madness, as Chaitanya exemplified it—a love that is normally uncontainable by the human affairs of this world.

Is There a "Theology" of the Chaitanya School?

Goswami, in this study, charges the word *theology* with great importance and seriousness, despite the associations and connotations, both positive and negative, that the word has carried. Indeed, it is worth underscoring here that our author, as a Vaishnava monk, worked with the Faculty of Theology at Cambridge University in order to discern powerful and compelling theological ideas presented by Prabhupāda that would ignite faith and the practice of Krishna *bhakti* in the minds and hearts of persons born to other faiths. Here, of course, I assume the tacit distinction between "a faith" as a religious tradition and "the faith" of a human being. The former is a word that can be found in the plural, but the latter is singular, denoting a human trait, a constituent, and a universal quality of being, feeling, and acting. A theology that becomes a *living* theology powerfully stirs the faith of humans to enter more deeply into a faith. Goswami sought to understand what elements of Prabhupāda's living theology achieved this, and thus the essential thrust of Goswami's analysis and examination of Prabhupāda's contribution is certainly theological.

It is important to note Goswami's easy employment of the word "theology." His study was to search for the "theological Prabhupāda." Throughout the volume, Goswami, in the ease with which he applies the word *theology*, perhaps appears to take for granted that the word is acceptable within the academic and the devotional communities for explicating Vaishnava thought. The discipline fell out of favor with most of the Western academic world several centuries ago.

It was a discipline that would be exercised only within the Christian community for the sole purpose of articulating its doctrine and tenets of its faith. Unlike other disciplines, theology was not an intellectual pursuit that entailed moving beyond the boundaries of the particular to the far reaches of the universal, going beyond the religious tradition that it served to look at all the data or information that could be considered "theological." This activity was more likely to be found in the phenomenological study of religion rather than theology.

Moreover, the term *theology* is simply not used by Western and Indian scholars or practitioners of Hindu traditions to describe the vision of the divine and ultimate reality. The English term *philosophy* has always been applied by Western and Indian scholars when they speak about Indian thought, despite the fact that Indic religion is clearly theological rather than merely philosophical. This has certainly been the case for practitioners of Krishna *bhakti* within ISKCON: Vaishnava thought is considered *philosophy* and not *theology*, if the latter word would even have any meaning for the members of the movement. Furthermore, the word *theology* would be unattractive to practitioners of Indian religion because it has been seen as the exclusive domain of Christian thought. But more importantly, it is a discipline that is seen as a very subjective and doctrinally closed system, without relevance to anyone outside of the tradition—a system that appears to be idiosyncratic and metaphysically baseless. While there is no doubt that the Chaitanya school engages philosophical approaches and tools in the service of its theological explications, the employment of the word *philosophy* was perhaps to reinforce what was perceived as universal tenets or truths of what was fundamentally theological in nature.

Theology in the West, over the past few decades, has been experiencing something of a rebirth and dramatic growth. It has begun to emerge and continues to grow into a discipline that speaks beyond an application for Christian traditions, a discipline that is even becoming more accepted by the academy. Christian theologians of the twentieth century have begun to see that a more sound theology must acknowledge the existence of other religious traditions and thus incorporate a comparative dimension. As David Tracy says, "A comparative theology in a particular tradition will insist on theological grounds that religious pluralism in the contemporary situation must receive explicit theological attention." He further says that "[a]ny theology in any tradition that takes religious pluralism seriously must eventually become a comparative theology" (1989:454).

The word *theology*, applied by Western scholars to non-Christian traditions, identifies discourses on the nature of their faith. Originally, before Chrisitanity existed, the word first appears in the Greek. And even after Christian traditions adopted the word, the history of the theological discipline since its early Christian applications has shown that, as it developed through time, it took on more types of intellectual tasks and became broader and broader in what its discipline incorporated. This elasticity of the word would anticipate its employment by someone like Goswami, who speaks freely of a Vaishnava theology.

Theology certainly has been and is being pursued by traditions other than Christianity, and here I am specifically speaking about such pursuits among Indic traditions. Just in the past century, the word *theology* has been applied to traditions outside Christianity by Christian thinkers. Perhaps the first time that a specifically Vaishnava tradition was regarded in the West as a serious and sophisticated theological tradition can be observed in the work of the German Lutheran theologian Rudolf Otto, in his book *India's Religion of Grace and Christianity Compared and Contrasted* (1930). And perhaps the first time the word was boldly applied by a Christian in the title of a serious scholarly work focusing on Vaishnava thought was when John B. Carman published *The Theology of Rāmānuja* (1974). Both these books focused on the specific Śrī Vaishnava tradition that had originated with the South Indian religious thinker Rāmānuja in the twelfth century.[7] According to Western Christian scholars, then, theology is a discipline in which Vaishnava traditions have engaged. Recently, Francis X. Clooney has made a case that Hindu traditions should identify their articulations of faith as specifically *theology*, in his notable chapter entitled "Restoring 'Hindu Theology' as a Category in Indian Intellectual Discourse" (2005). And now, currently, it can be said that serious and rigorous theological scholarship is being produced by contemporary Western Vaishnavas of the Chaitanya school.[8]

Is *theology*, then, a term by which the Chaitanya school of Vaishnavism should be identified? If theology is what can be basically understood from the etymology of the word itself, namely, a field of study that focuses on "the divine" (*theos*) and all "discourse" (*logos*) that articulates it, then yes; if theology concerns itself with the nature and existence of the divine and ultimate reality and the human relationship to it, then certainly yes; if theology is most fundamentally and necessarily grounded in the understanding of verbal revelation, and if it

7. Over the past few decades, the word *theology*, either in its forms as a noun or adjective, has found its way into various studies on Hindu traditions in general and into studies on the Vaishnava traditions specifically. For example, Jose Pereira in *Hindu Theology* ([1976] 1991) applied the word *theology* to Hindu traditions in general, and Guy Beck did the same, and focused on Vaishnava traditions in particular, in *Sonic Theology: Hinduism and Sacred Sound* ([1993] 1995). The works of two other scholars from a Christian background who have engaged with the word *theology* specifically in regard to Chaitanya Vaishnavism come to mind: Hein 1976 and Klostermaier's innovative article, "*Hṛdayavidyā*."

8. For examples of Western Vaishnava scholarhip, see Deadwyler 1996 and 2001, Edelmann 2012, Gupta 2007, and Valpey 2006.

seeks a view to salvation or the ultimate perfection of human life, then yes. And if it reveals and seeks the undistorted messages of divine revelation and if it functions to clarify and critique the religious tenets of a religious institution by bringing its doctrine more in line with such verbal revelational sources, then yes. Again, it is obvious that the field of theology is fundamentally different than that of philosophy, even though the English term *philosophy* is always applied in its place in India, intending to mean what I have meant here by the word *theology*. In spite of this displacement of terms, let us then simply declare that there is and has been a long and elaborate tradition of theology in the Chaitanya school of Vaishnavism, and thus it is no wonder that Goswami makes his inquiry for this work theological.

At the present time, as Vaishnava practice and thought continue to gradually blossom in the West and in key places around the globe, perhaps its tradition owes a debt to Christian development of theology and the Western study of religion, as they have assisted modern Vaishnava theologians in the further illumination of their faith through the evolved examples of Christian theology and interfaith encounters. This sharing of theological tools and visions has been one great virtue of the Hindu-Christian interfaith dialogues that have been occurring over at least the past two decades. Goswami participated in some these.

Goswami's project was not only to search for the theological Prabhupāda but also to establish some groundwork for building a contemporary systematic theology of Krishna *bhakti* for ISKCON. Since Prabhupāda did not equip the movement he established with specifically a contemporary systematic theology, Goswami perceived the lack of theological definition and clarity among the practitioners within ISKCON, who often struggle to find their way through the many, many volumes of translated text and commentary, recorded lectures, compilations of correspondence, anthologies, and so on. As both an academically and traditionally trained theologian, Goswami prepares the way for a systematic theology by making use of a theological palette that engages with current intellectual approaches: namely, those of history, philosophy, philology, the study of religion, even psychology, and so on. While Goswami engages with the available and useful intellectual fields for illuminating Prabhupāda's contributions, as good theology does, he does not subject the theology of Krishna *bhakti* to testing by secular knowledge or reduce it to that form. While theology will always make use of the scholarship of the time, it will also preserve and retain some of the theological approaches of its tradition. This practice is evident in Goswami's prominent engagement in his work with the three principal phases of practice in Krishna *bhakti: sambandha, abhidheya,* and *prayojana*. It is these three elements that I wish to expand further for gaining an overarching view of Chaitanya theology.

Three Foundational Sacred Texts

Prabhupāda's living theology is founded on the sacred texts that he translated into English from the Sanskrit and Bengali, scriptural writings to which he would give extensive commentaries. Goswami has drawn out the two pervasive *mahāvākyas* that run through Prabhupāda's translations and commentaries, and he offers ingenious analyses of the depth and significance of their theological meanings and implications. Given Prabhupāda's advanced age and wavering health, the three primary scriptural writings that Prabhupāda carefully selected and the specific order in which he presented them is significant.

Any theology of Krishna *bhakti* that comes through ISKCON must begin with Prabhupāda's literary presentation of the sacred texts coming from the earlier Chaitanya Vaishnava tradition, the tradition he was transmitting anew outside of India, first to the Western world. Each major work that Prabhupāda presented formed a kind of theological anchor for ISKCON, and thus it is important here to identify first the three revelational texts and discuss their essential value in building the theology of Krishna *bhakti* that Prabhupāda delivered. Next, it is important to grasp how they contributed essential and ultimate revelations of *prema,* the final stage of *prayojana* for Prabhupāda's theology and the traditional Chaitanya school.

The Bhagavad Gītā, the Bhāgavata Purāṇa, and the *Caitanya Caritāmṛta* are the three essential sacred texts that build a powerful theological edifice for ISKCON. They function as ISKCON's *prasthāna-trayī,* "the three foundational [theological writings]."[9] Prabhupāda made great sacrifices to produce translations and elaborate commentaries for each of these works, and each of the three received an abridged version that was published before production of the complete text and comprehensive commentary.[10] Although Prabhupāda produced many other

9. This phrase, *prasthāna-trayī,* meaning "the three foundational [texts]," is originally found in Vedānta, where the three groups of foundational writings are the Upanishads, the Bhagavad Gītā, and the Vedānta Sūtra. I borrow the term here and apply it specifically to ISKCON's three foundational writings to convey the authoritative weight these texts have for the community.

10. It is interesting to note that very shortly after Prabhupāda established ISKCON, he first produced short versions of these three texts: a much-shortened version of the Bhagavad Gītā; then a two-volume set summarizing and paraphrasing the tenth book of the Bhāgavata Purāṇa, entitled *Kṛṣṇa: The Supreme Personality of Godhead;* and a volume summarizing the *Caitanya Caritāmṛta,* entitled *Teachings of Lord Caitanya.* His interest in expeditiously producing ISKCON abridgments or a collection of the most important selections from these foundational texts before he could provide the complete versions of these works expresses both an urgency that Prabhupāda felt in transmitting these works as essential sacred texts and the weightiness that each of these three foundational texts possessed within the tradition that Prabhupāda represented.

smaller works, none has the theological presence and foundational authority that we find in any one of these three unabridged works. Indeed, around these three sacred texts, all other writings revolve, either by supporting them or by drawing from them in a vital way, or both.[11] Furthermore, these three specific works represent and contain the tradition's core theology of love, *prema*. When taken collectively, they build the tradition's exoteric and esoteric visions. They contribute different but overlapping and complementary revelations of the divine. And they express, at the core of each sacred text and collectively, what is at the very heart of the tradition's practice and way of life. These three principal revelational texts correspond to the three categories of *sambandha, abhidheya,* and *prayojana.*

The Bhagavad Gītā was one of the very first sacred texts to be presented by Prabhupāda. It was already one of the most widely read sacred texts in the world, having inspired well over one hundred translations or renditions by the time Prabhupāda produced his. He produced this work in 1968, only a few years after he arrived in America. But the Bhagavad Gītā was most often presented by non-Vaishnava schools of thought. In effect, Prabhupāda, with the publication of his translation, reclaimed it as a Vaishnava text when he presented it with his extensive commentary drawn from previous Vaishnava teachers. The practice and perfection of *bhakti* is most boldly presented in Prabhupāda's commentary and brought out in the verses themselves.

It is no wonder that Prabhupāda rushed to get the Bhagavad Gītā out first for the society he was building. The essential theological thrust of the Gītā constitutes the first, or *sambandha,* phase of Krishna *bhakti,* namely, the establishing of the relationship between the self and the divine. In fact, nowhere do we find such a preponderance of Krishna's voice relative to the length of the whole text, or even the sheer number of verses devoted to Krishna's words. Out of the approximate 700 verses of the Bhagavad Gītā, 585 contain Krishna's voice, which amounts to over 83 percent of the total text. It is the voice of the divine, as Krishna, who beckons souls to come to him. Indeed, in no fewer than 22 verses, Krishna expresses his desire for souls to come to him in various places dispersed throughout the text.[12]

---

11. There are other books that Prabhupāda himself wrote, and other books that have been compiled while he lived and posthumously in his name—often transcriptions of his lectures, talks, and interviews. Additionally, there are books that comprise the massive collection of his letters written mostly to his disciples, mostly individually and at times collectively. While there is much valuable material in these works that can shed further light on theological subjects, none, I would argue, can match the level of authority and ultimacy of the *Bhagavad-gītā As It Is,* the *Śrīmad Bhāgavatam,* and the *Śrī Caitanya-caritāmṛta,* all published by the Bhaktivedanta Book Trust.

12. See the chapter entitled "Krishna: Intimate and Infinite Divinity" (259–272) in my *Bhagavad Gītā: The Beloved Lord's Secret Love Song* (2007), especially 266 and n. 10.

In effect, these verses ultimately constitute a divine call to souls, ever beckoning souls to come to him. It is Krishna who is renowned as the deity who calls souls, especially by the music he makes on his flute. In fact, the most famous images of Krishna are of him directly gazing at the viewer while gently smiling and holding a flute to his mouth. We learn of this love call especially in the ultimate passage of the Bhāgavata Purāṇa known as the Rāsa Līlā, but in the Bhagavad Gītā, Krishna's love call takes the form of a song, or specifically a *gītā,* that attracts souls to him through the poetic and philosophical verses he speaks in intimate conversation with Arjuna. The ultimate message of the text occurs when Krishna expresses in the final chapter of the text a divine yearning that he has for all souls, which Krishna clearly expresses with the words "the greatest secret of all" and his "supreme message."[13] It is through Krishna's divine yoga that he embraces souls in various ways with his various divine, cosmic, and natural manifestations, and even by his personally manifest presence within the hearts of all beings, as he waits an eternity for souls to return the embrace. This reciprocated embrace of the soul for the divine is in essence what the yoga of *bhakti* is. What begins as a cosmic embrace becomes elevated into the intimate embrace between the soul and the divine as ideally exemplified by Krishna and the Vraja Gopikās—which is most celebrated in the second of the tradition's most treasured sacred texts.

The Bhāgavata Purāṇa, a text that was hardly known in the West (except by a few scholars who specialized in Hindu traditions), was presented by Prabhupāda because it is deemed the ultimate sacred revelation of Krishna's divinity. Prabhupāda had already published the first three volumes of the first book of the text in India before coming to the United States, but he was unable to complete the work. This work, comprising twelve books and having a total of 335 chapters among them, was almost completed by Prabhupāda, up to the fourteenth chapter of the large tenth book, after which point he passed away. It was his disciples who completed the remaining, untranslated 77 chapters of the tenth book and the eleventh and twelfth books. In this work of many thousands of pages, as he did with the Bhagavad Gītā, Prabhupāda brought together important theological information that he had heavily drawn from key traditional commentaries and to which he added his own vision and insights.

The tenth book reveals the much-loved stories of Krishna with those closest to him in his most intimate *līlās,* or divine acts. Among all of them, and among all the stories of the whole Bhāgavata, the five chapters dedicated to the *līlā* of the Rāsa dance are the most important and constitute the ultimate symbol of supreme love, *prema*. The running thread and focus throughout the text is

13. See "The Secret Love Song" in Schweig 2007:272–278.

the nature and practice of *bhakti*, with stories of how various *bhaktas* offer their hearts to Krishna. In this sense, the Bhāgavata represents the *abhidheya* phase of *bhakti*. But the ultimate *bhaktas* are the Vraja Gopikās, the cowherd maidens of Vraja, in the Rāsa Līlā. And the ultimate symbol of *bhakti* is the formation of the Rāsa dance: the cowherd maidens link arms forming a circle around Krishna, who stands at the center, while Krishna duplicates himself multiple times to personally dance with each maiden. This dance of divine love is itself the ultimate vision of *prema* for the tradition. This *līlā* of *prema*, for the Chaitanya school, brings all exoteric *līlās* together to this very point of the Rāsa Līlā, which then itself becomes the gateway into the esoteric visions of *prema* for the school, in which Rādhā, Krishna's dearest beloved, is revealed.[14]

Prabhupāda's theology is grounded within and generated from a very developed theological tradition going back to the sixteenth century, with the appearance of the ecstatic mystic Śrī Krishna Chaitanya (1486–1533 CE). Chaitanya wrote very little. Rather, his role was to provide the ultimate experience or paradigmatic example, life, and vision of devotion for Krishna and his feminine counterpart, Rādhā. Thus the very person of Chaitanya and his life story is divinely emblematic of the state of *prema* for the *bhakti* tradition he inaugurated. And it was Chaitanya's immediate disciples, known as the Six Goswamis, and their disciples, who provided the theological foundations for his lineage. Thus the most important biography on Chaitanya becomes itself the most critical work for forming the very theological basis on which the tradition was to be ultimately grounded, the specific tradition out of which ISKCON came.

That biography of Chaitanya is the *Caitanya Caritāmṛta*, written by Krishnadāsa Kavirāja Goswami in the latter part of the sixteenth century. It was the second major multivolume work that Prabhupāda presented in translation with elaborate commentary. It is important to note that the *Caitanya Caritāmṛta*, along with the significant life events of the person Chaitanya, presents a synthesis of the original key theological works of Chaitanya's immediate disciples, particularly those essential works of the Six Goswamis. It is therefore considered the comprehensive theological work for the Chaitanya school of *bhakti*. It is also no wonder that in the mid-1970s Prabhupāda interrupted his translation of and commentary on the tradition's most important revelational text, the Bhāgavata, in order to deliver Krishnadasa's work to the ISKCON movement he was establishing worldwide.

These three works, the Bhagavad Gītā, the Bhāgavata Purāṇa, and the *Caitanya Caritāmṛta*, progressively introduce the concept and experience of *prema*. Furthermore, these texts work synergistically and cumulatively in presenting the ultimate state of *bhakti*. This synergy of *bhakti* texts revealing *prema*

14. See my Schweig 2005a and its foreword by Norvin Hein.

was clearly intentional on the part of Prabhupāda. For example, it is interesting to note that in the Gītā, the specific term *prema* does not appear. Significantly, however, words derivative of the same root from which the word *prema* comes can be found—words such as *priya*, meaning "dearly loved" (22 instances found), and *prīti* or *prīta*, meaning "love" or "loved" (at least four instances). The Bhāgavata gives the word *prema* over 350 appearances in its approximate 14,000 verses, and there are well over 800 instances throughout the *Caitanya Caritāmṛta's* 11,556 verses.[15] Thus the three primary sacred texts offer a gradual introduction and cumulative revelation of *prema*.

Three Manifestations of the Loving Divinity

The humanity and divinity of the person of Chaitanya is certainly the focus of the *Caitanya Caritāmṛta*, and it is on his example of a *bhakta* and mentoring of his closest disciples that the theology of the Chaitanya school is based. But the *Caitanya Caritāmṛta* represents the greatest theological synthesis of the tradition. It constitutes the third and final phase of *bhakti: prayojana*. It reveals the ultimate vision of the *bhakta* and the perfection of devotional love, *prema*, which is that of Krishna and his beloved Rādhā, and the cowherd maidens who assist Rādhā in her devotions to Krishna. It further reveals through the external example of Chaitanya the ultimate life of *prema* and *bhakti-rasa*, a life no longer guided merely by the earlier Vedic strictures and the Hindu morés of the Bhāgavata, but rather a life in *bhakti* based on the transcendent power and ultimate value of Krishna *sevā*. Internally, Chaitanya himself, in his person, is declared to embody the very source of *prema*—the ultimate heights of love, that which is shared between Rādhā and Krishna. Let us more carefully look at these three foundational sacred texts and the ways they themselves deliver and symbolize dimensions of the theology they build.

The three most important sacred texts that Prabhupāda translated and those for which he provided the most commentarial teachings represent the three essential phases of *bhakti: sambandha, abhidheya*, and *prayojana*. These phases themselves also correspond to the three synthesized phases of Krishna's divinity as indicated and expressed by the three descriptive names for Krishna associated with each, respectively: Madanamohana, Govinda, and Gopīnātha. These three epithets for Krishna, in the simplest of terms, express the "beautiful," "playful," and "delightful" nature of the divine, respectively, or the three ways in which

15. The words *prīti* and *prīta* appear over 175 times in the Bhāgavata as well as the *Caitanya Caritāmṛta*. Additionally, the closely related words *bhakti* and *bhakta* also receive a greater frequency of attention, while taking into consideration the relative length of their respective texts. In the Bhagavad Gītā, these words appear 30 times. In the Bhāgavata Purāṇa, they appear 420 times. And in the *Caitanya Caritāmṛta*, they appear 1,120 times.

prema, or divine love, manifests in the divinity himself. As also with each of these phases of *bhakti*, these three manifestations of the divinity of Krishna correspond to the three foundational revelational scriptures, respectively, moving the *bhakta* more and more toward *prema*.

The epithet *Madanamohana* consists of two words, *madana* and *mohana*, and means "the one whose supremely magical charm [*mohana*] bewilders even the god of love [*madana*]." This epithet expresses the supremely irresistible and powerful nature of the beauty of God, the beauty that attracts souls to him. This phase of divinity also represents Krishna's divine love call of the flute, and the initial phase of the Rāsa Līlā story in which the Vraja Gopikās drop everything in their lives to run out to the forest when Krishna sends out his love call by making music on his flute. The Bhagavad Gītā as a whole represents this drawing souls to him, the divine yearning of Krishna to have souls come to him. Even the name Krishna has been understood by the school as "the attractive one," a meaning derived from the letters *kṛṣ*, which spells the Sanskrit verbal root, meaning "to draw to one's self" (MMW).

The epithet *Govinda* expresses the divine playfulness of *prema* in the divinity of Krishna. Specifically, it is literally understood to mean "the one who plays [*-vinda*] with the cows [*go-*]." The various *līlās* depicting Krishna's affection for cows are in the tenth book of the *Bhāgavata*. But the wider theological meaning of the name refers to full engagement within *bhakti* practice, and the full engagement of the divinity in his *līlā*, or divine displays of *prema*. In the Rāsa Līlā, Krishna's meeting with the Gopīs in the forest, their playful and coy dialogues, and their innocent playing throughout the forest of Vraja, including the great circle dance of the *rāsa*, all represent this phase of the divine. Thus the scriptural text associated with this phrase of divinity is the Bhāgavata Purāṇa, and the ultimate relationship of *prema* is that of Krishna and the Vraja Gopīkās.

The fullness of deity is represented by the epithet *Gopīnātha*, which expresses the blissfulness or "delightfulness" of the divine. The name means "the Beloved Lord [*nātha*] of the Gopīs." The Gopīs do not focus on Krishna in his manifestations of cosmic power and majesty (*aiśvārya*), or "Lord." Rather, they know Krishna primarily and essentially as the sweetest lord of their hearts (*mādhurya*), or simply as their Beloved. The sacred text that focuses on the love, or *prema*, between Krishna and the Gopīs, and even further, the love between Krishna and Rādhā, who is Krishna's favored cowherd maiden among all, is the esoteric vision of Chaitanya himself as revealed in the *Caitanya Caritāmṛta*. It is in this text that we find the culmination of the *bhakti* practice as *proyojana* in the achievement of *prema* for Krishna, and Krishna's love for the *bhakta* in *prema*.

At this final stage, the love of Rādhā and Krishna through the vision and person of Chaitanya completes the phases of divinity. Understanding the key phrase *rasika-śekhara*, which Krishnadāsa Kavirāja Gosvāmin provides, is critical for appreciating the divine role that the tradition imputes to the person of Chaitanya. Prabhupāda translates the phrase that describes Krishna's ultimate nature with a somewhat awkward wording as "the foremost [*śekhara*] enjoyer of loving exchanges [*rasika*]."[16] Because Krishna delights (*rasika*) supremely (*śekhara*) in the love, or *prema,* coming from the relationship he has with his *bhakta* (a "beloved" and "devoted" one), he desires to know the mysterious power of the love that his *bhakta* has for him, which can exceed, amazingly, even his supreme pleasure. The love of Krishna coming from his *bhakta* can conquer the heart of the divine, and therefore Krishna desires to empathically know and experience that love, which conquers even the supreme, by descending to this world to become a *bhakta* (*bhaktāvatāra*). The divine descent of Krishna as a *bhakta* is understood to be the person of Chaitanya, the consummate *bhakta.* To know, understand, and delight in the *prema* that the *bhakta* experiences in relation to Krishna, Chaitanya along with four of his close companions make up what is known as the *pañcatattva,* or "the five principles" of Krishna as a *bhakta* who experiences the supreme heights of *prema:* (1) the paradigmatic form of the *bhakta* (*bhakta-rūpa*), (2) the character and nature of the *bhakta* (*bhakta-svarūpaka*), (3) the divine descent of the *bhakta* (*bhaktāvatāra*), (4) the celebrated personality of the *bhakta* (*bhaktākhya*), and (5) the power of the *bhakta* (*bhakta-śaktika*) (see CC 1.1:14).[17]

Purest love, divine love, then, manifests as the "beautiful," "playful," and "delightful" states within the divinity of Krishna. These manifestations of *prema* in the divinity in turn correspond to the stages of *bhakti,* as *sambandha, abhidheya,* and *prayojana,* respectively. More specifically, the exoteric dimensions of sacred texts, particularly those of the Bhagavad Gītā itself, represent the *sambandha* stage, associated with the divinity of Madanamohana. Here the divinity

---

16. This particular translation of *rasika-śekhara* appears only once among the given instances in which the phrase appears in the *Caitanya Caritāmṛta.* I choose this translation among the others because it best expresses what I think is the theological force of this important phrase. In CC 1.4:16 we find the translation "the supremely jubilant"; in CC 1.4:103 we find the one I have used above; in CC 1.7:7, "the reservoir of all pleasure"; in CC 2.14:155, "the master of all transcendental mellows"; and in CC 2.15:140, "the summit of all transcendental humors." The widely varying translations in Prabhupāda's work certainly attest to the difficulty in bringing the phrase into English, as it is difficult to convey the richness of these two terms in conjunction with one another. The word *rasika* refers to a person who delights in *rasa* (referring to "the experience of the relationship with divinity or within divine *līlā,* or play"), and *śekhara* refers to the highest point, the pinnacle, the summit or peak of a mountain, for example. Since this phrase describes the divinity of Krishna, it describes him in the simplest of terms as "the one who supremely delights in *rasa.*"

17. Chaitanya and his close companions are associated with the five principles as their divine embodiments or personifications in the *pañcatattva* and are identified as follows: (1) Chaitanya, (2) Nityānanda, (3) Advaita, (4) Gadādhara, and (5) Śrīvāsa.

stands alone, sending out his love call to all souls, yearning for them to come to him. Then, the exoteric dimensions in sacred texts move to their ultimate level, the pinnacle of which constitutes the entrance into the esoteric world of envisioning the divine. This pinnacle is ultimately found in the Rāsa Līlā of the Bhāgavata Purāṇa, which represents the *abhidheya* stage, associated with the divinity of Govinda. Here, the playfulness of Krishna manifests as he interacts or "dances" with his most intimate *bhaktas,* his beloveds, the Vraja Gopīkās in his *līlā* of divine love. We have now progressed from the first unitive theism to the bipartite theism of Govinda and his feminine counterparts. When Krishna, as Gopīnātha, the Beloved Lord of the cowherd maidens, becomes delighted in his love with Rādhā, the most special to Krishna among all Gopīs, the tripartite theism emerges. In their love, Krishna discovers that Rādhā's pleasure in loving him exceeds even his in loving her. Since Krishna is *rasika-śekhara,* always "supremely delighted in *rasa* with his beloved [*bhakta*]," he manifests as the person of Chaitanya to preserve his divine supremacy and to enter more deeply into the mysteries of *prema.* This esoteric vision of divinity is represented in the most important biography of Chaitanya and most profound synthesis of the theology of the tradition. Love thus conquers both devotee and divinity, and the closeness between them knows no limits and no end to its depths.

In the complexity of the *bhakti* theology of the Chaitanya school, Prabhupāda gives ISKCON a pristine triangulating matrix within and from which the various relations in the divine and practices in *bhakti* form (see fig. 6.1). Beginning with Madanamohana, progressing to Govinda, and ending with Gopīnātha, this triangulating theological vision of the inner life of the deity resonates with the progression from the exoteric to esoteric, the call to *bhakti* and its practice, then perfection in *prema,* the beautiful, playful, and delightful dimensions of divinity, and their effects on souls as the attraction of souls to the divine, the interaction with the divinity, and the unification of the soul with the divine. The essence of

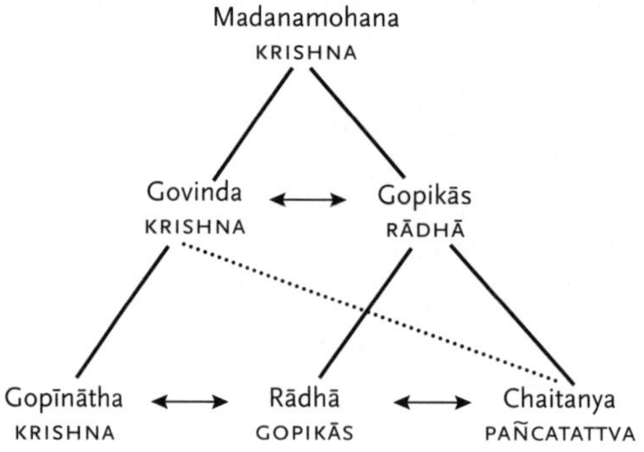

FIGURE 6.1 The tripartite theism within the Chaitanya school's theology of Krishna *bhakti.*

these unitive, bipartite, and tripartite structures within the school's theism is *bhakti*, or "the offering of the whole heart to the divine." As the *Bhakti Sūtra* of Nārada emphatically states, and conclusively exults toward the end of its text, "Of the tripartite formation of truth, the offering of all one's heart to the Beloved in *bhakti* is truly the most precious thing."

The Ultimate Theological Focal Point

The *Caitanya Caritāmṛta* provides a theological lens for ISKCON, a lens through which ISKCON can look in order to understand, interpret, and apply the teachings of the Bhagavad Gītā and Bhāgavata Purāṇa. It constitutes the ultimate theological statement of the Chaitanya school, and it is from this text that we can gain the greatest theological insight. And thus we might make the following critical inquiry: What is most sought, what is most ardently desired by practitioners in this tradition? How does this sacred text express these things? What is the highest experience for the Chaitanya school? What is it on which practitioners ultimately meditate? Among all the primary terms within this rich and sophisticated theological tradition, among all the phrases and key concepts within the Chaitanya school, what few words can possibly convey or express the ultimate focal point of the tradition?

Such a phrase or expression should be directly drawn from the tradition's theological textual resources. Thus to find such a representative key phrase, it would be to the *Caitanya Caritāmṛta* that we must turn to search for such expressions, because this text synthesizes the original theological teachings and vision for the school. If this core purpose of the tradition is articulated, then the very focal point of Prabhupāda's living theology is revealed. If this theological focal point can be identified and illuminated, then a more profound understanding of the rich and complex literary and theological expression within the tradition can be most clearly seen. This kind of theological work could affect the ways in which practitioners can most powerfully focus on the true essence of their practice, to deepen their vision of the gifts their tradition offers them, while it also better prepares the tradition to enter into deeper levels of dialogue with other traditions within the enterprise of a genuine comparative theology.

Let it be most boldly declared here about this theological focal point: The Krishna *bhakti* of the Chaitanya Vaishnava tradition celebrates a theology of the heart. Its practice cultivates the human heart for living a life oriented around pure love. One loves all beings and all humans, one has a special love for and fellowship with the lovers of the divine, and one experiences a most ardent love for divinity and the world of the divine. At the very center of this divine world dwells the imagery of the supreme masculine divinity, Krishna, and the supreme feminine divinity, Rādhā, whose exchanges of divine affection in *rasa* represent the supreme vision of love. And at the center of virtually every temple of worship that Prabhupāda and his disciples established within ISKCON worldwide are the three-dimensional figures of Rādhā and Krishna, who are supremely in love with one another, a supreme love that is itself worshiped by *bhaktas*. Thus what is prescribed for worship in *bhakti* is not ultimately the worship of a *person*, but the worship of a *relation:* the supreme relation of love between Rādhā and Krishna.[18]

It is significant that the classical, formal portraitlike way of presenting the imagery of Krishna with his beloved Rādhā in art and worship is not described or depicted in the narrations of sacred texts, in poetic verse, or in drama. The ecclesiastical context of the figures of Rādhā and Krishna, or their formal depictions in art, find them both standing next to each other, fully facing the viewer, with Krishna's gaze—and most of the time Rādhā's gaze as well—looking ahead into the eyes of the viewer. Krishna stands relaxed, with his right foot crossing the left one as it is firmly on the ground, while his head slightly tilts to his right, as he is about to play the flute that he lifts to his mouth with both arms to his right.

However, in the Bhāgavata's *līlās,* Krishna makes music with the flute without Rādhā by his side, for this flute music expresses a divine yearning to have souls closer to his own heart. It is most evident from the various *līlās* of Krishna that the purpose of making flute music is to call souls toward him, to attract souls, and indeed this he does in the famous Veṇu Gīta chapter (Bhāgavata 10.21) and at the start of the Rāsa Līlā Pañcādhyāya (Bhāgavata 10.29). Once the Vraja Gopikās respond to Krishna's melodious and irresistible flute music by dropping everything (household duties, care of family members, etc.) to run out of their homes to be with him, such flute music has fulfilled its purpose. When Krishna is in the presence of Rādhā, or the Vraja Gopikās, the flute is most often not engaged, and when they come, it is disengaged when in their presence. Various paintings of Krishna, when with the Vraja Gopikās and Rādhā, show him no longer holding

18. More work is needed on this most powerful yet subtle theological focus of the sect. Early theologians of the Chaitanya school, who begin to speak of a theology of divine relationality, invoke the great statement from the *Taittirīya Upaniṣad,* "*rasa* is truly this existence" (*raso vai saḥ*). In this statement the word *rasa* is likely to mean "essence." But from the perspective of the Chaitanya school, *rasa* takes on the meaning of "relationship" or more abstractly "relationality" at an onto-existential level. Additionally, a passage in Bhaktisiddhānta Sarasvatī's commentary on the *Brahmā Saṁhitā* indicates that the *kāma-bīja,* or "the primary cause of all-love" ([1932] 1985:10), is the very center or axis of the eternal realm of Krishna. The *yantra* geometry of which Rādhā and Krishna are the center points still further to the very center of them, between whom is "the principal seed, i.e., *klīṁ*...as the central pivot" (8) And finally, it must be affirmed that the person of Chaitanya is the full embodiment of a relation, the divine relation of Rādhā and Krishna.

the flute up to his mouth. Rather, he holds it with one hand away from his face while enjoying the company of and embracing his beloved.[19]

The question is, why is Krishna in a standing posture of playing the flute while in such close proximity of his supremely beloved Rādhā? How should the closely placed figures of Rādhā and Krishna standing side by side, facing forward toward worshippers with outward gazes, and with flute to Krishna's mouth, be construed? It is curious that here Krishna, in the context of worship, is always playing the flute when in the presence of Rādhā. I am suggesting here that Krishna's call of the flute is not just for the loved denizens of Krishna's eternal and perfect world. Now this love call is meant for Krishna's worshippers of *this* world. Both Krishna and his beloved Rādhā now call out to souls to draw their attention to the divine. Theologically expressed here in the concrete context of worship is not only the vision of supreme love as the divine relation of Rādhā-Krishna, but also, most poignantly and powerfully, by the sounding of Krishna's flute and the divine couple's ever-beckoning forward gaze, their joint call to all humans to come to them, to offer their love to all souls and to the supreme soul.

The core experience for which practitioners strive in this theology of love, what is envisioned and what is at the very heart of ISKCON's *prasthāna-trayī* sacred texts, is most potently expressed by the singular appearance of a three-word phrase found in the *Caitanya Caritāmṛta: prema-bhakti-rasa.*[20] In the briefest fashion, the meaning of these words taken together in this phrase may be understood as the following: With "purest love," *prema,* it is "the offering of the heart," *bhakti,* within "the most intimate dance of love between two hearts within the divine," *rasa.*[21]

---

19. See the reproduced painting by B. G. Sharma on the front cover of this book. While Krishna is surrounded by the Vraja Gopikās, and while Rādhā is standing closely next to him, Krishna's left arm, which is affectionately around the neck of Rādhā, holds his disengaged flute. Such depictions clearly express that the flute is no longer needed when Krishna's beloveds are present. It is primarily when Krishna's beloveds are absent that Krishna produces his alluring flute music.

20. CC 1.17:75: *jñāna-karma-yoga-dharme nahe kṛṣṇa vaśa | kṛṣṇa-vaśa-hetu eka—prema-bhakti-rasa |* ("Knowledge, action, and yoga—in these *dharmas* there is no pleasure for Krishna. Krishna's pleasure has one cause—*prema-bhakti-rasa*"). It is interesting to note that in this verse *jñāna,* karma, and yoga perhaps have some parallel relationship to *prema, bhakti,* and *rasa,* respectively. The ultimate realm of "knowing" or *jñāna* is that found in "purest love," or *prema;* the greatest way of "acting" is that of "offering of one's heart to the divine," or *bhakti;* and the highest form of union in yoga is that of the intimate relation between devotee and divinity in *rasa.* Krishna is not pleased by the "dharma" of each of these, implying that there is the *parodharma* (see Bhāgavata 1.2:6) in *prema-bhakti-rasa* by which souls are pleased as well as Krishna. This complete phrase appears only once in the whole text, and is found in the last chapter of the first of three books that comprise this text.

21. This rendition of the three-word phrase, *prema-bhakti-rasa,* conjuring the powerful connotations that these words carry individually and collectively, is offered here specifically

The meaning of each of these essential terms for the Chaitanya school can be briefly considered here. The word *bhakti* may be translated as that practice and natural disposition of the self that most essentially involves "the offering of the whole heart to the divine." It is significant, however, that *bhakti* first becomes a more external practice and discipline (*vaidhi-sādhana*), which then naturally develops and moves into the more internal life of the heart (*rāgānuga-sādhana*). This movement from the external to the internal is that process in which one is moved from being in the outer world to discovering the innermost world of the heart, which is filled with *prema* and *rasa*.[22]

The word *bhakti* often is contrasted with the paths, or *dharmas*, of "action" (karma), "knowledge" (*jñāna*), and "yoga" by philosophical Hindu schools. For this school, however, *bhakti* is not merely a path, or a means to attain union with the divine. It is also the ultimate end or perfection. Furthermore, *bhakti*, unlike the other paths, is not centered on the self. Rather, it is the loving dedication of the individual self (*bhakta*) to the supreme self (*bhagavat*) in which one becomes "selfless," in the sense that the heart of the individual self is wholly centered on the divine (*bhakti*). Additionally, the word *bhakti* is related to Bhagavān (or Bhagavat), the Lord who "possesses the parts [*bhaktas*] (of all reality)," conveying the sense that souls are his eternal constituent parts, but they experience themselves *apart*, as broken parts conditioned by this temporary world, who ultimately long to become *a part* within the whole of the divine. This longing of the soul begins when it realizes that the divine passionately desires such souls to come to him. The process of *bhakti* leads to a state of ecstatic self-forgetfulness in the process of utterly and totally offering the heart to the divine in *prema* and *rasa*. Finally, *bhakti* denotes the soul's offering of the heart as a response to the divinity's longing for souls.

For the Chaitanya school, the word *prema* is reserved for indicating the attainment of the highest and most purely cultivated love for God.[23] However, in the Bhāgavata, the word *prema* takes on a broad range of applications, expressing the

---

as it can be understood in the context of a *bhakti* theology. The word *prema* means literally "love" or "affection"; the word *bhakti* means "devotion" or "worship"; and the word *rasa* means "taste" or "a prevailing feeling."

22. What I refer to as the "movement" from the external practice of *vaiddhi* to the internal practice of *rāgānuga* is not saying that the external practice is given up or is no longer important. To the contrary, the external practice grows and evolves and is infused with importance precisely because it supports the developments of the internal states found within *rāgānuga*. Indeed, the two must work in conjunction with one another as constituents within *sādhana*, or the practice and discipline of *bhakti*.

23. In CC Madhya Līlā 23.14–15, *prema* is the eighth and last on a list of steps to the attainment of *bhāva* (see the first section of this chapter: "The Uncontainable Nature of Prema").

ubiquity of love in its purest form.[24] Words derived from the same Sanskrit verbal root indicate that residing within the hearts of beings is a pure love, yet it is a love that can be easily tainted by selfishness and the conditioned life.[25] It is a natural love that lies dormant, but has the potential to issue forth from the core of one's very being when a person is selflessly loving with one's whole heart, especially when a person is absorbed in a life steeped in devotion, or *bhakti*. Furthermore, the purest love of *prema* is not only *for* the divine but also *from* the divine. The divinity himself also experiences *prema* for souls, and thus the supreme love that divinity holds for souls is also described as *prema*. Thus love manifests its purest form as *prema* in both humans and the divine.

The word *rasa* indicates the experience of connecting with the divine in the most intimate exchanges of purest love. The dance of love between two hearts, that of the soul with the supreme Soul, is *rasa*. There are five principal types of eternal relationships in which divine love subsumes with its power both the soul and the divinity. Within these forms of *rasa*, the soul becomes immersed primarily in any one of five types of profound feelings possible within *prema* in direct relation to the divine: (1) reverential love (*śānta*), (2) subservient love (*dāsya*), (3) mutual love (*sākhya*), (4) nurturing love (*vātsalya*), and (5) passionate love (*śṛṅgāra*). The attainment of any one of these relationships constitutes the soul's greatest good fortune and pleasure for the divinity. It is born of *bhakti*, it is saturated with ever-increasing *prema*, and it is that divine activity in which supreme love displays both its power and sweetness.

The ultimate display of the highest *rasa*, the *śṛṅgāra-rasa*, occurs when *rasa* becomes the *rāsa*.[26] This ultimate expression of *rasa* manifests itself as the high-

---

24. It is not possible to explore here a comparison of the specific application of the word *prema* by the Chaitanya school and its various applications in the Bhāgavata Purāṇa. While the theologians of the early Chaitanya school reserve the word *prema* for a love so pure that it is attained after rigorous *sādhana* in *bhakti*, the Bhāgavata Purāṇa applies the word in an extraordinary range of loving relationships, divine and nondivine, even between animals and also between humans and animals, as well as objects of nature.

25. See the discussion on *prema* in Schweig 2005a, in the chapter section entitled "The Vision of Devotional Love," especially 168–169. Many of the ideas in this chapter are drawn from this book, and the five chapters of the Rāsa Līlā found in the Bhāgavata Purāṇa 10.29–33, which I present there in translation. I also present a translation of the Veṇu Gīta.

26. The word *rāsa*, which is a specific dance form performed by village cowherds in celebration of the harvest season, is technically not a derivative of the word *rasa*. However, teachers in the lineage of Chaitanya relate the two words, in how *rasa* between the Vraja Gopikās and Krishna in the *rāsa* dance represents the highest attainable level of intimacy possible. Thus the early theologians take *rāsa* to be a *vṛddhi* form of *rasa* to express a theological vision that is important for the school. I have noted elsewhere that this deeper significance of the word *rāsa* is recognized by Viśvanātha, in his commentary to the Rāsa Līlā chapters, specifically in his comment to the verse BhP 10.33:2, where he points out that

est *līlā,* or "the play of divine love," in the Rāsa Līlā. In the climactic portion of this *līlā,* Krishna duplicates himself multiple times to attend each one of the Vraja Gopikās, who are themselves the very embodiments of Rādhikā's emotions, in the great circular dance of divine love, the *rāsa.* This ultimate display of *rasa* is also found in the play of the divine figures of Rādhikā, the supreme goddess consort, and Krishna, her Beloved Lord, constituting the innermost realm of the divine. In Rādhā-Krishna *līlā,* or the Rāsa Līlā, divine love plays the players. Divine love ultimately dances within hearts, causing souls to become dancers, and between such dancers and the supreme dancer is the dance of love that dances through all hearts to one another. This is expressed no better than in the person of Chaitanya himself who is seen as the divine descent of Love. He is the very embodiment of Krishna's love for Rādhā and the Vraja Gopikās, or the embodiment of the Gopīs' and Rādhā's love for Krishna, or the embodiment of the divine love itself that eternally flows so intensely between them, or all three of these at once.[27]

The importance of each of the words, individually, in the phrase *prema-bhakti-rasa,* has been reviewed only briefly. It is important to note that each word separately and independently of the other two can be found in hundreds of instances throughout the *Caitanya Caritāmṛta,* indicating the vital ways that each word is employed, perhaps with greater frequency than most other terms in the text. Moreover, each word as it is coupled with one of the other words from this phrase forms three important compound terms: *prema-bhakti, bhakti-rasa,* and *prema-rasa.* While this full three-word phrase, *prema-bhakti-rasa,* amazingly, can be found only in a single instance within the text of the *Caitanya Caritāmṛta,* its power derives in part from the vitally important, individual terms themselves, and from the importance and pervasiveness of the compounding of those words as well. These words together, then, and these combinations of compounds embedded within this phrase as well as the weightiness of the individual words that comprise this phrase, make the whole greater than the sum of its parts.

This phrase expresses the ultimate theological focal point for the Chaitanya school, and the words collectively and individually express dimensions of divine love as the tradition's ultimate value against which everything else can be measured, and around which everything of greater or lesser signficance must revolve. It would be against this theological formula of *prema-bhakti-rasa* that all narratives, conceptions, visions, experiences, discourses, and so on would be measured. Within the total theological picture, as with any good art, there is within

---

Rāsa refers to the sum of all *rasas* or intimate experiences with the supreme. See Schweig 2005a:265 and Bhaktivilasa Tirtha 1940.

27. See ch. 4 of the Ādi Līlā of CC for the theology of Chaitanya's identity in relation to Rādhā and Krishna.

its composition a singular focal point, the very center of its composition, an ultimate place within such a picture on which the eyes may focus while seeing all the other contributing parts. Nothing distracts or detracts from the focal point of a good picture and the rest of its constituent compositional elements, and if it should, then such contrary elements should be eliminated. So it should be with the theological picture of Krishna *bhakti*. The focal point for this theology, then, is *prema-bhakti-rasa*. To the extent that something said or something written within the tradition, whether it be revelational, commentarial, or even ecclesiastical, moves closer to this formula, it would be imputed with importance and value. Something that is further away from it, then, would be considered not as important or central. If something detracts or distracts from this ultimate focal point, then this would be considered antithetical and would be rejected. Knowing what is at the very heart of the tradition's theology provides a kind of hermeneutic principle by which a practitioner or viewer of the tradition can develop a keen level of devotional discernment, a capacity that allows one to see and deeply appreciate the value and relevance of any revelational or personal vision. There is no other phrase that can better deliver the theological axiology of the Chaitanya school, the ultimate gift that this school has to offer.

The Divine Love Call

The particular deity of Krishna, among the many manifestations of the divine known to Hindu traditions, is revered as the ultimate personal aspect of the godhead by certain Vaishnava schools. The early Vaishnava theologians of the Chaitanya school, following a key verse from the Bhāgavata Purāṇa, establish three primary manifestations of the divine, of which Krishna is the highest, the ultimate, and the most intimate. These three primary manifestations are Brahman, Paramātman, and Bhagavān. Brahman is difficult to define or to describe. It may be understood as supreme spirit, the ultimate reality, the Everything, the ALL. There is not anything that is not contained within the divine, and thus there is nothing that exists outside of the divine.

At the core of Brahman, in which everything is contained by the divine, at the core of all existences and all beings, is the personal presence of the divine, identified by the word Paramātman, "the supreme self." This manifestation is the personal presence of the divine at the very core of every atom and all hearts, of all existences and all beings. Bhagavān is the singular, ultimate manifestation of divinity, its most loving and most intimate manifestation. At the heart of the very core of everything, the very essence and source of the ALL, is the very point from which everything originates and comes, and is constantly being sustained, including the Brahman and Paramātman manifestations of the divine. This is Bhagavān Śrī Krishna. Śrī Krishna has numerous names and epithets and is especially known as a deity of supreme beauty, supreme playfulness, and supreme love. Especially important for our discussion here is Krishna's distinguishing characteristic: he plays the flute, sounding divine music, lovingly attracting souls to come to him. This is Krishna's love call, for which he is so well known.

The Bhagavad Gītā, within the *prasthāna-trayī,* functions as the very foundation of the tradition's foundational texts and expresses a divine call to love most passionately, but subtly. It expresses *prema-bhakti-rasa* most prominently in Krishna's "song," or *gītā,* as a divine call to love, and expresses, mostly in Krishna's words, how *bhakti* is the most direct and personal response to this call.[28] The given title of the work begins to disclose the text's very purpose: It is a song (*gītā*) coming from the Beloved Lord (*bhagavat*). I have suggested in other work that "song" here does not indicate a literary genre; the word "song" here expresses what issues forth from the heart of the divine.[29] The Gītā presents a divine love call that ever beckons souls to become united with the divine. The divine desires us and loves us, and desires to attract us to himself.

This ultimate divine person within the Godhead, though the source of all divine manifestations—from whom all existences emanate and originate, on whom everything ultimately depends, and in whom everything is contained—most amazingly desires the love from human souls in this world. Bhagavān Śrī Krishna desires and loves humans, and desires souls to come to him. This is most passionately expressed in the philosophically dramatic conclusion and climactic portion of the Bhagavad Gītā, in the following simple words of Krishna to Arjuna: "You are so much loved by me!" (18.64).[30] The verse in which this ultimate expression of Krishna's appears, and verses leading up to it, become the subtle but ultimately most boldly presented divine love call of the Gītā.

Krishna represents that most central point of the Godhead from which all manifestations of the divine come, the point from which all existences are constantly being sustained. Yet Krishna simultaneously draws to himself the hearts

---

28. It is significant that in the formulation *prema-bhakti-rasa* the word *prema* appears as the first of the three terms. Indeed, the priority of *prema* in a Krishna theology must be brought out. It is often the case that in *bhakti-sādhana* emphasis is given to the love and devotion that the devotee or *bhakta* offers to the divinity in *bhakti,* even to the point of discounting or possibly excluding recognition of the most powerful and compelling love call of Krishna. However the sacred texts of *bhakti,* perhaps more subtly but certainly no less dramatically, say that without Krishna's *prema* for humans, there is no possibility for humans to develop *prema* for Krishna. It is *prema* coming from the divinity that is prior to *bhakti* itself, and the text of the Gītā most dramatically expresses this.

29. For a brief discussion on how the word *gītā* in the title *Bhagavad Gītā* constitutes a theological expression rather than an indication of a literary genre, see Schweig 2007: 3–4.

30. Translation from Schweig 2007. The words *iṣṭo'si me dṛdham iti* literally translate as "Desired you are by me so much!"

of those within his highest heaven, the supreme world in which he eternally dwells, and also draws to himself the hearts of those in this mixed and unhappy world by ever beckoning souls to turn toward him, to know him, and to love him. In both realms he does so through a most enticing divine love call. This divine call to love is one of the most powerful and distinguishing features of this theology: in everything, through everything, and in every event and in every part of existence, the divine is trying to reach us, to call us, to beckon us, if we will just hear it.

The divine love call also becomes the sounding of Krishna's flute in the most sacred revelational text for the Chaitanya school. At the very heart of the Bhāgavata Purāṇa's largest (tenth) book—that part of the text to which the other eleven books point—are the *līlās* of Krishna, of which those taking place in the paradisial, pastoral setting of Vraja are considered by the tradition to be the most intimate and most sacred. Among these, it is the five-chapter *līlā* of the Rāsa dance, the *rāsa-pañcādhyāyī,* that is considered the ultimate of all divine acts. It is the tradition's consummate vision of supreme love. Krishna draws the cowherd maidens, the Gopīs, to the forest at night to enter into the divine *līlā* of the Rāsa by the sounding of his flute. This call of the flute represents Krishna's call to all souls to come to him, to join him in his eternal dance of love. Indeed, one whole chapter appears several chapters prior to the five chapters of the Rāsa Līlā in which the cosmically alluring power of Krishna's flute music on all beings, animate and inanimate, is described.[31]

The *bhakta* responds to the call of Krishna's flute song and ultimately desires to enter Krishna's dance of divine love with the Vraja Gopikās. As Prabhupāda himself says, "This Kṛṣṇa consciousness movement is for approaching Rādhā-Kṛṣṇa, to be associated with the Supreme Lord in His sublime pleasure dance. That is the aim of Kṛṣṇa consciousness" (purport to "Nitāi-Pada-Kamala," 681221pu.la). The recitation of the *mahāmantra* is the soul's calling back to the divinity in response to the love call of the feminine and masculine forms of divinity: "*hare kṛṣṇa, hare kṛṣṇa, kṛṣṇa kṛṣṇa, hare hare / hare rāma, hare rāma, rāma rāma, hare hare.*" The name *hare* is the vocative of the feminine Harā, meaning "O Goddess, whose power of divine love inspires me (in the *seva,* or service, of the attractive Lord, Krishna, and the delighted Lord, Rāma)"; the name *kṛṣṇa* is the vocative of the masculine Krishna, meaning "O Divinity, whose supreme beauty attracts my heart," along with the other masculine vocative, *rāma,* meaning "O Divinity, whose supreme pleasure delights in my love." This mantra, the return call, the

---

31. See Schweig 2005a:78–85 for a translation of the chapter known as Veṇu Gīta (Bhāgavata Purāṇa 10.21). This chapter is solely dedicated to the transformative effects of Krishna's flute music on animate and inanimate beings.

central practice within *bhakti* for the Chaitanya school, increases the purest love, *prema,* which is eternally lived and enacted in *rasa.* Built into the response call of the soul's recitation of the *mahāmantra* is the divine's return reply to the soul's recitation response: When the soul meditates on the vocatively inflected names of the divine within the *mahāmantra,* the soul is effectively calling out to the divine while sonically recreating the Rāsa Maṇḍala, or the Rāsa dance of divine love within the heart.[32]

So the Gītā presents Krishna's love call through his teachings as a deeply felt passion for the love of humans, and he describes the human response to his love in *bhakti.* In the Bhāgavata, Krishna's love call is narrated and described as the sound of his flute, and the response of souls, namely the cowherd maidens of Vraja, as an irrepressible and intense attraction to Krishna. Here in the Bhāgavata, the emphasis is on the experience of *bhakti* on the part of the *bhakta.* In the *Caitanya Caritāmṛta,* there is the greatest emphasis on the soul's response to the love call of the divine in *bhakti,* as it is paradigmatically demonstrated by Chaitanya's life and teachings. Indeed, Chaitanya is considered the embodiment of the very love between Krishna and the Vraja Gopikās, or his most beloved Gopī consort, Rādhā. Chaitanya is the divine descent of Krishna, who himself desires to experience the love of his *bhakta,* and thus the ways the *bhakta* responds to his divine love call.

A Theology of Divine Secrecy

In the Bhagavad Gītā, a secret love song issuing forth from the heart of divinity for all souls is found. Through a secret love call, through a secret song of love, or *gītā,* issuing forth from the heart of divinity, he sends his love to souls. He is "secretly" or quietly loving souls. He displays manifestations of himself in order to love and embrace souls, and he softly beckons souls to know him, to love him, to come to him. His love is quiet or secret because we are unready to receive love from the divine, and he does not want souls to be pressured or forced to return his love. Indeed, Krishna's love is quiet to the point of his impartiality toward humans until they turn to him with their hearts (BG 9.29). Yet Krishna is ready to reciprocate the love of souls at any level in whatever way they turn to him:

In the way they offer
themselves to me,
in just that way

32. A discussion of the *mahāmantra* as the sonic representation of the Rāsa Maṇḍala is in Schweig 2005a:178–179.

I offer my love
to them reciprocally.
Human beings
follow my path
universally,
O Pārtha. (Schweig 2007: ch. 4:11)

This verse expresses well that Krishna's love patiently waits for the attention of humans. Significantly, Krishna says that all humans are on his "path" of divine love, but they are unaware of it until they submit themselves to him. Moreover, Krishna identifies himself as the *suhṛt,* "the innermost heart" or "one so dear to the heart" of all beings (BG 5.29), and proclaims that humans are already "dearly loved" by him, and thus he asks that they love him (BG 18.65).

In the intimate arena of *rasa* with the divinity, Krishna would not urge souls to love him if he did not already love souls. Indeed, in the dramatic anticlimactic event of Krishna's manifestation of his overwhelming and overpowering universal form in the eleventh chapter, Arjuna pleads for the "grace" of the intimate or *mādhurya* realm of *rasa* with Krishna in the following words:

As a father is to a son,
as a friend to a friend,
As a dearly loved one
to a dearly beloved—
be pleased to show your
loving kindness, O Divinity. (Schweig 2007: ch. 11:44)

The message in this portion of the Gītā is that Krishna wishes to inspire in Arjuna an appreciation for the ways in which he, as the supreme divinity, is so intimately present to receive such an intimate love. Krishna speaks of his humanlike form in the words, "Very rarely seen is this form of mine" (BG 11.52). And he further says that it is "[o]nly by the offering of one's love to none other... am I able, in such a form, to be known and to be truly seen, and to be attained" (BG 11.54). The tacit expression here is that divinity desires the love of humans who will love him in his most intimate humanlike form as Krishna, precisely because the heart of the divine holds a love for humans that he is desirous of their reciprocating.

Throughout the Gītā, Krishna lovingly acknowledges the many ways, the many paths, the many forms of worship, the many yogas, and so on, but nevertheless gently and quietly exhorts souls to know that he is the ultimate goal of all these—an exhortation that can easily be overlooked or missed because of Krishna's generosity of spirit in his acceptance of all the various indirect or even distracting processes that humans may take to eventually come to him. It is the soul's eternal nature to love divinity, but souls can become distracted or overwhelmed by what is temporary in the self and in the world and then act selfishly and thus turn away from divinity. He accepts all the various ways and practices in which souls can approach him, but ultimately desires for souls to give up all these ways and to fully love him. Throughout his teachings, therefore, Krishna weaves expressions of his desire for souls to know him, to love him, and to come to him, and these are the most poignant and powerful themes in the text.[33]

Divinity secretly longs for souls to come to him. This yearning of divinity in the Gītā is expressed in various ways. The reader is privy to a private conversation, a personal dialogue, between the narrator, Sanjaya, and Dhristarāshtra, the king to whom Sanjaya narrates the private conversation between Arjuna and Krishna. In this inner dialogue between Arjuna and Krishna, a gradual disclosure is presented throughout the text of what is the highest and most secret. The gradual disclosure takes several forms. One finds that expressions of the divinity's heart are gradually introduced throughout the text and in ways that are not prominent. One learns that the visions and descriptions of divinity's various manifestations are themselves ways in which divinity lovingly embraces all creation, all beings. Krishna's various divine identities become more and more personal and intimate as the dialogue progresses. In the Gītā there is an acceptance of any process or practice that gradually brings souls to divinity to love him. This gradual disclosure of divinity's love and his yearning for souls can be observed, subtly woven throughout all of Krishna's teachings, and it is often expressed more boldly in the last verse or last several verses of chapters. The purpose of this gradual disclosure is that divinity desires the unconditional love of souls. The love of Krishna must not arise out of fear of divine judgment and condemnation, or out of guilt or obligation. Krishna's eternally patient and divinely generous nature draws souls to his heart with an unconditioned love and purely out of their own natural affection and attraction to him.

Finally, in the eighteenth and last chapter of the Gītā, the "great secret," the "greater secret," and the "greatest secret of all" are disclosed. Krishna's simple words, "You are so much loved by me!" are *sarva-guhyatama,* the greatest secret of all, and moreover, *paramaṁ vacaḥ,* his "supreme message." The purpose of Krishna's secretiveness is to preserve his own love for souls until they are ready

33. The following are references to some verses expressing Krishna's desire for souls to know him: BG 5.13, 5.29, 7.3, 7.10, 7.12, 7.30, 9.13, 10.24, 10.27, 15.19, 18.55. The following are verses in which Krishna speaks about the soul's love for him: BG 4.3, 4.11, 6.31, 6.47, 7.21, 7.23, 7.28, 8.10, 8.22, 9.13, 9.29, 9.30, 9.31, 9.33, 9.34, 10.8, 10.9, 11.54, 11.55, 12.1, 12.14, 12.16, 12.17, 12.19, 12.10, 13.10, 13.18, 14.26, 15.19, 18.54, 18.55, 18.65, 18.68, 18.69. The following are verses in which Krishna speaks about souls coming to him: BG 4.9, 4.10, 4.11, 6.47, 7.14, 7.15, 7.19, 7.23, 8.7, 8.15, 8.16, 9.11, 9.25, 9.28, 9.34, 10.10, 11.55, 13.18, 14.2, 18.55, 18.65, 18.66, 18.68.

to receive his love. He waits an eternity for us to turn toward him. He asserts that he is impartial to all, while residing in the hearts of all, but he especially loves his *bhakta* (BG 9.29). His divine yearning is kept secret so that unqualified souls are excluded (BG 18.67). Divinity especially loves the souls who reveal this divine secret; he proclaims that there is no soul who loves him more than the one who reveals his divine secret, the greatest of all secrets (BG 18.68–69).

Secrecy is also connected to deeper levels of intimacy within *rasa* in several ways. The connection between two souls is something unique, something that belongs to the two personages within *rasa*. No matter how much we may observe persons in a relationship, it is always from the outside. The closeness and intimacy between two persons is closed and private to anyone else. When the Vraja Gopikās rushed off from their homes in the village to be with Krishna in the forest, they were secretly called to love (SB 10.29:4–9). They were the ones drawn to Krishna upon hearing his flute and no one else. Their families could not understand their attraction. Moreover, even the Vraja Gopikās, while among one another in the great *maṇḍala* of the Rāsa dance, individually felt Krishna's exclusive attention; each was utterly unaware of Krishna's attention to any other in the circle of Gopīs (SB 10.33:3). Yogamāyā, as love's most powerful force in the divine world and in this world, has a key role in deciding what is revealed to souls and what is concealed from them and thus what remains secret.

A theology of the Chaitanya school must take into account the undisclosable dimensions of divinity that are too profound and too intimate to verbalize. The school delights, but with caution, in disclosing intimate and more secretive dimensions of the Godhead, and yet always preserves a certain level of confidentiality and mystery about elements or realms that are too intimate for any kind of disclosure. An instance of the former is when the author of the *Caitanya Caritāmṛta* deliberates as to whether to disclose esoteric visions of Chaitanya's personality to his reader. Krishnadāsa Kavirāja Goswami at first hesitates to disclose intimate knowledge of Chaitanya, but then says that if this theological knowledge is not revealed, his worthy readers will not understand what is so critically important. He then decides to relate this esoteric knowledge in a disguised form, so that authentic devotees will receive it and foolish persons will not recognize it. He depends on the latter's ignorance to keep secret what is intended only for those who are qualified (CC 1.4:231–237). Thus ignorance and illusion have the positive element of keeping secret or confidential what is beyond disclosure in the theology of divine intimacy.

Even so, no matter how qualified one may be, the importance of preserving and respecting the secrecy and confidentiality of the most intimate aspects of the theology of Krishna is established. Moreover, such secrecy is itself both a tacit expression of a deep appreciation of the very depth and profundity of knowledge and an understanding of the most intimate and deepest aspects of the mystery of the divine. The utter necessity of divine secrecy can be observed in the dialogue between Rāmānanda Raya and Chaitanya in a kind of Vaishnava catechism, as presented in the *Caitanya Caritāmṛta*. After responding to many probing questions from Chaitanya, each one urging Rāmānanda to go deeper and deeper into the theological dimensions of Krishna and his beloved Rādhā, Rāmānanda is stopped by Chaitanya himself unexpectedly in a dramatic moment when Chaitanya covers his mouth with his own hand, not allowing him to go any further into the theology of divine intimacy (CC 2.8:193). Thus there are some aspects of intimacy within the divine that should not be expressed, even within the most personal and confidential settings, even within the exchanges between the most exalted beings, in word or in public. One loses the secret love song if one disrespects or ignores the necessity of divine secrecy in the theology of the Chaitanya school.

The Gifts of Theology

There is indeed a living theology of the Krishna movement that has moved the minds and hearts of persons from various cultures outside India to delve deeply into the practices and way of life of Krishna *bhakti*. This living theology can be found embedded in the powerful and compelling writings of A. C. Bhaktivedanta Swami Prabhupāda, a theology that energized him to bring the teachings of the Chaitanya school of Krishna *bhakti* to the West and to major cultural centers around the world. His spoken and written words transmitted a powerful theological vision that was established several hundred years earlier by the original teachers in the lineage of Śrī Krishna Chaitanya from the sixteenth century.

The most important theological work produced by the early teachers of the school was and remains the *Caitanya Caritāmṛta* by Krishnadāsa Kavirāja Goswami. This work recognizes the Bhāgavata Purāṇa as the most important sacred text on the life of devotion to Krishna as displayed in the lives of exemplary *bhaktas* and is also recognized as the most profound source of Krishna's various divine acts, or *līlās*. And the Bhagavad Gītā is recognized by the early school as foundational for its teachings. These three works provide a wellspring of theological information, inspiration, and revelation. They each reveal aspects of *prema-bhakti-rasa* as the school's theological focal point. Uniquely and synergistically, they each transmit dimensions of the divine love call. And by revealing secret or esoteric aspects of its theology, they each express the profundity and depth of knowledge to which this school's theology points.

What gifts does such a Krishna *bhakti* theology have to offer the world? This theology suggests that from the heart of every religious tradition there issues forth a secret love call, as it were, and that each tradition must search ceaselessly for the heart of its vision of the divine. At the very core and depths of every tradition are the resources for those inside the tradition to create the bonds of affection with those outside the tradition. And what flows to the practitioners from the very core of any tradition is a unique and sweet revelation of the most profound dimensions of love—*prema*. Yet there are depths of this divine love that will always remain secret, mysterious, and inexpressible, such depths to which the human heart is endlessly attracted and forever discovering. A genuine theology is fueled by this attraction and the unquenchable thirst for knowing these depths.

The sincere, genuine pursuit of and singular focus on this divine love—which is a boundless love that is grand, broad, and deep—necessitates that every tradition embrace and be embraced by other traditions for the ways in which they can reveal exclusive dimensions of divine love that would otherwise remain hidden from each. No longer are other traditions seen as truth conflicting or monopolizing, or as threatening the integrity of the other. On the contrary, the theologies of purest love, or *prema,* become invaluable and necessary partners in the quest for the supreme Beloved—just as the various Vraja Gopikās found it necessary to link arms to form the great circle around Krishna to create the magnificent arena of the Rāsa dance—and in the relentless search for all his infinite sweetness and greatness.

In this way, an interreligious theology engages with the unique experiences of the divine found within diverse religious traditions. Boundless love is then necessarily deeply realized within and reciprocally between traditions. Prabhupāda's living theology celebrates how this love (*prema*) forever dances between the hearts of divinity and souls (*rasa*), and how the practice of offering of one's whole heart to the divine (*bhakti*) constitutes the essential practice of religion. ISKCON's practitioners now only have to celebrate in practice and in life what is embedded within its own theology.

The founder and exemplary teacher of ISKCON, A. C. Bhaktivedanta Swami Prabhupāda, was himself a theological thinker whose living theology of Krishna *bhakti* would claim that *bhakti* itself is present in any authentic religious tradition (see Schweig 1998b). If *bhakti* can be found in other religious traditions, then surely something of *prema* as well as *rasa* will also be present in some form. Prabhupāda exemplifies the serious practitioner, who both delved within his or her own tradition to find that which most deeply moves the human heart toward the divine and also sought to contribute that as a gift to humanity by recognizing this dynamic of *bhakti* when it occurs in other traditions. Is this not what a genuinely *living* theology ultimately does? Traditions of *prema-bhakti-rasa* must be allowed to speak for themselves, and a comparative or interreligious theology does not compare for the purpose of judging and evaluating these traditions, nor does it compare them in the sense of a competition as Rudolf Otto attempted to do. Rather this kind of theological inquiry is meant to establish and inspire an even greater sharing and deepening of theological truths within and between traditions. Each tradition has something unique to disclose from its revealed vision of divine love, which will only enhance the experiences of divine love for those in other traditions, those who also contribute the gifts that their traditions offer.

What Tamal Krishna Goswami has offered to us is a gift. It was this interreligious contribution that he ultimately desired to engage in. It was his intention to examine essential aspects of Prabhupāda's teachings to afford a greater appreciation of Prabhupāda's contribution of a living theology of Krishna *bhakti* that could speak further to other traditions. Goswami provided the groundwork for building a more deeply probing and revealing constructive theology of *bhakti,* so that the Chaitanya school can enter more and more into the global conversation that will yield a greater revelation that can occur between hearts in *this* world. This sharing between hearts, which is at the heart of *bhakti,* consists of reaching from deep within one's own tradition to the point that one fully offers to those from other traditions the gift of total love, openness, and acceptance, which further reveals an elevated exchange in which participants are lifted up into the blessed state of a specially and unexpectedly shared theological moment.

Not only does Goswami's example compellingly demonstrate how a deeply committed practitioner can meet the expectations of the highest standards of scholarship when examining his or her own religious tradition but his sensitive study underscores the unique gift that theology can offer a world in great need, with a motive to nurture the vital role it must play within the total spectrum of human inquiry. I can think of no greater need and nothing more exhilarating for the world today: that very gift containing something of the experience and knowledge of the heart of the divine, most lovingly offered, received, and reciprocated, from one tradition to another, building a new global theology with the divine treasures excavated from the hidden depths of ultimately every personal vision and tradition of faith.

Works Cited

PUBLICATIONS OF A. C. BHAKTIVEDANTA SWAMI PRABHUPĀDA

———. 1968a. *The Bhagavad-Gita As It Is.* Abr. ed. New York: Collier Macmillan.

———. 1968b. *Teachings of Lord Caitanya.* New York: ISKCON Press.

———. [1960] 1970. *Easy Journey to Other Planets.* Rev. ed. Los Angeles: Bhaktivedanta Book Trust. Original ed., Delhi: author.

———. 1972. *Bhagavad-gītā As It Is.* Complete ed. New York: Collier Macmillan.

———. [1970] 1974. *Kṛṣṇa: The Supreme Personality of Godhead.* 3 vols. Los Angeles: Bhaktivedanta Book Trust. Original ed. 2 vols. Boston: ISKCON Press.

———. 1975. *The Nectar of Instruction: An Authorized English Presentation of Śrīla Rūpa Gosvāmī's* Śrī Upadeśāmṛta. Los Angeles: Bhaktivedanta Book Trust.

———. [1970] 1977. "The Krishna Consciousness Movement Is the Genuine Vedic Way: A Cogent Discussion between A. C. Bhaktivedanta Swami, Acarya: International Society for Krishna Consciousness, and Dr. J. F. Staal, Professor of Philosophy and South Asian Languages, University of California, Berkeley." Pp. 90–104 in *The Science of Self Realization.* Los Angeles: Bhaktivedanta Book Trust. Original ed., Boston: ISKCON Press.

———. 1979. *Life Comes from Life.* Los Angeles: Bhaktivedanta Book Trust.

———. [1970] 1982a. *The Nectar of Devotion: A Summary Study of Śrīla Rūpa Gosvāmī's* Bhaktirasāmṛta-Sindhu, 2nd ed. Los Angeles: Bhaktivedanta Book Trust. Original edition, Boston: ISKCON Press, 1970.

———. [1969] 1982b. *Śrī Īśopaniṣad.* Los Angeles: Bhaktivedanta Book Trust. Original ed., Boston: ISKCON Press.

———. 1982c. Śrī Nāmāmṛta: *The Nectar of the Holy Name.* Comp. and ed. Śubhānanda dāsa. Los Angeles: Bhaktivedanta Book Trust.

———. 1983. *Bhagavad-gītā As It Is,* 2nd ed., rev. Los Angeles: Bhaktivedanta Book Trust.

———. 1985. *Dialectic Spiritualism: A Vedic View of Western Philosophy.* Moundsville, WV: Prabhupāda Books.

———. 1987. *Śrīmad Bhāgavatam*. 12 cantos. Cantos 1–10, chapter 13 by Prabhupāda; canto 10, chapter 14–canto 12 by his disciples. Los Angeles: Bhaktivedanta Book Trust.

———. 1989. *Bhagavad-gītā As It Is*, 2nd ed., rev. and enl. Los Angeles: Bhaktivedanta Book Trust.

———. 1992a. *Renunciation through Wisdom*. Trans. by Sarvabhavana dāsa. Los Botany, Australia: Bhaktivedanta Book Trust.

———. 1992b. Śrīla Prabhupāda Śrīkṛṣṇāmṛta: *Nectarean Instructions from the Letters of His Divine Grace A. C. Bhaktivedanta Swami Prabhupāda*. 3 vols. Los Angeles: Bhaktivedanta Book Trust.

———. 1994. *"Back to Godhead"–1944–1960: The Pioneer Years*. Los Angeles: Bhaktivedanta Book Trust.

———. 1995. *The Jaladuta Diary*. Los Angeles: Bhaktivedanta Book Trust.

———. 1996. *Śrī Caitanya-caritāmṛta*. 9 vols. Los Angeles: Bhaktivedanta Book Trust.

———. 1998a. *The Bhaktivedanta VedaBase #1—Bhaktivedanta*. Version 4.11. Sandy Ridge, NC: Bhaktivedanta Archives.

———. 1998b. *The Bhaktivedanta VedaBase #2—Supplementary*. Version 4.11. Sandy Ridge, NC: Bhaktivedanta Archives.

———. 1998c. *The Bhaktivedanta VedaBase #3—Historical*. Version 4.11. Sandy Ridge, NC: Bhaktivedanta Archives.

SECONDARY SOURCES

Alper, Harvey P., ed. 1989a. *Understanding Mantras*. Albany: State University of New York Press.

———. 1898b. "A Working Bibliography for the Study of Mantras." Pp. 327–443 in *Understanding Mantras*, ed., Alper. Albany: State University of New York Press.

[Anūttama Dāsa]. 1999. Panel Discussion: "Can Cultic Groups Change? The Case of ISKCON." *ISKCON Communications Journal* 7, no. 2 (Dec.): 41–52.

Archer, W. G., n.d. *The Loves of Krishna in Indian Painting and Poetry*. New York: Grove Press.

Bābā Premānand Bhārati. 1904. *Sree Krishna: The Lord of Love*. New York: Krishna Samāj.

Baird, Robert D. 1986. "Swami Bhaktivedanta and the *Bhagavadgita* 'As It Is'." Pp. 200–221 in *Modern Indian Interpreters of the* Bhagavadgita, ed. Robert N. Minor. Albany: State University of New York Press.

———. 1987. "The Response of Swami Bhaktivedanta." Pp. 105–127 in *Modern Indian Responses to Religious Pluralism*, ed. Harold G. Coward. Albany: State University of New York Press.

———. 1988. "ISKCON and the Struggle for Legitimation." *Bulletin of the John Rylands University of Manchester* 70, no. 3 (Autumn): 157–169.

———. 1995. "Swami Bhaktivedanta and Ultimacy." Pp. 515–541 in *Religion in Modern India*, 3rd rev. ed., ed. Baird. New Delhi: Manohar.

Banerjee, Priyatosh. 1978. *The Life of Krishna in Indian Art*. New Delhi: National Museum.

Barbour, Ian G. 1990. *Religion in an Age of Science: The Gifford Lectures, 1989–1991*. Vol. 1. New York: Harper Collins.

Barker, Eileen. 1986. "World Congress for the Synthesis of Science and Religion: A Personal Account." Pp. 133–147 in *ISKCON Review* 2.

Basham, A. L. 1983. "Interview with..." Pp. 162–195 in *Hare Krishna, Hare Krishna: Five Distinguished Scholars on the Krishna Movement in the West*, ed. Stephen J. Gelberg. New York: Grove Press.

———. [1975] 1997. *A Cultural History of India*. New Delhi: Oxford India Paperbacks. Original ed. Oxford: Oxford University Press.

BBT Sankirtan Books. 1993. *The Nectar of Book Distribution: Statements by Śrīla Prabhupāda and His Followers on the Philosophy and Practice of Book Distribution*. Stockholm: BBT Sankirtan Books.

Beck, Guy L. [1993] 1995. *Sonic Theology: Hinduism and Sacred Sound*. Delhi: Motilal Banarsidass. Original ed., Columbia: University of South Carolina Press.

———. 1998. "The Devotional Music of Śrīla Prabhupāda." *Journal of Vaiṣṇava Studies* 6, no. 2 (Spring): 125–140.

———. 2005. *Alternative Krishnas*. Albany: State University of New York Press.

Beckford, James A. 1994. "The Mass Media and New Religious Movements." *ISKCON Communications Journal* 2, no. 2 (July–Dec.): 17–24.

Berwick, John. 1995. "Chātra Samāj: The Significance of the Student Community in Bengal c1870–1922." Pp. 232–293 in *Mind Body and Society: Life and Mentality in Colonial Bengal*, ed. Rajat Kanta Ray. Calcutta: Oxford University Press.

Bhakti Dayita Mādhava. 1982 [Caitanyābda 496]. *Śrī Yugala-nāma*. Mayapur: Sri Caitanya Gauḍīya Maṭh.

Bhaktikusum Sraman. 1983. *Prabhupāda Śrīla Sarasvatī Ṭhākura*. Trans. Gaurdas Brahmachari. Sri Mayapur: Sri Chaitanya Math.

Bhakti Pradip Tirtha. 1939. *Thakura Bhaktivinoda*. Ahol: Sri Sacinath Roy Chakravarti.

Bhakti Prajnan Keshab. [1950] 1981. Preface to the 1st ed. Pp. A–F in *Shri Chaitanya Mahaprabhu: His Life and Precepts*, 2nd ed., ed. Srila Thakur Bhaktivinoda. Nabadwip: Shri Goudiya Vedanta Samiti.

Bhaktisiddhānta Sarasvatī. 1933. Foreword. Pp.i–xix in *Sree Krishna Chaitanya*, ed. Nishikanta Sanyal. Madras: Bhaktihridaya Bana for Sree Gaudiya Math.

———. [1923–35] 1962. *Gauḍīya Bhāṣya*. 2nd ed. 12 vols. Mayapur: Caitanya Maṭha and Gauḍīya Maṭha.

———, ed. [1932] 1985. *Brahma Saṁhitā with Commentary of Jīva Gosvāmin*. Los Angeles: Bhaktivedanta Book Trust. Original ed., Madras: Bhakti Hṛday Bon.

———. 1993. *Prākrita Rasa Shata Dushini: A Hundred Warnings against Mundane Mellows*. Trans. Daśaratha-suta dāsa. Union City, GA: Nectar Books.

———. 1998. *Vaiṣṇava Ke? What Kind of Devotee are You?* 2nd ed. Trans. and comm. A. C. Bhaktivedanta Swami Prabhupāda and Jayapatākā Swami. Kuala Lumpur: Bhaktivedanta Victory Flag Press.

———. 1999. *Brāhmaṇa and Vaiṣṇava.* Trans. Bhumipati Dāsa. Vrindaban: Vrajraja Press.

Bhaktivedanta Book Trust (BBT). 1975. *The Krishna Consciousness Movement Is Authorized.* Los Angeles: Bhaktivedanata Book Trust.

———. 1981. "An Analysis of Bhagawat Geeta." Pp. xxv–xxxi in *Śrī Vyāsa-pūjā August 24, 1981.* Los Angeles: Bhaktivedanta Book Trust.

———. 1998. *Responsible Publishing: Why and How the BBT Publishes Revisions of Srīla Prabhupāda's Books.* Los Angeles: Bhaktivedanata Book Trust.

Bhaktivilasa Tirtha, ed. 1940. *Śrīmad Bhāgavatam* Tenth Book with Viśvanātha Cakravartī's Commentary. Śrī Māyāpura: Śrī Caitanya Math.

Bhaktivinoda Ṭhākura. 1959. *The Bhagavat, Its Philosophy, Ethics and Theology.* Ed. Bhaktivilas Tirtha, 2nd ed. Madras: Madras Gaudiya Math.

———. [1896] 1981. *Shri Chaitanya Mahaprabhu, His Life and Precepts.* 2nd ed. Nabadwip: Shri Goudiya Vedanta Samiti.

———. [1886] 1983. *Shri Chaitanya Shikshamritam.* Trans. Bijoy Krishna Rarhi. Madras: Sri Gaudiya Math.

———. 1988. *Śrīla Bhaktivinoda Ṭhākura's* Gaurāṅga-līlā-smaraṇa-maṅgala-stotra—*Auspicious Meditations on Lord Gaurāṅga.* Trans. Kuśakratha dāsa. Los Angeles: Kṛṣṇa Institute.

———. [1890] 1989. *Śrīla Bhaktivinoda Ṭhākura's* Śrī Navadvīpa-dhāma-māhātmya, Pramāṇa-khaṇḍa: *The Glories of Śrī Navadvīpa, Evidence from Scripture.* Trans. Kuśakratha dāsa. Los Angeles: Kṛṣṇa Institute.

———. [1900] 1990. Śrī Hari-nāma-cintāmaṇi: *The Beautiful Wish-Fulfilling Gem of the Holy Name.* Trans. Sri Sarvabhavana dasa Adhikari. Bombay: Bhaktivedanta Books.

———. [1893] 1994. *Gītāvalī.* Pp. 76–77 in *The Songs of Bhaktivinoda Ṭhākura.* Trans. Daśaratha-suta dāsa. Union City, GA: Nectar Books.

———. 1998. *Śrī Kṛṣṇa-saṁhitā.* Trans. Bhumipati Dāsa. Vrindaban: Vrajraj Press.

———. 2000. Daśa-mūla-tattva: *The Ten Esoteric Truths of the Vedas.* Trans. Sarvabhāvana Dāsa. Vrindaban: Rasa Bihārī Brothers.

———. [1893] 1975. Jaiva Dharma. Trans. Bhaktivedānta Araṇya Mahārāja et al. Mathura: Gauḍīya Vedānta Publications.

Bharadvāj, Banarasinath. 1989. *Kedāranath Datta.* Calcutta: Śrī Caitanya Research Institute.

Bharata Shrestha Das. 1998. "ISKCON's Response to Child Abuse: 1990–1998." *ISKCON Communications Journal* 6, no. 1 (June): 71–79.

Bhūrijana dāsa. 1997. *"Surrender Unto Me": An Overview of the Bhagavad-gītā.* Vṛndāvana: VIHE (Vaiṣṇava Institute for Higher Education) Publications.

Bolle, Kees W. 1979. *The Bhagavadgītā: A New Translation*. Berkley: University of California Press.

Boston, Rob. 1992. "Public Forum or Public Nuisance: Hare Krishna Prosetylizing Case Goes to Supreme Court." *Church and State* 45 (April): 4–7.

Breckenridge, Carol A. and Peter van der Veer. 1993. *Orientalism and the Postcolonial Predicament: Perspectives on South Asia*. Philadelphia: University of Pennsylvania Press.

Brockington, John. 1997. "The *Bhagavad-gītā:* Text and Context." Pp. 28–47 in *The* Bhagavadgītā *for Our Times*, ed. Julius J. Lipner. New Delhi: Oxford University Press.

———. 2005. "The Epics in the *Bhakti* Tradition." Pp. 31–53 in *Intimate Other: Love Divine in Indic Religions*, ed. Anna King and Brockington. New Delhi: Orient Longman.

Bromley, David G. 1989. "Hare Krishna and the Anti-Cult Movement." Pp. 255–292 in *Krishna Consciousness in the West*, ed. Bromley and Larry D. Shinn. Lewisburg, PA: Bucknell University Press.

Bromley, David G. and Larry D. Shinn, eds. 1989. *Krishna Consciousness in the West*, ed. Bromley and Shinn. Lewisburg, PA: Bucknell University Press.

Brooks, Charles R. 1986. Review of *I Am Not My Body: A Study of the International Hare Krishna Sect*, by Angela Burr. *ISKCON Review* 2: 148–164.

———. 1989. *The Hare Krishnas in India*. Princeton, NJ: Princeton University Press.

Brown, C. Mackenzie. N.d. "Misplaced Footprints: Convergent Tracks of Hindu and Christian Scientific Creationism." Ms. N.p.

———. 2003. "A Personal Reflection on Tamal Krishna Goswami." *The Tamal Krishna Goswami Memorial Volume*. Spec. issue of *Journal of Vaishnava Studies* 11, no. 2: 37–42.

Bryant, Edwin. 2007. *Krishna: A Sourcebook*. New York: Oxford University Press.

Brzezinski, Jan K. 1992. "Goloka Vṛndāvana: A Translation of Jīva Gosvāmī's *Gopāla-Campū* (chapter one)." *Journal of Vaiṣṇava Studies* 1, no. 1 (Fall): 61–98.

———. 1996–97. "The Paramparā Institution in Gauḍīya Vaiṣṇavism." *Journal of Vaiṣṇava Studies* 5, no. 1 (Winter): 151–182.

———. 1998. "What Was Śrīla Prabhupāda's Position? The Hare Kṛṣṇa Movement and Hinduism." *ISKCON Communciations Journal* 6, no. 2 (Dec.): 27–49.

BTG (*Back to Godhead*). 2001. [Advertisement] "Correspondence Courses: *Bhagavad-gītā As It Is*." Alachua, FL: *Back to Godhead* 35, no. 1 (Jan.–Feb.): 33.

———. 2002. "The Spiritual Beatle" and Śyāmasundara dāsa, "My Sweet George." *Back to Godhead* 36, no. 1 (Jan.–Feb.): 20–23 and 55–56.

Buitenen, J. A. B. van. 1966. "On the Archaism of the Bhāgavata Purāṇa." Pp. 23–40 in *Krishna: Myths, Rites, and Attitudes*, ed. Milton Singer. Honolulu: East-West Center Press.

Burr, Angela. 1984. *I Am Not My Body: A Study of the International Hare Krishna Sect.* New Delhi: Vikas.

Callewaert, Winand M. and Shilanand Hemraj. 1983. *Bhagavadgītānuvāda: A Study in Transcultural Tanslation.* Ranchi: Satya Bharati Publications.

Carman, John Braisted. 1974. *The Theology of Rāmānuja.* New Haven, CT: Yale University Press.

———. 1994. *Majesty and Meekness: A Comparative Study of Contrast and Harmony in the Concept of God.* Grand Rapids, MI: William B. Eerdmans.

Carney, Gerald T. 1998. "Bābā Premānanda Bhāratī (1857–1914), an Early Twentieth-Century Encounter of Vaiṣṇava Devotion with American Culture: A Comparative Study." *Journal of Vaiṣṇava Stuidies* 6, no. 2 (Spring): 161–188.

———. 1999. "Spirit in the World: Renunication/Affirmation: A Vaiṣṇava-Christian Dialogue—9–10 April 1999, Rockwood Manor, Potomac, Maryland, USA." *ISKCON Communications Journal* 7, no. 2 (Dec.): 84–86.

Case, Margaret, ed. 1994. *Vraja Conference 1994.* Spec. issue of *Journal of Vaiṣṇava Studies* 3, no. 1 (Winter).

———, ed. 1996. *Govindadeva: A Dialogue in Stone.* New Delhi: Indira Gandhi National Centre for the Arts.

Chaitanya, Krishna. 1991. *The Betrayal of Krishna: Vicissitudes of a Great Myth.* New Delhi: Clarion Books.

Chakrabarty, Ramakanta. 1985. *Vaiṣṇavism in Bengal.* Calcutta: Sanskrit Pustak Bhandar.

Chakravarti, Sudhindra Chandra. 1969. *Philosophical Foundation of Bengal Vaiṣṇavism: A Critical Study.* Calcutta: Academic.

Chatterjee, A. N. 1983. *SriKṛṣṇa Caitanya: A Historical Study on Gauḍīya Vaiṣṇavaism.* New Delhi: Associated Publishing.

Clooney, Francis X, S.J. 1994. "From Anxiety to Bliss: Argument, Care, and Responsibility in the Vedānta Reading of *Tattirīya* 2.1–6a." Pp. 139–169 in *Authority, Anxiety, and Canon,* ed. Laurie L. Patton. Albany: State University of New York Press.

———. 1996. "The Destiny of the Soul: A Vaiṣṇava-Christian Conference—East Freeport, Freetown, Massachusetts, USA, September 20–21, 1996." *ISKCON Communications Journal* 4, no. 2 (Dec.): 71–73.

———. 2000. Review of *Transcreation of the Bhagavad Gītā,* by Ashok Kumar Malhotra. *International Journal of Hindu Studies* 4, no. 1 (April): 64–66.

———. 2003. "Believers and Scholars: Reflections on an ISKCON-Jesuit Friendship." *The Tamal Krishna Goswami Memorial Volume.* Spec. issue of *Journal of Vaishnava Studies* 11, no. 2: 43–60.

———. 2005. "Restoring 'Hindu Theology' as a Category in Indian Intellectual Discourse." Pp. 447–477 in *The Blackwell Companion to Hinduism,* ed. Gavin Flood. Oxford: Blackwell.

Coburn, Thomas B. 1980. "The Study of the *Purāṇas* and the Study of Religion." *Religious Studies* 16: 341–352.

Coles, Rev. D. 1858. *Proceedings of the South Indian Missionary Conference, Ootacamund, 19 April–5 May 1858*. Pp. 161–212. Madras.

Copley, Antony. 1997. *Religions in Conflict: Ideology, Cultural Contact and Conversion in Late Colonial India*. New Delhi: Oxford University Press, Oxford India Paperbacks, 1999.

Corcoran, Maura. 1995. *Vṛndāvana in Vaiṣṇava Literature: History—Mythology—Symbolism*. Reconstructing Indian History and Culture, no. 6. Vrindaban: Vrindaban Research Institute and New Delhi: D. K. Printworld (P).

Cox, Harvey. 1977. "A Tribute to Kṛṣṇa Consciousness." *Back to Godhead* 12, no. 6 (June): 22.

———. 1983. "Interview with..." Pp. 21–60 in *Hare Krishna, Hare Krishna: Five Distinguished Scholars on the Krishna Movement in the West*, ed. Stephen J. Gelberg. New York: Grove Press.

Cracknell, Kenneth. 1996. "Conference Report on the Nature of the Self: A Vaiṣṇava-Christian Conference—Buckland Hall, Powys, Wales, 20–21 January, 1996." *ISKCON Communications Journal* 4, no. 1 (June): 77–82.

Cremo, Michael A. 1998. *Forbidden Archaelogy's Impact*. Los Angeles: Bhaktivedanta Book Trust.

Cremo Michael A. and Richard L. Thompson. 1993. *Forbidden Archeology: The Hidden History of the Human Race*. Badger, CA: Goverdhan Hill.

Daner, Francine Jeanne. 1976. *The American Children of Kṛṣṇa: A Study of the Hare Kṛṣṇa Movement*. New York: Holt, Rinehart and Winston.

Das, Rahul Peter. [1996] 1998. "'Vedic' in the Terminology of Prabhupāda and His Followers." *Journal of Vaiṣṇava Studies* 6, no. 2 (Spring): 141–159. Originally published in *ISKCON Communications Journal* 4, no. 2: 23–38.

Dasgupta, Surendranath. [1922] 1975. *A History of Indian Philosophy*. 5 vols. Delhi: Motilal Banarsidass. Original ed., Cambridge: Cambridge University Press. .

Davis, Richard H. 1997. *Lives of Indian Images*. Princeton, NJ: Princeton University Press.

Dayal, Jai. 1989. "The *Gurukula* System: An Inquiry into the Krishna Philosophy." EdD diss., Rutgers, State University of New Jersey–New Brunswick.

De, Sushil Kumar. 1961. *Early History of the Vaisnava Faith and Movement in Bengal: From Sanskrit and Bengali Sources*. Calcutta: Firma K. L. Mukhopadhyaay.

Deadwyler, William III [Ravīndra Svarūpa dāsa]. 1992. "The Saṁpradāya of Śrī Caitanya." Pp. 127–140 in *Vaiṣṇavism: Contemporary Scholars Discuss the Gauḍīya Tradition*, ed. Steven J. Rosen. Brooklyn, NY: Folk Books.

———. 1996. "The Devotee and the Deity: Living a Personalistic Theology." Pp. 68–87 in *Gods of Flesh, Gods of Stone*, ed. Joanne Punzo Waghorne, Normal Cutler, and Vasudha Narayanan. New York: Columbia University Press.

———. 2001. "Rādhā, Kṛṣṇa, Caitanya: The Inner Dialectic of the Divine Relativity." *Journal of Vaishnava Studies* 10, no. 1 (Fall): 5–25.

Delmonico, Neal Gorton. 1990. "Sacred Rapture: A Study of the Religious Aesthetic of Rūpa Gosvāmin." PhD diss., University of Chicago.

De Nicolas, Antonio T. 1976. *Avatara: The Humanization of Philosophy through the Bhagavad Gita*. New York: Institute for Advanced Studies of World Religions.

De Smet, Richard V., S.J. 1953. "The Theological Method of Śaṁkara." PhD diss., Pontifical Gregorian University.

Deutsch, Eliot. 1988. "Knowledge and the Tradition Text in Indian Philosophy." Pp. 165–173 in *Interpreting Across Boundaries: New Essays in Comparative Philosophy*, ed. Gerald James Larson and Deutsch. Princeton, NJ: Princeton University Press.

[Devamayī dāsi]. 1997. *Prabhupāda Saraswati Thakur: The Life and Precepts of Śrīla Bhaktisiddhānta Sasaswatī*. Eugene, OR: Mandala.

Dhanurdhara Swami. 2000. *Waves of Devotion: A Comphrehensive Study of the Nectar of Devotion*. N.p.: Bhagavat Books.

Dimock, Edward C. Jr. 1966. "Doctrine and Practice among the Vaiṣṇavas of Bengal." Pp. 41–63 in *Krishna: Myths, Rites, and Attitudes*, ed. Milton Singer. Honolulu: East-West Center Press.

———. 1972. Foreword to *Bhagavad-gītā As It Is*, complete ed., by A. C. Bhaktivedanta Swami Prabhupāda. New York: Collier Macmillan.

———. [1966] 1989. *The Place of the Hidden Moon: Erotic Mysticism in the Vaiṣṇava-sahajiyā Cult of Bengal*. Foreword by Wendy Doniger. Chicago: University of Chicago Press. Original ed., Chicago: University of Chicago Press.

Doniger, Wendy. 1998. *The Implied Spider: Politics and Theology in Myth*. New York: Columbia University Press.

Dr. Urquhart Farewell Committee. 1937. *Dr. Urquhart Commemoration Volume*. Calcutta: Dr. Urquhart Farewell Committee.

Eck, Diana L. 1979. "Kṛṣṇa Consciousness in Historical Perspective." *Back to Godhead* 14, no. 10: 26–29.

———. 1985. *Darśan: Seeing the Divine Image in India*. 2nd ed. rev. and enl. Chambersburg, PA: Anima Books.

Edelmann, Jonathan. 2012. *Hindu Theology and Biology: The Bhāgavata Purāṇa and Contemporary Theory*. Oxford Theological Monographs. Oxford: Oxford University Press.

Ellwood, Robert S. 1983. Foreword to *Hare Krishna, Hare Krishna: Five Distinguished Scholars on the Krishna Movement in the West*, ed. Stephen J. Gelberg. New York: Grove Press.

Entwistle, Alan W. 1987. *Braj Centre of Krishna Pilgrimage*. Groningen: Egbert Forsten.

Ewart, Rev. D. 1855. *Proceedings of a General Conference*. Pp. 67–79. Calcutta: Baptist Mission Press.

Farquhar, J. N. 1915. *The Crown of Hinduism*. Oxford: Oxford University Press.

———. [1915] 1998. *Modern Religious Movements in India*. New Delhi: Munshiram Manoharlal.

Fields, Rick. 1992. *How the Swans Came to the Lake: A Narrative History of Buddhism in America*. 3rd rev. and updated ed. Boston: Shambala.

Flood, Gavin. 1995. "Hinduism, Vaisnavism, and ISKCON: Authentic Traditions or Scholarly Constructions?" *ISKCON Communciations Journal* 3, no. 2 (Dec.): 5–15.

———. 1999. *Beyond Phenomenology: Rethinking the Study of Religion*. London: Cassel.

Fortshoefel, Thomas A. and Patricia Y. Mumme. 1999. "The Monkey-Cat Debate in Śrīvaiṣṇavism." *Journal of Vaiṣṇava Studies* 8, no. 1 (Fall): 3–33.

Ganga. 1990. *Kṛṣṇa Art*. New York: Ganga.

GBC Deity Worship Research Group. 1995. Pañcarātra Pradīpa—*Daily Service* (Nitya-seva)—*Method of Deity Worship for the International Society for Krishna Consciousness*. Vol. 1 and supp. vol. Mayapur: ISKCON GBC Press.

Geertz, Clifford. 1966. "Religion as a Cultural System." Pp. 1–46 in *Anthropoligical Approaches to the Study of Religion: The Social Anthropology of Complex Societies*, ed. Michael P. Banton. London: Tavistock Publications.

Gelberg, Stephen J. [Śubhānanda dāsa], ed. 1983. *Hare Krishna, Hare Krishna: Five Distinguished Scholars on the Krishna Movement in the West*. New York: Grove Press.

———. 1986. "The Catholic Church and the Hare Krishna Movement: An Invitation to Dialogue." *ISKCON Review* 2: 1–63.

———. 1992. "Vrindaban as Locus of Mystical Experience." *Journal of Vaiṣṇava Studies* 1, no. 1 (Fall): 9–41.

Ginsberg, Allen. 1968. "Swami Bhaktivedanta: Chanting God's Song in America." Pp. 13–15 in *The Bhagavad-Gita As It Is* by A. C. Bhaktivedanta Swami. New York: Collier Macmillan.

Gomatam, Ravi V. 1988. "Real and Artificial Intelligence: Can Machines Think?" Bombay: Bhaktivedanta Institute.

Gonda, Jan. 1960. *Die Religionen Indiens*. Vol. 1: *Veda and lterer Hinduismus*. Stuttgart: W. Kohlhammer.

Goodman, Nelson. 1968. *Languages of Art: An Approach to a Theory of Symbols*. Indianapolis: Bobbs-Merrill.

Goodstein, Laurie. 1998. "Hare Krishna Movement Details Past Abuse at Its Boarding Schools." *New York Times* Oct. 9: 1, 14.

Gordon, James S. 1989. "Psychiatry and Krishna Consciousness." Pp. 238–254 in *Krishna Consciousness in the West*, ed. David G. Bromley and Larry D. Shinn. Lewisburg, PA: Bucknell University Press.

Goswami, Asha. 2001. *The Kṛṣṇa Legend: A New Perspective*. Delhi: Motilal Banarsidass.

Goswami, C. L. and M. A. Sastri, trans. 1971. *Śrīmad Bhāgavata Mahāpurāṇa*. Gorakhpur: Gita Press.

Gupta, Ravi. 2007. *The Chaitanya Vaishnava Vedanta of Jiva Gosvami*. Routledge Hindu Studies. Oxon: Routledge.

Gupta, Sanjukta. 1989. "The Pāñcarātra Attitude to Mantra." Pp. 224–248 in *Understanding Mantras*, ed. Harvey P. Alper. Albany: State University of New York Press.

Haberman, David L. 1988. *Acting as a Way of Salvation: A Study of Rāgānugā Bhakti Sādhana*. New York: Oxford University Press.

———. 1994a. "Divine Betrayal: Krishna-Gopal of Braj in the Eyes of Outsiders." *Journal of Vaiṣṇava Studies* 3, no. 1 (Winter): 83–111.

———. 1994b. *Journey through the Twelve Forests: An Encounter with Krishna*. New York: Oxford University Press.

———, trans. 2002. *The Bhaktirasāmṛtasindhu of Rūpa Gosvāmin*. Delhi: Motilal Banarsidass.

Halbfass, Wilhelm. 1988. *India and Europe*. Albany: State University of New York Press.

Hardy, Friedhelm. 1983. Viraha-bhakti: *The Early History of Kṛṣṇa Devotion in South India*. Delhi: Oxford University Press.

———, ed. [1988] 1990. *The World's Religions: The Religions of Asia*. London: Routledge. Originally pub. as part of *The World's Religions*, ed. Stewart R. Sutherland et al. London: Routledge.

Hargrove, Barbara. 1978. "Integrative and Transformative Religions." Pp. 257–266 in *Understanding the New Religions*, ed. Jacob Needleman and George Baker. New York: Seabury Press.

Haridāsa Dāsa. 1941 [465 Gaurabda]. *Śrī Śrī Gauḍīya Vaiṣṇava Jīvana*. Vol. 2. Navadvīpa: Haribol Kuṭhir.

Hatcher, Brian A. 1999. *Eclecticism and Modern Hindu Discourse*. New York: Oxford University Press.

Hayagriva das [Howard Wheeler]. 1985. *The Hare Krishna Explosion: The Birth of Krishna Consciousness in America (1966–1969)*. Singapore: Palace Press.

Hein, Norvin J. 1976. "Caitanya's Ecstasies and the Theology of the Name." Pp. 15–32 in *Hinduism: New Essays in the History of Religions*, ed. Bardwell L. Smith. Leiden: E. J. Brill.

Herman, A. L. 1991. *A Brief Introduction to Hinduism: Religion, Philosophy and Ways of Liberation*. Boulder, CO: Westview Press.

Hiltebeitel, Alf. 1992. "Mahābhārata." Pp. 49–59 in *Vaiṣṇavism: Contemporary Scholars Discuss the Gauḍīya Tradition*, ed. Steven J. Rosen. Brooklyn, NY: Folk Books.

Holdrege, Barbara. 2003. "From the Religious Marketplace to the Academy: Negotiating the Politics of Identity." *The Tamal Krishna Goswami Memorial Volume*. Spec. issue of *Journal of Vaishnava Studies* 11, no. 2: 113–142.

Hopkins, E. Washburn. 1911. "The Epic Use of Bhagavat and Bhakti." *Journal of the Royal Asiatic Society of Great Britain and Ireland*, July: 727–738.

Hopkins, Thomas J. 1966. "The Social Teachings of the Bhāgavata Purāṇa." Pp. 3–22 in *Krishna: Myths, Rites, and Attitudes*, ed. Milton Singer. Honolulu: East-West Center Press.

———. 1983. "Interview with . . ." Pp. 101–161 in *Hare Krishna, Hare Krishna: Five Distinguished Scholars on the Krishna Movement in the West*, ed. Stephen J. Gelberg. New York: Grove Press.

———. 1989. "The Social and Religious Background for Transmission of Gaudiya Vaisnavism to the West." Pp. 35–54 in *Krishna Consciousness in the West*, ed. David G. Bromley and Larry D. Shinn. Lewisburg, PA: Bucknell University Press.

———. 1995. "A Response to Joseph Vekerdi." *ISKCON Communications Journal* 3, no. 2 (Dec.): 99–103.

———. 1998. "Why Should ISKCON Study Its Own History?" *ISKCON Communications Journal* 6, no. 2: 1–6.

———. 1999. Foreword. Pp. vii–x in *Hindu Encounter with Modernity: Kedarnath Datta Bhaktivinoda, Vaiṣṇava Theologian*, by Shukavak N. Dasa. Los Angeles: SRI (Sanskrit Religions Institute).

Hṛdayānanada dāsa Goswami. 1999. "For Whom Does Hinduism Speak?" *ISKCON Communications Journal* 7, no. 1 (June): 45–53.

———. 1996. *Our Original Position: Śrīla Prabhupāda and the Vaiṣṇava Siddhānta*. Mayapur: ISKCON GBC Press.

Inden, Ronald. 1990. *Imagining India*. Oxford: Basil Blackwell.

Ingalls, Daniel. 1966. Foreword to *Krishna: Myths, Rites, and Attitudes*, ed. Milton Singer. Honolulu: East-West Center Press.

Introvigne, Massimo. 1997. "Religious Liberty in Western Europe." *ISKCON Communications Journal* 5, no. 2 (December): 37–48.

Jagadīśa Goswami. 1986. Bhakti-Śāstrī *Study Guide for* Bhagavad-gītā As It Is. Dallas: ISKCON Gurukula Press.

Jaiswal, Suvira. 1981. *The Origins and Development of Vaiṣṇavism*. 2nd. rev. and enl. ed. New Delhi: Munshiram Manoharlal.

Jīva Gosvāmin. 1915. Bhāgavata-sandarbha. Śyāmalāla Gosvāmī. Calcutta: Śyāmalāla Gosvāmī.

———. 1951. Bhāgavata-sandarbha. 2 vols. Puridasa Mahasaya, ed. Vrindavan: Haridasa Sharma.

———. 1962. *Bhakti-sandarbha*. Ed. with Bengali trans. by Rādhāraman Gosvāmī and Kṛṣṇagopāla Gosvāmī. Calcutta: University of Calcutta.

———. 1986a. *Jīva Gosvāmin's Tattvasandharbha: A Study on the Philosophical and Sectarian Development of the Gauḍīya Vaiṣṇava Movement.* Trans. Stuart Mark Elkman. Delhi: Motilal Banarsidass.

———. 1986b. Kṛṣṇa Sandharbha *and Its Critical Study.* Ed. with intro. notes and *Sarvasamvādinī* commentary of Śrī Jīva Gosvāmī by Chinmayi Chatterjee. Calcutta: Jadavpur University.

Johnson, Gregory L. 1973. "An Alternative Community in Microcosm: The Evolution of Commitment to a Vedic Sect." PhD diss., Harvard University.

Jordens, J. T. F. 1998. *Gandhi's Religion: A Homespun Shawl.* London: MacMillan.

Judah, J. Stillson. 1974. *Hare Krishna and the Counterculture.* New York: John Wiley & Sons.

Kapoor, Oude Bihari Lal. 1976. *The Philosophy and Religion of Śrī Caitanya: The Philosophical Background of the Hare Krishna Movement.* Delhi: Munshiram Manoharlal.

———. 1992. "Vṛndāvana: The Highest Paradise." *Journal of Vaiṣṇava Studies* 1, no. 1 (Fall): 42–49.

———. 1993. *The Life of Love: Biography of Sri Srimat Radharamana Charan Das Dev.* Sarasvatī Jayaśrī Classics. Caracas: Badrīnārāyaṇa Bhāgavata Bhuṣaṇa.

———. 1995. *The Saints of Bengal.* Sarasvatī Jayaśrī Classics. Caracas: Badrīnārāyaṇa Bhāgavata Bhuṣaṇa.

Karambelkar, P. V. N.d. *Patanjala Yoga Sutras.* Lonavla, India: Kaivalyadhama.

Karṇāmṛta dāsa Adhikary. 1990. *Babaji Maharaja, "Two Beyond Duality": A Biography of His Divine Grace Śrīla Gaura-kiśora dāsa Bābājī Mahārāja and His Divine Grace Śrīla Jagannātha dāsa Bābājī Mahārāja.* Vol. 3 of *Live of the Vaiṣṇava Ācāryas.* Washington, MS: New Jaipur Press.

Kavi Karṇapūra. 1987. *Gaura-gaṇoddeśa-dīpikā.* Sanskrit, with trans. by Kuśakratha dāsa. The Kṛṣṇa Library vol. 11. Culver City, CA: Kṛṣṇa Institute.

Kennedy, Melville T. [1925] 1993. *The Chaitanya Movement: A Study of Vaishnavism in Bengal.* New Delhi: Munshiram Manoharlal. Original ed., The Religious Life of India Series, Calcutta: Association Press.

Kenney, J. Frank. 1976. "The Manifestation of A. C. Bhaktivedanta as Swami, Guru and Avatar." Paper presented at the annual meeting of the American Academy of Religion. Available online at: http://www.lotusimprints.com/new/pdf/TD5/td5_appendix_kenny-paper.pdf (accessed March 13, 2012).

———. 1980. "Krishna Consciousness as a Bengal Revitalization Movement." Pp. 14–16 in *Proceedings of the 1980 Southwest Conference on Asian Studies.* N.p.: n.p.

———. 1982. "'Dharma' and 'Tolerance' in Krishna Consciousness." Pp. 82–88 in *Proceedings of the 1982 Southwest Conference on Asian Studies.* N.p.: n.p.

———. 1990. "Is a Dialogue with ISKCON Possible?" *Jeevadhara* 20 (Spring): 405–411.

Kenney, J. Frank, and Tommy H. Polling. 1979. "Sexual Sublimation in Krishna Consciousness." Pp. 236–244 in *Proceedings of the 1978 Southwest Conference on Asian Studies,* ed. Lester J. Bilsky. Little Rock, AK: n.p.

———. 1986. *The Hare Krishna Character Type: A Study of the Sensate Personality*. Lewiston, NY: Edwin Mellon Press.

———. 1989. "Personality and Biographical Charateristics of Irish Hare Krishnas." Paper presented at the Annual Meeting of the Society for the Scientific Study of Religion, Southwest, Dallas, Mar.

Keśava Bhāratī dāsa. 1999. "A Storybook Ending: A Son Helps His Mother Prepare for the Ultimate Test." *Back to Godhead*, 33, no. 1 (Jan.–Feb.): 35–43.

King, Anna. 2003. "The Guru-Disciple Relationship in ISKCON." *The Tamal Krishna Goswami Memorial Volume*. Spec. issue of *Journal of Vaishnava Studies* 11, no. 2: 173–186.

King, Richard. 1999. *Orientalism and Religion: Postcolonial Theory, India and "The Mystic East."* London: Routledge.

Kinsley, David R. 1975. *The Sword and the Flute: Kālī and Kṛṣṇa—Dark Visions of the Terrible and the Sublime in Hindu Mythology*. Berkley: University of California Press.

Kliever, Lonnie D. 1981. *The Shattered Spectrum: A Survey of Contemporary Theology*. Atlanta: John Knox Press.

Klostermaier, Klaus K. 1972. "*Hṛdayavidyā*: A Sketch of a Hindu-Christian Theology of Love." *Journal of Ecumenical Studies* 9, no. 4 (Fall): 750–775.

———. 1980. "Will India's Past Be America's Future? Reflections on the Caitanya Movement and Its Potentials." *Journal of Asian and African Studies* 15, nos. 1–2 (Jan. and Apr.): 94–103.

———. 1988. "A Universe of Feelings." Pp. 123–139 in *Religions and Comparative Thought: Essays in Honor of the Late Dr. Ian Kesarcodi-Watson*, ed. Purusottama Bilimoria and Peter Fenner. Delhi: Satguru Publications.

———. 1996. "The Education of Human Emotions: Śrīla Prabhupāda as Spiritual Educator." *ISKCON Communications Journal* 4, no. 1 (June): 25–32.

Knott, Kim. 1986. *My Sweet Lord: The Hare Krishna Movement*. Wellingborough, England: Aquarian Press.

———. 1995. "The Debate about Women in the Hare Krishna Movement." *ISKCON Communications Journal* 3, no. 2 (Dec.): 33–49. Also published in *Journal of Vaiṣṇava Studies* 3, no. 4 (Fall 1995): 85–109.

———. [1997] 1998. "Insider and Outsider Perceptions of Prabhupāda." *Journal of Vaiṣṇava Studies* 6, no. 2 (Spring): 73–91. Originally published in *ISKCON Communications Journal* 5, no.1: 59–72.

———. 1999. *The Many Faces of ISKCON*. Audiotape no. 1 of a seminar presented at ISKCON Convention Europe 1999, Radhadesh, Belgium, June 29–July 3.

Kopf, David. 1969. *British Orientalism and the Bengal Renaissance: The Dynamics of Indian Modernization, 1773–1835*. Berkley: University of California Press.

Kṛṣṇadāsa Kavirāja. 1999. Caitanya Caritāmṛta *of Kṛṣṇadāsa Kavirāja*. Trans. and commentary Edward C. Dimock, Jr. Intro. Dimock and Tony K. Stewart. Ed.

Tony K. Stewart. Harvard Oriental Series, vol. 56. Cambridge, MA: Department of Sanskrit and Indian Studies, Harvard University.

Kṛṣṇa-kṣetra dāsa. (Kenneth R. Valpey). 2001. "Idolatry and Divine Manifestation." *Arcana* 3 (Mar.): 12–17.

Kurma dāsa. 1999. *The Great Transcendental Adventure: Pastimes of His Divine Grace A. C. Bhaktivedanta Swami Prabhupāda in Australia and New Zealand.* Botany, Australia: Chakra Press.

Langone, Michael D. 1999. "Cults, Psychological Manipulation and Society: International Perspectives—An Overview." *ISKCON Communications Journal* 7, no. 2 (Dec.): 53–60.

Lawrence, Bruce D. 1998. "Transformation." Pp. 334–348 in *Critical Terms for Religious Studies*, ed. Mark C. Taylor. Chicago: University of Chicago Press.

Levertov, Denise. 1968. "A Note of Appreciation for This Volume." Pp. 16–17 in *The Bhagavad-Gita As It Is* by A. C. Bhaktivedanta Swami. New York: Collier Macmillan.

Levine, Faye. 1974. *The Strange World of the Hare Krishnas.* Greenwich, CT: Fawcett Publications.

Lipner, Julius J. 1986. *The Face of Truth: A Study of Meaning and Metaphysics in the Vedāntic Theology of Rāmānuja.* Albany: SUNY Press.

———. 1989. "Śaṅkara on Metaphor with Reference to Gītā 13.12–18." Pp. 167–181 in *Indian Philosophy of Religion*, ed. R. W. Perett. Dordrecht: Kluwer Academic.

———. 1994a. *Hindus: Their Religious Beliefs and Practices.* London: Routledge.

———. 1994b. "ISKCON at the Crossroads?" *ISKCON Communications Journal* 3 (Jan.–June): 22–24.

———. 1996. "Avatāra *and* Incarnation?" Pp. 127–143 in *Re-Visioning India's Religious Traditions: Essays in Honour of Eric Lott*, ed. David C. Scott and Israel Selvanayagam. Bangalore: I.S.P.C.K. for United Theological College.

———. 1999. *Brahmabandhab Upadhyay: The Life and Thought of a Revolutionary.* Delhi: Oxford University Press.

———. 2000. "Lowering the Drawbridge: Are Hinduism and Christianity Compatible?" Pp. 333–348 in *A Great Commission: Christian Hope and Religious Diversity—Papers in Honour of Kenneth Cracknell on his 65th Birthday*, ed. Martin Forward, Stephen Plant, and Susan White. Bern: Peter Lang.

———. 2003. "The Pioneering Scholarship of Tamal Krishna Goswami." *The Tamal Krishna Goswami Memorial Volume.* Spec. issue of *Journal of Vaishnava Studies* 11, no. 2: 23–26.

Llewellyn, J. E. 2000. "The Clinging Spider Web of Context: A Review of *The Implied Spider* by Wendy Doniger." *Religious Studies Review* 26, no. 1 (Jan. 2000): 43–48.

Lorenz, Ekkehard. 2004. "The Guru, Māyāvādins, and Women: Tracing the Origins of Selected Polemical Statements in the Work of A.C. Bhaktivedanta Swami." Pp. 112–128 in *The Hare Krishna Movement: The Post-Charismatic Fate of a*

Religious Transplant, ed. Edwin Bryant and Maria Ekstrand. New York: Columbia University Press.

———. N.d. "Unzipping the Purports." Ms. Bhaktivedanta Book Trust.

Madsen, Finn. n.d. "Institutionalizing Varna in ISKCON." MS, n.p.

———. 2000. "Asrama, yukta-vairagya et structure d'organisation chez ISKCON." *Social Compass* 47, no. 2: 185–201.

Macnicol, Nicol. [1915] 1968. *Indian Theism: From the Vedic to the Muhammadan Period*. 2nd ed. Delhi: Munshiram Manoharlal.

Madhudvisa dasa. 1999. "108 Changes To Srila Prabhupada's Bhagavad Gita as It Is." *Vaisnava News Network* (VNN3273), March 8. Available at http://www.vnn.org.

Mahānidhi Swami 1996. *Appreciating Navadvīpa Dhāma*. New Delhi: Mahānidhi Swami.

Mahapatra, Sarat Chandra, ed. 1994. *Car Festival of Lord Jagannath Puri*. Puri: Sri Jagannath Research Centre.

Majumdar, A. K. 1969. *Caitanya His Life and Doctrine: A Study in Vaiṣṇavism*. Bombay: Bharatiya Vidya Bhavan.

Majumdar, Biman Bihari. 1969. *Kṛṣṇa in History and Legend*. Calcutta: University of Calcutta.

Majumdar, R. C., ed. 1965. *British Paramountcy and Indian Renaissance Part II*. The History and Culture of the Indian People, vol. 10. Bombay: Bharatiya Vidya Bhavan.

———. 1973. *History of Medieval Bengal*. Calcutta: Bharadwaj.

Malhotra, Ashok Kumar. 1999. *Transcreation of the Bhagavad Gītā*. Upper Saddle River, NJ: Prentice Hall.

Marglin, Frederique. 1999. "The Famous Ratha Jātrā Festival of Puri." *Journal of Vaiṣṇava Studies* 7, no. 2 (Spring): 131–173.

Marriott, McKim. 1966. "The Feast of Love." Pp. 200–212 in *Krishna, Myths, Rites and Attitudes*, ed. Milton Singer. Honolulu: East-West Center Press.

Matchett, Freda. 1993. "The Pervasiveness of *Bhakti* in the Bhāgavata Purāṇa." Pp. 95–115 in *Love Divine*, ed. Karel Werner. Richmond, England: Curzon.

———. 2001. *Kṛṣṇa: Lord or* Avatāra*?—The Relationship between Kṛṣṇa and Viṣṇu*. Richmond, England: Curzon Press.

Matilal, Bimal Krishna. 1986. *Perception: An Essay on Classical Indian Theories of Knowledge*. New York: Oxford University Press.

McDaniel, June. 1989. *The Madness of the Saints: Ecstatic Religion in Bengal*. Chicago: University of Chicago Press.

McDermott, Rachel Fell. "Remembering Tamal Krishna Goswami." *The Tamal Krishna Goswami Memorial Volume*. Spec. issue of *Journal of Vaishnava Studies* 11, no. 2: 27–32.

McFague, Sallie. 1982. *Metaphorical Theology: Models of God in Religious Language*. Philadelphia: Fortress Press.

———. 1988. *Models of God: Theology for an Ecological, Nuclear Age*. Philadelphia: Fortress Press.

Melton, J. Gordon. 1989. "The Attitude of Americans toward Hinduism from 1883 to 1983 with Special Reference to ISKCON." Pp. 79–101 in *Krishna Consciousness in the West*, ed. David G. Bromley and Larry D. Shinn. Lewisburg, PA: Bucknell University Press.

Mensching, Gustav. 1971. *Tolerance and Truth in Religion*. Tuscaloosa: University of Alabama Press.

Merton, Thomas. 1968. "The Significance of the Bhagavad Gita." Pp. 18–22 in *The Bhagavad-Gita As It Is* by A. C. Bhaktivedanta Swami. New York: Collier Macmillan.

Michael, R. Blake. 1989. "Heaven, West Virginia: Legitimation Techniques of the New Vrindaban Community." Pp. 188–216 in *Krishna Consciousness in the West*, ed. David G. Bromley and Larry D. Shinn. Lewisburg, PA: Bucknell University Press.

Miller, Barbara Stoler, ed. and trans. 1977. *Love Songs of the Dark Lord: Jayadeva's Gītagovinda*. New York: Columbia University Press.

Miller, Jeanine. 1993. "*Bhakti* and the Ṛg Veda: Does it Appear There or Not?" Pp. 1–35 in *Love Divine*, ed. Karel Werner. Richmond, England: Curzon.

Miller, Timothy, ed. 1995. *America's Alternative Religions*. Albany: State University of New York Press.

Minor, Robert N. 1986. Conclusion. Pp. 222–227 in *Modern Interpreters of the* Bhagavadgita, ed. Minor. Albany: State University of New York Press.

———. 1988. *Radhakrishnan: A Religious Biography*. Albany: State University of New York Press.

———. 1995. "The Bhagavad-gītā and the Reified 'Hinduism.'" *Journal of Vaiṣṇava Studies* 3, no. 2 (Spring): 71–89.

Moody, Jonathan Fredric. 1978. "Ethics and Colunter Culture: An Analysis of the Ethics of Hare Kṛṣṇa." PhD diss., Claremont Graduate School.

Mukunda Goswami. 1995. "NRM Is a Four-Letter Word: The Language of Oppression." *ISKCON Communications Journal* 3, no. 2: 73–75.

Mumme, Patricia Y., 1992. "Haunted by Śaṅkara's Ghost: The Śrīvaiṣṇava Interpretation of Bhagavad-gītā 18:66." Pp. 69–84 in *Texts in Context: Traditional Hermeneutics in South Asia*, ed. Jeffrey R. Timm. Albany: State University of New York Press.

Murty, K. Satchidananda. 1959. *Revelation and Reason in Advaita Vedānta*. Andhra University Series No. 64. Waltair: Andhra University and New York: Columbia University Press.

Muster, Nori J. 1997. *Betrayal of the Spirit: My Life behind the Headlines of the Hare Krishna Movement*. Urbana: University of Illinois Press.

Narayanan, Vasudha. 1996. "Arcāvatāra: On Earth as He is in Heaven." Pp. 53–66 in *Gods of Flesh Gods of Stone: The Embodiment of Divinity in India*, ed. Joanne Punzo Waghorne and Norman Cutler, with Narayanan. New York: Columbia University Press.

Niranjana, Tejaswini. 1990. "Translation, Colonialism and Rise of English." *Economic and Political Weekly* Apr.14: 773–779.

Nitya-svarupa Brahmachari, ed. 1907. Śrīmad Bhāgavata Purāṇam. Brindavan: Sri Devakinandan Press.

Nye, Malory. 1997. "ISKCON and Hindus in Britain: Some Thoughts on a Developing Relgionship." *ISKCON Communications Journal* 5, no. 2 (Dec.): 5–13.

———. 2001. *Multiculturalism and Minority Religions: Krishna Consciousness, Religious Freedom, and the Politics of Location.* Richmond, England: Curzon.

O'Connell, Joseph T. 1973. "The Word 'Hindu' in Gaudya Vaisnava Texts." *Journal of the American Oriental Society* 93, no. 3 (Jul. –Sep.): 340–344.

———. 1976a. "Caitanya's Followers and the *Bhagavad-gītā*: A Case Study in Bhakti and the Secular." Pp. 33–52 in *Hinduism: New Essays in the History of Religion*, ed. Bardwell L. Smith. Studies in the History of Religions (Supplements to *Numen*) 33. Leiden: E. J. Brill.

———. 1976b. Review of *Hare Krishna and the Counterculture* by J. Stillson Judah. *Journal of the Canadian Church Historical Society* 18, no. 1 (Mar.): 20–22.

———. 1989. "Were Caitanya's Vaiṣṇavas Really Sahajiyās?—The Case of Rāmānanada Rāya." Pp. 11–22 in *Shaping Bengali Worlds, Public and Private*, ed. Tony K. Stewart. East Lansing: Asian Studies Center, Michigan State University.

———. 1995. "*Karma* in the *Bhagavad-gītā*: Caitanya Vaiṣṇava Views." *Journal of Vaiṣṇava Studies* 3, no. 2 (Spring): 91–107.

———. N.d.. "The Sahajiya Problem: Chaitanya Vaishnava Bhakti vs. Tantric Yoga of the Left Hand." For "Caitanya Vaiṣṇava Studies II: Bhakti Texts and Teachings." N.p.

O'Flaherty, Wendy. 1987. "The Interaction of *Saguṇa* and *Nirguṇa* Images of Deity." Pp. 47–52 in *The Sants: Studies in a Devotional Tradition of India*, ed. Karine Schomer and W. H. Mcleod. Delhi: Motilal Banarsidass.

(Doniger) O'Flaherty, Wendy and J. Duncan M. Derrett, eds. 1978. *The Concept of Duty in South Asia.* London: School of Oriental and African Studies.

Otto, Rudolf. 1929. *Christianity and the Indian Religion of Grace.* Madras: Christian Literature Society for India.

———. 1930. *India's Religion of Grace and Christianity Compared and Contrasted.* New York: Macmillan.

Padoux, André. 1989. "Mantras—What Are They?" Pp. 295–318 in *Understanding Mantras*, ed. Harvey P. Alper. Albany: State University of New York Press.

Palmer, Susan Jean. 1994. *Moon Sisters, Krishna Mothers, Rajneesh Lovers: Women's Roles in New Religions.* Syracuse, NY: Syracuse University Press.

Patton, Laurie L., ed. 1994. *Authority, Anxiety, and Canon: Essays in Vedic Interpretation.* Albany: State University of New York Press.

Pepper, Stephen C. 1942. *World Hypotheses: A Study in Evidence.* Berkeley: University of California Press.

Pereira, Jose. [1976] 1991. *Hindu Theology.* Delhi: Motilal Banarsidass.

Pollock, Sheldon. 1993. "Deep Orientalism? Notes on Sanskrit and Power beyond the Raj." Pp. 76–133 in *Orientalism and the Poscolonial Predicament: Perspectives on South Asia,* ed. Carol A. Breckenridge and Peter van der Veer. Philadelphia: University of Pennsylvania Press.

Potter, Karl H., ed. 1970. *Encyclopedia of Indian Philosophies.* Vol. 3: *Advaita Vedānta up to Śaṁkara and His Pupils.* Delhi: Motilal Banarsidass.

Preciado-Solis, Benjamin. 1984. *The Kṛṣṇa Cycle n the Purāṇas: Themes and Motifs in a Heroic Saga.* Delhi: Motilal Banarsidass.

Prentiss, Karen Pechilis. 1999. *The Embodiment of Bhakti.* New York: Oxford University Press.

Puyang-Martin, Mi. 1996. "Kirtan: Devotional Music in the International Society for Krishna Consciousness." PhD diss., University of Maryland.

Radhakrishnan, Sarvepalli. [1948] 1993. The Bhagavadgītā*: With an Introductory Essay, Sanskrit Text, English Translation and Notes.* Delhi: Harper Collins Publishers India, Original ed., London: George Allen and Unwin.

Ramanujan, A. K. 1984. "The Myths of Bhakti: Images of Śiva in Śaiva Poetry." P. 212 in *Discourses of Śiva: Proceedings of a Symposium on the Nature of Religious Imagery,* ed. Michael W. Meister. Philadelphia: University of Pennsylvania Press.

Rambachan, Anantanand. 2001. "Hierarchies in the Nature of God? Questioning the *Saguna-Nirguna* Distinction in Advaita Vedanta." *Hindu-Christian Studies Bulletin* 14:13–18.

Ram das Abhiram das. N.d. "Krishna Art and the Scriptures." Pp. 147–162 in *Shri Krishna Caitanya and the Bhakti Religion,* ed. Edmund Weber and Tilak Raj Chopra. Studia Irenica no. 33. Frankfurt: Peter Lang.

Rāsamaṇḍala dāsa. 1994. "The Western Educationalists' Perspective on the Vedic Tradition." *ISKCON Communications Journal* 2, no. 2 (July–Dec.): 51–68.

Ravīndra Svarūpa dāsa [William H. Deadwyler III]. 1985a. "The Devotee and the Deity: Living a Personalistic Theology." Pp. 69–87 in *Gods of Flesh Gods of Stone: The Embodiment of Divinity in India,* ed. Joanne Punzo Waghorne and Norman Cutler with Vasudha Narayanan. New York: Columbia University Press.

———. 1985b. "The Scholarly Tradition in Caitanyaite Vaiṣṇavism." *ISKCON Review* 1, no. 1 (Spring): 15–23.

———. 1989. "Patterns in ISKCON's Historical Self-Perception." Pp. 55–75 in *Krishna Consciousness in the West,* ed. David G. Bromley and Larry D. Shinn. Lewisburg, PA: Bucknell University Press.

———. 1993a. "Modern Historical Consciousness: Its Causes and Cure—Part One." *ISKCON Communication Journal* 1, no. 2 (June): 44–50.

———. [1990] 1993b. "Religion and Religions." *ISKCON Communication Journal* 1, no. 1 (Jan.–June): 34–43. Originally pub. as "The Religions of Others in ISKCON's Eyes," Pp. 147–164 in *Attitudes of Religions and Ideologies toward the Outsider,* ed. Leonard Swidler. Lewiston, NY: Edwin Mellon Press.

———. 1995. "Modern Historical Consciousness: Its Cause and Cure—Part Two." *ISKCON Communication Journal* 3, no. 1 (June): 37–48.

Raychaudhuri, Hemchandra. [1920] 1975. *Materials of the Study of the Early History of the Vaishnava Sect.* New Delhi: Oriental Books Reprint Corporation. Original ed., Calcutta: University of Calcutta,

Reis, John Patrick. 1975. "'God Is Not Dead, He Has Simply Changed Clothes....': A Study of the International Society for Krishna Consciousness." PhD diss, University of Wisconsin–Madison.

Ricoeur, Paul. 1976. *Interpretation Theory: Discourse and the Surplus of Meaning.* Fort Worth: Texas Christian University Press.

———. 1977. *The Rule of Metaphor: Multi-disciplinary Studies of the Creation of Meaning in Language.* Trans. Robert Czerny. Toronto: University of Toronto Press.

———. 1984. *Time and Narrative.* Vol. 1. Trans. Kathleen McLaughlin and David Pellauer. Chicago: University of Chicago Press.

Robbins, Thomas. 1997. "Krishna and Culture: Cultural Exclusivity and the Debate Over 'Mind Control.'" *ISKCON Communications Journal* 5, no. 1 (June): 77–84.

Rochford, E. Burke, Jr. 1985. *Hare Krishna in America.* New Brunswick, NJ: Rutgers University Press.

———. 1995. "Family Structure, Commitment and Involvement in the Hare Krishna Movement." *Sociology of Religion* 56, no. 2: 153–175.

———. 1997. "Family Formation, Culture and Change in the Hare Krishna Movement." *ISKCON Communications Journal* 5, no. 2 (Dec.): 61–82.

———. 1998a. "Child Abuse in the Hare Krishna Movement: 1971–1986." *ISKCON Communications Journal* 6, no. 1 (June): 43–69.

———. 1998b. "Prabhupāda Centennial Survey Report." Submitted to ISKCON's Governing Body Commission. November.

———. 1999a. "Education and Collective Identity: Public Schooling of Hare Krishna Youth." Pp. 29–50 in *Children in New Religions*, ed. Susan Palmer and Charlotte Hardman. New Brunswick, NJ: Rutgers University Press.

———. 1999b. "Prabhupāda Centennial Survey Report: A Summary of the Final Report." *ISKCON Communications Journal* 7, no. 1 (June): 11–26.

Rohiṇī Kumār Svāmī. 1984. *Explanation of the Mahā-mantra.* Berkeley: Vaishnava Research Institute.

Rorty, Richard. 1989. *Contingency, Irony, and Solidarity.* Cambridge: Cambridge University Press.

Rosen, Steven J., ed. 1992a. *Focus on: Vraja, the Land of Kṛṣṇa.* Spec. issue of *Journal of Vaiṣṇava Studies* 1, no. 1 (Fall).

———. 1992b. Introduction to *Focus on: Vraja, the Land of Kṛṣṇa.* Spec. issue of *Journal of Vaiṣṇava Studies* 1, no. 1 (Fall): 1–8.

———. 1992c. Introduction (pp. 1–6) to *Vaiṣṇavism: Contemporary Scholars Discuss the Gauḍīya Tradition*, ed. Rosen. Brooklyn, NY: Folk Books.

———, ed. 1993. *Focus on: Rāgānugā Bhakti/Visualization.* Spec. issue of *Journal of Vaiṣṇava Studies* 1, no. 3 (Spring).

———. 1994. *Narasimha Avatar: The Half-Man/Half-Lion Incarnation.* New York: Folk Books.

Rothstein, Mikael. 1996. *Belief Transformations: Some Aspects of the Relation between Science and Religion in Transcendental Meditation (TM) and the International Society for Krishna Consciousness (ISKCON).* Aarhus, Denmark: Aarhus University Press.

Rudin, A. James. 1996. *A Jewish Guide to Interreligious Relations.* New York: American Jewish Committee.

Rūpa Gosvāmin. 1945. *Bhakti-rasāmṛta-sindhu.* Commentaries by Jīva Gosvāmin, Mukundadāsa Gosvāmin, and Viśvanātha Cakravartin. Ed. with Bengali trans. Haridāsa Dāsa. Navadvīpa: Haribol Kuṭhīr.

———. 1965. *Bhakti-rasāmṛta-sindhu.* Vol. 1. Trans. Swāmī Bhakti Hṛdaya Bon Mahārāj. Vrindaban: Institute of Oriental Philosophy.

———. 1989. *Śrī Śrī Laghu-bhāgavatāmṛta.* Ed. Haribhakta Dāsa. Vrindavan: Giridhari Patra.

———. N.d. Mathurā Māhātmya: *The Glories of Mathurā-Maṇḍala.* Sanskrit with trans. by Bhumipati Dāsa. Vrindavan: Rasibihari Lal and Sons.

Rūpa Vilāsa dāsa. 1988. *A Ray of Vishnu—The Biography of a Śaktyāveṣa Avatāra Śrī Śrīmad Bhaktisiddhānta Sarasvatī Gosvāmī Mahārāja Prabhupāda.* Vol. 1 of *Lives of the Vaiṣṇava Ācāryas.* Washington, MS: New Jaipur Press.

———. 1989. *The Seventh Goswami: A Biography of His Divine Grace Śrīla Saccidānanda Bhaktivinoda Ṭhākura (1838–1914).* Vol. 2 of *Lives of the Vaiṣṇava Ācāryas.* Washington, MS: New Jaipur Press.

Said, Edward W. 1979. *Orientalism.* New York: Random House, Vintage Books.

Saliba, John A. 1989. "Christian and Jewish Responses to the Hare Krishna Movement in the West." Pp. 219–237 in *Krishna Consciousness in the West,* ed. David G. Bromley and Larry D. Shinn. Lewisburg, PA: Bucknell University Press.

Sanātana Gosvāmī. 2001–2. *Śrī Bṛhad-bhāgavatāmṛta.* 3 vols. Trans. and commentary Gopīparāṇadhana Dāsa. Los Angeles: Bhaktivedanta Book Trust.

Satsvarūpa dāsa Goswami. 1980–83. *Śrīla Prabhupāda-līlāmṛta.* 6 vols. Los Angeles: Bhaktivedanta Book Trust.

Satya Nārāyaṇa dāsa and Kuṇḍalī dāsa. 1994. *In Vaikuṇṭha Not Even the Leaves Fall.* Vṛndāvana: Jiva Institute of Vaisnava Studies.

Śaunaka Ṛṣi dāsa. 1999. "ISKCON in Relation to People of Faith in God." *ISKCON Communications Journal* 7, no. 1 (June): 1–8.

Sax, William S. 2000. "Conquering the Quarters: Religion and Politics in Hinduism." *International Journal of Hindu Studies* 4, no. 1 (Apr.): 39–60.

Schmidt, Peter. 1999. *A. C. Bhaktivedanta Swami im Interreligiosen Dialog: Biografische Studien zur Begegnung von Hinduismus und Christentum.* Theion: Jahrbuch für Religionskultur, vol. 10. Frankfurt am Main: Peter Lang.

Schomer, Karine and W. H. Mcleod. 1987. *The Sants: Studies in a Devotional Tradition of India*. Delhi: Motilal Banarsidass.

Schweig, Graham M. 1998a. "Dance of Divine Love: The Rāsalīlā of Krishna as a Vision of Selfless Devotion." PhD diss., Harvard University.

———. 1998b. "Universal and Confidential Love of God: Two Essential Themes in Prabhupāda's Theology of Bhakti." *Journal of Vaiṣṇava Studies* 6, no. 2 (Spring): 93–123.

———. 2001. "The Essential Meaning of the *Bhagavad Gītā* According to Caitanyaite Vaisnavism." *Journal of Vaishnava Studies* 9, no. 2 (Spring): 227–239.

______. 2003. "Dying the Good Death: The Transfigurative Power of Bhakti." The Tamal Krishna Goswami Memorial Volume. Spec. issue of Journal of Vaishnava Studies 11, no. 2 (Spring): 77–111.

______. 2005a. *Dance of Divine Love: The Rāsa Līlā of Krishna from the* Bhāgavata Purāṇa, *India's Classic Sacred Love Story Introduced, Translated, and Illuminated*. Princeton, NJ: Princeton University Press.

———. 2005b. "Dying the Good Death: The Transfigurative Power of Bhakti." Pp. 369–408 in *The Intimate Other: Love Divine in Indic Religions*, ed. Anna S. King and John Brockington. New Delhi: Orient Longman,

______. 2007. *Bhagavad Gītā: The Beloved Lord's Secret Love Song*. New York: Harper Collins.

Schweitzer, Albert. 1911. *The Quest of the Historical Jesus*. 2nd ed. Trans. W. Montgomery. London: A. & C. Black.

Selengut, Charles. 1996. "Charisma and Religious Innovation: Prabhupāda and the Founding of ISKCON." *ISKCON Communications Journal* 4, no. 2: 51–63.

Sharma, B. N. K. 1962. *Philosophy of Śrī Madhvācārya*. Bombay: Bharatiya Vidya Bhavan.

Sharma, Krishna. 1987. *Bhakti and the Bhakti Movement: A New Perspective*. Delhi: Munshiram Manoharlal.

Sharpe, Eric J. 1985. *The Universal Gītā: Western Images of the Bhagavad Gītā—A Bicentenary Survey*. La Salle, IL: Open Court.

Sheridan, Daniel P. 1992. "Vyāsa as Madhva's Guru: Biographical Context for a Vedāntic Commentator." Pp. 109–125 in *Texts in Context: Traditional Hermeneutics in South Asia*, ed. Jeffrey R. Timm. Albany: State University of New York Press.

Sheth, Noel. 1982. "Krishna as a Portion of the Supreme." *Purāṇa* 24, no. 1 (Jan.): 79–90.

———. 1984. *The Divinity of Krishna*. New Delhi: Munshiram Manoharlal.

Shinn, Larry D. 1983. "Interview with. . . ." Pp. 61–100 in *Hare Krishna, Hare Krishna: Five Distinguished Scholars on the Krishna Movement in the West*, ed. Stephen J. Gelberg. New York: Grove Press.

———. 1987. *The Dark Lord: Cult Images and the Hare Krishnas in America*. Philadelphia: Westminster Press.

———. 1997. Foreword. Pp. ix–xiv in *Betrayal of the Spirit: My Life behind the Headlines of the Hare Krishna Movement,* by Nori J. Muster. Urbana: University of Illinois Press.

Shrivatsa Goswami. 1983. "Interview with. . . ." Pp. 196–258 in *Hare Krishna, Hare Krishna: Five Distinguished Scholars on the Krishna Movement in the West,* ed. Stephen J. Gelberg. New York: Grove Press.

Shukavak N. Dasa. 1998. "ISKCON's Link to Sādhana-Bhakti within the Caitanya Vaishnava Tradition." *Journal of Vaiṣṇava Studies* 6, no. 2 (Spring): 189–212.

———. 1999. *Hindu Encounter with Modernity: Kedarnath Datta Bhaktivinoda, Vaiṣṇava Theologian.* Los Angeles: SRI (Sanskrit Religions Institute).

Singer, Milton, ed. 1966. *Krishna, Myths, Rites and Attitudes.* Honolulu: East-West Center Press.

Singh, Chandralekha P. 1981. "Hare Krishnas: A Study of the Deviant Career of Krishna Devotees." PhD diss., New York University.

Singh, T. D. and Ravi Gomatam. 1988. *Synthesis of Science and Religion: Critical Essays and Dialogues.* San Francisco: Bhaktivedanta Institute.

Sinha, K. P. 1997. *A Critique of A. C. Bhaktivedanta.* Calcutta: Punthi-Pustak.

Sītā devī dāsī. 1995. Review of *Moon Sisters, Krishna Mothers, Rajneesh Lovers: Women's Roles in New Religions,* by Susan Jean Palmer. *ISKCON Communications Journal* 3, no. 1 (June): 83–86.

Śivarāma Swami. 1998. *The Bhaktivedanta Purports: Perfect Explanation of the Bhagavad-gītā.* Badger, CA: Torchlight.

Smith, Frederick M. 1994. "Purāṇaveda." Pp. 97–138 in *Authority, Anxiety, and Canon: Essays in Vedic Interpretation,* ed. Laurie L. Patton. Albany: State University of New York Press.

———. 1998. "Notes on the Development of Bhakti." *Journal of Vaiṣṇava Studies* 6, no. 1 (Winter): 17–36.

Smith, Wilfred Cantwell. 1978. *The Meaning and End of Religion.* London: SPCK.

Söderblom, Nathan. 1931. *The Living God: Basal Forms of Personal Religion.* London: Oxford University Press..

Soskice, Janet Martin. 1985. *Metaphor and Religious Language.* Oxford: Clarendon Press.

Spivak, Gayatri Chakravorty. 1993. "The Burden of English." Pp. 134–157 in *Orientalism and the Poscolonial Predicament: Perspectives on South Asia,* ed. Carol A. Breckenridge and Peter van der Veer. Philadelphia: University of Pennsylvania Press.

Staal, Frits. 1987. "The Ineffable *Nirguṇa Brahman.*" Pp. 41–46 in *The Sants: Studies in a Devotional Tradition of India,* ed. Karine Schomer and W. H. McLeod. Delhi: Motilal Banarsidass.

———. 1989. "Vedic Mantras." Pp. 48–95 in *Understanding Mantras,* ed. Harvey P. Alper. Albany: State University of New York Press.

Śubhānanda dāsa [Steven J. Gelberg]. 1978. *A Request to the Media: Please Don't Lump Us In.* Los Angeles: International Society for Krishna Consciousness, Office of Public Affairs.

Subrahmanyam, Korada. 1990. "*The Concept of* Mahāvākya." *Journal of Sanskrit Academy* (Osmania University, Hydrabad) 12: 42–48.

Suleri, Sara. 1992. *The Rhetoric of English India.* Chicago: University of Chicago Press.

Surya, Gerald. 1999. Review of *A Critique of A. C. Bhaktivedanta*, by K. P. Sinha. *ISKCON Communications Journal* 7, no. 2 (Dec.): 89–96.

Tamal Krishna Goswami. 1975. "You Can't Eat Nuts and Bolts." *Back To Godhead* 10, no. 4: 9–14.

———. 1984. *Servant of the Servant.* Hong Kong: Bhaktivedanta Book Trust.

———. 1985. *Jagannātha-priya Nāṭakam: The Drama of Lord Jagannātha.* Cambridge, MA: Bhaktivedanta Institute of Religion and Culture.

———. 1997. *Reason and Belief: Problem Solving in the Philosophy of Religion.* Dallas: Pundits Press.

———. 1998a. "The Dance of the Dexterous Hermeneute—Transformation and Continuity: Tensions in Scriptural Transmission—Hermeneutical Strategies in the Commentaries of A. C. Bhaktivedanta Swami Prabhupāda." *Journal of Vaiṣṇava Studies* 6, no. 2 (Spring): 61–72.

———. 1998b. "A Funny Thing Happened on the Way to Nirvana: When the Path of Vaiṣṇava-bhakti Crossed Amitābha's Pure Land." Pp. 187–203 in *A Hare Krishna at Southern Methodist University: Collected Essays 1995–1997*, by Tamal Krishna Goswami. Dallas: Pundits Press.

———. 1998c. *TKG's Diary—Prabhupāda's Final Days.* Dallas: Pundits Press.

———. 1999a. "Being Hindu in North America: The Experience of a Western Convert." Pp. 278–286 in *Religious Conversion: Contemporary Practices and Controversies*, ed. C. Lamb and D. Bryant. London: Cassell.

———. 1999b. "Servant of the Servant: A. C. Bhaktivedanta Swami Prabhupāda, Founder-acharya of the International Society for Krishna Consciousness." *Dialogue and Alliance* 13, no. 1: 5–17.

———. 2001. "Krishna and Culture." Paper presented at the annual meeting of the American Academy of Religion, Denver, November 20.

Thapar, Romila. 1985. "Syndicated Moksha." *Seminar* 313 (Sept.): 228.

Thompson, Richard L. 1981. *Mechanistic and Nonmechanistic Science: An Investigation into the Nature of Consciousness and Form.* Los Angeles: Bhaktivedanta Book Trust.

———. 1990. *Vedic Cosmography and Astronomy.* Los Angeles: Bhaktivedanta Book Trust.

———. 2000. *Mysteries of the Sacred Universe.* Alachua, FL: Govardhan Hill.

Towler, Robert. 1995. Statement against Alleged Misrepresentations by the German Federal Government. *ISKCON Communications Journal* 3, no. 1 (June): 71–73.

Tracy, David. 1989. "Theology: Comparative Theology." Pp. 446–455 in *Encyclopedia of Religion.* Vol. 14, ed. Mircea Eliade. New York: Macmillan and Free Press.

Trapnell, Judson. 1998. "The Everlasting Soul: A Vaiṣṇava-Christian Conference—Washington D.C., USA, 17 April, 1998." *ISKCON Communications Journal* 6, no.1 (June): 91–93.

Tubb, Gary. 2003. "Tamal Krishna Goswami's The Drama of Lord Jagannātha." *The Tamal Krishna Goswami Memorial Volume.* Spec. issue of *Journal of Vaishnava Studies* 11, no. 2: 143–154.

Underberg, Larry Ralph. 1987. "An Analysis of the Rhetoric of the International Society for Krishna Consciousness: An Implicit Theory Perspective." PhD diss., Pennsylvania State University.

Urquhart, William Spence. 1915. *The Historical and the Eternal Christ.* Edinburgh: Macniven and Wallace.

———. 1919. *Pantheism and the Value of Life: With Special Reference to Indian Philosophy.* London: Epworth Press.

———. 1928. *The Vedānta and Modern Thought.* Oxford: Oxford University Press.

Valpey, Kenneth R. [Kṛṣṇa-kṣetra dāsa]. 2004. "Krishna in *Mleccha-desh*: ISKCON Temple Worship in Historical Perspective." Pp. 45–60 in *The Hare Krishna Movement: The Post-Charismatic Fate of a Religious Transplant,* ed. Edwin Bryant and Maria Ekstrand. New York: Columbia University Press.

———. 2006. *Attending Krishna's Image: Chaitanya Vaishnava Mūrti-seva as Devotional Truth.* Oxon: Routledge.

Viśākhā devī dāsī, Sudharmā dāsī, Śītalā dāsī, Yamunā devī dāsī, Kuśa dāsī, Saudāmaṇī dāsī, and Rukmiṇī devī dāsī. 2000. "Women in ISKCON: Presentation to the GBC, March 2000." *ISKCON Communications Journal* 8, no. 1 (June):1–22.

Vṛndāvana dāsa Ṭhākura. *Caitanya Bhāgavata,* Antya, 4:126. P. 393 in *Śrīla Prabhupāda Ślokas: Selected Verses from the Teachings of A. C. Bhaktivedanta Swami Prabhupāda.* Sandy Ridge, NC: Bhaktivedanta Archives.

Wach, Joachim. 1944. *Sociology of Religion.* Chicago: University of Chicago Press.

Waghorne, Joanne Punzo and Norman Cutler with Vasudha Narayanan. 1985. Introduction to *Gods of Flesh Gods of Stone: The Embodiment of Divinity in India.* New York: Columbia University Press. 1–7.

Waldman, Marilyn Robinson. 1986. "Tradition as a Modality of Change: Islamic Examples." *History of Religions* 25, no. 4: 318–340.

Wallace, Anthony F. C. 1956. "Revitalization Movements." *American Anthropologist* 58: 264–281.

Weber, Edmund. 1997. "The Religion of ISKCON in the Perspectives of Diacritical Theology." *ISKCON Communications Journal* 5, no. 2 (Dec.): 49–60.

Weber, Max. 1964. *The Sociology of Religion.* Boston: Beacon Press.

Wheeler, Howard [Hayagriva Swami]. 1990. *Vrindaban Days: Memories of an Indian Holy Town.* Singapore: Palace Publishing.

Wilson, Bryan. 1982. *Religion in Sociological Perspective.* Oxford: Oxford University Press.

Wilson, H. H. 1862. *Essays and Lectures on the Religion of the Hindus.* Vol. 2. London: Trubner.

Wilson, J. 1883. *Report of the Second Decennial Missionary Conference Held at Calcutta, 1882–83.* Pp. 119–123. Calcutta.

Wolf, David Brian. 1999. "Effects of the Hare Kṛṣṇa Mahā Mantra on Stress, Depression, and the Three Guṇas." PhD diss., Florida State University.

Wright, Michael and Nancy Wright. 1993. "Baladeva Vidyābhūṣaṇa: The Gauḍīya Vedāntist." *Journal of Vaiṣṇava Studies* 1, no. 2 (Winter): 158–184.

Wulff, David M. 1991. *Psychology of Religion: Classic and Contemporary Views.* New York: John Wiley & Sons.

Yokum, Glenn. 1986. "Academics in Krishnaland." *ISKCON Review* 2: 120–132.

Young, Katherine. 1985. "Response to Papers." *ISKCON Review* 1, no. 1 (Spring): 29 33.

Zaehner, R. C. 1968. *Hinduism.* New York: Oxford University Press.

———. [1969] 1973. *The* Bhagavad-gītā: *With a Commentary Based on the Original Sources.* Oxford: Oxford University Press.

Zaidman-Dvir, Nurit. 1994. "When the Deities Are Asleep: Processes of Change in the Hare Krishna Temple." PhD diss., Temple University.

Index

Hair (musical drama), 180
Halbfass, Wilhelm, 107n53, 160n7
Harappans, 75
Hardy, Friedhelm, 124, 141, 164n20
hare (name), 225
Hare Krishna *mahāmantra,* 72n75, 146
as centering, 110n66
and Chaitanya school, 33n29, 178–179, 181, 204, 226
and Krishna fundamentalism, 76n85
and Prabhupāda, 181, 183n78, 193, 225
as response to Krishna's call, 225–226
See also chanting; Krishna; mantras
Haridāsa Ṭhākura, 181, 182, 192
Harijans, 168
Harmonist, 111
Harrison, George, 65, 187
"The Hare Krishna Mantra," 180
"My Sweet Lord," 180
Hatcher, Brian, 121, 147
haṭha-yoga, 171
Hayagriva das
See Wheeler, Howard (Hayagriva Swami)
Hegel, G. W. F., 100n36, 101
Hein, Norvin J., 207n7
Hemraj, Shilanand, 58n39
Herman, A. L., 77, 166n24
Brief Introduction to Hinduism, 75–76
Herzig, Carl, 9–10
Herzig, James Joseph, 9
Hiltebeitel, Alf, 125
Hinduism, 72, 121, 151
and Bhagavad Gītā, 117
and Chaitanya, 78
and colonial/missionary context, 3
and Herman, 75
and Hindu-Christian dialogues, 208
and ISKCON, 77–78
and orthopraxis, 57, 158
and Prabhupāda, 78
and Protestant missions, 95–97
reformers in, 151
as religion of sensate myths and rites, 63
Hindu-Muslim unity, 168
hippies, 53
Baird on, 68
and Bernhard, 42n7
and cult controversy, 51
freedom from, 45, 46
and Krishna consciousness, 44
stigma of, 43n9, 47
Hiraṇyakaśipu, 62n49
hlādinī-śakti, 133
Holdrege, Barbara, 5, 8
holy place, residence in, 187–190
Hopkins, E. Washburn, 167
Hopkins, Thomas J., 24n12, 48, 56, 90n9, 158
and *bhakti,* 130
on Prabhupāda's achievement, 36–37, 71, 74, 103, 103n44, 184
on Prabhupāda's translations, 57–59
and worship, 193
Hṛdayānanda dāsa Goswami (Howard Resnick), 77
Hunter, Edward, 51n28

idols, 155, 156
impersonalism, 67n61
and Chaitanya, 138
and *jñāna,* 165
and *nirviśeṣa,* 121
and Prabhupāda, 26, 101, 102
and Prabhupāda's purports, 116
and Prabhupāda's translations, 116, 141
Sharma on, 161
and Urquhart, 102
inattention (*pramāda*), 88
India, 56, 156, 173
foreigners in, 74
and Gauḍīya Maṭh, 175
guru in, 176
independence of, 168

India (*Cont.*)
and ISKCON, 73–74
racism in, 130
seen as inferior, 57
South Asian Hindus in, 8
and Urquhart, 99
International Society for Krishna Consciousness (ISKCON)
and academe, 8, 52
as alternative, 72
ancient spiritual tradition of, 56
and association of devotees, 173–177
as authentic Indian missionary movement, 53
as Bengal revitalization movement, 46–47n21
and *bhakti*, 208
binding narratives about, 39
as bona fide religion, 54
and books, 59–60, 186
and chanting, 194
and Christianity, 79
as Christian-Vaishnava hybrid, 98
conspiratorial theory about, 52
contextualization of, 56–57
and counterculture, 50, 123
and cults, 51, 52, 55, 56, 59, 63–64, 123
and *daiva-varṇāśrama*, 170
Daner on, 47
as deceptive, 60–61
and dialogue with people of faith, 79
and dissemination of knowledge, 85
and establishment values, 52
ethnographic studies of, 46–48
expansion of, 114
and family life, 177
fear of, 54
finances of, 60
and Gauḍīya Maṭh, 115
and Goswami, 3, 8
Governing Body Commission of, 176
and gurus, 174n51
and Hinduism, 77–78
Hopkins on, 57–59
hostility toward, 52
and India, 73–74
and Indian population of North America, 52
Indian temples of, 11
indifference toward, 71, 72, 123
initial public reception of, 38
Judah on, 44–46
as kitchen religion, 197–198
and Knott, 65
and Krishna-Balaram Temple, 74
and Krishna Consciousness, 55
"The Krishna Consciousness Movement Is Authorized," 52
literature distribution by, 60
and love of Krishna and Rādhā, 218
as mainstream Hindu faith and practice, 8
and Māyāpur, 190
and Māyāpur-Vṛndāvana festival, 189
and middle-class youth forums, 51
and modernity vs. tradition, 79–80
Moody on, 49–50
and music, 180–181
name of, 26
as new religious movement, 50, 56
and Nityānanda, 196
and origin of soul, 135n49
and other religious traditions as *bhakti*, 79
as otherworldly, 57
and philosophy vs. theology, 206
and physical and psychological isolation, 60
popular devotional praxis of, 56
and Prabhupāda, 2
Prabhupāda as identifying with, 40
public denial and private rationalization by, 60
public reception of, 21
and *rāgānuga-bhakti*, 82n98, 199
and Rathayātrā, 197

hupāda (*Cont.*)
heritance of, 27
novation of, 7, 30, 31, 157, 170–172
intolerant, 122
vocational prayer to self, 26
tana performance by, 10–11
he Krishna Consciousness Movement
Is the Genuine Vedic Way," 43
ṇa, The Supreme Personality of Godhead,
26, 35–36n32, 89, 114, 209n10
dership of, 24–25, 37
rs to Judah, 45n17
r to editor of *Los Angeles Times*, 43
r to Gandhi, 168
r to Goswami, 60n43
r to Nandarāṇī, 138
Comes from Life, 80n95
ies Rādhārāṇī Datta, 33
ion of, 5, 25, 36, 101, 150, 159, 173, 196
mother (Rajani), 32, 33, 90, 91
of, 22, 32
Nectar of Devotion, 35–36n32, 49n25,
119, 165, 173, 193, 198
ectar of Instruction, 118
w York, 2, 122
ork storefront temple of, 36
l contributions by, 159
her religious traditions, 78, 231
intings, 184–185
of, 32–33, 89–91
emical debate, 67–70, 83
t, 37
s of, 35, 36, 41, 46, 67, 116
ka-śekhara, 215
of degree by, 95, 102
er of religion, 37
a Gosvāmin, 165
rancisco, 122
krit, 113–114
krit canon, 129–131
Deluded," 151
ip of, 42
at Scottish Churches' College, Calcutta, 33
as self-consciously religious thinker, 66
situational character of thought of, 87
Śrīmad Bhāgavatam, 48n24, 179
Śrī Nāmāmṛta, 145n85
succession controversies following death
of, 60
summary of Rūpa Gosvāmin,
Bhakti-rasāmṛta-sindhu, 114
teachers of, 89–92
Teachings of Lord Caitanya, 35–36n32,
209n10
theology of, 6, 7, 24, 25, 55, 113, 116, 122,
123, 208, 216–217
time spent in India, 73–74n79
and title Bhaktivedānta, 34
and tradition, 7, 23, 25, 27, 29, 30, 117, 159
translation of Bhagavad Gītā, 35, 75–76,
140–141, 148
translation of Bhāgavata Purāṇa, 26, 35,
113–114
translation of Īśopaniṣad, 35, 118
translations of, 4, 24, 25, 48n24, 58, 118,
134n47, 140–141, 157, 166–167, 174, 215
travel to America, 35
and Urquhart, 92–95, 98–102
Vaishnava upbringing of, 94
voluminousness of thought of, 39
and West, 71n68, 74
and Western cultural hegemony, 36
Prahlāda, 62, 74–75
pramā (valid knowledge), 87
pramāṇa (sources of knowledge), 69n65, 85
and Prabhupāda's early life, 87–119
See also knowledge
prameya (that which is knowable),
84–85n102, 87, 123
prasāda, 197–198
prasthāna-trayī, 209
prayojana, 210
and *bhakti,* 208, 209, 215
Caitanya Caritāmṛta as, 213

Kṛṣṇadāsa Kavirāja, *Caitanya Caritāmṛta,* 123,
195–196n112
and Bhagavad Gītā, 117, 230
and Bhāgavata Purāṇa, 230
and *bhakti,* 162, 171n44, 172, 173, 177
and Bhaktivinoda, 105
and Buddhism, 121
and Chaitanya tradition, 118
and chanting, 179, 182
and Krishna and Chaitanya, 203, 216
and Krishna's love call, 226
and love, 202
and Prabhupāda, 209–210
and Prabhupāda's *mahāvākya,* 127,
129n30, 143n78, 145
and Prabhupāda's study program, 119
Prabhupāda's summary of, 35–36n32
Prabhupāda's translation of, 185–186
and *prema,* 209–210, 215
prema-bhakti-rasa in, 219, 222
and *rasika-śekhara,* 214–215
and *sambandha,* 126
secrecy in, 229–230
and theology, 212, 213, 217
Kṣīrodakaśāyī Vishnu, 134
Kurukshetra, Battlefield of, 41

Lakṣmaṇa, 195
Lalita Prasad Datta, 104n45
Levertov, Denise, 40, 41, 42n6
Levine, Faye, *The Strange World of the Hare Krishnas,* 44n15
Lifton, Robert Jay, 51n28
Lipner, Julius, 79, 88n2
on Goswami, 4–5
on Goswami's dissertation, 17, 18, 200
on Goswami's integrity, 16
and innovation, 31
and language, 32
and Rāmānuja, 100n37
and Śaṅkara, 148
tutelage of Goswami by, 13
Lorenz, Ekkehard, 79, 113, 114, 116, 176n60
love, 198
and *bhakti,* 217–223
from every religious tradition, 230–231
of Godhead, 49
and Judah, 45
and Moody, 49
and selfishness and conditioned
life, 221
theology of, 201
and Yogamāyā, 229
See also Krishna; *prema*
Luther, Martin, 25

Macaulay, Thomas Babington, 102, 105n47
Macnicol, Nicol, *Indian Theism,* 97n29
Madanamohana, 126, 191, 213–214
and tripartite theism of Krishna, 215–216
Madhva, 23, 67n61, 70, 100n37, 113, 127n22,
154n110
Mādhvas, 125, 169–170n42
Madsen, Finn, 79
Mahābhārata, 59, 164
mahābhāva, 133, 203–204
mahābhāva-svarūpa, 133
mahāvākyas (great utterances)
defined, 128–129
and mantras, 145, 146, 147, 148, 150n97
of Prabhupāda, 4, 25, 127–132, 150,
153, 209
single purpose of, 142
mantras
and deities, 155
and *mahāvākyas* (great utterances), 145,
146, 147, 148, 150n97
and mind-control techniques, 52
and women, 175
See also Hare Krishna *mahāmantra*
manvantara-avatāras, 135–136
Mariott, McKim, 74n80
married couples, 111n68
Matchett, Freda, 164

theology (*Cont.*)
and Prabhupāda, 6
as relational, 32
Rochford on, 59
social theories based on, 49
Vaishnava, 207
wholeness in, 6
theology, living, 5–8, 205
and *bhakti*, 85, 170
of Krishna *bhakti*, 15
of Prabhupāda, 3, 4, 25, 122, 230
total material energy (*hiraṇmaya-mahat-tattva*), 134
Towler, Robert, 72n73
Tracy, David, 206
tradition
and amalgam of past and present, 18
and Bhaktisiddhānta Sarasvatī, 108, 110
and Bhaktivinoda Ṭhākura, 108
commentarial, 7
cumulative, 18, 27n20
and disciplic succession, 116
as fixed code or techniques and values, 30
Hopkins on, 57–58
and innovation, 7
of interpretation, 150
interpretation of, 76
as modality of change, 30–31, 159
and modernity, 30
and Prabhupāda, 7, 23, 25, 27, 29, 30, 117, 159
preservation and adjustment of, 27
as style, 30
ten foundational truths of, 84–85n102
those outside vs. inside, 27
transcendental meditation (TM), 81
Tubb, Gary, 15

Underberg, Larry R., "Analysis of the Rhetoric of ISKCON," 60–61
universal dissolution (*pralaya*), 134
universalism, 57, 110, 168, 175
Upaniṣads, 25n14, 43n12, 209n9
authority of, 163n16
and *bhakti*, 164
and Bhaktivinoda Ṭhākura, 105
and Herman, 75
meaning in, 28–29
and *śabda* and *śruti*, 88
saguṇa and *nirguṇa* in, 161n11
Urquhart on, 101
Urquhart, William Spence
and *bhakti*, 159
and God's personality, 138
influence of, 79
and Jesus, 93
and morality, 105, 163
Pantheism and the Value of Life, 98
and Prabhupāda, 94, 98–102
and Prabhupāda's *mahāvākya*, 150
and theology, 92–95, 97
Uttar Pradesh, 188

vaidha-bhakti-sādhana, 79
vaidha sādhana, 189
vaidhī bhakti, 49, 74n81, 86, 199
Vaikuṇṭha planets, 198–199
vairāgya (renunciation), 165, 191n100
Vaishnava Saṁhitās, 192
Vaishnavism, 44, 59, 67, 77–78, 125
and Bhagavad Gītā, 210
and Bhaktisiddhānta, 110
and Goswami, 2–3
and ISKCON, 3
and Judah, 45
as monotheistic, 23
and Prabhupāda, 102
Shinn on, 57
and Urquhart, 101n39
Vallabha, 125, 167
van der Veer, Peter, 39
Varāha Purāṇa, 193
varṇa, 171n47